# Beauty and Brutality

EDITED BY MARTIN F. MANALANSAN IV,
ROBERT DIAZ, AND ROLANDO B. TOLENTINO

# Beauty and Brutality

*Manila and Its Global Discontents*

TEMPLE UNIVERSITY PRESS
*Philadelphia • Rome • Tokyo*

TEMPLE UNIVERSITY PRESS
Philadelphia, Pennsylvania 19122
*tupress.temple.edu*

Library of Congress Cataloging-in-Publication Data

Names: Manalansan, Martin F., 1960– editor. | Diaz, Robert, Jr., editor. |
  Tolentino, Roland B., editor.
Title: Beauty and brutality : Manila and its global discontents / edited by
  Martin F. Manalansan IV, Robert Diaz, and Roland B. Tolentino.
Description: Philadelphia : Temple University Press, 2023. | Includes
  bibliographical references and index. | Summary: "This edited volume
  deconstructs popular generalizations of Manila. Bringing together
  scholars from across the humanities and social sciences, this volume
  presents a series of multidisciplinary lenses to understand the
  complexities and contradictions of Manila, illustrating the breadth of
  experience it represents and that its citizens live"— Provided by
  publisher.
Identifiers: LCCN 2022024967 (print) | LCCN 2022024968 (ebook) | ISBN
  9781439922279 (cloth) | ISBN 9781439922286 (paperback) | ISBN
  9781439922293 (pdf)
Subjects: LCSH: Manila (Philippines)—Social conditions. | Manila
  (Philippines)—In popular culture. | Manila (Philippines)—Politics and
  government.
Classification: LCC HN720.M33 B43 2023  (print) | LCC HN720.M33  (ebook) |
  DDC 306.09599/16—dc23/eng/20220912
LC record available at https://lccn.loc.gov/2022024967
LC ebook record available at https://lccn.loc.gov/2022024968

Printed in the United States of America

9  8  7  6  5  4  3  2  1

# Contents

# Acknowledgements in Three Parts

This section is a series of seemingly disparate individualized messages of gratitude and musings about Manila. In fact, the messages are entangled with each other with lives and loves finding a common ground in the city. Like Manila itself, the editors' voices travel across divergent borders between feelings of longing, hopefulness, nostalgia, anger, and shifting events of beauty and brutality. All these affective and geographic routes end up with a Manila that has been, is, and will be.

Manila again and again. Like the nostalgic incantations in Jessica Hagedorn's essay "Homesick," Manila figures as a central yet repeating node in my life and the heart of my own worldly urban wanderings. I was born and raised in Manila, and I plan to return there for my golden years in the future. Despite an ongoing itinerant life in New York, Chicago, and Minneapolis, Manila remains my affective terra firma. It is the main point of departures and arrivals in a life enriched by people in multiple places and times.

I can only enumerate names for now, so I cannot adequately convey the joys and deep emotional support they have brought into my life. The list is incomplete like many things, always partial and always aspirational. I extend my deep gratitude to my fellow urban travelers who buoyed this project: Paul Michael Atienza (researcher extraordinaire), Shaun Vigil of Temple University Press, and, of course, my coeditors, Robert Diaz and Rolando B. Tolentino. I relish the support and memories of people far and wide who always evoke the idea of home wherever I may be: Gary Devilles, Celia Antonio, Laura Samson, Bebon Gatuslao, Bobby Abastillas, Manolo Tanquilut, Rick Bonus, Ria Vera Cruz, Monica Santos, and Kiko Benitez.

As of this writing, Manila remains a very distant, forbidding place because of the pandemic. I yearn to visit, but I cannot. Through this work, I send a tender message of affection to my brothers, sisters, nephews, and nieces "right here" and "over there"—we are and will always be together in various ways via Zoom or phone and, hopefully, face-to-face very soon.

The past year and a half has been one of loss and tragedy. My mother and youngest brother, Earl, four of my aunts, a couple of cousins, and numerous friends have tragically succumbed to COVID. I write this section with waves of bittersweet remembrance of intimate moments mixed with fits of anger at the cruelty and mortal ugliness of it all. But I refrain from offering a mournful dirge, and instead I wish to celebrate with the many voices contained in this volume. I want to remember and cherish my memories of a formerly noisy and vibrant city that has been muted due to the passing of the colorful and warm presences of many dear people who have passed on: Papa, Mama, Earl, and my *titas* and *pinsans*. I dedicate my work to them and to the lives we have led together and apart, communing in a city in which I have loved and will continue to love them.

Martin F. Manalansan IV
Minneapolis, Minnesota, USA
September 30, 2021

I was born in and spent most of my childhood in Cabanatuan, a town far removed from Manila's speed and intensity. Because of this, I often dreaded regular trips to Manila since they ended somewhere far too overwhelming for my liking. The city's traffic, smell, and noise were all too much. Looking back, it's ironic that the things I initially despised about this maligned city of my youth eventually became the very things I longed for in the aftermath of enforced distance as an adult. I left the Philippines when I was seventeen and could not return until I was thirty. During this period of separation, memories of Manila's chaos sustained my intellectual curiosity as well as fueled bursts of happiness when I needed them. Manila's contradictions made it the only destination worth going to in my recurring desires. Wanting to feel the city again made me encounter artists whose metropolitan dreams enriched my own. The novels of Jessica Hagedorn, R. Zamora Linmark, Gina Apostol, and Ninotchka Rosca encouraged me to discover a gritty metropolis filled with irreverent humor and unyielding resistance. The films of Lino Brocka, Marilou Diaz Abaya, Nick Deocampo, Gil Portes, and Jun Lana invited me to experience a vibrant place filled with wayward intimacies and unruly sexualities. Thus, this collection is an attempt to thank them and other artists whose many Manilas continue to energize and nourish.

Aside from these artists, I was also fortunate to glimpse Manila's vitality through the mentorship and intellectual kinship numerous scholars near and far gave. I could not ask for better coeditors and collaborators than Martin Manalansan and Rolando Tolentino. Their academic and community work inspire me to understand the value of urban, cultural, and diasporic willfulness. I've also been fortunate to "revisit" many versions of Manila alongside Allan Isaac, Lucy Burns, Christine Balance, Selmin Kara, Michelle Cho, Christine Kim, Hae Yeon Choo, Ferdie Lopez, and Gary Devilles. Their scholarly and emotional comradery make "traveling" anywhere worth undertaking. On that note, the multiple Manilas that appear across the pages of this book could not have come together without Paul Michael Atienza's administrative support. Through his scholarly writing and those of others featured in this collection, we are able to envision Manila's ongoing contributions to numerous fields of study. Their versions of Manila are thankfully mine now too.

And despite the multiple migrations that have marked my life, family members and friends have made Manila the only place that I can truly call home. Pia Bagamasbad, Cia Hermosa, Allen Tan, GA Fallarme, Janir Datukan, and Oliver Gutierrez remind me of why distance during this pandemic is filled with sorrow. Josefina De Jesus, Emilia Desphy, Jeanna Teves, Ada Garcia, Mai Garcia, Anya Garcia, Elenita Adia, Adeth De Guzman, as well the entire Garcia and Adia clan encourage me to see Manila as a place to rest and rejuvenate. And lastly, Michael Adia makes me realize that no version of Manila is worth dreaming or living in without him in it. From the moment we met in the city, he has been a constant source of support and joy. All roads to my many Manilas lead to him, and any version of a just world I can envision inhabiting has intrinsically been touched by his kindness.

Robert Diaz
Toronto, Canada
October 27, 2021

Though I spent my early childhood in San Leonardo, Nueva Ecija, I grew up in Mandaluyong and got my education in Makati when these were just municipalities. My family moved to Manila in 1969, and I was the first of my siblings to complete an education in Manila, a big deal for my parent's middle-class aspiration. When Manila became Metro Manila in 1975, it engulfed fifteen cities and municipalities of the National Capitol Region. Imelda Marcos became its governor until the Marcoses were deposed in 1986. Metro Manila's current population in 2021 is some 13.5 million people, the second to Calabarzon or the nearby economic hub of five provinces.

Manila no longer has the feel of a small livable and manageable place. Its skyline fluctuates as it has yet to fully First World–develop, with urban poor communities staking their contrary claims to the city. It has no master planning and is choked by traffic, housing, and massive poverty issues with very little public and open spaces. Yet I chose to live and work here in Quezon City, moving very infrequently, especially in the pandemic lockdown, outside the confines of the campus and my residence. The cities and municipality of Metro Manila have their distinct feel and affect to both its residents and passersby. Each has become its own insular island. Despite the rising cost of living, Metro Manila remains the hub of capital, value-added labor opportunities, governance, education, telecommunication, film, media, and culture.

I no longer recognize the Manila I had known in 1969 or during visits to Luneta prior to settling here. And I have no nostalgia for that time and place, nor do I have a desire to move elsewhere to another time and place outside Metro Manila at this time. I chose, like its 13.5 million residents, to last it here. I am sustained by personal and professional relationships formed and transformed in the decades of living and working in Metro Manila. Many thanks to those who lived and worked here, especially to Bienvenido Lumbera, who passed away in September 2021 and still stands as the inspiring shade for younger generations of scholars he has mentored, and to other friends, scholarly partners, and activists who share in the living and the struggle here. Many thanks, too, to those who have lived here and continue to periodically return here—exemplary scholars and collaborators Martin Manalansan in Minnesota and Robert Diaz in Toronto, to Paul Michael Atienza for making the book happen, and Shaun Vigil for shepherding the manuscript in Temple University Press. To the scholars who contributed their work and their commitment to a transformative cultural politics in their essays, many thanks for articulating the contrariness of the Philippine state formation.

It is in the making of the book on Manila that Manila can be unmade. It is having lived and continuing to live—or return—that sustains the struggle and resistance to the choking hold of Manila. The uneasiness and precarity of individual and collective life and living in Manila also create the necessity to voice out what is wrong, what may be righted, and what is right and just. In spite of and despite Metro Manila's woes, especially in the peril of life and living in the pandemic and the longest and strictest lockdown in the world, still ongoing as of this writing, we dare to live, to create, to protest, to struggle, and to win.

Rolando B. Tolentino
Quezon City, Philippines
November 3, 2021

# Beauty and Brutality

# Manila in the World

MARTIN F. MANALANSAN IV,
ROLANDO B. TOLENTINO,
AND ROBERT DIAZ

A city is a machine with innumerable parts made by the accumulation of human gestures, a colossal organism forever dying and being born, an ongoing conflict between memory and erasure, a center for capital and for attacks on capital, a rapture, a misery, a mystery, a conspiracy, a destination and point of origin, a labyrinth in which some are lost and some find what they're looking for, an argument about how to live and evidence that differences don't always have to be resolved, though they may grate and grind against each other for centuries. (Solnit 2016, 1)

Metro Manila in 2006 is a labyrinthine, megalopolitan fortress of foreclosure. Almost all the main arteries of metropolis have become virtually enclosed corridors of free-flowing vehicular traffic, without regulated crossings where pedestrians and cross-street flow might momentarily interrupt the stream of hundreds of thousands of cars, buses, and trucks careening down these roads every day. With the help of numerous "flyovers," or overpasses, and underpasses built by the metropolitan government over the last decade and a half, these ten-lane roads have become highways that coast and tunnel through the thick of the city, connecting the scattered, archipelagic commercial centers and gated communities where the upper-class and upwardly mobile sectors work, live, shop, and socialize. (Tadiar 2007, 316)

Manila is a chaotic machine (Solnit 2016), a messy space (Manalansan 2015), a political patchwork (Garrido 2019), and a city with no central vantage (Tadiar 1996). With no overall grid and as a veritable sensorial morass or "assault" (Tadiar ibid.; Devilles 2020), people always expect Manila to be on various lists of the "worst cities"—worst traffic, worst pollution, worst hygiene, worst infrastructure, worst violence, and the lists go on. These expectations of the worst in Manila and the relative complacency about the city's inadequacies and excesses that come along with it have become stale commonsense assumptions that often are pathetic ideological cul-de-sacs. Wearily cyclical. Bound for nowhere.

*Beauty and Brutality* is about Manila, the fabrication and unraveling of this much maligned, often endearing, sometimes frightening capital city of the Philippines. This collection aims to exfoliate and unpack the persistent desiccated layers of conflicting images and ideas ensconced in this "Noble and Ever Loyal City" (a moniker given by Spanish colonialists) or the "City of Man"—a label given by an infamous First Lady who was the first governor of Metro Manila (a conglomerations of districts, cities, towns, and neighborhoods). Questions around these historical appellations remain: Loyal to whom and for whom? Who gets to be human amid the city's stark inequalities?

Because of its official and imperial designation as the nation's capital and its long history, Manila often stands in for the Philippine nation and people. For better or for worse, the stories of Manila are seen to represent and at the same time obscure the variegated national landscape (see the following books for divergent examination of the city: Barbaza 2019; Doeppers 2016; Pante 2019; Wise 2019; Wiselius 2016). This anthology is a critical encounter with this city's imagined and material contours. More appropriately, the essays are limnings of the divergent ways one can talk about Manila and its varied stories. To encounter Manila or any city is to engage with a language constituted by codes enshrined in physical and social densities, paradoxes, and assemblages (Sudjic 2016). This collection offers a particular energized language of urban "worldings" in the Global South, a specific city's coming into being and its relentless undoing (Simone 2001; Roy and Ong 2011; Wilson and Connery 2007; Tadiar 2004).

## Locating Manila: Infrastructural Mappings

Latitude: 14.6042004
Longitude: 120.982206
Northern Hemisphere

These bare-naked numbers are the geographic coordinates of Manila. But such numbers disregard the messy, fleshy, recalcitrant, mercurial, and immeasurable qualities of the city. If we take location not as a fixed site but as an itinerary (Clifford 1997, 11) and a narrative unfolding, then we should consider Manila's location as a series of discrepant stories, manifold optics, and multifaceted processes that involves unpacking layers of paradoxical and enmeshed practices, violent hierarchies, institutions, bodies, and histories that make up this city's past, present, and futures.

The celebrated writer Jessica Hagedorn (2013, 9) described Manila as "a woman of mystery, the ultimate femme fatale. Sexy, complicated, and tainted by a dark painful past, she's not to be trusted. And why should she be? She's been betrayed time and again, invaded, plundered, raped and pillaged."

Hagedorn is referring to Manila's long, violent colonial occupations by Spain, Japan, and the United States. Each regime has left its mark on the architectural and psychic landscapes of the city. But beyond these unfortunate histories, she says, "Manila is a city of survivors, schemers and dreamers . . . [it] is a city of extremes" (12).

Hagedorn's raw yet affectionate portrait of Manila is an invitation to unravel its mysteries and banalities and to confront the city's extremes. Placing Manila in time and space is an archeological endeavor. Excavating through "mysterious" layered strata of meanings and unwieldy concatenations of events and images, Manila encompasses the pulsating embodied experiences of teeming millions living amid cramped aging infrastructures that involve alleys (*eskinitas*), highways, flyovers, corners (*kantos*), dead ends, gateways, and crossroads (*sangandaan*)—these elements make up what is at first glance the legible face of the city (Tolentino, Baquiran, and Aguirre 2002; Tadiar 2004).

This anthology stands as a major attempt to delve into and wade through its liquid modernity (Baumann 2000) with the city's murky ambivalences and paradoxes. Time and space are entangled in Manila's complicated narratives, especially those stories sedimented into the built environment. Manila's imaginative and material landscapes belie prehistoric, Hispanic, and American colonial pasts that resonate with contemporary attempts at presentist struggles and futurist longings. Some writers and scholars romanticize these foreign imperial influences through ruins and rebuilt structures of colonial times, gesturing to an ornate tropical baroque and quaint oriental fusion (Joaquin 1999). Others have critically pointed out that the American baroque exemplified in the city plans by the architect Daniel Burnham is no more American than an awkward, deficient, and vestigial aesthetic sensibility—or to put it in slang words, *barok*, not baroque (Tolentino, Baquiran, and Aguirre 2002, 19). This *barok* sensibility is based on the uncomfortable impositions and mistranslations of designs and urban imaginings that have no place for the local and the indigenous (Tolentino, Baquiran, and Aguirre 2002). At the same time, the "mall-ification," or "malling," of this crowded city has created unwieldy interiors that are less about an internal refuge and more of public masquerades of the dwindling bourgeois wishes of its citizens. These sprawling malls are air-conditioned paeans to capitalist consumerism. They are a testament to the calcification and erosion of memory and collective action, acting as material and ideological "paramnestic" insulators from the violence and suffering that persist within and without (Hedman and Sidel 2000, 118–139; see also Tolentino 2001).

Manila's modernist soaring "flyovers" are elite vantages that provide some respite from the unpaved longings and desperate dreams of the million daily commuters lying underneath. These urban natives are left to jostle in the crowded streets below to get into buses and jeepneys amid the unrelenting heat and choke-provoking exhaust fumes, smells, and noise. Neferti Tadiar (2004) considers these forbidding structures as metaphorical and material stand-ins for the Philippine state's machinations in the late twentieth and early twenty-first centuries, particularly in its inability to absorb its citizen into the national body and instead expels them in a kind of bulimic reaction to the morass of the global service industry. The Philippine state, through its failing infrastructures, has shaped the troubled contours of the city. Overall, Manila displays its histories and spatialities in the manner of a discomfiting palimpsest, composed by erasures, overwriting (overbuilding), floodings, and ruinations.

## Manila's Beauty and Brutality

Given all its cacophonous properties, it is perhaps odd for any collection of works to collectively frame Manila as beautiful. Yet we invoke *beauty* here as a complex, tenuous, and contingent term that both incorporates and moves beyond the specific material elements of the city. Writing about beauty's relationship to the social, Mimi Nguyen suggests that beauty can act as an imperative discourse that "determines what conditions are necessary to live, what forms of life are worth living, and what actions we must follow to preserve, secure, or replicate such conditions and forms" (Nguyen 2016). It is precisely this notion of beauty as ethos, aspiration, and capacity for achieving the "good life" that conjoins it with the political, the social, and the material. In the context of Manila, beauty saturates sedimented dreams of a livable life continually denied for some and made possible for others. Beauty sets the stage for the contradictions that can make Manila brutal, violent, and disciplinary. Manila's beauty is brutal inasmuch as the city's inequities are often justified through harsh invocations of beauty as a material and social good. If anything, beauty lays bare the differential power dynamics that affect how people navigate Manila with uneven levels of mobility and ease.

Such notions of beauty have historically been wielded in Manila as a site of political power. For instance, with an eye toward the United States, the Marcos regime deployed facile notions of beauty to justify the restructuring of an entire metropolis, to censor representations of systemic brutality, to buttress the mythic domesticity of Ferdinand and Imelda Marcos's conjugal dictatorship, and to maintain martial law, all in the name of what Imelda Marcos (herself a former beauty queen) calls the "true, the good, and the beautiful." As Mina Roces notes, in the context of martial law Manila, "the relationship between beauty and power is dialectical: beauty can be a source of power, but closeness to power is also a source of beauty" (Roces 1998, 18). A key impetus for Imelda Marcos's propagandistic attempts to transform the city's infrastructure was the consolidation of material wealth to her office as the governor of Metro Manila, a consolidation that required the joining of multiple cities and municipalities into one body that she could then govern. Marcos strategically used beauty as a political tool, mining the dialectical relationship between power and beauty to fashion an image of herself as the ideal national citizen (as a "star and slave") while also transforming Manila's contours, flows, and facades. Thus, for better or for worse, Imelda Marcos's invocations of beauty continue to haunt the Manila we know today. Her notions of beauty are imbedded in its very built environment, affecting how people transect this ever-changing space.

Efforts to beautify the urban space to consolidate political power and to streamline the flow of capital have continued even after Imelda's governorship. Lito Atienza, for instance, sought to "light up" Manila's multiple thoroughfares as he refashioned the city's coastal highway, Taft Avenue, so that the city could become destination for foreign tourists. Proceeding Atienza, Alfredo Lim self-fashioned himself as a "Dirty Harry" figure whose slogan, "*Magaling na Lider, Disiplonado*," became the primary justification for efforts to "clean" the city of petty crime. If, as Vanita Reddy notes, beauty lends itself to the language of capitalist accumulation (Reddy 2016), then the shaping and the priming of Manila for the flow of commerce has historically been deployed through narratives of beauty, narratives that are ultimately conditioned by the country's larger economic aspirations.

At the same time, the dialectical relationship between beauty and power in Manila has also produced the conditions for enacting different ways of resisting the inequities that continue to mark both the city and the larger country. Returning to the Marcos regime, Mina Roces suggests that one of the main reasons that Corazon Aquino unseated Ferdinand Marcos as president in 1986 was her self-presentation as Imelda Marcos's antithesis, as a simple housewife who did not desire beauty and instead desired to right the wrongs of the country. Roces also points out that "while Mrs. Imelda Marcos alone epitomized the almost palpable links between beauty and power, political activism bred in the atmosphere of a repressive authoritarian regime encouraged the blossoming of the woman as political activist" (Roces 1998, 3). Thus, Marcos's gendered deployment of beauty also ironically created the conditions of possibility for multiple invocations of feminist critique that continue to work its way in the streets of Manila today. Such critique is certainly present in significant and oft-cited cinematic and literary representations of the city. Films like *Manila in the Claws of Neon* (dir. Lino Brocka, 1975) and *Manila by Night* (dir. Ishmael Bernal, 1980) or diasporic novels like *Dogeaters* (Jessica Hagedorn, 1990) and *Leche* (R. Zamora Linmark, 2011) produce moments of beauty that do not only mark the aesthetic or creative value; beauty in these works also serves as a foil to critique the brutalities of governmental policies, poverty, and social neglect that exist in Manila.

Beauty animates modes of pleasure, fun, and joy that are wedded to the very messiness of Manila. These artists portrayed sexually and economically marginalized characters that saw beauty in muck, pleasure in trash, and joy in crossing the boundaries of class difference. Artistic depictions of beauty (from the opulent to the gritty, from the mundane to the sexual, in the streets and on the skin) enabled subtle critiques of dictatorial policies and of the continued existence of U.S. colonialism under unquestioned militarism. Beauty is everywhere, and it can be a resource for new ways of existing amid the limits placed on the people living in the city.

In one of the most pivotal moments of the film *Manila by Night*, Kano, a lesbian drug pusher, states her love for a chaotic Manila. She stands on a rooftop, proclaiming: "I love you, Manila, no matter what you are. Young, old, smelly, ugly, woman, man, *bakla*, or lesbian!" With a hint of euphoria in her voice, and before she smokes a joint, Kano scans the dim glow of Manila under the neon lights of motels, beer houses, and other spaces for pursuing forbidden pleasures. Through this scene, Bernal offers a version of Manila far removed from what the Marcos regime wanted to present abroad. Thus, the film was the first and only one to be banned unless reedited to its existing edition with a voice-over smoothing issues of drug use and good citizenship in the closing scene for international screening. Kano's love for this chaotic and vibrant metropolis enables Bernal to provide a critique of the regime's beautification efforts, as seen from the vantage point of a sexually and economically marginalized inhabitant. Kano sees beauty not in the repaved, rezoned, and reclaimed streets of Manila, whose globalized aspirational ethos ultimately mask the realities of poverty and disciplinary violence. She instead sees beauty in the rawness and grit of a city whose chaos engenders different kinds of intimacies and pleasures and different ways of living, being with, and reproducing the urban.

The political meaning of this iconic moment is made eerily resonant in the present. As many local and international social justice organizations have noted, the Rodrigo Duterte government (2016–2022) has precisely justified and rationalized the extrajudicial killing of individuals (mostly from the economically disadvantaged areas) through sanitary narratives that seek to "clean up" Manila of the vagaries of drugs, addiction, and immorality. As Human Rights Watch points out, Duterte's "war on drugs" has led to the death of twelve thousand people, mostly from the urban poor (HRW 2019). Amnesty International has recently called such killings a "large-scale murdering enterprise" (Amnesty International 2019), one that involves multiple governmental institutions and the police as they mark specific individuals and communities for dehumanization and death. Imbedded within such narratives of "cleanliness" are, of course, assumptions about dirt, obsolescence, and uselessness. Given such modes of dehumanization, this collection thus sees Manila as a significant and timely physical and ideological space to explore the dialogic nature of beauty and brutality—as these concepts intertwine in the exhilarating, painful, and complex urban repertoires of the Global South. As a city that has experienced the multiple vestiges of empire, the disciplinary machinations of dictatorial rule, the current effects of the "war on drugs," and the continued realities of uneven resource distribution, Manila is a key site from which to understand how urban realities in the Global South emerge from the transnational movement of goods, bodies, and ideas within and outside of the metropolis. This work revisits multiple versions of Manila to track what forms of beauty and brutality foreground the human and the inhuman, the disposable and the useful, the free and unfree.

## Diaspora and Re-turn: Else-wheres, Other Manilas

Manila is no longer just a circumscribed place objectified in maps, lists, guidebooks, movies, songs, and other cultural genres. It is not only a cumulative effect of lives lived within its own parameters. The typical Manileño, or Manila native, is a minor node within a vast global network of bodies, currencies, and technologies. Such emotional, economic, and political "connectivities" have transformed the city, like others in the Global South, with the emergence of call centers and expatriate/returnee communities that transformed real estate market, social life, and the skyline (Pido 2017; Padios 2018; see also Huyssen 2008).

Filipinos may have left the country in droves, and some have returned, but Manila itself has migrated or more appropriately dispersed—to other places as mini facsimiles located in the Filipino diasporic elsewhere. Manila is not a mere object of cool scrutiny, it can be a mournful refrain, a level of intensity, and an unwieldy nostalgic orientation. Manila is not a site for the classic realization of diasporic return but rather becomes an arena for its contestation. Manila is about a re-turn.

Various media outlets have long been involved in enticing Filipinos working and residing in parts of the world by showing airbrushed and decluttered images of Manila as a stand-in for the homeland. Television shows and songs among others have become fertile vehicles for cultivating this form of banal nostalgia for a long time. In 1976, the Filipino pop band Hotdog, composed of elite youth from exclusive private schools, topped the charts with a song entitled "Manila." For people who lived in Manila in the late twentieth century, the song may evoke a familiar cringe or even a distancing moment while succumbing to a kind of nostalgic pleasure. Time has passed—the Marcos martial law regime was toppled, but the song itself may also be an unwitting archival vantage that may open up the limitations and possibilities of understanding and confronting the various faces of the city.

In the lyrics of the song, there is an abrupt slide from Tagalog to an aspirational (Filipino upper class) American-accented English pays homage to the postcolonial city. The band members painted a Manila that was deemed to be different from other world cities because of its delightful noisy urbanity, and they likened it to a female lover whose arms awaited their embrace. That is, a return to Manila is to be enfolded back to the nation after a worldly romp across other cities and with other women. In other words, it is a song of unbridled, youthful heterosexual masculinity—mobile, promiscuous, and carefree. The song marked not only the emergence of a new musical trend called the "Manila sound," but it also heralded the historical unfolding of a Filipino global migration that has made "leaving home" the order of the day, and homecomings have become pivotal visceral and economic necessities (e.g., the Balikbayan program). The song is based on a failed yet eager heteronormative masculinist cosmopolitanism and an unbridled sense of privileged elsewhereish-ness tempered by an imagined rootedness to sexy female bodies, delicious sounds, cramped spaces, and the colorful images of a chaotic metropolis. However, the Hotdog anthem, in all its problematic undercurrents and strange mixture of eloquence, sappy nostalgia, masculine toxic bravado, and youthful awkwardness, speaks to the troubled notion of return (*pagbabalik*) to this metropolis.

What constitutes the national mythologies of and allegedly visceral compulsion to return? How does return shape visions, fantasies, and realities of the Noble and Ever Loyal City of Manila? Despite many turgid scholarly dissections of return within the context of diaspora where return is always figured as a penultimate, necessary, and teleological node in a predictable cycle, Manila defies such formulaic assessments.

Manila is not a strictly bounded geographic place within a particular latitude but rather is constructed through affective evocations echoed in unexpected places and times, such as the streets of Woodside in the New York City borough of Queens, in the streets of Jersey City, National City in San Diego, in Daly City, in Stockton (Mabalon 2013), Los Angeles (España-Maram 2006), and in the interstices of other urban areas such as Madrid, Toronto, London, and other world cities. Here, these affective evocations resonate in the fleeting moments of atmospheric recognition, jolting déjà vu, and surprising intimate connections in otherwise foreign spaces. We see fragments and traces of lives and dreams lived in Manila and now transported to these corners and neighborhoods in these other world cities. While some of us have the privilege to a diasporic homecoming, some can only look to or "turn to" such corners, neighborhoods, and districts for the momentary solace of the familiar despite the strange forlornness it might evoke. Here are social sites where one can speak in one's language, buy home comfort food, and shop for various items from "over there." These are spaces one can go back to again and again without the problem of "legal" travel documents and money. Such visits become habitual and repetitive; then they become occasions for firing up emotional and affective energies beyond the everyday. These enclaves provide both the material and symbolic fulcrum for mobilizing ethno-nationalist sentiments, critical conviviality, and, in many cases, community and long-distance activism.

In this sense, diasporic return could be better understood as re-turn. *Re-turn* is not just a change of orientation, trajectory, or maneuver or a "moving back to a place of origin" as in *return*, but rather it is imperative to think of re-turn in terms of repeated turning or repetition in language and travel where the act of repeating is not just a lazy droning of the same morpheme but rather marking a persistent tension, an escalating intensity of an enactment, and the relative virtue or lack thereof of an object or a subject. In Tagalog and other Austronesian languages, the repetition of a word is not just a mere reprising of the same sound. Rather, it denotes a shift in emphasis and meaning. Repetition shapes directionality, intensity, valuation, and orientation. For example, *ganda*, which means "beautiful," is intensified by repetition so that *ganda-ganda* means "*very* beautiful."

Re-turn is never a singular process or event. It is multivalent. Re-turn then speaks to an affective accretion of disparate ambitions, desires, stances, and interests that meld into an imagined space called Manila. The anthropologist Benito Vergara (2009) in his excellent ethnography of Daly City in the Bay Area spoke about the idea of re-turning in terms of the competing demands of citizenship. Daly City is a Filipino ethnic enclave that has been derisively seen as a ghetto, an elsewhereish Manila or an Americanized version of the original. Culling from Kachig Tölölyan's assertion that diasporic existence does not necessarily involve actual physical return, Vergara asserts that re-turn is really "repeated turning . . . through political activism, assertions of ethnic pride, nostalgia, consumerism or just vague remembering. Re-turn is obliquely opposed to the narrative of assimilation. The tension between this remembrance and the demands of citizenship in the new homeland, the obligations in different directions, constitute a predicament for the Philippine immigrant . . . [in how they] negotiate—or indeed fail(s) to find a balance between the two" (Vergara 2009, 4).

Manila is constituted by various tensions: between attachments and detachments, between the pendulum swings of movement and immobility, between being mobile and (un)settled, between failures and fulfillment, and between return and re-turn. These tensions compel us to think of how seemingly antipodal sites, narratives, and processes can become a melancholic incantation, a reverie of spatial and temporal incompleteness, a psychic restlessness, and a vital necessary itinerancy. Manila is neither an original departure point nor a penultimate destination. It is not the culmination of a diasporic cycle. Manila is a repeating node, a continuous waystation, and an invocation not toward a dead end but rather to persistent unending journeys buoyed by intensified, enduring desires and longings. These affective geographies and temporalities are best exemplified by the haunting lines of Jessica Hagedorn in her essay "Homesick." This section of the introduction ends with these lines not as a definitive conclusion but as a lively segue to animate readers' engagements with the essays that follow and to also intensify hopes for a Manila that will persist and survive in its various future incarnations:

> I leave one place for the other, welcomed and embraced by the family
> I have left—fathers and brothers and cousins and uncles and aunts.
> Childhood sweethearts now with their children, I am unable to stay.
> I make excuses, adhere to tight schedules. I return only to depart. I
> am the other, the exile within, afflicted with permanent nostalgia for
> the mud. I return, only to depart: Manila, New York, San Francisco,
> Manila, Honolulu, Detroit, Manila, Guam, Hong Kong, Zamboanga,
> Manila, New York, San Francisco, Tokyo, Manila again, Manila
> again, Manila again. (Hagedorn 1991, 326)

## Sitings and Citings of Manila's Beauty and Brutalities

The essays in the anthology conjure Manila and its larger amalgamated entity, Metro Manila, in their immense representational forms and various contents that substantiate the worlding of its modernities usually imbricated in its beauty and brutalities and in its rendering of metropolitanisms and cosmopolitanisms. The city's beauty is situated in the experience of its madness and brutalities, and its persistent brutalities render an aestheticization of the experience of beauty—one that recalls the violence of colonialisms, neocolonialities, U.S. imperialism, Third Worldism, development, dictatorship, neoliberalism, and tyranny, among others. The essays examine the translocalities of Manila as represented in literary texts, films, SOGIE (sexual orientation, gender identities and expressions), use of hookup apps, and urban poor performances of their precarity and strength that foreground reiterations of urban, national, and global histories, geographies, and modernities. The essays discuss the creative responses from the ground level to Manila's insistence on beauty and brutality, allowing alternative and contrary claims of hope. The power of the essays is their capacity to site and siting or the mapping out of geographies of insistence and resistance in the urban war of classes, genders and sexualities, ethnicities and races, and generations, especially of those obfuscated in this war, and to cite and citing or laying bare the oftentimes conjectural, discrepant, and intermittent histories, disciplines, texts, and contexts that attempt to cohere a worlding of other possible worlds of and in Manila.

The essays examine the cartographies of Manila, its metropolitanizations and imbrications in the nation, local and the global. Oscar Tantoco Serquiña Jr.'s "Scenes Not So Fair: Poetic Representations of the Philippine Capital City" examines the literary metaphors of the city to discuss its competing epochal histories and its refusal to be shaped and to find a coherent shape. It is in the insistence to represent the unrepresentable in Manila's politics—the socialities of the urban poor—that locates another Manila within Manila. The essay foregrounds the city as a battleground between classes and class interests, especially to what would transpire to a consumption politics since the 1990s that segues to an affect of being stuck, as in Metro Manila's notorious traffic and the daily rendering of a biopolitics of docility, especially for its middle class and in its middle-class aspirations. The selection of poems results in an urban aesthetics that allows for a discussion of the divergent and dialogical forms of Manila's imbrication in colonial, imperial, dictatorial, and multinational power relations. The contemporary poets provide a critique of these social relations in power, foregrounding a site of negotiation and relief in the everyday that bears the weight of the violent histories and spatialities.

An olfactory mapping and navigation of the city is offered in "Smelling Manila" by Gary C. Devilles, who mobilizes this sensorial regime to explore its unique urban forms and configurations. Devilles examines the symbolic dimensions of Manila's smell and the materialization of scents of the city through colonial and postcolonial conjectures of personal, literary, and filmic experiences of the factory odors and foul aromas in the production of soaps and the popularity of soap operas in the local national context and the scent of apples and the smelling sensibilities of the Filipino immigration in the postcolonial context. Wittingly foregrounded in the experience of the sense and sensing of the city is the privileging of the smell of Americanization, where the economic postcolonial presence of the United States' mode of manufacturing allows for an intergenerational site of citizenry working class formation. The consequence of the downside and downsizing of the United States' economic ventures in the Philippines allows for labor migration also to be institutionalized in the 1970s, with work migration in the United States as the most privileged among other labor hosting nations. The materialization of America's worlding through smell both in the national and transnational landscapes becomes a metonym of colonial and postcolonial identity formation and transformation of becoming and being a Filipino labor.

Bliss Cua Lim's "A Tale of Three Buildings: The National Film Archive, Marcos Cultural Policy, and Anarchival Temporality" conceives of the Marcos martial law period as the propensity to meld all necessities of authoritarian nation-building in the doomed film and cultural archive Marcos has initiated, becoming the very analogue that forecasted the doomed trajectory of the Marcos dictatorship and usurpation of power of the succeeding elite factions of the newer national administrations. The lack of closure on Marcos authoritarianism in the post-Marcos era becomes the register in the continuing failing quests for a national film archive. Marcos's enforcement of archival time haunts the continuing failure in the amnesia to deal with what will become this national trauma—so painful was its register of experience in its time yet so unresolved or even erased in the present. The archival void is mobilized in the post-Marcos era and its continuing and failed quests and questings for a national film archive. Lim's analysis of the tales of the arts and culture and film buildings reify the logic and violence of archival time of Marcos's edifice complex, including lost lives in the tragedy of the collapse in the construction of the National Film Center and in the continuing failed and some hopeful mobilizations in the post-Marcos era of archival time and the national film archives. In contrast, Lim uses anarchival time as the flip side of Marcos's megalomaniac pursuits and mobilization of archival perpetuity time, a sensed "time of collapse and precarity," though directly linked with state power allowing a reflexive gesture and gesturing of ephemerality. This timeliness of time allows for a newer temporality of archiving, maintenance of, and everyday negotiation with state power, especially in a current time when historical revisionism about the Marcoses, martial law, and the Marcos dictatorship has been systemically at work, leading to the big-time political and social comebacks of the Marcoses.

Ferdinand M. Lopez's essay "Wayward Informality, Queer Urbanism: Manila, the Dark and Decadent City" further evokes the filmic conversation of the Marcos dictatorship and the *bakla*, a noncompliant gay male figuration of insistence and resistance. The filmic representations of gay Manila and the authoritarian Philippine state allow for a contestation of desires and claims to darkness, making possible a rendering of the relationship of visibility and invisibility in the formation of the state and its transformation in and by the *bakla*. Lopez analyzes the ingenuity of the film and its *bakla* heroine in the morass of Imelda Marcos's social engineering of Manila, which is nestled, too, in the quagmire of Ferdinand Marcos's mobilization of martial law in the city and the country. The figures of the *bakla* and Manila in film and the lived experiences of the *bakla* in martial law allow for a contrary claim and claiming of national identities in state formation.

The state disavowal and counter-reclaiming of the *bakla* identity in Lopez's essay is relationally mobilized in the discourse of Metro Manila's urban poor and sites in Christine Bacareza Balance's "This Is Our City: Manila, Popular Music, and the Translocal." Balance uses sonic and music texts and sensing to differentially analyze the state citification drive and the alternative music and urban poor reclaiming of the city, scenes, and sites and their resultant translocal urbanity and identity. The essay is initially replete in the descriptions of the translocal music scene as interactive cultural negotiations of the foreign and its use and adaptation in the lives of the people that embody and choose to mobilize this as their own. The translocality of the music scene and its local actors is further teased out in the more violent site of staking claim in the city, that of the urban poor and their settling in intermittent city sites, which unsettles the state's ventures of the beautiful progressive city and nation-formation. Local musicians embody their lived negotiations—the "Manila sound," which is symptomatic of a larger national-transnational nexus—accommodating and inhabiting their origin and progression of their music evolution and divergence in this nexus of the conditions of the possible in their music and in the Philippine popular and alternative music scenes. Balance rightly complexifies the origins and rise of these multitudes of claiming and reclaiming of the city through music, music sites, and music publics, but she also renders the class specificity of the younger musician intelligentsia in the territorialization and re-territorialization of the city's sonic and music subcultures.

If for Balance, the city is ours, then for John B. Labella, the city can never be theirs, which is what Balance foregrounds and Labella unpins in their essays on the city and its poor. John B. Labella's essay, "Nodes of a City Labyrinth," analyzes the version of the city novel *Smaller and Smaller Circles* by F. H. Batacan as an imagined and lived Manila of mountains of trash and landfill, sewer riverways, and trashed humanity as critical sensing of the urban imaginary representations, including dreams of what Metro Manila produces, discharges, and trashes and what literature and creative responses reclaim and redeem. The essay uses the novel as a rendering of a theory of the lived experiences of Metro Manila, using the detective fiction novel to investigate and unravel the paradoxical Manila's "disputed coherence." The city labyrinth is one of nodes, a man-making endeavor that restricts flows and enhances flooding and fixes people and their dreams in standstill traffic and uninterchangeable social classes on the one hand but also allows for pedestrians to seize the streets, proliferate violence as a counter-state act, and realize their existence outside the state purview. It is mostly the underclass that outmaneuvers the city as labyrinth, allowing detection and to sense places in tight spaces even as the labyrinth insists and is insistent in its dislocations and mapping or can only be mapped out and experienced in its nodes and nodal spaces. What the novel does and Labella navigates are the insistent ways the abject subjects reclaim other state-instigated daily ways of life—Metro Manila's notorious traffic, pedestrian seizures of the streets, and contradictions of flow—to a city that can never be theirs.

Faith R. Kares elaborates and analyzes the violence of urban life and growth in "Of Demolitions and Dispossession: The Everyday Violence of Metro Manila's Growth Politics." Her essay anchors the state's obfuscation of the urban poor and their reclaiming of the interstitial city on the larger national problem of pro-elite agrarian reform programs that have insufficiently addressed the land issue for Filipino farmers victimized by the hacienda system introduced during the Spanish colonial times and remaining intact, for most part, during the American colonial and contemporary periods. The landless farmers in the countryside form the reserve army of surplus labor in the city, though remaining a vital component that runs Metro Manila and other cities and the nation itself. Through ethnography and immersion in urban poor communities, the tales from below of how the dispossessed urban workers negotiate with the artificial poverty alleviation schemes of the national government, neoliberal machinations of national development that privileges large private businesses, including the current propensity for public-private partnerships (PPP) to build and operate infrastructures of public services at assured profit margins for the winning proponents, the continuity of the agrarian reform issue in the current continuing dispossession of the urban poor, and how progress and privatization affects the Metro Manila's poor unfold. It is the last section that weaves stories told by the urban poor that provides a contrapuntal narrative of struggle, survival, minute triumphs and wholesale victimization, and creative daily undertakings to the state imperative of rendering the urban poor as an invisible yet a vital force that moves the nation's economy. What is foregrounded in the essay is the machination of the city's urban poor and their conditionalities, especially their being dispossessed of land, that allow these bodies for another government policy—contractual labor migration and export.

In the meantime, in the waiting game of finding work overseas or business process outsource work in the key cities and to what is claimed as the "sunshine industry" in the Philippines that is targeted to employ two million call center agents, the daily living of the surplus army of reserved labor in urban poor communities abound even as urban poor dwellers are periodically demonized in political and elite rhetoric and even as their sites are demolished or threatened with demolition in the greater demand for gentrified business spaces in Metro Manila and other key cities. In the convolutions of neoliberalism and the unsettling settled claims of inner ghetto claim to rightful existence, especially of Manila's urban poor, Vanessa Banta's "Recalling to Sitio San Roque: Countermapping Urban Spaces in Quezon City" examines the creative impetus and response to the drastic and violent urbanization in neoliberal Metro Manila. The essay relationally signifies the more violent and rising creativity of the lived negotiations of the urban poor as narrativized in one such effort and scene in Sitio San Roque, "at the heart" of the proposed business district of Quezon City. This essay also marks the imposing and contending notions of beauty and brutality in the experience of city planners and state power on the one hand and the urban poor dwellers laying claim to their sites and communities on the other hand. The state's neglect and obfuscation of the urban poor and their communities as unsightly, or even "un-sitely," allow a taking on of life and living by the community members, transforming house by house, alley by alley, daily life by daily life, and creative performance by creative performance the necessity of individual existence and shared community claims that reconstitute what often is rendered invisible and powerless, their claiming of their site in the city—a literal and figurative undertaking of the city as battleground.

The rendering of invisible and powerless of the urban poor as discussed in the essays of Kares and Banta are integral in the imagination of a truly metropolis Metro Manila. The rendering of a First World metropolis is discussed in Paul Nadal's "Infrastructural Futures: Arroyo's Philippines in a Technological Frame." Nadal examines the future-making drive of then-President Gloria Macapagal Arroyo in again another attempt to transform the Philippines into a First World nation and Metro Manila as its primary showcase of megalomania. The essay traces the recent First Worlding attempts of past national administrations, using this drive to get elected into power, propelling the kinetics of their programs, terms, and visibility of the presidential bodies, and implementation of global neoliberalism in the country and focuses on Arroyo's infrastructural future of a Philippine First World imaginary. This essay tacitly links and differentiates Arroyo's infrastructure-driven development with the Marcoses' edifice complex, that modernizing infrastructures translates to economic growth. What end-results from this infrastructural future necessitates a technological framing, allowing structures, networks, and sites to exude a dreamworld of the First World possible. As philosophically drawn out in the essay, technology is a poetic form of worlding, and Arroyo's drive becomes a kind of un-worlding of the country's maldevelopment realities into a First World technological frame, with herself as the messianic evocation of this turn. Nadal examines a counter-representational claim to technologizing the infrastructural future by way of a poetry collection that writes "beyond the time of development."

The elaboration of a technological future is further elaborated in the next two essays, focusing on Metro Manila's SOGIE concerns. Roland Sintos Coloma's "The Struggle Continues . . .": On the Cruel Optimism of LGBT Organizing" traces the origin, rise, and conundrum of Ladlad, the first lesbian, gay, bisexual, transgender political party in the Philippines along its enactments of "parrhesiastic pedagogy," or an oppositional form of learning proposed by subordinated subjects seeking to present a counter-hegemonic discourse. In campaigning for party-list representation, Ladlad has moved from Metro Manila to form a provincial network of voters and advocates; it has negotiated with political parties, realities, and exigencies for the elections it has participated in. The confluences of other SOGIE gains in the electoral process and how this perseverance and educational drive for the elections and an LGBT-future is a "cruel optimism," a relation to the "compromised conditions of possibility." Paul Michael Leonardo Atienza's "Sociotechnical Infrastructures: Tracing Gay Socio-Sexual App Socialities in Manila," on the other hand, examines a class-based use of gay dating apps in Metro Manila, elaborating on the use and movement of science-based technological infrastructuring that allow the specific gay individuals and sectors to circulate and negotiate within and outside their community. The essay maps out the contending coding networks of engagement that marks bodies and identities among Metro Manila's rich gay individuals and their communities, allowing them to negotiate and reconfigure solitude and intimacies. Although gay dating apps have normativized the parameters of gay male engagements, these have also provided world-making possibilities for its users, allowing within their communities a restitution of inclusivity and exclusivity. Through an ethnography of networks that form distinct blue-collar and elite gay male users' communities in Metro Manila, tales of cloistered solitudes and new intimacies are retold, allowing for a network to establish shared platforms of negotiating tactics and an imagination of other possible worldings of their gay male positionalities and futures.

The lived creative response to urban hegemony of Metro Manila life and existence is further teased out in two specific texts and endeavors to negotiate, critique, and come into terms with the national development drive instigated in the city. In Louise Jashil R. Sonido's "*Halimaw*: A Hauntology of Manila in Street Art," the modalities of street photography art by the Ang Gerilya collective are examined on its representational counterclaims to the city. Usually known for its political street murals, Ang Gerilya draws from the transgressive erasures of mural making to a transmediated photographic contemplation and occupation of Metro Manila's streets. In the *Halimaw* series, the rich mythic and folk creatures present in the Filipino collective consciousness are mined and reinvented for the city sites, contemporizing growing up and into tales and creatures in the visibility of the urban landscape. As part of the "postcolonial fixation on identity-formation," the *Halimaw* series in the essay is examined in its translayering of its power to haunt and its power to represent a hauntology of Metro Manila. In Jema Pamintuan's "*Endo*, Manila Kentex Fire, and Contractualization under Global Capitalism," the independent film *Endo* becomes the starting point and nexus to expound on the imagined and real perils of the intensification of flexible labor in the Philippines, a neoliberal policy normalized to favor business owners. The essay traces the genealogy of Philippine films that have represented the laborer and their conditions of labor and how the overt political rendering in these films has morphed into *Endo*, a romance film set in Metro Manila with the capacity to provide commentary to this current mainstreamed structure of contractual employment. Pamintuan asks the ethically vital and charged question, "For whom?" and debunks the labor practice's illusion of bridging the socioeconomic gap. Not just withstanding the lack of security of employment with the possibility of regular worker benefits, the hazardous conditionalities of flexible labor have yielded to catastrophic accidents. The fire that engulfed seventy-two workers in the Kentex factory relates to other tragic fires that killed huge number of workers in South Asian factories, highlighting the culture of impunity in late capitalism.

The final essay, by Rosa Cordillera A. Castillo and Raffy Lerma, "Regime-Made Disaster in Metro Manila: Beyond an Aesthetics Reading of Photographs of Duterte's 'Drug War,'" examines the discourse of President Rodrigo Duterte's war on drugs that has claimed thousands of lives, mostly from the poor and abject poor of the country, and the photojournalism that documented and provided a contrary representation, mostly from the positionality of the victims and their loved ones. As part of a campaign promise, Duterte harped on, among other things, the enormity and monstrosity of the "drug problem," which catapulted a regional candidate into the presidency, thereby reactivating the strongman rule of Marcos. In power, Duterte continues to echo the drug problem and validity of the war-on-drugs solution that has allowed his administration and military to implement a martial law political and everyday environment. Yet, his presidency and his policies remain popular with the masses of people primarily affected by his violent solutions. Rosa and Lerma examine the political rendering of the war on drugs by Duterte, police, and the primarily poor people directly affected and instigate a contrary claiming at the ground level, the photojournalists' documentation of the lethal quality of the war. The essay details the modalities of extrajudicial killings, justifications, and tactics of sustainability of this war. What rose as a creative response to the coverage of the war on drugs are photographs by persevering photojournalists covering nightly the daily toll of the war. Lerma is one such photojournalist, and it is primarily his coverage photographs that highlight a contrarian claim, visuality, and storytelling to this war, allowing for the humanity of the victims and their families to be represented.

By and large, the essays and anthology talk about the modalities of state beauty and brutality and the tactics of negotiation and critique in the lived and representational experiences at the ground level or by responses of artists, writers, photographers, and cultural workers or by both marking a contrarian notion of beauty and brutality in Metro Manila and in the Philippines, implicating the historical evolution of Manila and the Philippines under colonial rules to its postcolonial development, highlighting the Marcos dictatorship as a benchmark to the contemporary rise of populist administrations in Duterte and Ferdinand Marcos, Jr. This anthology involves the re-infrastructuring and social re-engineering of tales and analyses of bodies, identities, communities, and sites of complicity and resistance. The overbearing weight of state formation in the intensification of neoliberalism, neoconservatism, and fascism that secures the profit of the 1 percent seems to allow little breathing space for those in the majority whose lives, social relations, and city-making efforts are directly and violently affected in the everyday. But as the essays also foreground, there is something hopeful, too, in the compounding ways of Philippine state formation in Manila and Metro Manila—in the creative everyday lives and tales of the urban poor, gay communities and political party, and the other disenfranchised individuals and sectors, in the politicized artistic intervention of performing groups in abject communities forging an organization of resistance, in the photographs providing stories from the street and the violent scene of daily life and death, and in the scholars themselves represented the beauty and violence of the city, nation, and state that has also represented the creative and real claims and stakes to these violent ventures. In these texts, artifacts, and mnemonics, hope abounds, and in the real responses and struggles, a hundred flowers and discourses bloom.

## BIBLIOGRAPHY

Amnesty International. "Philippines: Duterte's 'Large-Scale Murdering Enterprise' Amounts to Crimes Against Humanity." Amnesty.org.au, 2019, https://www.amnesty.org.au /philippines-dutertes-large-scale-murdering-enterprise-amounts-to-crimes-against -humanity/.

Barbaza, Remmon E., ed. *Making Sense of the City: Public Spaces in the Philippines.* Quezon City: Ateneo de Manila University Press, 2019.

Baumann, Zygmunt. *Liquid Modernity.* London: Polity, 2000.

Clifford, James. *Routes: Travel and Translation in the Late Twentieth Century.* Cambridge, MA: Harvard University Press, 1997.

Devilles, Gary. *Sensing Manila.* Quezon City: Ateneo de Manila University Press, 2020.

Doeppers, Daniel F. *Feeding Manila in Peace and War, 1850–1945.* Madison: University of Wisconsin Press, 2016.

España-Maram, Linda. *Creating Masculinity in Los Angeles's Little Manila: Working-Class Filipinos and Popular Culture, 1920s–1950s.* New York: Columbia University Press, 2006.

Garrido, Marco Z. *The Patchwork City: Class, Space and Politics in Metro Manila.* Chicago: University of Chicago Press, 2019.

Hagedorn, Jessica. "Homesick." In *Visions of America: Personal Narratives from the Promised Land,* edited by Wesley Brown and Amy Ling, 326–328. New York: Persea Books, 1991.

———, ed. *Manila Noir.* Manila: Anvil Press, 2013.

Hedman, Eva-Lotta, and John T. Sidel. *Philippine Politics and Society in the Twentieth Century: Colonial Legacies, Postcolonial Trajectories.* New York: Routledge, 2000.

Human Rights Watch. "World-Report." HRW.org, 2019, https://www.hrw.org/world -report/2019/country-chapters/philippines.

Huyssen, Andreas. *Other Cities, Other Worlds: Urban Imaginaries in a Globalizing Age.* Durham: Duke University Press, 2008.

Joaquin, Nick. *Manila, My Manila*. Manila: Bookmark, 1999.

Mabalon, Dawn. *Little Manila Is in the Heart: The Making of Filipina/o Community in Stockton California*. Durham, NC: Duke University Press, 2013.

Manalansan, Martin. "Queer Worldings: The Messy Art of Being Global in Manila and New York." *Antipode: A Radical Journal of Geography* 47, no. 3 (June 2015): 566–579.

Nguyen, Mimi. "The Right to Be Beautiful." *Account Magazine*, 2019, http://theaccount magazine.com/article/the-right-to-be-beautiful.

Padios, Jan. *A Nation on the Line: Call Centers as Postcolonial Predicaments in the Philippines*. Durham, NC: Duke University Press, 2018.

Pante, Michael D. *A Capital City at the Margins: Quezon City and Urbanization in the Twentieth-Century Philippines*. Quezon City: Ateneo de Manila University Press, 2019.

Pido, Eric. *Migrant Returns: Manila, Development and Transnational Connectivity*. Durham, NC: Duke University Press, 2017.

Reddy, Vanita. *Fashioning Diaspora: Beauty, Femininity, and South Asian American Culture*. Philadelphia: Temple University Press, 2016.

Roces, Mina. *Women, Power, and Kinship Politics: Female Power in Post-War Philippines*. Westport, CT: Praeger, 1998.

Roy, Ananya, and Aihwa Ong. *Worlding Cities: Asian Experiments and the Art of Being Global*. Malden, MA: Wiley-Blackwell, 2011.

Simone, AbdouMaliq. "On the Worlding of African Cities." *African Studies Review* 44, no. 2 (2001): 15–41.

Solnit, Rebecca. "Introduction: Center and Edges." In *Nonstop Metropolis: A New York City Atlas*, edited by Rebecca Solnit and Joshua Jelly-Schapiro, 1–15. Berkeley: University of California Press, 2016.

Sudjic, Deyan. *The Language of Cities*. London: Penguin, 2016.

Tadiar, Neferti. *Fantasy Production: Sexual Economies and other Philippine Consequences for the New World Order*. Manila: Ateneo de Manila University Press, 2004.

———. "Manila's Assaults." *Polygraph* 8, no. 9 (1996): 12–24.

———. "Metropolitan Life, Uncivil Death." *PMLA* 122, no. 1 (2007): 316–320.

Tolentino, Rolando B. *Sa Loob at Labas ng Mall Kong Sawi / Kaliluha'y Siyang Nangyayaring Hari: Ang Pagkatuto at Pagtatanghal ng Kulturang Popular* [Inside Outside of My Country's Malls, Treachery Is What Reigns: The Pedagogy and Performance of Popular Culture in the Philippines]. Quezon City: University of the Philippines Press, 2001.

Tolentino, Rolando B., R. P. Baquiran, and A. C. Aguirre. *Kuwentong Siyudad* [City Story]. Manila: Ateneo de Manila University Press, 2002.

Vergara, Benito M. Jr. *Pinoy Capital: The Filipino Nation in Daly City*. Philadelphia: Temple University Press, 2009.

Wilson, Rob, and Christopher Leigh Connery, eds. *The Worlding Project: Doing Cultural Studies in the Era of Globalization*. Santa Cruz, CA: Atlantic Books, 2007.

Wise, Edwin. *Manila, City of Islands: A Social and Historical Inquiry into the Build Forms and Urban Experience of an Archipelagic Megacity*. Quezon City: Ateneo de Manila University Press, 2019.

Wiselius, Jacob Adolf Bruno. *A Visit to Manila and its Environs*. Translated by Geert van der Linden. Quezon City: Ateneo de Manila University Press, 2016.

# Scenes Not So Fair

*Poetic Representations*
*of the Philippine Capital City*

Oscar Tantoco Serquiña Jr.

In the sonnet titled "Manila" (1965), Filipino poet Federico Licsi Espino imagines the Philippine capital city in all its postcolonial struggles with cultural identity and social development. In Espino's poetic rendering, Manila is "a hermit crab beside the tide of times," which not only bears "the traces of her former homes, / the shells of foreign cultures and the slime," but also forages a natural environment bereft of provisions and proofs of other life. Amid this scarcity is the sharp and mocking sound from a seagull overhead, whose freedom to soar above the sky and survey the terrain underneath stands in stark contrast to the muteness and dullness of the crab.

Espino's poem depicts Manila as a city continuously haunted by its erstwhile encounters and one that currently exists in a visibly careworn state. That Espino renders Manila as a crustacean whose carapace carries the residues of "former homes" and "foreign cultures" is telling of how the poet makes sense of the aftereffects of history on the much-vaunted Pearl of the Orient. Traces of slime are seen on the crab's thick covering, serving as its constitutive parts on the one hand, but also causing this crustaceous creature's slow progression on the other hand. In highlighting these residual components bearing on this clawed animal's shell, the poem primarily illuminates issues on what makes and affects the crab's physical constitution.

Espino's poem points its readers to the fact that Manila's sociohistorical encounters with the foreign have reconfigured the old city's native shores. Such confrontations have not only caused tremendous destitution on the part of the city's colonized people whose resources were profoundly exploited. Additionally, these entanglements have brought into existence these people's dismal living conditions, their cultural predicaments, and, not least, their "hungry quest" for food, livelihood, and identity. Espino alludes to this when he writes about how the crab's displacement causes its feelings of inferiority in relation to the seagull's form, flight, and sonic register. While the crab crawls sluggishly in its search for nutrition and refuge, the bird freely and gracefully flies above. Relatedly, Manila's brokenness, fragmented identity ("she finds nothing in her hungry quest"), and elusive progress ("the sidewise movement") are due in large part to its placement under long and tumultuous years of consecutive colonial subjugations and its contemporary imbrications with neocolonial formations.

Manila was the principal city of Spain's farthest colony that played a crucial role in organizing Hispanic relations in the whole Philippine archipelago as well as with other countries. Because of its considerable human density, strategic geographic position, already thriving commercial trade, and extensive hinterlands, Manila was easily the perfect permanent location of the Philippines' colonial capital. As Robert Reed (1978, 12) notes in his masterful book *Colonial Capital: The Context of Hispanic Urbanism and Process of Morphogenesis*, the emergence of Manila as the colonial capital was pivotal to its rise as the archipelago's multifunctional center in the seventeenth century (Reed 1978). Reed documents how Manila, as the capital city of the first big European colony in Southeast Asia, reigned supreme during the Spanish occupation of the Philippines, especially because it exceeded all other economic activity, population size, social complexity, political reach, as well as religious significance of other towns and cities in the country. Not only did Manila, particularly the Spanish quarter of Intramuros, become the seat of Spanish imperial power, but it also served as the "morphological model" that authorities mimicked in other urban areas across the Philippine islands (Reed 1978, 12).

When the American naval fleet defeated the Spanish Armada in Manila Bay on May 1, 1898, and after the Philippines was ceded by Spain to the United States of America for $20 million through the Treaty of Paris, the Spanish imperial forces finally surrendered to the Americans. With the formalization of the Spanish-American pact and the establishment of a civil government in the islands by U.S. President William McKinley, the American empire took over its new colony and consequently placed it under its bureaucracy. Manila, in no time, became a chief recipient of the urban aspirations of city planners and developers. The American regime, through Secretary of War William Howard Taft, hired Daniel Burnham, the master designer of the Chicago World's Fair in 1893, to make a design that would integrate the representations of the American nation's dignity and might with American interests in modernity. Burnham was quoted to have said in 1906, "Possessing the bay of Naples, the winding river of Paris, and the canals of Venice, Manila has before it an opportunity unique in [the] history of modern times, the opportunity to create a unified city equal to the greatest of the Western world, with [the] unparalleled priceless addition of a tropical setting" (Zialcita 2006, 31). Burnham's plans of building a civic center at the heart of Manila, a boulevard around Manila Bay, and recreational parks across the metropolis did not materialize.

Manila soon came to be the battlefield on which a generation-defining combat between the American and Japanese military forces occurred. This event razed the city to the ground and left it in utter ruins after the Second World War. Since then, Manila has failed to recover from its devastation. It has, instead, become the home to informal settlements, to unimaginable poverty, and to political and social divisiveness, even while it also saw the emergence and explosion of some fortified enclaves, private and commercial industries, and other capitalist developments. All of these major historical events made Manila into a geopolitical consequence of colonial rule and modernist aspirations.

Espino's poem indicates Manila's bad shape, to be sure. But it also intimates how this primate city continues to overcome its impasses. In the sonnet's final strophe, Espino writes that "Yes, this city is a pair of claws, / Creeping, crabbing with all its tragic flaws." These concluding lines suggest that despite its agonizing struggle for the right to life, as well as its long-standing battles with the historical and social afflictions weighing on its back, the hermit crab, like the city of Manila for which it stands, continues to endure, if not contend with, pulchritude and squalor, plenitude and penury. As with the crustacean that crawls across the littoral landscape without surrender, Manila persistently withstands the constant tension between its backward and forward motions.

Certainly, Espino's poetic allusion to Manila is neither a novel nor pathbreaking literary venture. Manila, after all, has frequently appeared—and continues to do so—in the country's national literatures. Although fiction writer Cristina Pantoja-Hidalgo (2002, 303) laments that the nation's capital generally figures only as a mere backdrop for stories and essays, and not so much as the character or event that moves the narrative forward, there remains a whole body of literature—from novelistic prose, to creative nonfiction, to poetry, up to comics—that centers on the city of Manila and demonstrates the complexity of its historical, political, and social configurations. These writings have a role in creating Manila, especially because they provide the means through which city dwellers may remember the city. In simulating and stimulating the city's psychosocial life through a semiotic string of symbols, these literary texts undeniably put Manila, to use the words of cultural studies scholar James Donald (1997, 185), in a "structure of visibility."

Manila is typically seen as novelistic in its intensity, extensity, and velocity. As such, prose fiction and cinema are often the nominated cultural forms in apprehending the polyphonic tones and variegated cones of vision in the Philippine capital city (see Pantoja-Hidalgo 2002; Tolentino 2001b). In this essay, I deviate from these prevailing preferences and instead turn to Philippine poetry in English in sensing representations of a city like Manila. Poetry is deemed fit in analyzing Manila because of how this literary genre demands intense linguistic compression of tropes and idioms, soundscapes and subgenres (see Ramazani 2009). Unlike poetry, however, that operates on the strict forms that render this genre scriptable and sensible, Manila seems to refuse well-defined methods to its general madness. In contrast to poetry that finds organic unity on the page and whose rhetorical devices cohere into comprehensibility, Manila has yet to reconcile itself with a strict order of things, if not a clear-cut land use plan. At present, the city vertiginously accumulates mass and volume, fuse and diffuse cultures, and contradicts itself almost to no end.

This essay explores Philippine poems in English from such writers as Federico Licsi Espino, Bienvenido Lumbera, Emmanuel Torres, Marne Kilates, and Isabelita Orlina Reyes, who bring into critical expression the experiences specific to a dense and massive city like Manila. These texts not only treat Manila as their muse and metaphor. Rather, they also discursively facilitate, if not contribute to, what cultural studies scholar Ben Highmore (2005, 5) refers to as "the tangle of physicality and symbolism, the sedimentation of various histories, the mingling of imaginings and experience" transpiring in this metropolitan space of colonial, modern, and global import. Other than foregrounding these poetic representations and discourses, I shall likewise enfold them in the particular sociohistorical juncture from which they have sprung and to which they allude. These junctures traverse colonialism (Espino), the martial law period (Torres and Lumbera), modernization (Kilates), and globalization (Reyes). In rethinking poetry vis-à-vis the Philippine capital city's interfaces with these phenomena, it is my intention to demonstrate how points in history, aspects of culture, and forces of society bear on poetic labor, structure, and content.

## Urban Representations

If Espino's poem renders the historicity of Manila through the image of a crab, literary historian, poet, and National Artist for Literature Bienvenido Lumbera allegorizes the city's desolate population using a primitive, pesky, and persistent insect in his poem "Eulogy of Roaches" (1965).

EULOGY OF ROACHES[1]
*Bienvenido Lumbera*

Blessed are the cockroaches.

In this country they are
the citizens who last.
They need no police
to promulgate their peace
because they tolerate
each other's smell or greed.

Friends to dark and filth,
they do not choose their meat.
Although they neither sow
nor reap, a daily feast
is laid for them in rooms
and kitchens of their pick.

The roaches do not spin,
and neither do they weave.
But note the russet coat
the sluggards wear: clothed
at birth, roaches require
no roachy charity.

They settle where they wish
and have no rent to pay.
Eviction is a word
quite meaningless to them
who do not have to own
their dingy crack of wall.

Not knowing dearth or taxes,
they increase and multiply.
Survival is assured
even the jobless roach;
his opportunities
pile up where garbage grows.

Dying is brief and cheap
and thus cannot affright.

A whiff of toxic mist,
an agile heel, a stick
—the swift descent of pain
is also final death.

Their annals may be short,
but when the simple poor
have starved to simple death
roaches still circulate
in cupboards of the rich,
the strong, the wise, the dead.

That Lumbera eulogizes his subjects reveals his sympathies for the poor—
"the citizens who last"—and his acknowledgment of the tenacity of this
social class as Manila's "living dead" (Mbembe 2003, 40). The eulogy works
as both prayer and praise for those who have less or nothing in life. On the
one hand, it places these people in the shadows of death, if not buries them
in the graveyards of the city, and highlights the inhumanity they confront
day per embattled day. As a necrological message, the poem indeed grieves
for the lives that, though not totally extinguished, are placed under various
stages of precarity and collapse. On the other hand, the eulogy signifies a com-
memoration of the poor's resourcefulness, flexibility, and survivability. Mor-
ibund as they are in their suspended life and death, the poor are eulogized
as cockroaches: creepy-crawlies feared for their toxins, their pernicious appearances, their long life spans, and their adaptability in a range of environments. This comparison gestures toward an understanding of these people
as parasitic to society, but who nevertheless remain enduring in a habitus
like Manila, whose authorities always outlaw and evict them to no avail.

Like informal settlers who have claimed huge tracts of land on which
they have long-established their self-governing communities, livelihoods,
and cultures ("They need no police / to promulgate their peace / because
they tolerate / each other's smell or greed."), cockroaches are mobile species
that breed and dwell in random residences and move around aimlessly
("They settle where they wish / and have no rent to pay. / Eviction is a word
/ quite meaningless to them / who do not have to own / their dingy crack of
wall"). Similar to the much-abhorred vermin, Manila's urban poor are not
made to count, despite their multitude, pervasiveness, and the many services that they deliver to formal and informal economies alike. Comparable
to immutable colonies of cockroaches, the urban poor, "not knowing dearth
or taxes," just "increase and multiply" without end as the city's remainders
and excesses whose survival, employment, and opportunities largely come
from spaces "where garbage grows."

Manila's urban poor are marginalized crucially because of their "smell and greed," their friendship to "dark and filth," their incapacity to "sow or reap" or "spin and weave," and their alleged sluggishness and status of homelessness. Bearing these traits, the lifetimes of the urban poor are deemed unworthy and disposable, while their deaths are "brief and cheap," thereby can neither be formally mourned nor officially memorialized. Akin to cockroaches that are easily killed and mindlessly discarded, the poor that Lumbera personifies are vulnerable to the degree that "the swift descent of pain / is also [their] final death."

Squatter colonies, as they are commonly called, have resulted from the imbalanced development happening between Manila and the countryside. With Manila's advancement as the key urban environment for the country's social, political, cultural, and economic affairs, people from the regions flock to the capital city, where they hope to relocate, find employment, and eke out a living to survive. In his landmark book *The Origins of Metropolitan Manila: A Political and Social Analysis*, Filipino scholar Manuel Caoili (1999, 46–47) writes that Manila has experienced rapid growth through the resources, labor, and surplus that it takes from the hinterlands. Manila has also been at the receiving end of streams of people who are, over the years, "pushed" from the rural areas by colonialists, bourgeois capitalists, military powers, and rapacious landlords whose prohibitive and abusive practices have engendered an unimaginable impoverished quality of life in the countryside. In this vein, the Philippine capital takes in more inhabitants than it can sustainably house and manage. This has turned the capital city into the major location of sprawling low-income shanties, *barong-barongs*, and other informal and low-income communities.

With their growing size and ubiquitous presence in almost every metropolitan space available, squatter colonies have become one of the most persistent and disruptive images in Manila's claim to urban modernity. As cultural studies scholar Rolando Tolentino (2001a, 167) argues in his essay "The Capital Infrastructuring and Technologization of Manila," squatter colonies are sites of disruption in the transnational economy's idealized spaces where manifestations of poverty are sought to be erased for utopian ideals of a modern city. Inasmuch as the entirety of Manila is greatly sustained by capital that streams mainly from multinational companies that facilitate the speedy development of high-rise buildings, the vast transformations of lands into spaces for private housing and mass consumption, and the intense urban renewals that aspire for "smart" and "clean and green" cities, squatter colonies are demonized in the popular imagination as dregs, abject figures, public menaces, as well as human refuse (Tolentino 2001a). As a repercussion of this prejudice against the poor, city leaders and other officials venture into civic drives with the aim of eradicating any indication of abjection, scarcity, and commotion in Manila.

Written as a response to how the urban poor and their homes were concealed by the Marcosian state in a desire to project a sanitized city during the papal visit of Pope Paul VI in Manila from November 27 to December 3, 1970, Emmanuel Torres's "Another Invitation to the Pope to Visit Tondo" (1972) is a poetic and political critique of how society's most marginalized sectors are pushed to the wayside by biopolitical control. An esteemed poet and art critic, Torres alludes to how the Marcos dictatorship kept behind whitewashed walls the urban slums teeming in Tondo, an old city district in the northwest portion of Manila considered to be one of the most destitute, most densely populated, and most underdeveloped in the country. In his poetic piece, Torres gives voice to the poor and makes them speak back with so much ironic flare against the repressive schemes of a dictatorship.

ANOTHER INVITATION TO THE POPE TO VISIT TONDO[2]
*Emmanuel Torres*

Next time your Holiness slums through our lives,
we will try to make our poverty exemplary.

\*

The best is a typhoon month. It never fails
to find us, like charity, knocking on
all sides of the rough arrangements we thrive in.
Mud shall be plenty for the feet of the pious.

We will show you how we pull things together
from nowhere, life after life,
prosper with children, whom you love. To be sure,
we shall have more for you to love.

We will show you where the sun leaks on our sleep,
on the dailiness of piece meals and wages
with their habit of slipping away
from fists that have holes for pockets.

We will show you our latest child with a sore
that never sleeps. When he cries,
the dogs of the afternoon bark without stopping,
and evening darkens early on the mats.

Stay for supper of turnips on our table
since 1946 swollen with the same hard tears.
The buntings over our one and only window
shall welcome a short breeze.

And lead prayers for the family that starves
and stays together. If we wear rosaries round our necks,
it is not because they never bruise our fingers,
(Pardon if we doze on a dream of Amen.)

But remember to remember to reward us
with something . . . more lush, greener than all
the lawns of memorial parks singing together.
Our eyes shall bless the liveliness of dollars.

Shed no tears, please, for the brown multitudes
who thicken on chance and feast on leftovers
as the burning garbage smuts the sky of Manila
pile after pile after pile.

       *

Fear not. Now there are only surreal assassins about
who dream of your death in the shape of a flowering kris.

President Ferdinand Marcos resorted to urban cleansing and renewal to
ordain Manila as the City of Man, which the dictator's wife, former First Lady
Imelda Romualdez Marcos, the self-proclaimed principal dreamer of Philippine urban modernity, governed with much ambition and lavishness. Under
this regime, the general task was to stave off all forms of urban ugliness and
transform the capital city in accordance with the perverse Marcosian logic of
"the true, good, and beautiful." Reengineering the whole city into a built and
regulated environment necessitated the erection of modernist structures—
such as the Cultural Center of the Philippines, the Manila Film Center, and
the Philippine International Convention Center, to name only a few—across
Manila's reclaimed and cultivated landscape. These efforts were testaments
to how the conjugal dictatorship treated the Philippine capital city not only
as the "crown of its civilization," but more importantly as the major gateway
through which the Philippines may access and may be accessed by the rest of
the world (see Benedicto 2014; Lico 2003).

On November 7, 1975, President Marcos signed Presidential Decree No.
824, which integrated the seventeen local governments of the Metropolitan
Manila Area (MMA) under the Metropolitan Manila Commission (MMC).

The city of Manila was linked to other nearby cities and municipalities to create "a single, shining metropolis" that served as the premiere show-off project of the authoritarian regime's aspiration for a New Society (see Tadiar 2007, 319). Metropolitan Manila's new form sought to address the deteriorating conditions of the city. Additionally, it served as a national economic strategy that could invite foreign investors, boost Manila's image as a hub of multinational corporations, and promote the tourism industry. This kind of urban refurbishment, however, brought about what literary scholar Jini Kim Watson (2011, 207) calls a "concentricity of power," which concerns the unremitting, overwhelming, and alienating dwarfing and compression of the city's entirety to give way to fast-rising business kingdoms and domiciles. Such an urban renewal, according to Caoili (1999, 152), also intended to neutralize, if not quell, efforts of radical groups that strongly opposed the brazen oppression, corruption, and abuse that took place under military rule. In other words, the creation of the MMA may be viewed as the simultaneous concentration and intensification of power that the Marcos regime rapaciously enacted.

Although the Marcos regime successfully maneuvered the city's sand, sea, and sky to turn, rather fantastically, a Third World nation into a dreamscape of First World stature (see Tadiar 2004, 2), it failed in alleviating the lives of the Filipino people. Under the watch of the Marcoses, the slums of Manila grew bigger in proportion, social unrest became more intense, and the streets of Manila, though often sanitized, turned into the locus classicus of class antagonisms. The Marcosian vision of a City of Man tried to suppress all of these social realities by deploying armed forces and barricading the entirety of the Philippine capital with outstanding infrastructures that catered to national and international gatherings as well as to social and public services (Tadiar 2007, 318).

In Manila, there is a big chasm between the rich and the poor, the powerful and the powerless, the state and the citizenry. The privileged lord over the city, whereas the underprivileged barely matter, merely keep mum, or simply fall apart. In Torres's poem, however, these binaries are challenged and reimagined to the extent that who is often perceived as the aggrieved party now derives power from a collective voice that does not deny its marginalization but in fact finds dignity in it. In this sense, the poem offers an affirmative and agentive perspective of the poor, one that perceives them not as inactive, helpless, and docile members of a city besieged by a bureaucratic and tyrannical government. Rather, they are humans with a powerful resolve and ability to expose in full view the aspects of their life-worlds that the Philippine state chooses to ignore or conceal, namely, their insufferable paucity, their cramped and dilapidated abodes, their lack of proper employment and decent sources of income, their limited access to health services and social welfare, as well as their unstable land ownership and tenure.

Celebratory and proud in tone, the poem plays with the Filipino people's "warmth" and "hospitality" to evolve a social critique about religion, politics, and the urban environment, especially in poverty-stricken Manila. Like Lumbera's biblical allusions, Torres's poem brings to the fore the same Bible-inspired narratives revolving around travel and search for home, destitution and holiness, and the hypocrisy of the rich and the generosity of the unjustly deprived. Here, it is the poor that accommodate the pope and unabashedly show him their makeshift houses, the scarcity of food on their table, and their family members who remain sick and vulnerable. In this regard, the poem not only exposes what has been kept from the public eye; it also goes against the very state-sanctioned rendering of a beautiful city, with all its man-made landscapes, top-of-the-line amenities, and world-class events, which the Marcos regime aggressively supported, funded, and endorsed.

Torres's poem is thus exemplary in five fronts. First, it represents the poor as articulate subjects of history and society who do not apologize for their poverty but rather embrace it even as they try to make sense of the social structures that underpin it. Second, it gives a cognitive mapping of Manila's underbelly, or the other side of its modern facade, that remains repressed in statist depictions of the city. Third, it sullies Manila's state-flagged image as an orderly and well-managed city by foregrounding dearth, dirt, and disease. Fourth, it addresses the prevailing disdain of the ruling classes for the grim realities in the streets. And lastly, the poem provides a ground-level view of Manila, especially its people who, despite being "the brown multitudes / who thicken on chance and feast on leftovers / as the burning garbage smuts the sky of Manila / pile after pile after pile," demand neither pathos nor wealth, only what they think is deservingly theirs: land, "more lush, greener than all / the lawns of memorial parks singing together," on which they may build their houses and lead their lives in peace. Taken together, these arguments challenge discursive constructions of Manila that are predicated upon what Donald (1997, 192) calls a "therapeutic modernism," or "the desire for a space cleansed of all uncanny mental disturbances, or even, it seems events."

With the downfall of a dictatorial regime in 1986 and the ascendancy of an elite democracy thereafter, Manila has rapidly changed its configuration to suit the demands of neoliberal market industries. With the slow demise of the Philippine state's responsibility and accountability to its citizens, with the surge of global investments in Manila, the Philippine capital city embraces a postcolonial urban modernity that is no longer largely propelled by government bureaucrats, as in the time of Marcos, but by multinational companies taking a strong hold of key areas in the whole of Metro Manila. Gavin Shatkin (2005/2006, 590) argues that not only has the private sector come to serve an intensive role in defining the patterns of the city's development through implementation of "mega-projects," more importantly, national governments have also become savvy in promoting urban development that caters to the interests of "the economically and politically influential"—the middle class, multinational businesses, tourists, and expatriates. Tolentino (2001b, 135–136) further observes that this shift in the urban environment concerns a turning from developmental schemes that the American colonial empire and an authoritarian government perpetuated. At this point, Manila shifts from being a geopolitical space that necessitated elites or technocrats to manage its territory to becoming a global city that depends on multinationals and their offerings of premature dreams of overarching modernity and urbanity.

The changes have become most apparent via Manila's unstoppable and rapid spatial reconfiguration as a city dotted with modern fortresses more commonly known as shopping malls. These edifices at once materialize and symbolize Manila's modernity to the degree that they serve not as the most obvious landmarks encroaching upon the cityscape but also the most visible manifestations of transformation in a metropolitan market space where commodities unstoppably turn into a fetish and consumerism becomes the national pastime. Furthermore, the emergence and expansion of meccas of conspicuous consumption signify how Manila is no longer just the colonial city of the past nor a grub Third World urban center of the present. Instead, it has ascended into becoming a neoliberal and global city that services and mediates for dominant and advanced economies across the world.

Manila's hurried urbanization is captured in Marne L. Kilates's "Python in the Mall" (1993), a poem that taps into a widespread urban legend in the early 1990s about a half-serpent, half-human creature that purportedly resided in the stealthiest spaces of one of Manila's major malls and victimized its much-desired targets. Such legend came into wide prominence especially because a famous actress allegedly fell prey to this enigmatic entity but was fortunate enough to escape captivity. This unverified incident fast circulated as gossip, and Kilates utilizes this whole controversy in his poem to launch a commentary about the entanglement of mythmaking and city building.

PYTHON IN THE MALL[3]
*Marne Kilates*

A serpent-like creature has taken residence
in the dark recesses of a new shopping mall.
Supposedly the offspring of the mall tycoon
himself, the creature feeds, by preference,
on nubile virgins.

—Tabloid story

She hatched in the dank
Basements of our gullibility,
Warmed in the gasp of our telling,
Curling in the tongues
Of housewives and clerks.

We gave her a body half-serpent,
Half-voluptuary, and a taste
For maidens and movie stars
Who began to vanish mysteriously
Behind the curtains of boutique
Fitting rooms and water closets,
Never to be seen again,
Or only to be found in the parking
Cellars, wandering dazed
Into the headlights of shoppers' cars.

How she fed on our thirst
For wonders, fattened on our fear
Of vacant places. Slowly
We embellished the patterns
On her scales and admired
The sinuous grace of her spine.

Avidly we filled our multifarious
Hungers at her belly, and lapped
The marvelous tales of her forked
Tongue. And as the gleaming temples
Of her worship rose in the midst
Of our squalor, how we trembled
At the seduction of her voice,
O what adoring victims we became.

This poem, at first glance, can merely be a straightforward accounting of a long, unresolved, and extremely hyped-up mystery. But my argument is that the python in the mall may also stand for the Philippine capital city. Both lure their objects of interest to go deep into their lairs ("a taste / For maidens and movie stars / Who began to vanish mysteriously"). Like the python whose "embellished patterns" and "sinuous grace" pique the curiosity of mall goers, the city also keeps its dwellers in a daze via its copious promises and enchantments. Both urban lore and urban location are invested in spectacle, beauty, and glamour. Both are curiously thought and talked about as signs for wonder. Both are propped up, embellished, and sustained by all sorts of human intervention: the former acquires weight through the stories told and passed on about it, while the latter obtains purchase through the infrastructural developments transpiring within and around its zones.

Additionally, Manila and the shopping mall where this beast supposedly hides are comparable in that they are go-to places for city dwellers in need of various nourishment and entertainment ("Avidly we filled our multifarious / Hungers at her belly, and lapped / The marvelous tales of her forked / Tongue"). Shopping malls expand and improve their operations, their structural appearances, and their commercial offerings to further fire up the patronage, marvel, and investment of their customers. Relatedly, the city develops over time according to its residents' civilizational aspirations for progress and development ("gleaming temples / Of worship rose in the midst / Of squalor"). Indeed, both derive value from people's broadly conceived "hungers," their lingering curiosities for "gleaming temples," and their bottomless adoration for all that is spectacular and solid.

Another crucial aspect of this poem is the way it sheds light on how financial capital—akin to the gossip, folklore, and mythologies that pass from one person to another—circulates in the lifeline of market industries within the city. While gossip is the means through which the urban myth of a serpent-like creature is established and embedded in the urban consciousness, capital or money is the primary means and the intended end through which capitalist modernities are structured, sustained, and perpetuated in the city and, even more widely, across the nation. Related as they are by the social and financial streams through which they flow, gossip and capital are also the means to create the desires and satiate the various appetites of both the city and its residents. The operation of malls, to borrow words from scholar and poet Rajeev Patke (2000, 13), "continues to condition consciousness and invite us to make a fetish of the commodity, on an ever-grander scale and in a more phantasmal space." The circulation of gossip, on the other hand, continues to structure the social imaginary of people and elevate a certain reality to the status of a legendary narrative or an overarching myth. In the poem of Kilates, gossip and capital are not mutually exclusive from each other. They, in fact, complement and interpenetrate, not only in according mileage and value to someone or something, but also in facilitating the movement of ideas, bodies, and objects in the city. Kilates exemplifies how speculative thoughts and presences, all of which hatch "in the dank / Basements of our gullibility" and are "warmed in the gasp of our telling," serve very well Manila's rise as a city brimming with privatized mega infrastructures, securitized business districts, and other fortified enclaves. The poet also illustrates how Manila's new commercial and capitalist form shapes and is, in turn, shaped by an array of viral scripts and stories, of valuable constructions and currencies.

If Kilates touches on the boom of Manila as a site of capital in the last decade of the twentieth century, Isabelita Orlina Reyes exposes the social, economic, and ethical impasses that Manila faces in the twenty-first century. In "Where It Resides" (2005), Reyes cites scenes concerning "elusive, evanescent wisps of lives" that exist above "the concrete hollows and highways" of the Philippine capital city in order to foreground how Manila, in the words of cultural studies scholar Bobby Benedicto (2013, 28), "elicits a lost sense of progress, optimism, globalism, while [also] inducing feelings of terror and dread."

WHERE IT RESIDES[4]
*Isabelita Orlina Reyes*

In our faces, actually,
in the disappearing

peso and our mounting debt,
our morning death toll of labor,

the bribe between his and hers,
the ride between this ritzy bar

and that carinderia, and how we fawn
over blond hair and brand names,

and how we dream to escape
everyday, we inhale it

and it doesn't have to be
drug-induced, murderous,

heinous, it's the usual lie,
the news, the passable meme,

a veneer of facts jigsawed
superglued until it has the hardness

of truth, these days, you don't have
to look too far, it's there in the garbage,

laced with maggots, at the back
of the mall where scavengers scrounge

for leftovers, the naked
taong *grasa* in the middle of the road,

at the back of the FX, the knife
in your side, your stolen phone,

the muddy floor of the public rest
room, you can't make much

for yourself or anyone
on edsa, under the flyovers

where people live in carts, hide
and collide, hold their breath,

close their eyes, stop their ears
against the metal

passing overhead—it's there
and it doesn't sing or roar. It drones.

Reyes catalogs snippets about urban life to unravel Manila's financial crisis ("in the disappearing // peso and our mounting debt, / our mounting death toll of labor"); the glaring gaps in the lifestyles of the city's human fragments ("the ride between this ritzy bar / and that carinderia"); and the fraudulence ("the bribe between his and hers") and obsession of Manila's residents in the ways and means of their previous colonial masters ("and how we fawn / over blond hair and brand names, / and how we dream to escape / everyday"). Stifling, suffocating, and seething with crime, Manila and the whole nation for which this capital city metonymically stands are diabolic traps from which Filipinos want to flee but cannot. Stuck at the nexus of a bleak past that cannot be forgone, a present that perennially passes without fulfillment, and a future that looms large in the horizon without much certainty and clarity, Manila indeed signifies physical erosion, material debris, and plundered social relations. The capital city continues to turn in its multilayered sociopolitical failures even while it also takes pride in its intimacies with global economies, market industries, and foreign capital.

Reyes unfolds incidents and images constituting the everyday life in the city. She at the same time allows these images to pile up one after another and cohere into a coherent frame containing Manila's disconnected, dizzying, and daunting landscape. Through this rhetorical technique, Reyes effectively evokes the tense fragmentation for which Manila is known, at one point, and the undeniable interconnection among the city's institutions, infrastructures, and inhabitants, at another point. These evocations accentuate Manila's uneventful absorption into schemes of globalization, or the late stage of capitalism, and this city's aspiration for a kind of progress that has yet to come to full fruition.

With the rise of Manila as one of the "global cities of the South" (Dawson and Edwards 2004, 1), financial investments and market economies take center stage. From this view, subjective experiences come under the orchestrations of business and commerce. Human relations, in addition, are subjected to principles such as objectivity, productivity, and efficiency, if not reduced into the quantifiable formulations of data, numbers, and statistics. And yet, Manila's urbanity is far from unified, organized, and smooth as a locale of life and labor. It is, in fact, an exemplary test case for the contradictory nature of cities in the Global South that largely evolve from the rubbing along and the rubbing against of power emanating from different parties. Reyes's poem spotlights some of these power sources, specifically those who, in the words of Watson (2011, 200), can be referred to as "the marginalized human remainders left over from the nation's rush to modernize." Populating Manila, according to Reyes, are those who "live in carts, hide / and collide, hold their breath, // closing their eyes, stop their cars / against the metal // passing overhead." Composing this humungous cityscape, furthermore, are the palpable proofs of uneven qualities of life ("at the back / of the mall where scavengers scrounge // for leftovers, the naked / taong *grasa* in the middle of the road, // at the back of the FX, the knife / in your side, your stolen phone, // the muddy floor of the public rest / room, you can't make much // for yourself or anyone"). As Reyes brings to the fore via her human subjects who are concurrently pivotal and peripheral to the Philippine capital city's urban systems and operations, Manila is the locus of aimless bodies and uncertain lives. In this environment that does not "sing or roar but drone," the dying refuse to succumb to complete death—in the sense that they cannot be completely purged or vanished into total oblivion—while the living cannot fully attain a dignified life.

## Urban Aesthetics

In the poems of Espino, Lumbera, Torres, Kilates, and Reyes, Manila takes on discrepant forms and yields multiple metaphors. It is not a perfectly charted, controlled, and coordinated city. It brims, instead, with despair and decay, crime and grime, discordant cultures and discrepant life forms. It is full of blight and blunder, terror and adversity, danger and delicacy, rubble and refuse, as well as all the things and beings that Tadiar (2007, 318) has referred to as the city's "visible artifacts and ruins of war." It is also simultaneously hospitable and resistive to the full throttle of modernity. While drowning in its fantasies of a good life, Manila also overflows with unbearable modes of existence. These contradictions come to the fore in the poems I have analyzed in this essay, which collectively put forward several "views from below" that counter the vantage points largely coming from what Henri Lefebvre (quoted in Highmore 2005, 3) calls "technocratic subdividers and social engineers," such as urban architects, planners, geographers, and surveyors. An aesthetics of postcolonial urban modernity may thus be gleaned from these poems that have presented Manila as a creature (especially in the works of Espino, Lumbera, and Kilates); as a world of scavengers (for identity in Espino, for social justice and a right to the city in Torres, and for a quality life in Reyes); and finally, as a cityscape of simultaneous lifetimes.

Rendered as a crab, a cockroach, and a snake, Manila is in itself a living and breathing entity. It has its own body parts that are functional or dysfunctional. It has both natural and artificial ecologies of its own. It carries a set of physical traits and pursues its own acts and movements. Indeed, though this urban environment advances slowly, it nevertheless continues to move up, down, and sideways, albeit not without struggle, to maintain and replenish its own life.

As a world of scavengers, Manila is no alien to the survival strategies of marginalized inhabitants who continue to persist amid state abandonment. Tolentino (2001a, 168) argues that scavenging is a feature of self-reliant urban communities and subjects. It is, in addition, an everyday practice and a source of livelihood that entails a making "sense of the literal and figurative garbage dumped" on the face of Manila (ibid.). As the poor maintain their lives through their transactions with and dependence on informal economies and the surplus of others, scavenging may be perceived as a creative tactic of going through and digging deep into the layers of society to find not only material resources but also social alliances and additional means to survive (see Tadiar 2009). In other words, scavenging may be seen as a gesture of marginalized individuals to symbolically or materially expose the city's chaos, if not bring to the open what remains underneath its metropolitan mayhem.

It is vital to remember, however, that such mode of urban survival occurs within and against a city that is perennially being enclosed both by political endeavors to development and by market-driven aspirations to modernity. In Torres's poem, the city is cordoned off to conceal the poor during the pope's visitation to the Philippines. In Kilates's poem, malls and, by extension, rising business enclaves and fortified communities are gating the city. These enclosures—or these processes of enclosing Manila, to be exact—may be perceived in conjunction with the overwhelming attempts at urban makeovers that are nothing but aesthetic pursuits to gentrify spaces in accordance with the market industries and at the expense of venues in which social encounters are fashioned or lived out.

As a cityscape of simultaneous lifetimes, Manila witnesses how the past, the present, and the future overlap with one another. Reyes's poem, for instance, accounts for the convergence and divergence of social worlds; the unified and contradictory flows of labor and capital; and the intimacies and clashes among social classes. Manila's urban lifetimes, as Reyes's poem carves into high relief, is composed of human lives and activities that simultaneously exist in the city but do not necessarily possess the same status or significance in the larger scheme of things. In this vein, Manila's lifetimes are neither chronologically ordered nor properly synched. Lifetimes in this city involve the developmental schemes of the business market on the one hand and the day-to-day rhythms and maneuverings of those "inassimilable" urban elements and excesses that the Philippine state, in particular, has been wanting to expel or eliminate from the city on the other hand (see Tadiar 2007, 318–319). There is, in other words, a glaring contradiction and a wide gap between the lifetimes of businessmen, capitalists, bureaucrats, and the bourgeoisie and the lifetimes of people who Emmanuel Torres, in another poem titled "Making Out" (1972), calls the "retazos" of society, or the "multitudes who go without horizons."

The poetic imaginations of Espino, Lumbera, Torres, Kilates, and Reyes have provided different understandings of *living* and *breathing* in Manila. By centering on issues such as cultural identity, poverty, violence, and globalization, these poems differ greatly from the hubristic rationalism of city planners, the mathematical calculations of geographers, and the political instrumentalism of technocratic leaders. These poems clarify how Manila's modernity is composed of flawed encounters with progress and drowns in premature if not totally aborted dreams to realize First World stature. Additionally, they underline the fact that a postcolonial city's modernity cannot be swiftly categorized in the same manner as other modernities, not least those in imperial centers, from which it frequently takes inspiration. More importantly, these literary texts call attention to what the Philippine state tends to neglect in its conceptualization of the city or in its mapping of the urban imagination: the asymmetry is at the heart of urban development transpiring in the Philippine capital.

Apart from the pieces included in this essay, several Philippine poems in English correspondingly chronicle and challenge the existing and emergent conditions in Manila. The work of Jose Lacaba, for instance, is situated in a long tradition of protest poetry that renders Manila as the ground on which Filipinos mobilize themselves against a season of authoritarian duress. In her poetry collection *Dark Hours* (2005), Conchitina Cruz writes about contemporary Manila, especially its middle-class sector and this sector's most personal and poignant concerns. Vincenz Serrano, in *The Collapse of What Separates Us* (2010), experiments with poetic forms to take into consideration the layered textures, the unpredictable configurations, and the irrepressible turmoil of Manila. Some poems in Mabi David's *You Are Here* (2009) keep an eye on the traces of war in the Philippine capital city. State-commissioned projects such as the National Book Development Board's *Tulaan sa Tren* (National Book Development Board 2008; Abad, Lumbera, and Yuson 2009; see also Serquiña 2014) have collected poems about Manila from different Filipino writers and subsequently posted them inside train coaches for the enjoyment of passengers who travel across the metropolitan area day by day. This string of literary outputs are testaments not only to Abad's (2008, 16) assertion that most of Filipino writers in English since the 1950s deal with life of the urban upper and middle classes, but also to the centrality of the city in the creation and circulation of identities, subjectivities, discourses, and practices in the Philippine nation.

In dealing with Manila's issues about cultural identity, its contested notions and embodiments of citizenship, its dynamic yet compromised public life, its unstoppable expansion and lopsided growth, as well as its failures, fractures, and flaws, the five poems included in this essay bring into clear focus the city not as an ideal haven for the powerful and the privileged alone, nor as a site wiped out of strangeness, difference, and otherness. Instead of dwelling on what Donald (1997, 197) calls the "joyous potential of cities," these poems clarify the grave urban conditions that at once get excised from and frustrate Manila's attempts to participate in global modernity. More specifically, these poems speak about Manila's burial under the weight of foreign debt, its erasure under cultural amnesia, its embroilments in poverty, its confrontations with colonizers, its complicities with capitalist developers, as well as its egregious errors and excesses. Indeed, there is a gesture in all of these poems to flesh out Manila's constitutions, to free this capital city from illusions of regalities, and to ground it back in grit and grime. Ultimately, the poems throw into high relief the fact that as the noble and ever-loyal colonial city, as the repercussion of a dictatorial dreamwork of modernity, and as the default center of a yet to rise Southeast Asian tiger economy, Manila has died and continues to die a thousand deaths. And yet, especially in the company of its people who forge ahead and valiantly fight for their rights to the urban environment, Manila persists and lives on.

## NOTES

1. "A Eulogy of Roaches." Reprinted with permission of the author.
2. "Another Invitation to the Pope to Visit Tonto." Reprinted with permission of the author.
3. "Python in the Mall." Reprinted with permission of the author.
4. "Where It Resides." Reprinted with permission of the author.

## BIBLIOGRAPHY

Abad, Gémino H. "Mapping Our Poetic Terrain: Filipino Poetry in English from 1905 to the Present." In *The Likhaan Anthology of Philippine Literature in English from 1900 to the Present*, edited by Gémino H. Abad, 3–21. Quezon City: University of the Philippines Press, 1998.

———. *Our Scene So Fair: Filipino Poetry in English, 1905–1955*. Quezon City: University of the Philippines Press, 2008.

Abad, Gémino, Bienvenido Lumbera, and Alfred Yuson, eds. *Off the Beaten Track*. Quezon City: National Book Development Board, 2009.

Benedicto, Bobby. "The Queer Afterlife of the Postcolonial City: (Trans)gender Performance and the War of Beautification." *Antipode* 47, no. 3 (2014): 580–597.

———. "Queer Space in the Ruins of Dictatorship Architecture." *Social Text* 31, no. 4 (2013): 25–47.

Caoili, Manuel A. *The Origins of Metropolitan Manila: A Political and Social Analysis*. Quezon City: University of the Philippines Press, 1999.

Cruz, Conchitina. *Dark Hours*. Quezon City: University of the Philippines Press, 2005.

David, Mabi. *You Are Here*. Quezon City: High Chair, 2009.

Dawson, Ashley, and Brent Hayes Edwards. "Introduction: Global Cities of the South." *Social Text* 22, no. 4 (2004): 1–7.

Donald, James. "This, Here, Now: Imagining the Modern City." In *Imagining Cities: Scripts, Signs, Memories*, edited by Sallie Westwood and John Williams, 179–199. London: Routledge, 1997.

Espino, Federico Licsi. "Manila." In *A Native Clearing*, edited by Gémino Abad, 393. Quezon City: University of the Philippines Press, 1993.

Highmore, Ben. *Cityscapes: Cultural Readings in the Material and Symbolic City*. United Kingdom: Palgrave Macmillan, 2005.

Kilates, Marne L. *Poems en Route*. Manila: University of Santo Tomas Press, 1998.

Lacaba, Jose. *Mga Kagila-gilalas na Pakikipagsapalaran: Mga Tulang Nahalungkat sa Bukbuking Baul*. Quezon City: Office of Research and Publications, School of Arts and Sciences, Ateneo de Manila University Press, 1996.

Lico, Gerard Rey A. *Edifice Complex: Power, Myth and Marcos State Architecture*. Quezon City: Ateneo de Manila University Press, 2003.

Lumbera, Bienvenido. "A Eulogy of Roaches." In *A Native Clearing*, edited by Gémino H. Abad, 258. Quezon City: University of the Philippines Press, 1993.

Mbembe, Achille. "Necropolitics." *Public Culture* 15, no. 1 (2003): 11–40.

National Book Development Board. *Train of Thought: Poems from Tulaan sa Tren*. Quezon City: National Book Development Board, 2008.

Pantoja-Hidalgo, Cristina. "Metro Manila: City in Search of a Myth." *Philippine Studies* 50, no. 3 (2002): 303–326.

Patke, Rajeev S. "Benjamin's *Arcades Project* and the Postcolonial City." *Diacritics* 30, no. 4 (2000): 2–14.

Ramazani, Jahan. *A Transnational Poetics*. Chicago: University of Chicago Press, 2009.

Reed, Robert R. *Colonial Manila: The Context of Hispanic Urbanism and Process of Morphogenesis*. California: University of California Press, 1978.

Reyes, Isabelita Orlina. *In Transitives*. Quezon City: University of the Philippines Press, 2005.

Serquiña, Oscar Tantoco Jr. "Across the City, Toward the Nation: Philippine Poetry, Metropolitan Trains, and the *Tulaan sa Tren* Project." *Humanities Diliman* 11, no. 1 (2014): 30–56.

Serrano, Vincenz. *The Collapse of What Separates Us*. Quezon City: High Chair, 2010.

Shatkin, Gavin. "Colonial Capital, Modernist Capital, Global Capital: The Changing Political Symbolism of Urban Space in Metro Manila, the Philippines." *Pacific Affairs* 78, no. 4 (2005/2006): 577–600.

Tadiar, Neferti. *Fantasy-Production: Sexual Economies and Other Philippine Consequences for the New World Order*. Quezon City: Ateneo de Manila University Press, 2004.

———. "Metropolitan Life and Uncivil Death." *Modern Language Association of America* 122, no. 1 (2007): 316–320.

———. *Things Fall Away: Philippine Historical Experience and the Makings of Globalization*. Durham and London: Duke University Press, 2009.

Tolentino, Rolando B. "Cityscape: The Capital Infrastructuring and Technologization of Manila." In *Cinema and the City*, edited by Mark Shiel and Tony Fitzmaurice, 158–170. Oxford, U.K.: Blackwell, 2001.

———. *National/Transnational: Subject Formation and Media in and on the Philippines*. Quezon City: Ateneo de Manila University Press, 2001.

Torres, Emmanuel. "Making Out." In *A Native Clearing*, edited by Gémino Abad, 276–279. Quezon City: University of the Philippines Press, 1993.

———. *Shapes of Silence*. Mandaluyong: Wherehouse, 1972.

Watson, Jini Kim. "Seoul and Singapore as 'New Asian Cities': Literature, Urban Transformation, and the Concentricity of Power." *positions: east asia cultures critique* 19, no. 1 (2011): 193–215.

Zialcita, Fernando N. "Revitalizing the City through Heritage." In *Quiapo: Heart of Manila*, edited by Fernando Nakpil Zialcita, 15–39. Quezon City: Ateneo de Manila University and Metropolitan Museum of Manila, 2006.

# Smelling Manila

Gary C. Devilles

## A Scent of Pandemic

The year of the coronavirus pandemic will definitely be momentous, as the whole world is still reeling with the upsurge of COVID-19 cases despite the production of vaccines and as nations compete for its procurement. With the growing number of almost half a million COVID-19 cases in the Philippines, Metro Manila cities and other local government units have boosted their efforts and plans for vaccine purchase, with P250 million to be used from the Manila City's 2021 budget, P1 billion for Makati, and P300 million for Pasig City, giving the impression that the fate of Filipinos is in the hands of these city mayors and the more affluent local government units that can afford the vaccines.

As the pandemic has highlighted systemic failings, fragilities, and inequalities, it seems that our efforts to curb this problem are still symptomatic of the same malaise. We are failing to reimagine our future, and the transformative shift that ought to happen in our thinking with this new normal is not happening. It is in this context that I draw our attention to sensing the city, in particular, how an olfactory geography can help us deal with the growing desensitization of the city and its inhabitants, which is both the effect of the pandemic and our desperate response for survival.

Even before the pandemic, a lot had already been said about the lack of study on sensory modalities, the slow repression of emotional activities, and the greater rationality of human behavior, starting with Lucien Fevre's call for a history of sensibilities in 1938 (Corbin 2014, 128) to Michel Serres's *Les cinq sens* in 1985, which derides the urban-dwelling scholars who sit huddled over their desks, basing their notions of perception on the bit of the world they glimpse through the window—and no doubt thereby overemphasizing the role of vision in their intercourse with the world (Howes 2014, 2). But now that we find ourselves in a very restrictive environment with physical-distancing protocols, along with face masks and face shields, Fevre's and Serres's calls for an embodied approach to scholarship is becoming unsurmountable, and even worse is the fact that dealing with this crisis is rearing its ugly head, turning us into blasé individuals, accepting or condoning the militaristic approach to our problem and sometimes really helpless against the state's fascistic agenda. How can we claim back our sensibilities, and how can we regain slowly our humanity amid the threat of natural and man-made calamities?

The recent Marciano Galang Acquisition Prizes of Ateneo Art Gallery was held with its theme on COVID-19, and artists were invited to reflect on the turmoil, struggles, initiatives made, and hopes as the country continues to navigate the pandemic. The gallery received an overwhelming total of 329 entries after closing its call June 2020. From those entries, fifty-four works on paper, using different media, were selected by a jury for exhibition, and I was drawn to the work of Tom Bauya's *Shroud*, which is a rendered white face in a white canvas, with its lips strewn as revealed by an unfastened facial mask. Bauya's work reminds me of various levels of shrouding, whitewashing, and concealment that we are experiencing right now with the pandemic and state repression, but at the same time, it is also a painful reminder of the possibility for uncovering. In an article he wrote for *Sun Star* in Cagayan de Oro, he talks about how he was fascinated with smelling crayons, which reminds him of familiar things, but he was also traumatized one day when in art class he was scolded for submitting a traced drawing of an eagle. Bauya's work reminds us that aesthetic contemplation is never really divorced from the context of harsh conditions of living, whether on the daily basis or on calamitous situations. As the late art critic John Berger brilliantly articulates it, nature is fearsomely indifferent—its harshness exists without promise—but it is also where beauty is encountered not in what is happening, but in the hidden, intangible signs, even in the simple white bird kitchen decorations on long winter nights in Haute-Savoie.

It is in this context, too, that I draw my sensorial explorations of Manila, my attempt to make sense of my city out of this senselessness that we are all in right now. I would like to make the connection primarily on how I grew up loving everything about the United States as sort of this fascination with the scent of American products or how we were captivated by this American perfumery, and in doing so, we were also drawn to the lies of martial law during the Marcos regime. But just like any perfume, the American Dream and martial law are evanescent; they do not linger long until we begin to realize the stench of our poverty, inequality, and pain. This is also why I endeavor to be mindful of our present situation under Duterte's regime and its fascistic approach to his so-called cleansing the city, with his war on drugs campaign, red tagging, silencing his critics, and blaming the communists for all our ills. Much of this "deodorizing" or "cleaning" is always an attempt to conceal contradictions or our real problems, and once the perfume wears off or the state withers, we are left to our devices, reeking with their undoing. I am interested in why fascism can be captivating at first and how it falters eventually, especially with the global economic and sociopolitical crises. Our experience of lockdown and physical distancing in this pandemic can open up avenues by which we can articulate what it means to strengthen our resolve never to forget our pain and to use these excruciating memories to cultivate an active ethical self. Throughout this paper, I argue that scent is about people, our struggles and political conflicts, and how we also come to terms with and negotiate this particular sensorial dimension of the city, creating or recreating the very city we live in (Cowan and Steward 2007, 13–14).

## The Olfactory of Factories

Although I grew up in Taguig, it is in Pasig, the eastern part of Metro Manila, where I studied from grade school to high school and where my parents first met and worked as factory workers. Pasig City is bordered to the west by Quezon City, north by Marikina City, south by Taguig City, and to the east by Antipolo City. In the 1970s, Pasig officially became part of the metropolis because of its development and urbanization; and its financial resources were concentrated on the western part, which is closer to the river, providing accessibility and convenience for factory shipments and deliveries. It was here where long and bigger roads were built, such as Ortigas Avenue, which connected Pasig to EDSA. These highways were home to numerous factories, warehouses, establishments, and commercial facilities.

My father worked at Warner-Lambert, an American pharmaceutical company founded in 1856 in Philadelphia by William R. Warner. In 1955, Lambert Pharmaceutical, the makers of Listerine mouthwash, merged with Warner to form Warner-Lambert. By the 1960s, a large number of American companies were relocating their manufacturing plants to the Philippines, for the obvious reason that the labor here was cheaper. It was around that time, too, when factories sprung up in Pasig and in Quezon City, as Manila was getting more congested, while Pasig and Quezon City were fast becoming sites of new development and urbanization. Small communities on the fringes were slowly being built. Rows of small two-story apartment houses were constructed for factory workers and their families in the area. Our small barrio was divided into zones, and we were in the fourth zone. We lived in a small apartment, where the lounge, dining area, kitchen, and bathroom were all on the first floor and the bedroom was on the second. Our apartment houses were like duplex-type houses that had thin walls, so we could hear everyone and practically smell what my neighbors were cooking. The residents of the apartment blocks bonded like a community, and eventually everyone knew each other. My friends and playmates had parents who also worked, if not in the same company, in one of the factories along the road. E. Rodriguez Avenue was a line of factories, from the Alaska Milk factory, followed by Ovaltine, to Ajinomoto, a Japanese food and chemical factory, and Union Republic Glass, a glass and cement factory. Further down, near Barrio Bagong Ilog, there were the Universal Robina Corporation, which manufactured animal feed, Pepsi Cola Bottling, and Coca-Cola Bottling, both makers of the famous sodas. There was also a local chocolate factory, Ricoa, near a public hospital in the southernmost part of Pasig.

I remember these factories well because of the odors they emitted whenever I commuted from our place to the downtown area. My dad was a confectionery maker of Halls, Chicklet gums, and Dynamints, and their smells are usually lemon, peppermint, strawberry, and menthol. Eventually, I would learn that these are all artificial flavors, but at that time I had no way of knowing the synthetic from the real. For me, those scents were overpowering, and every time he came home from work, the smell of gum and candies on his uniform filled our rooms. Strangely, these factory scents have shaped my family's identification with American culture. Most American factories, including my dad's company, were producing deodorizing products, and their factory odors tended to be pleasant, while local factories that were producing poultry and husbandry feeds sent off foul (fowl!) odors. These American factories played on the olfactory psychology as part of their highly effective practice of marketing and manufacturing. In truth, the use of olfactory psychology was not an uncommon practice in the U.S. manufacturing industry. There was an experiment in 1966, for example, in which marketers tested the impression produced on consumers by the addition of a lemon scent to Joy laundry detergent. Even though the lemon scent in no way altered the substance of the detergent, the consumers agreed that the scent of lemon increased the soap's cleaning and grease-cutting power (Classen et al. 1994, 192–193). It is highly probable that American factories in the Philippines concentrated on deodorant and perfumed soap products since these products emitted pleasant odors that were more likely to win customers.

My dad had a strong sense of loyalty to his company, and he believed American products were superior to any local brands, although there were very few local counterpart companies, because American goods had already dominated the market even before the 1970s. It would take some time for us to produce our own soaps and deodorizing products. And although the country was expanding its manufacturing industry, most local factories ended up manufacturing processed primary commodities to be exported back to the industrialized countries (Kim and Young 1987, 30–31). Such uneven practice had dire effects on the economy, and by the 1980s, the Philippines was lagging behind other Asian countries because of the prolonged dependence on and overvaluation of American goods.

The growth of the American manufacturing industry in the Philippines in the 1970s was part of global capital and labor flows. Capitalism works in terms of uneven geographical development, which means that as there were pockets of development in the United States, there were vast areas of underdevelopment; with urban decline in United States, there was a sort of urban growth in the Philippines and other Asian countries; and as the manufacturing industry moved to the service industry, there was mobility of capital and labor (Harvey 1982, 373–376). The proliferation of American factories can be understood in terms of the contradictory nature of capitalism. As much as it paved the way for standardized, low-cost goods and just compensation for factory workers, these have always been executed in the interest of capital and not necessarily for the welfare of the workers. Such movement of capital was driven by its logic of accumulation and its growth, no matter the ecological, social, or geopolitical consequences (Harvey 2006, 121).

This is the reason for the short-lived industrialization patterns in one country. By the late 1980s, factories were already relocating to China and other Asian countries. The industrialized country then had no choice but to move to the service-oriented industry, as evinced by the proliferation of malls, call centers, and the migration of people to other countries to work. Capital mobility is about expansion and seeking surplus, and as the Philippines in the 1970s provided cheap labor for American factories, the country generated a culture of consumerism. Aside from the contradictory nature of capital flow, the factories were the result of extending the Fordist principle of efficiency and mass production. By the 1950s, the model of Henry Ford's mass production spread across the oceans to new industries and extended to new kinds of production, from house building to junk food manufacturing. Goods and services were now produced for a mass market (Hobsbawm 1994, 263–264).

I remember my dad working in two shifts with overtime rates. For my dad, overtime payment meant savings, and he was saving to build a house and settle in Taguig. His aspiration was the typical working-class American Dream: work hard, save, build a house, and then retire. The factories made it possible for workers like my dad to create and realize this sense of lifestyle. Fordist principle is not just about the efficacy of production; it is about creating this working middle-class fantasy, exalting man for his heroic self, to be productive and provide for his family. Gramsci accounts for these seemingly progressive conditions, saying that among such conditions like the introduction of more efficient machines, the formation of a new type of worker through high wages and benefits is inevitable. He notes, however, that such phenomenon also has saturation limits and is followed by declines in the production of consumer and capital goods (1995, 433–434). Working-class "American" Dreams are sustained by capitalism, and this was institutionalized during the U.S. Depression era, when a counsel on public relations was created and headed by Edward L. Bernays, a nephew of the founder of psychoanalysis, Sigmund Freud. As a public relations consultant, Bernays was tasked to create public opinion, spreading an impression to the public, in other words, to work on propaganda (Bernays 1961, 11–12). Bernays used many of Freud's findings in psychoanalysis, including an understanding of the unconscious desire, which he aimed to tap into. He sought the help not of politicians but of capitalists in producing fantasies, in making people want things, in appealing not to their rational side but to the irrational aspect of their lives, such as dreams and fears.

Together with Fordism, therefore, the counsel on public relations was manufacturing public consent, feeding their fantasies, allaying fears, and turning workers into desiring "happy machines." The goal of a factory is not just to produce surplus but also to turn workers into virtual factories that perpetually produce or reproduce, consume, and distribute fantasies and commodities. Bernays was not alone in using and manipulating public opinion; Hitler and his party, the National Socialists, were on the same track of manufacturing public consent, of rationalizing the public's collective desire and unconscious.

In the Philippines, the manufacturing of public consent worked very well with Marcos's dictatorial regime. Dictatorship thrived on the Fordist principle of urbanization in the 1970s, and fetishism of American goods worked because it was supported or backed by such a manipulative and oppressive political system. Robert Stauffer argues that the Philippine government was in cahoots with international financial institutions to the extent that they created the preconditions to the authoritarian political direction of the type imposed by President Marcos himself. Much of this control came in the form of debt accumulation from multilateral banking institutions, encouraged from outside and by Filipino economists who share the same developmental models as foreign lenders', which ultimately resulted to a total of USD $1.96 billion in debt. The mounting debt brought strong pressure from the International Monetary Fund, forcing the Philippines to devalue its currency and adopt a "floating rate" for the peso (Stauffer 1986, 1–3).

Marcos maintained continuity with the established political tradition, with his domestic base that included military officers, civilian technocrats, and the elite, securing, at the same time, crucial external support from the U.S. government, skillfully manipulating its preoccupation with the military bases and personally investing in the electoral campaigns of key U.S. politicians (Boyce 1993, 8). Foreign companies dominated the Philippine industry, and even the so-called Filipinization of the industry was also an extension of this Americanization since the American companies turned over their companies to their rich Filipino friends and allies: for example, Manila Electric was sold to the Lopez family in 1961, and the General Telephone and Electronics Corporation of New York was sold to Ramon Cojuangco of the landed Cojuangco family of Tarlac (Doronila 1992, 87–88). Marcos would definitely woo these oligarchs, both the Americans and the Filipino elite, hence, his rule was no different from oligarchy. But when he could not win the oligarchs to his side, he eventually sequestered their properties and replaced them with his own cronies. In effect, Marcos extended this Americanization, and the companies or industries, whether owned by Filipinos or partly owned by American firms, were all instruments of this domination, creating a sense of cultural hegemony in the process, as the goods produced by these companies created also the consumers like me and my dad, who would desire them and grew up loving anything made by American companies. In our own parlance, we would say that everything U.S.-made is "stateside."

Most of these American factories would also make the efforts to integrate their employees into their systems and help create communities. I remember that the company where my dad worked would always sponsor family activities, sports festivals, summer outings, etc. They also made their presence felt and visible through advertisements and sponsorships of our local basketball leagues. During town fiestas, the companies would donate confetti and banners stamped with their logo. In short, the factories were shapers of our everyday culture and sensorium.

The domination of American factories and their goods in the 1970s came as well with the denigration of local companies, as local products were considered cheap and a poor imitation of their U.S. counterparts. Furthermore, local companies were considered to have substandard, hazardous, and poorly sanitized working areas. To a certain extent, American factories tried to be as different as possible from their local counterparts. It was not accidental that, compared with the local ones, most American factories emitted pleasant smells and avoided goods that emitted unpleasant odors—thus convincing us of their perfumed superiority.

Local factories could not compete with American factories, and they ended up producing effluvial by-products. When I was in grade school, one local factory would discharge a sharp stench that reached all over the school premises. We hated this factory, and I remember this was how we reckoned with the worth of local goods. We learned to distinguish between local and American factories, a sense that eventually was extended to comparing local goods to imported goods, our inferiority to American superiority, and our stinking identity to the American's perfumed superiority. It took some time, of course, before we realized the folly of such distinctions, and in the process, we also neglected our Pasig River, which was starting to emanate offensive smells. Most of the factories, local and multinational, were discharging their refuse into the Pasig River.

The name Pasig can be an allusion to *dalampasigan*, which literally means "shore," and since early communities were around or near the river, Pasig, historically, is one of the oldest communities in Manila. The Pasig River connects Laguna de Bay to Manila Bay, stretching for about twenty-five kilometers. Its major tributaries are the Marikina and San Juan Rivers. Before the mass urbanization, the Pasig River served as an important means of transport. During Spanish colonization, the walled city of Intramuros was built on the southern bank of the Pasig, near its mouth. After World War II, however, the river was soon neglected amid the massive population growth, the widespread construction of infrastructures, and the dispersal of economic activities to the suburbs. Informal settlements were built on the riverbanks, and the factories dumped their wastes into the river, turning it into an effective, huge sewer system.

By the 1980s and through the 1990s, the Pasig River was considered biologically dead, a fitting expression of the short-lived benefits of Fordism and the country's stinking economy. Factory wastes dumped in the river accordingly accounted for 45 percent of its total pollution; about 315 of the 2,000 or more factories situated on the river basin have been identified as its principal polluters, dumping an average of 145 tons of biochemical oxygen demand per day. By the 1990s, most of these factories would close down and relocate to China and other Southeast Asian countries that offered cheaper labor. The factories have disappeared, but the stench in the river lingers.

Records show that the textile and food manufacturing industries are the greatest water polluters among those considered in the study. Domestic liquid waste contributes another 45 percent of the pollution load in the Pasig River. Untreated wastewaters from the remaining 88 percent of the population flow through canals and estuaries into viaducts leading into the river. It is estimated that 148 tons of biochemical oxygen is added to the river every day, and this entirely from the sewage outlets scattered along its banks (Helmer and Hespanhol 1997).

People had already stopped using the river's water for laundering in the 1960s, and ferry transport had declined. Despite the pollution, however, we still played on the riverbanks. The river was murky, and there were times when my parents scolded me, forbidding me to play along the banks because they feared for my health after my elder brother had earlier suffered from diphtheria, which my parents believed he contracted from the polluted water. Despite the constant warnings not to play near the river, we would nonetheless sneak away from our apartments in the afternoon and play there. I must have become so accustomed to the smell of the river that I do not recall being sickened by it.

But what fascinated me then about the river was the flooding during the typhoon season, in the months of June until August. Floods destroyed houses and properties, and in Pasig, we experienced two big floods. What I recall is seeing from my window the strong muddy current flowing toward the western part of Pasig City. I saw debris of logs, uprooted trees, and appliances floating in the river. People were in panic. My dad made sure that we were all secure on the second floor of our apartment. Water rose chest-deep on the ground floor, but dad had to help our neighbors. Flooding and calamities have their way of bringing out the best in people. They helped each other, and I remember how our neighbor who owned a convenience store around the corner gave us food. But the most striking thing about flooding was the day after, when people were starting to rebuild everything. I remember a clear morning, as if sunlight were particularly crystal and all around was exceptionally brilliant. Moreover, there was a palpable absence of stench, and the clearing of the air made breathing pleasant. I know how much damage a storm can cause; the Philippines suffers twenty-six to thirty storms every year. Flooding continues to be a perennial problem in Pasig, but, ironically, nature has a way of deodorizing the air, and it is through this natural deodorizing that I remember the city as well. Even the smell of the briny bay disappears for a moment after a storm, as what an Australian friend who lived in Makati City for five years has told me of what he remembers about the Philippines. Natural calamity is not the only way of deodorizing the air in Manila. American factories invested heavily in deodorizing products in the Philippines to the point that deodorization became a distinct feature of American colonialism, the propagation of its culture, and the construction of our docility.

## A Scent of American Colonization

Warwick Anderson's *Colonial Pathologies* (2006) demonstrates how sanitation has always been a preoccupation of the United States in colonizing the Philippines, as the Americans had eagerly taken up the burden of cleansing us, attempting to purify not only our public spaces, water, and food but also our bodies and conduct The emergence of factories in the 1970s was a continuation of the logic of their operation.

In the 1970s, when the United States was suffering an economic crisis, it was logical for the industries to relocate to countries like the Philippines in search of surplus and cheaper labor. The United States continued to exercise its hegemony over the Philippines despite having granted it its independence after World War II. This is one contradiction of my colonial experience—we were told that the country was democratic, but we always sensed otherwise. I consider the United States' relation to the Philippines one that can be sensed literally and metaphorically by its scents, by the paradoxical nature of scent as being invisible yet manifestly present.

I grew up with my parents working in American factories, and they were conditioned by the very movement of capital, by its dynamics, and by its logic of accumulation. Accordingly, in the domination of capital, the laborer is nothing but a variable capital, an aspect of capital itself, which means that as capital is indifferent, the laborers are forced to accept that their labor always produces the same product and money and must be in principle always ready and willing to accept every possible variation of labor that promises higher rewards (Harvey 1982, 380–381). High rewards, the American Dream, and upward social mobility are the very desires by which capital accumulation works, and these were also the pervasive themes in TV soap operas. Hence, domination can be sensed in American cleansing soaps and the proliferation of TV soap operas, in which cleansing soaps and soap operas are entangled, not just as commodities, but as the very instrument themselves in making commodities out of consumers.

My mom worked in the Johnson & Johnson factory that made rubbing alcohol, body oil, shampoos, and soaps. Though she resigned when she got married to my dad, her loyalty to the American company and its products was as indisputable as my dad's. I grew up with the company's brand of herb-scented soap called Heno de Pravia, which came in a pale green box. After a morning bath and before I dressed for school, I would apply Johnson & Johnson baby powder to my chest and back for relief from the heat. I would brush my teeth with Colgate toothpaste. As grade school students, we were also taught basic grooming and hygiene with the use of rubbing alcohol and cologne.

Coming home from school in the afternoon, I deodorized by washing hands and feet and applying rubbing alcohol. Later, we tried other soaps like Irish Spring, Palmolive, and Dove. These deodorizing products have made their way onto my body and into my sensorium, shaping it through smell and touch. They were so much part of my day-to-day ritual that even the brand names were powerful enough to be generic household names. We called toothpaste Colgate, detergent soaps Tide or Mr. Clean. These American goods had a mystical and mythical quality—for instance, soaps, whether detergent or soft, were imbued with the aura that Roland Barthes discusses in *Mythologies*. Barthes uses the brand name to talk about the *Omo euphoria*, the mystifying process that consumes the consumers, as though they become like the soap itself, a commodity (Barthes 2009, 31). In other words, as we immerse ourselves in these commodities, feeling and smelling them, we become part of the system of exchanges so that our consumption of goods is seemingly converted into a value and that, ultimately, even relationships and subjectivities become tainted with it. *Omo euphoria* works on supplanting social relations and values as these goods "magically" transform us into little Americans—smelling like them.

The U.S. goods thus specifically targeted our bodies. Most of them were cleaning and whitening products designed to make body pliable, desirable, and recognizable. Hence, the goods generated the same *Omo euphoria*, an exaggerated feeling of happiness akin to soap bubbles that exuded luxury despite their lack of substance. Soaps and other American goods created an ensemble of abstraction by which consumption became a form of reproduction, an endless duplication of the object where the consumer became like the soap bubbles or the commodity itself.

Our Americanization is not far from the phenomenon that Anne McClintock discusses in her erudite work *Imperial Leather* (1995) about soap and its advertisements in the nineteenth century. As she argues, the advertisements captured the hidden affinity between domesticity and empire, the undervaluation of women's work, the overvaluation of commodity in the industrial market, and the disavowal of colonized economies in the arena of empire. Accordingly, soap flourished not just out of necessity but as a form of mediation for Victorian poetics of racial hygiene and imperial progress (McClintock 1995, 208–209). The same case happened in the Philippines, as the proliferation of these commodities governed our daily lives and consumption ultimately became ideological (Baudrillard 1996, 3). Hence, what was being circulated in our market was the very ideology of the American way of life. American colonization of the Philippines did not stop when the country became an independent republic. Rather, it continued, persisted, and became even more insidious. It lingered like smell.

Yet what the ideology promised, ironically, and what, at a superficial level, it provided was a pleasant smell. Americanization in this period was sustained by the illusion of abundance, the saturation of goods, mass production, fantasy and mythmaking, bombardment of images and signs, activation of desires, and the tapping into the collective unconscious. Even an image became a commodity, a desire, and an identification. At that time, I did not understand how temporary or fleeting the expansion of the manufacturing industry was, how the factories were predicated on cheap labor, and how ironic globalization and the rise of transnational companies were. I did not understand why my dad was retrenched from his work in the late 1980s and why he had to leave and work in Saudi Arabia. But considering the logic of capital movement, I see urbanization as a big bubble, a big soapy bubble, like the one that gets in your eyes and blocks your vision or goes up your nose and overpowers your smell.

By the time my dad lost his job in the American factory in Manila, he had already bought the land in Taguig. He used the money he got from his retrenchment package to build our house and saved the rest of it in Banco Filipino, which shortly thereafter suffered a bank run because of political instability. We could not get our money then, and dad had no choice but to apply and work abroad in Saudi Arabia. I was in the second year of my high school at the time. I remember this particularly well because my dad told us that one of us, one of my siblings, would have to stop schooling. I would note that what was happening to us was not unusual. By the late 1980s, the Philippines had moved into the service-oriented industry and had become an exporter of labor. It is said that, presently, overseas Filipino workers number at ten million, about 10 percent of our population, and more than a million leave every year to work abroad. This exodus also includes a number of skilled workers taking on unskilled work overseas, and their combined remittances in 2015 were estimated to be USD $20.117 billion, representing 13.5 percent of our gross domestic product, thereby being the main source of our so-called economic growth.

The year 1986 was a promising one, politically, for the country, as the People Power ousted Marcos, but that was the very year we as a family felt financially devastated. We started selling our appliances, and we borrowed money from our relatives and friends to make both ends meet. I recall one incident when a convenience store in our neighborhood just canceled our credit line because of our mounting debts. Mom was truly upset, and for the first time I believed I understood what economic crisis meant—growing up with a dad who was working overseas, trying to maintain my grades to qualify for a scholarship, being different from my classmates who enjoyed much more comfort and luxury. The momentary relief of industrialization as we understood and sensed it was indeed very much like a lingering scent: we could not anymore smell it.

## A Political Anosmia

I tried to show how a sensorial approach can be useful in making sense of the place I grew up during martial law, and I draw on how an olfactory geography can reveal the contradictions of Americanization and by extension the martial law that sustained it. Our sense of smell can be a powerful mode of perception in revealing crucial contradictions and conflicts of our lived experience. But our sense of smell is a layer of multifaceted experience, and connected to our present circumstances, I reiterate the call earlier for a history of sensibilities and sensory ethnography to ground our experiences and ideas and to make connections, especially now, that everything and everyone is threatened by the invisible COVID-19 virus.

It is quite fortuitous that one of the symptoms of this viral infection is the loss of sense of smell, or anosmia, and scientists all over are trying to understand if this loss of smell can be a key aspect of understanding the nature of the virus. But along with this imminent and real threat is the degrading loss of sensibilities in dealing with this pandemic, as the precautionary measures we have to take during lockdown, such as work from home, physical distancing, and facial masking, are making it difficult for us to relate as embodied beings in a sensorial environment. This situation is even made more complicated by the militaristic and jingoistic approach of this government, "waging war" without any regard to human life or easily dismissing viral infection cases as casualties in statistics.

I go back to Tom Bauya's *Shroud*, which suggests that precisely in these trying times we should endeavor to remember, to put back the face on all forms of defacement and erasures, to insist on the value of life, and to reclaim our human dignity. The shroud is the manufactured layered assault that should never be forgotten and that is constantly in dialectic with making sense of the hidden and experiential truth. In other words, even if there are attempts at perfumery, to deodorize or to conceal the real situations and problems, absence of smell does not necessarily mean nonexperience. The olfactory space is a combative space of aromas and bad odors, potent enough to remind us of contradictions and contesting forces in our society. An acute sense of smell whether in the everyday or the political is able to discern the real from artificial and pierce through the envelop of perfume and *Omo euphoria*. Americanization, fascism, and martial law are dominant scents that linger in countries like us, and they remain persuasive and ever seductive. As of this writing, the Department of National Defense has abrogated its 1989 pact that prohibits the unauthorized entry of police and military personnel in University of the Philippines' campuses. The accord was a hard-won right of student activists who fought for police-free campuses and the restoration of their rights after the late President Ferdinand Marcos lifted martial law. This move of the Department of National Defense is in line with the state's logic of criminalizing dissent and criticism at a time when the government is disintegrating and cannot anymore conceal their inefficiency, corruption, and failings. The state is not only withering, but its putrefaction is also intensifying. UP is fighting back to preserve its academic freedom, and this behooves us never to forget, to put sense back, to wake up from a perfumed nightmare, and to join the clamor against all forms of state repression.

## BIBLIOGRAPHY

Anderson, Warwick. *Colonial Pathologies: American Tropical Medicine, Race, and Hygiene in the Philippines.* Durham, NC: Duke University Press, 2006.

Baclig, Cristina Eloisa. "COVID-19 Vaccine Procurement Projects of Metro Manila." *Philippine Daily Inquirer*, January 4, 2021, https://newsinfo.inquirer.net/1379245/covid-19-vaccine-procurement-projects-of-metro-manila-lgus#ixzz6jyG5sLqJ.

Barthes, Roland. *Mythologies*. Translated by Annette Lavers. New York: Vintage, 2009.

Baudrillard, Jean. *The System of Objects*. Translated by James Benedict. London and New York: Verso, 1996.

Bauya, Tom. *Shroud*. Ateneo Art Gallery, Marciano Galang Acquisition Prizes Exhibit, 2020, https://ateneoartgallery.com/exhibitions/marciano-galang-acquisition-prizes-and-aag-klfi-essay-writing-prizes.

Berger, John. *Ways of Seeing*. London: British Broadcasting Corporation and Penguin Books, 1972.

Bernays, Edward. *Crystallizing Public Opinion*. New York: Liveright, 1961.

Boyce, James K. *The Philippines: The Political Economy of Growth and Impoverishment in the Marcos Era*. Quezon City: Ateneo de Manila University Press, 1993.

Classen, Constance, David Howes, and Anthony Synnot. *Aroma: The Cultural History of Smell*. London and New York: Routledge, 1994.

Corbin, Alain. "Charting the Cultural History of the Senses" In *Empire of the Senses*, edited by David Howes, 128–139. London and New York: Bloomsbury, 2014.

Cowan, Alexander, and Jill Steward, eds. *The City and the Senses: Urban Culture since 1500*. Burlington: Ashgate, 2007.

Doronila, Amando. *The State, Economic Transformation, and Political Change in the Philippines, 1946–1972*. Singapore: Oxford University Press, 1992.

Kim, W. Chan, and Philip K. Y. Young, eds. *The Pacific Challenge in International Business*. Ann Arbor, MI: UMI Research Press, 1987.

Harvey, David. *The Limits to Capital*. Oxford: Basil Blackwell, 1982.

———. *Spaces of Global Capitalism: Towards a Theory of Uneven Geographical Development*. London and New York: Verso, 2006.

Helmer, Richard, and Ivanildo Hespanhol, eds. *Water Pollution Control: A Guide to the Use of Water Quality Management Principles*. London: E&FN Spon, 1997.

Hobsbawm, Eric. *The Age of Extremes: A History of the World, 1914–1991*. New York: Vintage International, 1994.

Gramsci, Antonio. *Further Selections from the Prison Notebooks*. Edited and translated by Derek Boothman. Minneapolis: University of Minnesota Press, 1995.

McClintock, Anne. *Imperial Leather: Race, Gender and Sexuality in the Colonial Contest*. London and New York: Routledge, 1995.

Santos, Eimor. "UP-DND pact Soto-Enrile Agreement." *CNN Philippines*, January 19, 2021, https://www.cnn.ph/news/2021/1/19/UP-DND-pact-Soto-Enrile-agreement-.html.

Stauffer, Robert B. *The Philippines under Marcos: Failure of Transnational Developmentalism*. Sydney: University of Sydney, 1986.

# A Tale of Three Buildings

*The National Film Archive, Marcos Cultural Policy,*
*and Anarchival Temporality*

BLISS CUA LIM

ollowing the deadly collapse of the Manila Film Center five months into
its frenetic construction, strident anti-Marcos critic and former University of the Philippines President Salvador P. Lopez voiced the nation's
diagnosis of the First Lady's mania for architectural construction: "There's no
question about it: Mrs. Marcos is a compulsive builder. She has a bad case of
the edifice complex, though fortunately non-Oedipal and non-fatal."[1] The term
*edifice complex* was the pun-loving Filipino public's shorthand for the massive
state-sponsored architectural reinvention of Manila during the twenty-year
rule of Ferdinand and imelda Marcos, from December 1965 to February1986.

From the mid-1970s to the early 1980s, as state power, public funding, and
cultural authority were increasingly concentrated in the First Lady's hands
as governor of Metro Manila, representative to the Interim National Assembly, and Minister of Human Settlements, Imelda Marcos promulgated
a utopic vision of Metropolitan Manila reborn as the "City of Man," a humane city "able to bring out what is true, good and beautiful in man and his
environment."[2] The dictatorship's urban vision attempted to reclaim the nation's capital from the alternative geography of student dissent that had culminated in the First Quarter Storm of January to March 1970, when anti-
Marcos youth protesters were violently suppressed by police and military
forces. In contrast to student activists' "fearful geography" of street protest,[3]
the Marcosian edifice complex erected grandiose buildings that, as Gerard
Lico argues, were "propaganda realized in architectural form," asserting
state power through megalithic "spectacles of legitimation." The Cultural

Center of the Philippines Complex, built on reclaimed coastal land along Roxas Boulevard, was the nucleus of the regime's ambitious architectural overhaul of Manila's urban space. In practice, the City of Man entailed the forcible displacement of sixty thousand slum dwellers as well as a Beautification Program that spray-painted parched foliage green and hid the capital's squatter colonies from the gaze of visiting foreign dignitaries.[4]

Weaving together strands of spatiality, temporality, and cultural legislation, this essay suggests that the catastrophic effects of Marcos-era cultural policy on Philippine film archiving can be apprehended as a tale of three buildings. Completed in 1969 during the early years of the Marcos regime, the first of these structures is the Cultural Center of the Philippines (CCP) Performing Arts Theater. Institutionally, the CCP functioned as the dictatorship's central implementing agency for cultural policy initiatives; the fledgling Film Archive of the Philippines was initially subsumed under its auspices. Funding for the construction of the CCP theater was riddled with fiscal malfeasance from start to finish,[5] and CCP practices exemplified a neocolonial politics of patronage that often devalued the Filipino artistic labor it claimed to celebrate.[6] Nonetheless, in hindsight, the CCP is not only the first but also the most enduring realization of dictatorship architecture and cultural policy. In contrast, the Manila Film Center, erected in the twilight of the dictatorship, exemplifies the failure and decay that haunts the Marcoses' edifice complex. Built to house several government film entities, the Manila Film Center—and with it, the Film Archives of the Philippines (FAP)[7] situated on its premises—was the most memorable casualty of Imelda Marcos's characteristically rushed construction timetable, an *Imeldific temporality* that proved not only unrealistic but also lethal. In the wee morning hours of November 17, 1981, the scaffolding of an upper floor of the Manila Film Center collapsed under the weight of quick-drying cement, burying and killing the construction workers beneath who had been working around-the-clock to complete the building. Following the Manila Film Center's completion in 1982, members of the First Family participated in numerous exorcisms in response to accounts of haunting.[8] Despite criticism that proximity to the sea air would harm the film archive's collection, the FAP was housed on the ground floor of this purportedly haunted film center until 1986, when the conjugal Marcos dictatorship was swept away by popular revolt. In the post-Marcos era, the Manila Film Center has alternated between periods of disuse and dereliction. In 2001, it became the unlikely site of queer reoccupation and renewal by the performers, tourist audiences, behind-the-scenes workers, and organizers of the Korean-owned *The Amazing Show*, touted as "the largest transvestite show in Asia."[9]

The CCP Performing Arts Theater and the Manila Film Center—two emblematic edifices that bookend the dictatorship—actualize Marcosian cultural policy in built form. In addition to these two structures, I triangulate a third edifice that never was (or has not yet been): a permanent building to house the nation's film archive under suitable archival conditions. Though never built, this structure has been frequently envisioned by a tenacious advocacy movement for audiovisual archiving. Since the 1990s, stakeholders and advocates of audiovisual archiving have collectively imagined and fervently anticipated what one sociologist might call a "place that does not yet exist."[10] Throughout, I invoke these three edifices as not only material structures of built space but also as institutions that emblematize and operationalize cultural policy.

In juxtaposing the three buildings, I reflect on the question, "How does architecture govern?"[11] Architecture is plaited together with Marcosian cultural policy in the long struggle to establish and sustain a national film archive in the Philippines. Since a building to permanently house the national film archive has been repeatedly planned but never erected, this phantom edifice demands a notion of architectural governmentality open to instances of failure:[12] as of this writing, this building still belongs to the virtual genre of unrealized architecture. Its unrealized architecture points to negotiated histories forged by state bureaucracy, cultural policy, and the heterogeneous players of a persistent audiovisual archive advocacy.

Triangulating these three buildings to explore the first FAP's articulation within the dictatorship's cultural policies, I argue that the continued instability of the present-day National Film Archives of the Philippines (NFAP), established in 2011 and subsequently renamed the Philippine Film Archive (PFA) in 2018, has deep roots in the political culture of the Marcos era. The conjugal dictatorship of Ferdinand and Imelda Marcos demonstrated an unprecedented investment in culture, but cultural policies under the dictatorship sought to bring the film industry under direct presidential control rather than creating the conditions for Philippine cinema to thrive. Despite having been historically excluded from founding state cultural policies,[13] film suddenly occupied center stage through a succession of initiatives[14] introduced in the twilight of the Marcos era as the Philippine economy plummeted. Forged in the context of economic, social, and political chaos, the first, short-lived FAP was subjected to multiple organizational reshufflings and mired in the patronage politics of the Marcos regime, what Doreen Fernandez has aptly called a cultural politics of "whim and memorandum."[15] Founded in 1981, the FAP withered in 1986, its collection dispersed amid the dictatorship's presidential decrees, since its fate and funding had never been secured by an act of Congress.[16]

Excavating the ironic legacy of Marcos cultural policies and institutions, this essay identifies two enduring problems bequeathed by the Marcos-era film archive to the present day: first, the established but deeply problematic practice of presidential appointments to state film entities; and second, the issue of *anarchival temporality*. Contravening the more conventional notion of archival temporality as an impossible fantasy of permanence, the anarchival temporality of the FAP—a time of precarity, loss, and unsustainability—is the flip side of the Marcos dictatorship's frenetic pursuit of perpetuity.

## Anarchival Temporality, Cultural Policy, and Presidential Appointments

Historically, advocates of audiovisual archiving have fought a losing battle to preserve what remains of Philippine cinema. Of more than 350 films produced before the outbreak of World War II, only five complete feature-length Filipino films from the American colonial period survive, all feature films produced in Manila using the official national language, Tagalog-based Filipino.[17] The institutional precarity, scarcity, and circumscribed circulation that subtend Philippine cinematic history create a situation that is simultaneously archival and *anarchival*. Jacques Derrida's "archive fever" is the internal contradiction that burns at the heart of every archive and "threatens . . . every archival desire": the inevitable destruction, forgetfulness, and loss that "menaces" the institutional drive to preserve and remember. Derrida writes, Freud's "death drive is above all anarchivic. . . . It will always have been archive-destroying."[18] Extrapolating from Derrida, Akira Lippit defines the *anarchive* as the necessary complement to the archive, the inevitability of loss that shadows historical survival. For Lippit, the prefix *cine* in cinema refers not only to movement but to cinders, to the ashes to which photochemical film will inevitably be reduced. Deterioration, degeneration, and ruin comprise every archive's anarchival shadow.[19] Limited access, the diminution of surviving works, and the instability of key film collections are anarchival in the sense of running contrary to temporal fantasies of perpetual preservation and untrammeled retrieval. Archivists are well aware that any guarantee of all media being accessible and inviolable "forever" is a fantasy,[20] indispensable attempts to safeguard, restore, and disseminate selected works notwithstanding.

The particular form of anarchival temporality that shadows Philippine cinema, I argue, is historically rooted in Marcos-era cultural policies and practices. Ferdinand Marcos, the first Philippine president to evince a keen interest in film, established the film archive via Executive Order 640-A under the supervision of the CCP in 1981. Exemplifying the dictatorship's fickle approach to cultural policy, the FAP was reclassified under the newly created Experimental Cinema of the Philippines (ECP) the following year, 1982. Three years later, in August 1985, the ECP was dissolved and the FAP transferred to a censorship agency, the Board of Review for Motion Pictures and Television (BRMPT).[21] But the censorship board was itself unstable. Denounced by a vigorous anti-censorship movement helmed by filmmaker Lino Brocka and the Concerned Artists of the Philippines (CAP), Marcos's censorship entities were subjected to numerous reshufflings, forced resignations, and rushed appointments.[22] In October 1985, a month after the archives had been transferred to the censors, the censorship board was itself abolished by a dictator struggling to pacify the opposition.[23]

This chaotic timeline and the FAP's "unsettled organizational status"[24] tell us that although the Marcos regime was the first administration to be seriously interested in Philippine cinema, its erratic and self-contradictory policies were ultimately deleterious for film archiving. The FAP changed hands three times in four years and was defunct in five. The last organizational move in particular was excoriated by critics who rightly noted that BRMPT censors who "cut and delete footage from pictures" are diametrically opposed to archivists, who painstakingly "collect and conserve every single part of motion pictures."[25] Those objections notwithstanding, the FAP was turned over to the censorship board a year before the Marcos regime itself collapsed, overthrown by the EDSA People Power Revolt. Lasting a mere five years (1981–1986), the first FAP remains the grimmest example of the many ephemeral film archiving initiatives subsequently undertaken by the Philippine government.[26]

Following the dictatorship's ouster by the 1986 EDSA People Power Revolt, the five-year-old FAP eventually withered under the new government of Marcos's successor, President Corazon "Cory" Aquino, its collection subject to dispersal and attrition. The withering of the first FAP was followed by twenty-five years of state neglect that irreversibly damaged the majority of the Philippines' film holdings. In those gap years, a nongovernmental organization, the Society for Film Archivists, later renamed the Society of Filipino Archivists for Film (SOFIA), spearheaded film preservation and restoration efforts and called for the establishment of a national audiovisual archive.[27] In 2011, the National Film Archives of the Philippines (NFAP) was revived under the auspices of the Film Development Council of the Philippines (FDCP), an industry-focused state film entity whose archival mandate consists of a single sentence.[28] Historically, the FDCP's weak archival mandate has meant that the degree to which the state film council pursues or neglects archiving is at the discretion of the particular FDCP chair appointed by the sitting Philippine president. Upon President Rodrigo Duterte's election in 2016, the NFAP was deprioritized by the FDCP and rebranded the Philippine Film Archive (PFA) in 2018, its pace of restorations and activities slowing markedly.[29] The NFAP/PFA remains on uncertain ground, having been reestablished without the security of a legislative bill that would assure ample funding, autonomous governance, and a permanent repository for the archive—all long-standing demands voiced by advocates and stakeholders.[30]

Among the enduring problems bequeathed by the Marcos era to contemporary cultural policies on film is the continued reliance on presidential appointees for key positions in state film agencies. The current NFAP/PFA inherits the organizational structure of its predecessor since its current administrative chain puts it directly under the Office of the President via the Film Development Council of the Philippines (FDCP). This makes the state film archive vulnerable to changes in presidential administration; without relative autonomy from the state, projects and sometimes whole government agencies do not survive changes in Malacañang. The now-established practice of presidential appointments to head the FDCP (itself a latter-day version of the Marcos-era ECP)—based on the appointees' ties to the sitting president rather than their qualifications—has been pernicious for film archiving since few FDCP chairs have appreciated the significance of archiving, acknowledged its complexities, or been open to consultation and feedback from archivists and stakeholders. It follows that NFAP/PFA initiatives are often short-lived, as projects prioritized by the FDCP under one leadership are often discontinued by the next presidential appointee.

Putting culture and especially the film industry directly under presidential control did not begin with Ferdinand Marcos but was inherited from the first postwar censorship body established in 1961 by President C. P. Garcia.[31] It was the Marcoses, however, who shrewdly used the practice to amplify authoritarian, personalistic control over the cinema. Historically, the problematic practice of presidential appointees for government positions stems from the Marcos regime's wholesale cooptation of the civil bureaucracy. Appointing candidates selected by the president to plum government posts was a key tactic through which state officials became enmeshed in the Marcos dictatorship's patronage politics.[32]

In the aftermath of Marcos's ouster, a position paper on the Aquino government's newly created Presidential Commission on Culture and the Arts notes a major problem with presidential appointments to key cultural positions: the danger that they might serve the cultural agenda of influential individuals, creating a nondemocratic culture of censorship or suppression.[33] Ignoring such critiques, all successive presidential administrations in the aftermath of the Marcos dictatorship have continued the fraught practice of presidential appointments for film-related state agencies.

## The CCP Performing Arts Theater

Noting that the state has a vital stake in "preserving and promoting" all aspects of Philippine culture, Ferdinand Marcos created the Cultural Center

Cultural Center of the Philippines, Theater of the Performing Arts (Architect: Leandro Locsin, 1969). (From the author.)

of the Philippines by executive fiat in 1966,[34] thus circumventing the need for congressional approval. Designed by National Artist Leandro Locsin, the CCP's Performing Arts Theater opened in 1969. (It was renamed the Tanghalang Nicanor Abelardo in the post-Marcos era and is now popularly referred to as the CCP Main Theater.) Over the years, contradictory accounts emerged about the CCP's genesis. In early interviews, the First Lady had publicly given the credit to her husband, in keeping with a gendered conception of national/familial labor emphasized in publicity surrounding the First Couple.[35] However, as the CCP became a reality, state propaganda and Imelda Marcos herself vigorously asserted her sole authorship, claiming that the CCP was her brainchild.[36] Popular journalism dubbed the CCP Main Theater "the Imelda Project,"[37] unwittingly portending the Marcoses' extreme personalization of cultural policy in years to come.

Locsin's vernacular architectural design for the CCP Main Theater was a unique departure from the cityscape of postwar Manila. While other Filipino architects mimicked the foreign architectural trend of working with steel and glass, Locsin embraced inexpensive concrete to create a dramatic structure of formidable scale based on the iconic Filipino rural house on stilts, the nipa hut. The humble nipa hut's "raised floors" and "massive overhanging eaves" were approximated in "the massive cantilevered block . . . [that] serves as a protective eave over the balcony that surrounds the lobby" of the

CCP Main Theater.[38] Locsin's architectural achievement launched a fetish for indigeneity in state architecture in the service of the Marcoses' mythmaking. Over time, the regime's exoticization of folk motifs, ethnic symbols, and vernacular iconography was belied by their glaring neocoloniality and land grabbing from indigenous minorities.[39]

Marcos propaganda alleged that the CCP Main Theater had been erected solely through the charismatic fundraising of Imelda Marcos.[40] In fact, CCP funding was sourced from U.S. government sources and private loans and was riddled with fiscal malfeasance. U.S. President Lyndon Johnson, on Imelda's urging, had diverted war damage funds slated for Filipino veterans' education to the CCP as well as apportioning special Senate funds in exchange for Marcos's promise of Philippine support for the Vietnam War.[41] In addition, a loan of between $5 and $7 million was secured from the Chemical Bank of New York by the CCP Board of Trustees, for which the newly created Philippine National Bank subsidiary served as guarantor.[42] Thus, from the outset, an initiative whose declared objective was to foster and safeguard Filipino cultural heritage was mired in a highly politicized, questionable allocation of funds from American war damage payments, federal aid, and loans from private banks. Despite its corrupt origins and the Imeldific politics of patronage it emblematized in the Marcos years, in hindsight, the CCP has turned out to be not only the first but also the most substantive example of dictatorship architecture and cultural policy.

The CCP's enduring relationship to Philippine cinema originates in the Marcos years, when it served as the dictatorship's primary cultural policy apparatus.[43] As the principal cultural policy instrument of the Marcos state, the CCP had a seat at the table for all significant film-related state initiatives.[44] In the post-Marcos period, as artists and intellectuals who had previously protested the CCP's cultural politics of patronage, elitism, and neocolonialism took the helm under Cory Aquino's administration, the CCP's cultural policy frameworks pivoted toward "Filipinization, democratization, [and] decentralization."[45] From the late 1980s onward, the considerably democratized, still monumental, though increasingly dilapidated CCP has become a vital hub for the arts community. In 2005, the CCP coorganized the annual Cinemalaya Independent Film Festival, which, together with other key film festivals, spearheaded a renaissance of the domestic film industry by providing production grants and a distribution and exhibition platform for talented indie digital filmmakers, though Cinemalaya has its share of controversies and detractors.[46] And in the long gap years between the demise of the FAP in 1986 and the founding of the NFAP in 2011, film archivists and historians at the CCP worked closely with SOFIA, the Philippine Information Agency (PIA), the University of the Philippines Film Center, the Movie Workers

Welfare Foundation (Mowelfund), and the National Commission on Culture and the Arts (NCCA) to pursue urgent film preservation and restoration projects and to call for the reestablishment of the NFAP.[47]

## The Manila Film Center

The *New York Times* calls the Manila Film Center "the ultimate symbol of Marcos decline."[48] From 1978 to 1983, the half decade leading up to the assassination of Benigno Aquino Jr., underemployment tripled under the debt crisis. At about the same time, from 1976 onward, capital outlays for government construction projects—such as those erected in the CCP Complex under Imelda's Ministry of Human Settlements—increased fourfold. Economists surmise that the Marcos regime might have survived the 1980s, "when world recession came and exports were hit hard," were it not for government overspending on lavish construction projects that caused the country's external debt to balloon to $15 billion—the steep cost of the Marcosian edifice complex.[49] On the orders of Imelda Marcos, who also chaired the Filipino Motion Picture Development Board, the film center was built at breakneck speed to be completed in time for the opening of the Manila International Film Festival (MIFF) in January 1982. The scale of the project proved both massive (costing an estimated 200 million pesos) and corruption ridden (construction went forward in the absence of a building permit, qualified contractors, or government oversight of the blueprints).[50] Five months into the hurried construction, at 2:00 A.M. on November 17, 1981, the scaffolding that held up concrete slabs and beams on the sixth floor of the nine-level structure buckled under the weight of the quick-drying cement being poured over it, burying construction workers on the floors below. This was the second fatal accident at the site.[51] The official cover-up that followed means that no accurate tally of the fatalities exists, although it was reported that of 204 workers assigned to that overnight shift, 100 were still missing two days after the accident.[52] Philippine newspapers in the Marcos-controlled mediascape minimized the death toll, but foreign journalists painted a grisly portrait of the tragedy. Recounting the accident for *Film Comment*, Elliott Stein writes:

> More than 200 persons were buried under fast-drying cement. A security blanket was immediately imposed; nothing could be done until an official statement, minimizing the accident, had been prepared. Ambulances were not permitted access to the scene of the disaster until nine hours after the cave-in. . . . Orders were given to slice in half those caught unconscious in the quick drying porous cement. Had they been dug out or drilled out whole, construction would have been further delayed. This graveyard shift claimed well over 100 lives.[53]

Manila Film Center (Architect: Froilan Hong, 1982). (From the author.)

The first home for the FAP had caved in even before it had opened, boding ill for its long-term prospects. Undeterred, Imelda Marcos announced that the film center would be "finished on schedule" and that the MIFF would go on as planned, enumerating the benefits to the domestic film industry and to the national economy that the festival would generate.[54] The Manila Film Center was rebuilt from the rubble of its deadly collapse. In the final phase of the frantic construction—between Christmas Day in 1981 and the MIFF's opening night on January 18, 1982—seven thousand workers surged onto the construction site working in nonstop shifts, an unforgettable sight variously described by journalists as a human "swarm" of workers[55] looking like "huge colonies of ants"[56] at work on a mammoth undertaking. Although Imelda Marcos initially hyped the MIFF as a regional counterpart to the Cannes Film Festival that would catapult the Philippines to the center of Asian film-making,[57] the MIFF would only be held twice at the Manila Film Center before permanently closing its doors. Once underway, the first Manila International Film Festival was, by all accounts, a letdown. The recent tragedy cast a pall over the festival, and several international guests canceled, boycotted, or withdrew their films.[58]

To Filipino moviegoers, however, the MIFF represented an appealing departure from a suffocating norm: in a context of strict state censorship over domestic film production and exhibition, the MIFF (administered by the ECP) took advantage of its censorship exemption to screen uncut soft-core sexploitation films.[59] Known colloquially in the Philippines as *bomba*, or "bold," movies, these films' combination of sex and violence provoked the Marcos regime's infamous censorship campaigns.[60] The soft-core porn screenings at the second and final MIFF in 1983 were an attempt to recover the massive expenses incurred by the Manila Film Center.[61] Though the Marcos government was initially bankrolled by foreign debt–financed government funds, the World Bank and International Monetary Fund insisted that the country tighten its fiscal belt and abandon frivolous projects. When Prime Minister Cesar Virata cut government subsidies for the MIFF, Imelda Marcos turned to the lucrative exhibition of *bomba* films at the film center to raise funds. Yet the state's hiatus from censorship did not last. A few months after the close of the 1983 MIFF, police squads confiscated negatives and arrested the very producers whose profitable *bomba* films had saved the MIFF and the Manila Film Center from financial ruin. Ferdinand Marcos proceeded to widen the jurisdiction of the censorship board with another executive decree.[62] In the long run, public outcry against *bomba* at the Manila Film Center and the dictatorship's arbitrary censorship policies set in motion a chain of events that would lead to the dissolution of the Film Archive's umbrella agency, the ECP, and destabilize as well its eventual home under a censorship body, the BRMPT.[63]

The archival fragility of Philippine cinema hummed in the background of the controversial international film festival. Tucked away in an auxiliary theater at the second MIFF was a retrospective screening of Filipino film classics from 1951–1982 that the festival should have spotlighted. Instead, what Stein called "by far the most interesting section of the festival" was sadly "the most poorly attended, most badly projected" part of the program. Several films were shown in the wrong aspect ratio, with the result that "heads and/ or subtitles [were] lopped off." Film reels were projected out of order, and "some of the 16mm prints were so dupey that time spent watching them was as time spent watching a blank bedsheet." The abysmal condition of the archival screenings leads Stein to the heartbreaking conclusion that "the festival spent millions on fripperies, but treated its own national cinema as a poor relation."[64] Despite technical consultations with UNESCO prior to the construction of the building's archival section,[65] the FAP had clearly taken a back seat to the Manila Film Center's flashier divisions.

In his discussion of the co-constitutive dynamic between *space* and *place*, Michel de Certeau characterizes place through the law of the "proper," that is, via notions of ordered, stable positionalities. In contrast, space is processual and brought into being by practice, "caught in the ambiguity of an actualization." Constantly and conflictually transformed, space "has none of the univocity or stability of a 'proper.'" The apparent dichotomy between *place* and *space*, however, is continually undone by the push-and-pull dynamic between them: "*Space is a practiced place.*" Spatial stories are powerful everyday practices that articulate place and space: "Stories . . . carry out a labor that constantly transforms places into spaces or spaces into places." While space is determined by "the actions of historical *subjects*," stories of the dead have, for de Certeau, a place-making function, since places "are ultimately reducible to the *being-there* of something dead."[66]

The November 17 tragedy, the multiple exorcisms performed in its wake, and the film center's enduring tales of haunting are "spatial stories" in de Certeau's sense, everyday practices that produce the Manila Film Center as place. "This Film Center is the only *palais du festival* which is also a mass mausoleum," wrote Stein. At the MIFF's gala opening in 1982, the air "thick with thousands of flies" and the stench of putrefaction were tangible memento mori of the construction workers slain by Imeldific temporality, their bodies decomposing beneath the glitz of the film festival.[67] Within a year of the fatal accident, six exorcisms—variously observing Catholic, Chinese, and Igorot rites—had been held to rid the building of rumored ghosts and to halt the "freak fatal accidents" that plagued the Manila Film Center.[68]

Against the vigorous disavowals of the Marcos dictatorship, ordinary Filipinos' spatial stories about the Manila Film Center insist on remembering that the laboring dead are there; the erstwhile film palace is a mass grave. The undervalued workers who built the film center, only to be entombed within it, grimly attest to the layered materiality, the ineluctable archival dimension at work in all cities. If "a city is a memory machine," then the city-as-archive points to an accretion of historical events that gain significance in the collective memories of those who live there. Moreover, the "politics of urban naming" are key to the commemorative practices of all cities.[69] Imelda Marcos shrewdly realized this when, in the wake of the November 17 tragedy, the former "Manila Film Palace" was more modestly renamed the "Manila Film Center."[70]

On Imelda Marcos's orders, hastily completed architectural structures had transformed Manila in less than a decade, resulting in a spatiotemporal oxymoron: the *rushed monument*. Rather than commemorating authoritarian accomplishment, however, Imeldific temporality leaves behind a legacy of hauntings that cannot be exorcised and the failure of two Marcos-era initiatives, both bound up with the Manila Film Center from their inception—the MIFF and the first FAP.

## A Building to Be (or Not to Be)

Institutional dislocation engulfed the FAP upon the abolition of the ECP and its transfer to the BRMPT in September 1985, less than five months before the conjugal dictatorship was itself dethroned. The Marcos government was deposed before the orphaned FAP found a secure institutional home. In his May 1986 report to the recently installed Aquino administration, FAP Director-General Ernie de Pedro recounted that under the jurisdiction of a newly reconstituted censorship body, the Movie and Television Review and Classification Board (MTRCB), staff salaries for the FAP had gone unpaid since December 1985.[71] My research has uncovered no official response to de Pedro's request for state support from the Aquino government.

The post-Marcos state's silence, inaction, and neglect augured the beginning of the twenty-five-year gap between the demise of the first FAP and its long-awaited revival as the NFAP in 2011. In 1999, what remained of the FAP collection in the censors' hands was summarily returned to the films' rightsholders; unclaimed films were "turned over to other archives who may be able to give better care and attention to the films";[72] further deterioration and dispersal of the former FAP collection ensued.

In those gap years, SOFIA emerged as the lead nongovernmental "coordinating body" for an archival advocacy movement that remains active to this day.[73] SOFIA founding member Annella Mendoza recounts that in 1996, "a consensus was reached by various government and film related agencies to build a national storage facility to house our national collection. Within a span of one year, the national AV storage site was identified and the technical design and construction specifications were drawn."[74] Mendoza is referring to a 1996 report conducted by Australian media preservationists Mark Nizette and Guy Petherbridge that suggested another Marcos edifice, the National Arts Center in Mount Makiling, as the most suitable site for a national audiovisual archive, not least because of its "lower average temperature" and "lowered pollution levels."[75] Nearly two decades later, in 2013, the reopened NFAP also commissioned architectural plans for a permanent archival compound, possibly to be located in the cooler climate of Tagaytay City.[76] In August 2020, the PFA announced that the FDCP's planned "construction of the Film Archive Heritage Building in Intramuros," a historic district in Manila, had been delayed due to the COVID-19 pandemic.[77] As of this writing, none of these plans have come to fruition.

Nonetheless, this nonexistent archival building has been the focus of longstanding collective imaginations about place and an anticipatory temporality of future outcomes in which not only the NFAP but also the wider community of stakeholders in the Philippines' and Southeast Asia's decentralized audiovisual archive movement are deeply invested. The discursive trail of this edifice-to-be is by now considerable: it dates from UNESCO consultant Christopher Roads's technical specifications for the archival section of the Manila Film Center in 1981, to Nizette and Petherbridge's 1996 feasibility study, and the Leandro V. Locsin Partners' architectural design concept in 2013. Where "places that do not exist, yet" are concerned, "time, especially individuals' anticipation of potential and imagined future events, is of paramount importance for understanding perceptions of place."[78] As such, I recognize the profound necessity for keeping alive the anticipatory collective demand for this spectral-archive-to-be. At the same time, however, this expectant optimism is inevitably counterweighted by anarchival temporality, which forms the focus of this essay's closing section.

## Imeldific, Martial, and Anarchival Temporalities

The Philippines' first National Film Archive was an oxymoron: it was an archive that did not last. This is a sticking point because the durative sustainability of archives goes to the heart of a state archive's promise to the public. As Ray Edmondson astutely remarks, archives that "fail to survive" do "immense damage," "destroying public confidence in the whole idea of preservation."[79] The anarchival temporality manifested by failed archives is the very opposite of the temporal fantasy of certainty, security, and permanence that archives stand for.

Anarchival time is the flip side of Imeldific time, the dictatorship's frenetic pursuit of perpetuity through the rushed construction of urban monuments. In his 1969 profile of Imelda Marcos, Joaquin describes the First Lady as a "beautiful dynamo" who was almost fatiguing to watch, so impelled was she by an overwhelming sense of temporal scarcity.[80] Hints of what Lico calls the "Imeldific timetable" of state architectural construction under the dictatorship emerge in 1974, when the Folk Arts Theater, "an arena-type ten thousand seat-theater," was completed in seventy-seven days to host the Miss Universe Pageant and to impress foreign dignitaries during their brief stay in the city. The now-defunct PhilTrade complex, composed of more than 250 "vernacular-inspired pavilions" that served as kiosks and booths for a UN trade conference, was completed in a mind-boggling twelve days in 1979, anticipating the frenetic pace of construction on the Manila Film Center in 1981.[81] Architect Froilan Hong's account of the final, frenzied days of the Manila Film Center's construction, which reads like a bizarre game of "beat the clock," remains the most vivid account of what Imeldific temporality was like for those who labored under its strictures. A thousand workers toiled to "finish in 72 hours a lobby that would normally take six weeks, and a 1,400-seat theater that would usually take three months to complete."[82] For the First Lady, time always seemed to be on the verge of running out; this emphasis on speed might have been fueled by an underlying defensive fantasy of staying one step ahead of the increasingly restive anti-Marcos movement.

Imeldific time was also darkly implicated in the indefinite temporality of martial law, the simulated legitimacy that allowed Ferdinand Marcos to hold on to the presidency instead of relinquishing it at the end of his second term as the 1935 Constitution mandated.[83] First declared by Ferdinand Marcos in September 1972, martial law ushered in military-backed authoritarian rule without an end date in sight, as Ferdinand and Imelda attempted to extend their hold on power into perpetuity and become, in Benedict Anderson's memorable phrase, "Supreme Cacique[s] for Life."[84] The era of abusive martial power, 1972–1981/1986,[85] were years in which the Marcoses governed on stolen time,[86] which may partly explain the conjugal dictatorship's hurry to erect, as quickly as possible, a monumental—but ultimately haphazard—legacy. My hunch is that the anarchival time of government film archives is the penumbra of martial and Imeldific temporalities: a time of collapse and precarity directly linked to the conjugal dictatorship's longing to quickly yet perpetually personify state power.

The collapse of archival permanence under the Marcos dictatorship involves a temporal inversion: constitutionally, political power is constrained by defined term limits, while the temporal fantasy of archival permanence imagines that archives can preserve collective memory by going on forever. In declaring martial law to bypass the constitutional term limits of the Philippine presidency, however, the Marcos regime created conditions under which archival longevity became its opposite: anarchival ephemerality. The conjugal dictatorship's repressive pursuit of permanent power doomed many of its cultural policy initiatives, including the first FAP, to transience.

Derrida warns that the archive is far from an "assured" concept; it is emphatically not a "question of the past," nor a concept that we already have unproblematically "at our disposal." Rather, archiving always raises the question of an undecided and radically open future: the "question of a response, of a promise and of a responsibility for tomorrow."[87] Indeterminacy shrouds the possibility of the NFAP/PFA ever having a permanent long-term home. In one sense, indeterminacy is common to all archives in their struggle against forgetting, obsolescence, and loss. In another, as I hope to have shown, Philippine cinema's anarchival temporality has deep roots in the cultural policies and practices of the Marcos era, subtended by the temporal rhythms of martial law and the Imeldific-Marcosian city.

## NOTES

Note: This is an abridged version of the first chapter of my forthcoming book, *The Archival Afterlives of Philippine Cinema* (Duke University Press).

1. Lopez, "Who Says Rome," 7.

2. Nolledo, "A Human Settlement," 38. After the conjugal dictatorship of Ferdinand and Imelda Marcos was ousted from power in February 1986, Imelda Marcos faced several trials for racketeering and corruption in the United States and the Philippines, many of which continue. She has enjoyed an extensive political career, having been elected for three consecutive terms as member of the Philippine House of Representatives for Ilocos Norte's 2nd District, from 2010 to 2019.

3. Joaquin, "Before the Blow," 372.

4. Lico, *Edifice Complex*, 45–54, 66–67.

5. Aquino, "A Pantheon," 218–219.

6. Fernandez, "Mass Culture," 492–493; Baluyut, *Institutions*, 35.

7. Referred to only as the "Film Archive" or "Film Archives" in Marcos's Executive Order No. 640-A, the Film Archives' first director-general, Ernie de Pedro, referred to the agency as the "Film Archives of the Philippines" with the acronym "NFAP" (despite the lack of "National" in its designation) in his 1986 report. Marcos, Executive Order No. 640-A; de Pedro, "Overview." I refer to the Film Archives of the Philippines (1981–1986) as the FAP to distinguish it from the National Film Archives (NFAP) re-established by the Film Development Council of the Philippines (FDCP) in 2011 and renamed the Philippine Film Archive (PFA) in 2018.

8. "Marcos' Daughter," n.p.

9. Benedicto, "Queer Space," 27. By June 2019, the dilapidated Manila Film Center was undergoing renovation; *The Amazing Show* went on hiatus during the global COVID-19 pandemic.

10. Borer, "From Collective Memory," 96.

11. Abramson et al., "Introduction," vii.

12. Many articles in Abramson et al.'s *Governing by Design* "address failures, points in the historical record when projects went unrealized. They suggest that plans, schemes, books, journals, objects, buildings, and technologies often emerge less from pure intentionality as out of negotiation with the radical indeterminacy of a given situation." Abramson et al., xi.

13. In the Macapagal era, Republic Act 4165 to create the National Commission on Culture did not list film among the country's various arts. During the Marcos era, Republic Act No. 4846 in 1966 also fails to mention film in its list of cultural properties in need of preservation.

14. See Ferdinand Marcos's Executive Orders 640-A and 770, signed into law in 1981 and 1982.

15. Fernandez, "Mass Culture," 492.

16. Republic Acts (i.e., congressionally approved legislation) regarding cinema are few and far between, and they cluster not around archiving and preservation, but around censorship and taxation, the two most enduring—and narrowly income-centered—interests of the Philippine state with regards to the domestic film industry. It comes as no surprise, then, that archiving should be marginalized since preservation and access correspond to neither the government's disciplinary (e.g., censorship) nor revenue-generating (e.g., taxation) agendas. The Philippine Congress had a complicated history in the martial law years. Marcos's Proclamation 1081 declaring martial law in 1972 dissolved the bicameral congress; an Interim Batasang Pambansa, or Interim National Assembly, was convened in 1978. In the final years of the Marcos regime, the official Batasang Pambansa held its first session in 1984 and was terminated by President Corazon Aquino in 1986 after the ouster of the dictatorship.

17. The five surviving Filipino full-length feature films from the prewar period are the following: *Zamboanga* (1937), *Tunay Na Ina* (True Mother, 1939), *Giliw Ko* (My Dear, 1939), *Pakiusap* (Lover's Plea, 1940), and *Ibong Adarna* (Adarna Bird, 1941). See Junio, "Movie in My Mind," 7–8; del Mundo, *Native Resistance*, 7–8; and Deocampo, "*Zamboanga*." In 2009, archival sleuthing by cinephile-archivists Teddy Co and Martin Magsanoc established that footage from two Filipino silent films from 1931, *Moro Pirates* and *Princess Tarhata*, had been reedited as a single film and released in the U.S. market under the title *Brides of Sulu* in 1934. See San Diego, "Archivists Reclaim."

18. Derrida, *Archive Fever*, 10–12.

19. Lippit, *Atomic Light*, 8–9, 12, 33.

20. Kumar, "National Film Archives," 16. Even under the best possible storage conditions, with temperature and humidity regulated, the temporality of film preservation is one that continually *defers* an inevitable process of decay. *Deferral* here means that films' degradation, while inevitable, can be delayed; under ideal conditions, films can last for over a century or more. Edmondson, *Audiovisual Archiving*, 53–54.

21. F. Marcos, Executive Orders 640-A, 770, and 1051.

22. Tiongson, "Filipino Film," xx–xxiii; Salazar, "Philippines' Marcos Orders"; Giron, "Trial Begins"; Giron, "Only One Oppressor," 109.

23. Giron, "New Bill"; Giron, "Marcos Plucks."

24. de Pedro, "Overview," 22.

25. "Archives Shift," 339, 413.

26. The history of the FAP/NFAP has broad parallels with the tragic dissolution of other key government media collections. See Lim, *Archival Afterlives*, chapter 2.

27. SOFIA was incorporated on June 27, 1993, in the same year that the ASEAN Conference-Workshop on Film Retrieval, Restoration, and Archiving was held in Manila. Mendoza, "Seven Years," 1.

28. The FDCP's archival mandate reads: "to ensure the establishment of a film archive in order to conserve and protect film negatives and/or prints as part of the nation's historical, cultural, and artistic heritage." Congress, "Republic Act No. 9167."

29. By 2020, four years after Duterte's appointment of Mary Liza B. Diño as the new Chair of the FDCP, the PFA had seen increased turnover of leadership and staff positions and had completed far fewer digital film restorations than the prior NFAP. PFA restorations include a pre-war film, *Zamboanga* (Eduardo de Castro, 1936). By her own admission, Diño "had no prior knowledge about film archiving" at the time of her appointment. Many of the film restorations listed as PFA accomplishments were actually undertaken by the NFAP under the prior FDCP Chair. Diño-Seguerra, "The Vision."

30. Lim, "Analysis," 27.

31. Joaquin, "Press Discovers," 5.

32. Celoza, *Ferdinand Marcos*, 87.

33. Victor Ordoñez, "The Neglect of the Past," background paper on the Presidential Commission on Culture and the Arts (PCCA), quoted in Fernandez, "Mass Culture," 495.

34. F. Marcos, "Executive Order 30."

35. Nolledo, "First Lady," 8; Fernandez, "Mass Culture," 492–493.

36. Baluyut, *Institutions*, 13; Maramag, *Cultural Center*, 9.

37. Coseteng, "Imelda Project," 16–17.

38. Polites, *Architecture*, 9–13.

39. Lico, *Edifice*, 49–50.

40. Coseteng, "Imelda Project," 16–17.

41. Aquino, "Pantheon," 218–129; Baluyut, *Institutions*, 14–15.

42. Baluyut, *Institutions*, 15.

43. In addition to functioning as a premier performing arts venue and a museum exhibition space for modern and contemporary art, it was also "endowed with authority and extra-legal powers" because Imelda Marcos chaired its Board of Trustees. Baluyut, *Institutions*, 11.

44. F. Marcos, Executive Orders 640-A, 770, and 1051.

45. Tiongson, "Winds," 30.

46. Young Critics Circle, "Statement." Both established in 2005, the two major Philippine festivals credited with jump-starting the upsurge in digital indie filmmaking are the partially state-supported Cinemalaya Philippine Independent Film Festival and

the corporate-funded Cinema One Originals Festival, a subsidiary of media conglomerate ABS-CBN. See Villarama, "Current Film Distribution."

47. PIA-SOFIA, "Consultation Meeting;" Mendoza, "Seven Years," 1.
48. Whaley, "Brisk Walk."
49. De Dios, *Analysis*, 12, 34; Bello, Kinley, and Elinson, *Development Debacle*, 14.
50. "Gov't Takes Over," 1; "First Lady: Filmfest," 6.
51. "Film Center's 6th Floor Falls," 1, 10.
52. "Gov't Takes Over," 1–2.
53. Stein, "Manila's Angels," 48.
54. "First Lady: Filmfest," 1, 6.
55. Benigno and Zapanta, "'Instant' Film Center," 13.
56. Tatad, "MIFF," 8.
57. "First Lady: Filmfest," 1, 6; "Film Center Collapses," 4.
58. Lacaba, "Misadventures," 17.
59. F. Marcos, "Executive Order 770"; Lacaba, "Misadventures," 17.
60. Espiritu, *Passionate Revolutions*, chapter 3.
61. The *bomba* films screened at the Manila Film Center and in 153 other Manila movie theaters affiliated with the festival attracted record crowds and raised an estimated $6 million. They also drew the ire of the Philippine Catholic Church and prominent filmmakers like Brocka and Mike de Leon, who castigated the festival for its extravagance and hypocrisy. Stein, "Manila's Angels," 54.
62. Stein, "Manila's Angels," 54; F. Marcos, "Executive Order 868."
63. F. Marcos, "Executive Order 1051."
64. Stein, "Manila's Angels," 49, 51.
65. Roads, "Manila National Film Centre."
66. de Certeau, *Practice*, 117–118; italics in original.
67. Stein, "Manila's Angels," 49.
68. "Marcos' Daughter," n.p.
69. Sheringham, "Archiving," 10–14.
70. Lacaba, "Misadventures," 17.
71. de Pedro, "Overview," 2–3.
72. Mendoza, "Audio-Visual Archiving," 4
73. Capul, "Annex H: Toward a National Film Archive."
74. Mendoza, "Seven Years," 7.
75. Nizette and Petherbridge, "Assessment of Potential Sites," 1–3
76. Leandro V. Locsin Partners, "Architectural Design Concept," 10–12.
77. Diño-Seguerra, "Vision."
78. Borer, "From Collective Memory," 96–97.
79. Edmondson, "Notes on Sustainability," 25.
80. Joaquin, "Woman of the Year," 123, 127.
81. Lico, *Edifice*, 50–53, 115.
82. Benigno and Zapanta, "'Instant' Film Center," 13.
83. Ferdinand Marcos was nearing the end of his second and final presidential term, per the 1935 Constitution, when he invoked a constitutional provision to proclaim martial law in Proclamation 1081, officially dated September 21, 1972. Marcos's televised declaration of martial law aired at 7:00 PM on September 23, in the wake of several high-profile bombings in Manila and a staged ambush of Secretary of Defense Juan Ponce Enrile. This spate of state-orchestrated violence, allegedly the work of communists, provided Marcos with a pretext for the imposition of martial law. "Declaration of Martial Law."

84. Anderson, "Cacique Democracy," 18.

85. Though martial law was officially terminated via Marcos's Proclamation 2045 in 1981, key aspects of martial law remained in effect until the dictatorship was deposed in 1986 (e.g., provisions for military suppression of "violence, insurrection, rebellion, and subversion" as well as the suspension of the writ of habeas corpus).

86. I thank my partner Joya Escobar for pointing out that the martial law years were a form of "borrowed time" that may have something to do with the feverish pace of Imeldific temporality.

87. Derrida, *Archive Fever*, 29, 33, 36. Steedman has explored both the powerful appeal and the inherent limitations of Derrida's exploration of the archive as a "capacious metaphor." Steedman, *Dust*, 4.

## BIBLIOGRAPHY

Abramson, Daniel, Arindam Dutta, Timothy Hude, and Jonathan Massey for Aggregate. "Introduction." In *Governing by Design: Architecture, Economy, and Politics in the Twentieth Century*, vii–xvi. Pittsburgh: University of Pittsburgh Press, 2012.

Anderson, Benedict. "Cacique Democracy in the Philippines: Origins and Dreams." In *Discrepant Histories: Translocal Essays on Filipino Cultures*, edited by Vicente L. Rafael, 3–47. Philadelphia: Temple University Press, 1995.

Anonymous. "Archives Shift to Snippers Hit." *Variety*, October 16, 1985: 339, 413.

———. "Declaration of Martial Law." *Official Gazette of the Republic of the Philippines*. July 28, 2015, http://www.gov.ph/featured/declaration-of-martial-law/fm-declaresmartial-law/.

———. "Film Center Collapses; 20 Workers Feared Dead." *Business Day*, November 18, 1981: 4.

———. "Film Center's 6th Floor Falls; At Least 3 Dead." *Bulletin Today*, November 18, 1981: 1, 10.

———. "First Lady: Filmfest to Go On as Scheduled." *Daily Express*, November 20, 1981: 1, 6.

———. "Gov't Takes Over Film Center Work; Toll Now 8." *Daily Express*, November 19, 1981: 1–2.

———. "Marcos' Daughter Takes Part in Rites to Appease Spirits." *Korea Herald*, July 21, 1982.

———. "Only One Oppressor." *Village Voice*, November 15, 1983.

Aquino, Benigno S. Jr. "A Pantheon for Imelda." In *A Garrison State in the Make and Other Speeches*, edited by Makati: Benigno S. Aquino, Jr., 117–127. Foundation, 1985.

Baluyut, Perlie Rose S. *Institutions and Icons of Patronage: Arts and Culture in the Philippines During the Marcos Years, 1965–1986*. Manila: University of the Philippines Publishing House, 2012.

Bello, Walden, David Kinley, and Elaine Elinson. *Development Debacle: The World Bank in the Philippines*. San Francisco: Institute for Food and Development Policy, 1982.

Benedicto, Bobby. "Queer Space in the Ruins of Dictatorship Architecture." *Social Text* 31, no. 4 (2013): 25–47.

Benigno, Nena C., and P.A. Zapanta. "The 'Instant' Film Center." *Weekend*, February 21, 1982: 12–13.

Borer, Michael Ian. "From Collective Memory to Collective Imagination: Time, Place, and Urban Redevelopment." *Symbolic Interaction* 33, no. 1 (2010): 96–114.

Capul, Belina. "Annex H: Toward a National Film Archive for the Philippines." Unpublished paper presented at the Workshop/Consultative Meeting on the Development Plan for AV Archiving in the Region: The ASEAN Catalogue of Film and Television Productions. Quezon City, December 1–5, 1997.

Celoza, Albert. *Ferdinand Marcos and the Philippines: The Political Economy of Authoritarianism.* Westport, Connecticut, and London: Praeger, 1997.

Congress of the Philippines. "Republic Act No. 4165. An Act Creating the National Commission on Culture and Providing Funds Therefor." August 4, 1964.

———. "Republic Act No. 4846. An Act to Repeal Act Numbered 3874, and to Provide for the Protection and Preservation of Philippine Cultural Properties." June 18, 1966.

———. "Republic Act No. 9167. An Act Creating the Film Development Council of the Philippines, Defining Its Powers and Functions, Appropriating Funds Therefor, and for Other Purposes." June 7, 2002.

Coseteng, Alice M. L. "The Imelda Project." *Weekly Graphic* 32, no. 42 (April 13, 1966): 16–17.

de Certeau, Michel. *The Practice of Everyday Life.* Translated by Steven Rendall. Berkeley: University of California Press, 1984.

De Dios, Emmanuel, ed. *An Analysis of the Philippine Economic Crisis: A Workshop Report.* Quezon City: University of the Philippines Press, 1984.

de Pedro, Ernie A. "Overview of the Film Archives: Report for Hon. Joker C. Arroyo, Executive Secretary from Ernie A. de Pedro, Director-General, Film Archives of the Philippines." May 22, 1986.

del Mundo, Clodualdo Jr. *Native Resistance: Philippine Cinema and Colonialism, 1898–1941.* Manila: De La Salle University Press, 1998.

Deocampo, Nick. "*Zamboanga:* 'Lost' Philippine-Made Film Discovered in US Archive." *Movement* (February 2004): 2–7.

Derrida, Jacques. *Archive Fever: A Freudian Impression.* Translated by Eric Prenowitz. Chicago: University of Chicago Press, 1996.

Diño-Seguerra, Liza. "The Vision for FDCP's Philippine Film Archive." *Sunday Times Magazine*, August 9, 2020, https://www.manilatimes.net/2020/08/09/weekly/the-sunday-times/arts-awake/the-vision-for-fdcps-philippine-film-archive/752670/.

Edmondson, Ray. *Audiovisual Archiving: Philosophy and Principles.* 3rd ed. Paris and Bangkok: UNESCO, 2016.

———. "Notes on Sustainability of Audiovisual Archives." In *Proceedings of the Philippine Cinema Heritage Summit: A Report*, 24–25. Manila: National Film Archives of the Philippines, 2013.

Espiritu, Talitha. *Passionate Revolutions: The Media and the Rise and Fall of the Marcos Regime.* Athens: Ohio University Press, 2017.

Fernandez, Doreen. "Mass Culture and Cultural Policy: The Philippine Experience." *Philippine Studies* 37 (1989): 488–502.

Giron, Marietta V. "Marcos Plucks Censor Thorn After Filipino Trade Tirade." *Variety*, October 16, 1985: 336, 413.

———. "New Bill Proposing an End to Pic Censorship Stirring Up Philippines." *Variety*, March 27, 1985.

———. "Trial Begins for Filipino Film Directors." *Variety*, February 6, 1985.

Joaquin, Nick. "Before the Blow: Ninoy's Senate Years." In *A Garrison State in the Make and Other Speeches*, edited by Benigno S. Aquino Jr., 355–390. Makati: Benigno S. Aquino, Jr. Foundation, 1985.

Joaquin, Nick [Quijano de Manila, pseud.]. "The Press Discovers the Cinema." *Philippines Free Press*. September 18, 1965: 5, 37, 65, 68.

———. "Woman of the Year." In *Reportage on the Marcoses: 1964–1970*, 122–132. Manila: National Media Production Center, 1979.

Junio, Arnulfo. "The Movie in My Mind: A Film Archivist's Reflection." In *Philippine Audiovisual Archives Collections: An Inventory*. Unpublished report. National Commission for Culture and the Arts (NCCA)-Committee on Archives and Society of Film Archivists (SOFIA), 2003.

Kumar, Ramesh. "National Film Archives: Policies, Practices, and Histories. A Study of the National Film Archive of India, EYE Film Institute Netherlands, and the National Film and Sound Archive, Australia." Ph.D. dissertation, New York University, 2016.

Lacaba, Jose F. "Misadventures in the Dream Trade." *Mr. & Ms. Magazine*, February 2, 1982, 15–17.

Leandro V. Locsin Partners, Architects (LVLP). "Architectural Design Concept." In *2013 Philippine Cinema Heritage Summit: A Report*, 10–12. Manila: National Film Archives of the Philippines, 2013.

Lico, Gerard. *Edifice Complex: Power, Myth, and Marcos State Architecture*. Quezon City: Ateneo de Manila University Press, 2003.

Lim, Bliss Cua. "Analysis and Recommendations in the Wake of the 2013 Philippine Cinema Heritage Summit." In *2013 Philippine Cinema Heritage Summit: A Report*, 26–32. Manila: National Film Archives of the Philippines, 2013.

———. *The Archival Afterlives of Philippine Cinema*. Durham, NC: Duke University Press, forthcoming.

Lippit, Akira Mizuta. *Atomic Light (Shadow Optics)*. Minneapolis: University of Minnesota Press, 2005.

Lopez, Salvador P. "Who Says Rome Can't Be Built in a Day?" *Mr. and Ms. Magazine*, February 16, 1982: 6–7.

Maramag, Ileana. *Cultural Center of the Philippines*. Manila: Cultural Center of the Philippines, 1970 [?].

Marcos, Ferdinand E. "Executive Order No. 30. Creating the Cultural Center of the Philippines." June 25, 1966.

———. "Executive Order No. 640-A. Prescribing Guidelines to Promote and Enhance the Preservation, Growth, and Development of the Motion Picture Art and Science in the Philippines." January 5, 1981.

———. "Executive Order No. 770. Creation of the Experimental Cinema of the Philippines and Placing the Film Archives Under the Umbrella Organization of the ECP." January 28, 1982.

———. "Executive Order No. 868. Reorganizing the Board of Review for Motion Pictures and Television Created Under Republic Act No. 3060, as Renamed and Reconstituted Under Executive Orders Nos. 585, 745 and 757, and Expanding Its Functions, Powers and Duties." February 1, 1983.

———. "Executive Order No. 1051. Re: Abolition of the Defunct Experimental Cinema of the Philippines and the Transfer of the Functions and Personnel of the Film Archives to the Board of Review for Motion Pictures and Television." August 8, 1985.

———. "Proclamation 1081. Proclaiming a State of Martial Law in the Philippines." September 21, 1972.

———. "Proclamation 2045. Proclaiming the Termination of the State of Martial Law Throughout the Philippines." January 17, 1981.

Mendoza, Annella M. "Audio-Visual Archiving: Frequently Asked Questions." *Society of Film Archivists (SOFIA) Newsletter* 1, no. 1 (August 1999): 4–5.

———. "Seven Years of the Society of Film Archivists." *Society of Film Archivists (SOFIA) Newsletter* 1, no. 1 (August 1999): 1, 7.

Nizette, Mark, and Guy Petherbridge. "Assessment of Potential Sites for a Philippines National Audio Visual Archives Facility." Unpublished report, July 1996.

Nolledo, Wilfrido D. "The (First) Lady of the House." *Focus Philippines*, June 30, 1979, 8, 10, 12, 14, 16, 38–40.

———. "A Human Settlement for the Tao." *Focus Philippines*, June 23, 1979, 24–25, 32, 38.

Philippine Information Agency (PIA) and Society of Film Archivists (SOFIA). "Consultation Meeting Establishing the National Film/Video Archive Facility, Annotated Agenda." Unpublished report, 1997.

Polites, Nicholas. *The Architecture of Leandro Locsin.* New York: Weatherhill, 1977.

Roads, Christopher. "The Manila National Film Centre." Report Prepared for the Government of the Philippines by the United Nations Educational, Scientific and Cultural Organization (UNESCO). Unpublished report, Paris, 1981.

Salazar, Oskar. "Philippines' Marcos Orders Review of Exec. Order 868." *Hollywood Reporter*, February 22, 1983.

San Diego, Bayani Jr. "Archivists Reclaim 2 Silent PH Films 'Pirated' by US." *Philippine Daily Inquirer*, August 26, 2011, http://entertainment.inquirer.net/11043/archivists-reclaim-2-silent-ph-films-'pirated'-by-us-film-fest-opens-friday.

Sheringham, Michael. "Archiving." In *Restless Cities*, edited by Matthew Beaumont and Gregory Dart, 1–17. London and New York: Verso, 2010.

Steedman, Carolyn. *Dust: The Archive and Cultural History.* New Jersey: Rutgers University Press, 2002.

Stein, Elliott. "Manila's Angels." *Film Comment* 9, no. 5 (1983): 48–55.

Tatad, Francisco S. "The MIFF Passes." *Mr. & Ms. Magazine*, February 16, 1982, 8–9.

Tiongson, Nicanor G. "The Filipino Film in the Decade of the 1980s." In *The Urian Anthology 1980–1989*, edited by Nicanor G. Tiongson, xvi–xxxv. Manila: Antonio P. Tuvera, 2001.

———. "The Winds of Change: 1986–1994." *Genesis* (2010): 28–39.

Villarama, Baby Ruth. "Current Film Distribution Trends in the Philippines." In *Art Archive 02: A Collection of Essays on Philippine Contemporary Literature and Film*, 98–105. Manila: The Japan Foundation, 2019.

Whaley, Floyd. "A Brisk Walk Featuring Imelda." *New York Times*, October 15, 2012, http://travel.nytimes.com/2012/10/15/travel/in-manila-livin-la-vida-imelda.html.

Young Critics Circle Film Desk. "Statement of the YCC Film Desk on the Disqualification of Emerson Reyes' Entry from the 8th Cinemalaya Independent Film Festival." March 8, 2012, https://yccfilmdesk.wordpress.com/tag/cinemalaya-controversy/.

# Wayward Informality, Queer Urbanism

*Manila, the Dark and Decadent City*

Ferdinand M. Lopez

## A Placemaking of One's Own

My friends tell me that I am poor in directions. That I'm bound to get lost every time I travel. Perhaps my internal compass is ruptured most of the time. I have a rather vague notion of space, its metrics for calculating distances, its globular orientations, and temporal coordinates. That is why, finding myself suddenly in the Land of Immigrants and away from the reassuring presence of the familiar, I easily get discombobulated by spatial directives. I don't know how to navigate using cardinal directions as reference points. I am not versed in the metrical measures of distance to steer me correctly to my destination. Where I come from, spatial directions are detailed narrations embellished with sensorial details, personal memories, intertwining relationalities, and cultural allusions.

For more than half a century now, my recollections of the city have been tied to a sensorial mapping of Manila—the peculiar stench of blood, feces, and urine of animals slaughtered in the abattoir of Tondo; the blaring jeepney horns and startling sonorous chimes of horse-drawn *calesas* (rigs) plying the route of C. M. Recto Avenue; the melancholic amber sunset bleeding the knifed horizon at the Manila Bay; the sweet scent of ripe papaya, marang, and jackfruit wafting from the fruit stalls in Padre Rada; the tangy-tasting pomelo and dalandan sold along Asuncion Street in Divisoria; the congested, dilapidated, and fuggy boarding houses in the university belt area of Sampaloc; the delectable aroma of freshly steamed pork and shrimp dumplings at the fast food restaurants along Calle Ongpin in Binondo, the world's oldest Chinatown; the colorful assortment of tropical cut flowers—azucena, lilies, orchids, and birds-of-paradise along Dimasalang and Laong-laan Streets; the squat baroque San Agustin church, and the neoclassic Manila Cathedral in the historic Walled City of Intramuros; the cloud of dust particles in the workstations of marble gravestone engravers in Blumentritt; the rhythmic frenzy of brass bands in the Buling-buling festival at Paco and Pandacan; the sea of sweat-drenched devotees during the *translasyon* of the Black Nazarene, the Jesus Padre Nazareno from Luneta to Quiapo; and the joyful Manila sounds of the 1970s made popular by Cinderella, VST and Co., Rico Puno, Hajji Alejandro, Rey Valera, and the Hotdog's "I keep coming back to Manila / simply no place like Manila / Manila, I'm coming home"—these are my memory prompts engendered by sensing the city. They are the workings of memory constructed through urban *citysenseship*. A sensing of the city, which is also a sense-making of urbanism—oscillating between clarity and ambiguity, legibility and incomprehensibility, location and dislocation, integration and fragmentation, and the proverbial common sense and the sensing of the uncommon (Nancy 1997; Devilles 2019).[1]

These synaesthetic images that reside and survive in the heart of the individual and communal imagination is what the urban planner Kevin Lynch described as "imageability," persisting smells, sights, textures, sounds, touches, and tastes conjured simultaneously in the intersecting axes of spatiality and temporality. It is both cognitive and affective. It sustains the flow of synergy, collectivity, and belonging among city dwellers in the spaces of the metropolitan imaginary (1960, 9). What's more, these are the visual-mental pictures of the city that we cherish. These are the images that we keep in our hearts endearing the place to us. They become alive in our memories and imagination. In the same way, places that are forlorn and forgotten somehow fade away and die. Places and spaces are enlivened through sensorial apprehension, energized by relational encounters, and sustained through lived experiences (Tuan 1977).

To grasp the indissoluble connectedness between peoples and places, Aaron Betsky talks about how queer people are affected by their surroundings—their exclusion, oppression, and marginalization. In the process, members of the queer community strategically transform inhospitable spaces to accommodate their desires, ideals, and aspiration. Accordingly, the sexualization of space indicative of contemporaneous contestations by gendered subjects has been poignantly explored by Aaron Betsky in *Queer Space: Architecture and Same-Sex Desire*. Betsky argues that spaces are reused, redesigned, and refunctioned by the people occupying a given locus. In defining queer space, Aaron Betsky shares:

[Queer Space] is a kind of space that I find liberating, amoral, and sensual . . . space that lives only in and for experience. It melded Utopian and corporeal escape, a movement inward with a movement outward. The city was rewritten by men cruising and refusing to accept strictures. . . . In all these ways, queers queered the city. They made it their own, they opened it up on the margins and they performed it. (1997, 5–13)

It is by the presence of a gendered subject that a given space assumes its gender identity. In queer geography, the transgressive sexuality of the *bakla* is performed in the negotiated spaces of Manila's urban life. The *bakla* opens the spaces where they are previously unwanted. They occupy, liberate, and use these spaces in queer time. They unapologetically perform their *kabaklaan* in spite of intense sexual regulation and moral admonition. Meanwhile, the conventional representation of space as an ahistorical, asexual, and immobile locus of cultural contestations remains problematic in the light of how the tripartite connectedness of time, place, and ideology inform both individual subjects and collective identities through a complex web-work of social relations and exchange (Soja 1993). Space informs subjects. Subjects, in return, affect and constitute the character of a given place.

In this essay, I will heuristically employ the terms *bakla, gay, transgender,* and *queer* interchangeably for strategic reasons and practical purposes, notwithstanding the specificities of their cultural provenance, possible translation slippages, and their overdetermined formation. The traditional connotation of the *bakla* in the Philippines refers to a male who desires another male because the core of *kabaklaan* is femininity. This cross-gendering and cross-dressing *bakla* is aligned with the Western notion of the transgenderism (Garcia 2003; Manalansan 2003; Diaz 2015). In truth, the umbrella term *bakla* covers a panoply of practices and expressions of nonnormative sexualities as locally conceived in the archipelago. Most of my informants believe that *bakla* is translatable into English as "gay," despite the difference in sexual politics as pointed out by some Filipino gay scholars. Apart from this, *bakla* as a gender category in the islands shares with *queer*, as an identity critique of "multiple social antagonisms," a long history of persecution and suffering in relation to institutions of control and regimes of power (Eng, Halberstam, and Muñoz 2005). In the Philippines, *bakla* is a capacious term embracing nuances of gayness, transness, queerness, bisexualness, and the 2spiritness common among indigenous communities in Asia-Pacific and in the Americas.

This essay reads the filmic representations of queer Manila during the Marcos regime using Ishmael Bernal's *City after Dark* (*Manila by Night*) as a celluloid cartogram exposing queer spaces in the city film. The articulation of refusal and resistance of the *bakla* against heteropatriarchy, heteronormativity, and homonationalism of the martial law period is exemplified in Bernal's work. This film's representations of queer Manila will be read in conjunction with the ethnographic narratives of fifteen Tondo[2] queer subjects who performed their *kabaklaan* in the heterotopic spaces of the city during the Marcos regime. In film and in real life, *lamyerda* (walking, tracing, cruising) and the *mujeran* (drag balls and pageantry) are types of wayward informalities that enunciate the aesthetic refunctioning and cultural reclaiming of the streets of Manila, the City of Contradictions. These perceived, conceived, and lived spaces in real life and in the film *City after Dark* emplaced decadent desire through the film's mise-en-scène as analogs of queer urbanism.

I deploy the term *wayward informality* by invoking Saidiya Hartman's notion of the wayward as insurgent, subversive, wild, liberated, and rebellious, which are oftentimes construed as pathological, deviant, and criminal by formal social institutions. And yet, they are visionary, beautiful, and colorful—representing the reckless dynamism of the city (Hartman 2019). Synonymous with the term *wayward* is the concept of the wild. Jack Halberstam refers to it as the undisciplined, disobedient, deviant, degenerate—descriptive signifiers often yoked with queerness. The wayward is wild, abject, uncivilized, uncouth, cut off, and separated from its *other*. Besides, it is untethered and autonomous from colonial management and compulsory policing. Halberstam opined that "wildness is not limited to the natural world, and it has an extensive life elsewhere too—in aesthetics, politics, theory and desire" (2020, ix).

Informality, on the other hand, refers to life practices, cultural activities, and modes of production existing outside the legal framework of state control, government administration, and the global neoliberal development scheme (Jabareen 2014). It is both a critical and a creative intervention in the utilization of public spaces and resources to accommodate the needs, values, and desires of "undesirable" and "unwanted" individuals who make up the city. It provides marginalized subjects freedom and access to resources through creative interventions and critical maneuverings. As such, wayward informality fastens radical imagination with the ordinary, everyday, and practical modes of survival.

Meanwhile, queer urbanism is predicated on the active political participation of nonnormative individuals and queer communities in the highly contested spaces of the city. I follow the leads of Eng, Halberstam, and Muñoz in their use of the term *queer* to indicate the multiple forms of social antagonism against institutions and the social processes that produce, recognize, sustain, stabilize, and normalize identities (Eng, Halberstam, and Muñoz 2005). Conversely, *urbanism* refers to the various ways in which people relate with each other and how they react to their built environment (Wise 2019, 4). Thus, the participatory, appropriative, alternative, and insurgent queer urban politics is based on Henri Lefebvre's notion of "right to the city" (1996), purportedly enjoyed by all members who inhabit and reshape the metropolis (Iveson 2013).

For this reason, Natalie Oswin believes that a queer space is a concrete space carved out of sexual dissidence. Queers continue to negotiate, resist, and rapture the hegemonic, homonationalist, and heteronormative control of geopolitical spaces (2008). These contested sites, where forms of nonnormative practices occur, are radically reconceptualized, relived, and reembodied by the *bakla*'s performative world-making and life-affirming practices such as the *mujeran* (drag balls and pageantry) and *lamyerda* (walking, tracing, and cruising). Specifically, they are forms of wayward informalities in queer, modern, and urbanized Manila.

Similarly, this emplacement is what Jacques Ranciere alludes to in the triangulations of the self, the world, and the meaning-making sensibility of people as the distribution of the sensible. He contends that "this distribution and re-distribution of places, and identities, this apportioning and reapportioning of spaces and times, of the visible and invisible, and of noise and speech, constitutes what I call the distribution of the sensible. Politics consists in reconfiguring the distribution of the sensible which defines the common of a community to introduce into its new subjects and objects, to render visible what has not been, and to make heard as speakers those who have been perceived as noisy animals" (2004, 25). The capacity to see, think, and do are available politically and aesthetically to the individual and the collective. When the individual or the community sense, apprehend, and act based on a common desire, they politically revise the distribution of the sensible. In fact, this occasions otherwise—a condition of possibility. The collective aspiration of those who were previously marginalized in the distribution can potently destabilize the forces and contexts that can lead to a better station in life. In this regard, the *bakla*, who previously were not heard and seen, are rendered visible and audible as they liberally inscribe their public presence through *lamyerda* (walking, tracing, cruising) and *mujeran* (drag ball). By queer appropriation of time and space, the sensible is redistributed to embrace the wild and wayward *bakla* politics and aesthetics in the city, where they were written off, cast aside, and rendered insignificant by those who police and manage strategically the distribution of the sensible.

Meanwhile, Gaston Bachelard argues that "space that has been seized upon by the imagination cannot remain indifferent to the measures and estimates of its surveyor. It has been lived in, not in its positivity but with all the partiality of the imagination. Particularly, it nearly always exercises an attraction for it concentrates on being within the limits of that which surrounds and protects" (2014, 19). The city, when grist to the artist's imagination, is affectively constituted with memory and experience assigning value to every crevice, corner, nook, and cranny of the geopolitical unit (Yi-Fu Tuan cited in Cresswell 2004; Bachelard 1969). To write about a place is to record the personal and the political. Each page is a documentation of an affective rumination, an attempt to memorialize what otherwise is fleeting and passing. Queer time, after all, according to Judith Halberstam, is contingent, evanescent, and transitory—moments appear, disappear and reappear. Memories come and go evocative of queer conjuring (2005). Placemaking, meaning-making, and homemaking belong to every one of us. Memories and meanings flow in and out or flow on and on even in the *elsewhereness* of human imagination.

This relational approach in sensing Manila is what Faranak Miraftab recognizes as affective mapping of the global heartland, a sociality, and a confluence of peoples, processes, and emotional relations between borders and beyond barriers. She explains, "Through such an approach, I recover voices and stories often hidden, made invisible, or left out of the picture, to theorize place and place-making relationality" (2016, 210). This in-placement reveals the complexity of everyday lives, networks of care, dynamics of interaction, tactics of survival, and conditions of possibility that inform social relations. This sense of place and placemaking prompted me to write about wayward informality and queer urbanism of Manila, imagined and remembered in the formidable distances of space and time.

## Queering Methodology

I have always been drawn to the streets. Even at a tender age of ten, I would manage to sneak out of the house and join my friends as we took over streets. We transformed every available space into our playground. Parks and recreation centers were seen only in the make-believe world of film and television. I grew up in the slums of Tondo, where streets teem with so much vibrancy, life, and beauty.[3] As children of the city, we owned the streets. The streets opened other worlds for us. It was quite different from that carefully curated universe spawned by the family. My friends and I would be on the streets from 5:00 in the morning until 10:00 in the evening. We practically lived in the streets. We would go home to have breakfast at 8:00 A.M., lunch at 12:00, and dinner at 6:00 P.M. Then we would go back to play, tell tall tales, gossip, quarrel, eat, walk, and gallivant. We had always been out on the streets. No coming out was required. Everyone belonged. We took care of each other. No one was alone on the streets. As I was growing up, I got to know a lot of places beyond our neighborhood by walking in the streets. Only adults, I daresay, are afraid of the streets.

The best way to know people and places is by walking. Luckily, friends and I would map the geography of relations everywhere we would go by walking. Everyone seemed to know everyone. Because everybody had the right to the streets, it was easy for the *bakla* to walk, cruise, and take over. On a hot September 21, 1972, afternoon, while on my way home as a third-grade student in the elementary, I heard over the radio in the jeepney I rode with my younger sister that the martial law period[4] had been declared. I did not know what it was all about. When my sister and I reached home, I saw my mother frantically take down the three laminated certificates of my father. He got them after several months of trainings under the National Federation of Labor Unions. After that day, my aunts and my mom were always in a huddle. They were always whispering, afraid that the walls in the house might hear them. We were not allowed to go out anymore. She said that the members of the Philippine Constabulary patrol would jail us if they found us in the streets. Nobody went out. The streets were finally quiet.

State institutions started to regulate the streets. The surveillance machinery of the martial law regime took the streets away from us. Suddenly, it was no longer safe to walk, especially at night. Then there were rumors of *aswangs* (ghouls, bloodsucking monsters) roaming the dark alleys of Tondo at night. It was an attempt to control and regulate our movements. The epidemic of fascism forced everyone to be on house arrest during the curfew hours. Several months after, walking revealed a totally different image of the streets. It was one of persisting inequalities, grinding poverty, squalor, violence, and death. Victims of salvaging or summary executions were dumped in deserted corners or remote places after dark. Drug addicts would raid fly-by-night pharmacies for their supplies of cough syrups and downers. People had to line up for the government ration of third-rate, poorly milled rice from the barangay. Cats also disappeared in the neighborhood. Rumor had it that they ended up in the freezers of a famous siopao (steamed bun) restaurant in Quiapo. Showdown of warring gangs like Commando, Sigue-sigue Sputnik, Batang City Jail, and the Low-Waist Gang became a frequent spectacle. The wooden bridge in Romana Street connecting Labasan and Ibayo became more difficult to cross after pillboxes were thrown on it by clashing cabals. Frequent saturation drives or zonings were conducted to flush out suspected criminal elements in Tondo.

But the informal people persisted, endured, and survived, among them the *bakla*, who managed to make do with the available resources to make a living and find fugitive pleasures in the militarized spaces of the martial law period. In the slums, the *bakla* lived side by side with other marginalized subjects condemned to a life of abjection. They were interpenetrating communities bound by economic exigencies. They colluded, relied on each other, forged values and norms based on their dynamic interactions on the streets (Pasco 2019). They were the unwanted presence in the genteel and gentrified City of Man/Madame.

Charles Baudelaire used the image of a traveling man to appraise and evaluate the effects of modernity in European cities. The rapid urbanization of the metropolis casts its detrimental effects on people's quality of life. There is a pervading sense of loneliness, looming sense of gloom, and quiet desperation that typify the nameless crowd in the modern city (Laing 2016). The brutal indifference that characterized the anonymous masses were palpably represented by nineteenth-century city artists in their works. These amorphous crowds encounter each other on the streets. With lordly unconcern, they dismiss each other and perfunctorily rush to their respective destinations every day. They jostle each other, walk past each other, ignore each other. The flaneur sets himself apart from the daily crowd of passersby and anonymous public in the big city. Compared to the masses, the flaneur moves in and out with much ease and flair in his milieu. An ambulatory person of leisure, the flaneur indulges in the art of seeing and sensing the urban environment, rising above the throng (Benjamin 2019). Born in the life of privilege, the aimless surveyor and wanderer in the streets is often male. Women walking the street are often construed as hookers and prostitutes plying their trade in the dark street corners of the city (Elkin 2016).

Here, I provisionally use the terms *lamyerda* as "queer walking"—a methodology suggesting an alternative way of producing knowledge on the city. The *bakla*, a queer complex figuration of persistent individual and resilient community, walks with graceful familiarity the labyrinthine lanes and byways of the Third World city. Through this *bakla* methodology, I extend Baudelaire's concept of *flanerie* (Benjamin's flaneur, de Certeau's walking rhetoric, Lefebvre's rhythmanalysis, and Francesco Careri's walking as an aesthetic practice), Derrida's formulation of impression and tracing, and Muñoz's idea of cruising in mapping the contact zones of *kabaklaan* elided in the archives of quotidian life in the city. By tracing the roots, routes, rites, and rituals of *kabaklaan*, I reclaim the invisible, silenced, and erased spaces of *kabaklaan* in the genealogy of Philippine community life, urban planning, and city development.

*Lamyerda* (queer walking, roaming, tracing) in *bakla*-bulary (queer lexicon) suggests a psychic remapping of queer fantasy, mobility, and itineracy. Traces of queer life are reviewed and redrawn to render visible, albeit fugitively and fleeting, renegade desires (Muñoz 1996). *Lamyerda* is a term derived from the Spanish phrase *a la mierda*, which means "to fuck," "to shit," "to hell," or everything that suggests vulgarity and profanity. From its obscene genesis, the *bakla* refashioned the term to critically describe their multiple types of wayfaring and forms of meandering. *Lamyerda* (tracing, cruising, roaming) as a type of urban informality underwrites the performativity of desire taking over public metropolitan spaces previously codified by the hegemony for heteronormative functions.

*Lamyerda* is a form of queer tracing (*pagtunton*, *pagtalunton*). It is a mobile quest provoked by erotic desires and fueled by queer energies. It is attended by *chikahan*, a blithe, barb, bitchy, mundane, convivial conversation that involves the dynamic exchange between individuals and communities. It is ignited by *kalandian*, an archipelagic flirtation. It involves *aurahan*: surveying, interacting, and assessing, contacting, and booking as messy and complex transactional gestures. It is further propounded by *rampahan*, akin with cruising or navigating. Kibitzers' use the term *hunting* to describe this queer searching, where the *bakla* is constituted as a predator like the *aswang*[5] in local lore. However, I think *haunting* is more appropriate to describe this queer spectrality because, as Derrida suggests, "haunting implies places, a habitation," (1995, 86) a spatial familiarity and personal fondness rooted from an uncanny connection with a site, object, and people. What's more, *lamyerda* as tracing implies a complex form of sashaying marked by messy forms of turning and re-turning in search of fleeting pleasures amid peril. A habitual movement of queer passion and desire.

Similarly, queer tracing is a reencoding of disobedient desires, punished and erased by heteropatriarchal and heteronormative institutions steeped in double-standard morals. Seismic flirtation, the shape of queer archipelagic desire born in the Pacific Ring of Fire, is tidal. *Lamyerda* erupts from the crevices of the social regulation, discipline, and control. It disrupts the normative practices of inclusion, which is also the politics of exclusion. Tracing interrogates the notion of centering, which oftentimes results in marginalizing. It tracks social processes that empower some and disenfranchise *others* within the social structures. Tracing reappears the specters of archipelagic flirtations that cannot be contained because it always exceeded itself in auto-erasures and self-obsolescence, a desire that keeps on moving and re-moving its dark and decadent impressions in the city of local restrictions and legal sanctions.

*Lamyerda* is a cartography of queer intimacies revitalizing the erotic of queer remembering to uncover the persistent violence on queer lives. It is a memorialization of the multiple ways in which the *bakla* cope with precarious conditions in the city. It is remapping of queer (be)longing in spaces where they are systemically excluded and excised. Queer tracing documents the ephemeral practices of sexual delight and danger and tracks down the vestiges of *kabaklaaan*, disappeared under the bright and blinding lights of gay globality (Benedicto 2014).

In the same vein, *lamyerda* is a repetitious act. A mnemonic prompt characterized by an unconscious turning and re-turning to exhume and uncover imprints of recalcitrant libidinal practices and subversive sexual acts. As a performance of ephemerality, *kalandian* and *kabaklaan* are self-extinguishing, self-dissolving, and self-vaporizing. They leave impressions of desires that are distinct, singular, personal, and irreplaceable as the moments of erotic yearnings (Derrida 1995). *Lamyerda* is an instinctive tracing of immanent desires iterating incommensurable intimacies. It follows a genetic script as the queer tracker pursues the hint with no promise. The *bakla* is always in search for what was before nuanced desire—a seduction, a hinting, a beckoning to decode. "Trace travels, with no guarantees. Trace teaches, lessons that the subject soaks up" (Spivak 2012, 503).

If cities are created primarily for safety and convenience, walking underwrites security. People who are walking get to look out for each other and care for each other (Careri 2002). *Lamyerda* facilitates this renewal of social bonds as communities touch base with each other while roaming the streets. The *bakla* remaps the disappearing paths by wandering in the city. Walkscapes are primarily designed for being lost, for being adrift, for discovering and opening new undiscovered worlds within the city (2002, 14). In an archipelagic city, drifting enables the queer subject to steer from shore to shore, point to point in constantly shifting tides of affective exposure and emotive encounters. It is in this indeterminacy, wild abandon, and openness to instability that queer subjects are able to learn new things about themselves and about the city, for instance, to understand how queer intentions and actions collide with normative social proscriptions and moral regulations—in a place or space, where desires, values, and beliefs constantly clash and exist in perpetual tensions.

By walking, a queer method of reorganizing and refusing the script of intense social proscription and sexual regulation, the *bakla* subverts heteropatriarchal hegemony (de Certeau 1984, 100; Springgay and Truman 2018). *Lamyerda* reinforces the queers' right to the city. Besides, *lamyerda* is navigating the archipelagic city, taking full control of steering the temporal and spatial course, movement, and destination in the thoroughfares of the Global South (DeLoughrey 2007). In fact, *lamyerda* as critical place-based research methodology uncovers how space is affected by the complexity of overlapping social phenomena such as globalization, urban modernity, neoliberalism, queer globality, and environmental destruction (Tuck and McKenzie 2015). Furthermore, *lamyerda* (queer walking) accounts for the messy interconnected social dynamics of place and time manifested in transitioning and passing (Gozlan 2015; Berlant 2016; Manalansan 2014). Contemplating on queer durability, flexibility, and resilience, Aaron Betsky is correct when he said, "Queers queered the city, otherwise, they could not have survived"(1997,12).

## Of Art, Culture, and Society: *Manila by Night*

In *"Ang Pelikula sa Lipunang Filipino, ang Lipunang Filipino sa Pelikula,"* or "Film in Philippine Society, Philippine Society in Film," noted critic and

Philippine National Artist Bienvenido Lumbera prefaces his argument on the interface of art and life by invoking two film metaphors in his native tongue, Tagalog: "*mga aninong gumagalaw*," roughly translated as "moving shadows," and secondly, "*sa pinilakang tabing*," or "on the silver screen," which exhort the nature and modality of filmic representations. He posits that people, places, and events unfolding on the big screen are merely silhouettes of strangely familiar figures, recognizable locations, and well-known realities refracted creatively through the director's "optical unconscious" and power optics (Yu 2005).

The city film *Manila by Night* constructs the geopolitical entity not merely as locus of action but as a living catalyst and pivotal agent. Manila engages and stirs the other characters to personally resist and communally respond to life's constant clobbering in the asphalt jungle. After all, as Lumbera observes:

> Bernal's Manila is certainly not everybody's Manila, least of all city planners and social workers who might want a scrubbed-up and deodorized version of the primate city. Those who know Manila through glossy posters and color supplements intended for the eyes of tourists, and those who know it through lifetime residence in any one of its districts are both bound to be disconcerted by *Manila by Night*. The first would be dismayed that their image of the city has been tarnished by Bernal's sense of authenticity which is dominated by the squalor of slums and the reek of poverty. The second group would be offended perhaps by the selectiveness of Bernal's imagery which omits scenes and sights of warmth and wholesomeness which, no doubt, have managed to survive the darkest corners of the city. Indeed, anyone who sees *Manila by Night* expecting to find in it the actual topography and demography of the real city will come out of it quarreling with Bernal on many points about Manila. (1997, 211)

Bernal's dark and decadent Manila is one of the many representations of the "noble and ever loyal" city.[6] As a metropolis practically enveloped in darkness—which I argue is a metaphor of a nation abject in poverty (of the body, soul, and spirit)—nighttime ironically exposes the lives of these urban settlers, whose motives and actions are otherwise concealed in darkness. Night embraces and vitalizes its own inhabitants. The Marcos regime has created a nation of nocturnal creatures: prostitutes—young and old, male and female, professional and amateur—all trying to survive the economic squalor and moral putrescence of the Sin City[7] (Tadiar 2004, 37–75). As a metonymic representation of the nation, the city in the film is populated by prostitutes, drug addicts, pimps, masseuse, pedophiles, and drug pushers, who are part of the city's informal economy. Their lives transect and connect with the life of gay fashion designer Manay Sharon and her *bakla* cohorts through a vicious cycle of lust, manipulation, and betrayal. Thomas Elsaesser, in his study of the New German Cinema of the 1970s, came up with a parallel observation regarding the value of film as an archive of people's memory. He believes that film:

> was an attempt to gather, record, and report the images, sounds, and stories—including those that cinema itself produced—which make-up the memory of a generation, a nation and a culture, and to translate them, from their many perishable supports in people's minds to the one medium that, after all promises paradoxically to be the most permanent: the cinema. Literature, popular culture, architecture, fashion, memorabilia, and the contents of junk shops have all been enlisted in a vast effort to preserve the traces of lives lived for oblivion. This hastily accumulated visual wealth has not yet been tapped or even properly inspected for its meanings or uses. (1989, 322–323)

Film, as both historical artifact and cultural signifier, corroborates what otherwise has been elided in the officially recognized representations of the nation and its people. Artists register fragile memories and evanescent lives in film to preserve what otherwise could have been erased and destroyed by time's demolishing hands. In Bernal's *City after Dark*, the Filipino viewers participate as meta-spectators watching their own escapist narratives unfold on the silver screen of cinema houses enveloped in darkness. Film narratives make us understand the social, economic, historical, cultural, and political world we live in. The stories in cinema give insights regarding the loss, pain, difficulties, and struggles that confront marginalized individuals and disenfranchised communities. These stories offer "methods of social inquiry," enabling people to comprehend the various roots, forms, and occasions of harm and injury on queer bodies caused by power asymmetry (Georgis 2013).

Meanwhile, the *bakla*, or non-gender-conforming Filipinx, are perceived in urban popular imagination as nocturnal monsters or "bloodsucking" creatures. This is a common perception among outsiders of the *bakla* community based on a cursory assessment of the *bakla*'s late-morning arising as well as their relatively enervated and lackluster presence at day compared with their invigorated countenance as darkness prevails. Filipinx queers cruise the asphalt jungle as night settles in, together with other shadowy shape-shifters of Philippine social reality. In the regime of blood and beauty, the conjugal dictators, Ferdinand and Imelda, are the arch-impalers and symbolic bloodsuckers who drain the national coffers, the lifeblood of the nation, sapping the life force of the people who precariously live in the state of terror and horror. This couple from hell siphon the democratic force and libertarian energies of the national body polity. They leave behind in the wake of their feeding frenzy (to satisfy their insatiable greed for money, fame, and power) heaps of tortured and dead bodies, scores of national debt, and throngs of economically depraved and culturally displaced citizens immolated on the altar of tyranny.

In writing a "history of difference," Joan Scott explains how narratives from the edge challenge the prevailing notions of gayness. These queer narratives present a world of alternative sexualities and values that subvert the hegemonic constructions of the social world. Scott proposes the documentation of the lives of those overlooked and omitted in the accounts of the past because it can occasion a crisis in traditional historiography. Scott elaborates that:

> [the] histories that document the hidden world of homosexuality, for example, show the impact of silence and repression on the lives of those affected by it and bring to light the history of their suppression and exploitation. . . . In these stories, homosexuality is presented as an expressed desire (experience denied), made to seem invisible, abnormal, and silenced by a "society" that legislated heterosexuality as the normal practice. (1993, 400)

In postmodern retelling, reinstalling historical context to filmic images became significant because it critically engages the social institutions and social structures of the past by reexamining their forms of administrative control, surveillance, and social regulations. In this paper, I will interrogate the trope of darkness, which ironically renders visible the decadent desires of the *bakla* characters in the city film under consideration.

## Martial Law Manila: Dark and Decadent City

The gentrification of Manila, a salutary aftermath of Imelda Marcos's visionary project, the City of Man, or more properly, the "City of Ma'am," the cornerstone of the Marcosian New Society. As a beautifully dressed window, this historical capital exhibits Imeldific excesses and delusional aesthetics. To achieve this gentrified look, the city is aggressively purged of lawless elements using military might. Madame Marcos strategically purified her ideal city from economic putrescence and squalor by invoking the use and abuse of artistic license to build edifices that memorialized the new political order.[8] Concomitant to this, throngs of urban poor settlers were periodically displaced. The rest of shanty town was purposely enveloped in pristine walls that palisaded the pestering eyesores of the city. No wonder the self-instituted Patroness of Philippine Arts, the governor of Metro Manila, the

Human Settlement Commissioner, and the First Lady of the Republic of the Philippines, Madame Imelda Romualdez Marcos, endowed with a string of political epithets emblematic of unbridled authority, successfully persuaded the producers of the Ishmael Bernal film *Manila by Night* to change the movie title to *City after Dark* in 1980. By doing so, it purportedly obliterates any allusion to the decadent center of Philippine political and cultural life during the martial law era.

The city, instead of being a passive witness, becomes actively involved in the lives of all the characters in the film. The film successfully presents multiple narratives that are structurally suspended on a peg. The seven narratives gravitate around the central intelligence gay character, Manay Sharon, a fashion designer, perhaps modeled after the late popular fashion iconoclast Santiago de Manila. Ernest Santiago (a.k.a. Santiago de Manila) was couturier by day and operator of the Coco Banana disco bar, where Manila's who's who in arts and entertainment gathered in the company of Manila's outlandish gay performers.

In the film, Manay Sharon is the embodiment of the city in perpetual quest for meaning behind the absurdity of existence—forever searching for authentic love in a hapless and uncaring universe. Inextricably linked in the life of Manay are two opportunistic men, Pebrero, a taxi driver who has a utilitarian relationship with Adelina, a female prostitute disguised as a nurse, and Baby, an innocent provincial lass whom he impregnates and abandons after. The other lover is Alex, the wayward son of Virgie, an obsessive-compulsive reformed prostitute who tries to build a perfect family. She and her family live in House No. 7. In biblical numerology, the number seven is a signifier of perfection, but in the film, it ironically reveals a dysfunctional and degenerate family. Alex has a romantic entanglement with Vanessa, a student from an exclusive girls' school, whom he forsakes because of drugs, and Bea, the blind masseuse with whom Alex has a sexual encounter at the instigation of Kano, the lesbian drug pusher, whose love interest is none other than the blind Bea.

These motley characters inhabit the evanescent spaces of *City after Dark*. As "living dead," they roam the city in search of their next victim—someone who will feed their insatiable thirst and hunger for love, understanding, and acceptance. Instead, they attract those who mirror the same appetite, albeit in varying degrees of aspiration. Darkness awakens manifold impulses and longings in her denizens, which daytime refuses to acknowledge and fulfill. These nocturnal beings are portrayed alive and kicking—walking, hiding, running, gossiping, copulating, and negotiating walkways, dark alleys, massage joints, gay bars, motels, and brothels—in the asphyxiated streets of Tondo, Binondo, Santa Cruz, Blumentritt, Paco, Libertad, Sampaloc, and Ermita in the Sin City.

In the film, the *bakla* inhabit practically every dark street and alley of the city. They cruise the city venturing in zones of pleasure and pain, safety and danger. In the Philippines, the *bakla* have been popularly constituted as *aswangs* (ghouls and vampires), nocturnally active but asleep and immobile by day. They rewrite the heteronormative scripts of discotheques, parks, comfort rooms, or the streets, opening them up for homosexual encounters and queer consumptions. Here, the victimizer is also a victim, and vice versa, prone to manipulations and harassment and vulnerable to erotic provocations and pleasures. What is interesting is Manay Sharon's self-knowledge of this machination of erotic reciprocity. She accepts her queer predicament, thus diminishing any conjected pain resulting from a jolting epiphany. Robert Diaz in "Queer Love and Urban Intimacies in Martial Law Manila" points out the complexity of these queer liaisons that foreclose relational possibilities. These dissident forms of intimacies account for the rich textures and robust nuances of queer reckoning of disobedient desires, evanescent pleasures, residing in the insurgent sexcapades (2012, 18).

At the heart of the city is Manay, a sister to an extended-family relation defined more by sexual proclivities and sympathetic filiations. Manay Sharon is a do-gooder who tries to help the blind Bea regain her sight. She provides for the needs of her boyfriends, Pebrero and Alex. She tries to recover the dead body of Adelina, Pebrero's mistress who was strangulated by an irate sex partner. This does not at all mean that Bernal is cashing in on the good, funny, hysterical gay stereotype. In the film, Bernal manages to show the underside of her character as cynical, promiscuous, and gullible. According to Bienvenido Lumbera, Manay Sharon is the first gay character in Philippine cinema who is not a caricature (1997, 210). Prior to Manay Sharon, the *bakla* in Philippine cinema were loud, flamboyant, tragic-comic characters who were limp-wristed and pathetic figures. Bernal's sympathetic portrayal of Manay Sharon is a celebration of *kabaklaan* in a film that performs his own sexual politics. Bernal's deep psychological probing of the complexity of gayness, as well as the characters' existential search for meaning behind quotidian existence, are manifestations of his profound philosophical insights, political convictions, and aesthetic moorings.

Another aspect of the city enunciated in the film is that of a dark embryo—a womb where initial life is nourished and sustained. It is a space of life that enables Manay Sharon to express her sexual desires and experience sexual intimacies. Her bedroom is her metaphorical womb where her homosexual yearnings are born and sustained. In the privacy of this enclosure, she negotiates blissful pleasures, albeit momentarily. In this enclosure, she is both vulnerable and safe: vulnerable to the manipulations of her partners not without any agency; safe from the puritanical eyes of a society that has demonized, criminalized, and pathologized her.

As opposed to the other morally degenerate, desperate, and depraved characters in Bernal's dark city—pimps, prostitutes, drug addicts, and drug pushers sinking in the quagmire of despair and anguish, using sex as a way to escape from the dystopic city—Manay Sharon is the only character who finds redemption by embracing and celebrating her queer faith and identity.[9] What Manay was able to accomplish in the film is to reconcile spirituality and sexuality. At the end of the movie, she enshrines the image of the Child Jesus, the Santo Niño, the iconic representation of gender fluidity and shiftiness in her atelier abode. The venerated image of popular devotion has been transformed by the faithful to a queer religious icon. Garbed in satin, silk, lace, and lamé and adorned with semiprecious stones, glass beads, rhinestones, corded appliqués, ostrich feathers, and metallic trimmings, the androgynous Holy Child becomes a queer representation of the Incarnate God. Gay theoretician J. Neil Garcia notes:

> In so many ways, the flamboyantly bedecked and royally coutoured Boy Jesus—in these islands, the object of so much pious adulation—struck me as being sissy as I was. That this image of the Holy Child should have to bear the full brunt of all my identificatory politics should not sound so strange in a culture that, as a whole considers it a sacred plaything. (1998, 181–182)

## Manila: The Carnivalesque City

Tondo is a metonymy of Manila, Carnivalesque City. This coastal town enclosed westward by the Manila Bay and eastward by the Estero de San Lazaro probably derived its name from either the Tagalog word *tundo*, meaning to "bait" or "catch a fish," or, better yet, from *tundoc*, a violet-colored banana species that abounded in this fishing community before the onset of rapid urbanization (Ira and Medina 1977). Tondo mirrors Manila as an archipelagic city. Both are composed of land masses rising from the Pasig River and the Manila Bay. Tondo remains an outsider inside Manila—a disintegrating figure in the body polity of the city. This paradoxical disposition eventuates from Manila's uneven development, where Tondo languishes continuously under the shadows of socioeconomic depravity. Ironically, Tondo's strategic location as hub of Manila's business activity, as crossroads of cultures, and as a significant historical site could not trenchantly efface its shady reputation as an impoverished neighborhood populated by hapless criminal elements.

In Tondo, one of Manila's most economically depraved districts, the image of the Conquistador Prince, the Santo Niño, is regally enshrined amid economic declension and moral degradation. It is in this part of the metropolis where the most lavish and grandest fiesta celebration in the city is held every third Sunday in January. In this impoverish neighborhood, the most garish fiesta processions are routed showcasing the most flamboyant articulations of *kabaklaan* in the city.

The recalcitrant nature of the *bakla* thrives in and partakes of this rhetoric of democratization and counterculture, which Mikhail Bakhtin calls the "carnival." He explains:

> In the world of carnival all hierarchies are cancelled. . . . All castes and ages are equal. . . . All the elements—the peculiar festive character without any piousness, complete liberation from seriousness, the atmosphere of equality, freedom, and familiarity, the symbolic meaning of indecencies, the colonial crowning and uncrowning . . . all of these are contained in the [carnivalesque] world, and they all have the same philosophic meaning.
>
> Popular festive form . . . presents—peoples material abundance, freedom, equality, brotherhood . . . the whole world is triumphantly *gay* and fearless. (Underscoring supplied; 1987, 251–256)

In this Bakhtinian revelry, the most spectacular expressions of the *bakla* body are repossessed from the consumptive male gaze through its "double positivity"—as medium conveying the inversion and also as performative vehicle of heteroglossic projection that evades heterosexist imagination.

In the film, a similar Bakhtinian impulse is echoed in the statements, "*Sino ang Diyos ngayon?* [Who is God tonight?]," and "Who wants to join me?" uttered by a gay character wearing the toga of a Roman god or emperor. Bacchus, the god of wine and merrymaking, is embodied by the despotic Philippine president, drunk with power and military might. As god to his comrades, this *bakla* appropriates the character of a Roman ruler and challenges the Filipino demigod residing in Malacañang Palace. Marcos, the Filipino Bacchus, inaugurates and presides over the longest bacchanalia in Philippine history by creating a national sex tourism industry.

Moreover, this *bakla*, together with his cronies of drunk and drugged cross-dressers, lesbian pimp, and other drug dependents, invades and appropriates the off-limits breakwaters of the Manila Bay on New Year's Eve. This is a symbolic baptism of queer bodies in the New Society. This right to buffoonery permits the resurgence of inverted folk wisdom that allows people to see the carnivalesque world with foolish eyes exacerbated by hallucinogens, alcohol, and nicotine ingestion. This is amplified by the camera's slow-motion focusing on surreal images of floating candles, a colorful fireworks display, an alienating night sky, the murky water of desolation, and a land engulfed by a sense of void, dramatically intensified by the Vanishing Tribe's psychedelic sounds (Baytan 2010). The coarseness and grotesqueness of this orgiastic merrymaking affirms the indestructible character of the dregs of society amid the regime of military surveillance and fascist rule (Bakhtin 1987).

Another queer aspect of the film *City after Dark* is the *mujeran*, or the gay ball. In one passing scene, Alex and his friends make fun of a disabled *mujerista* whom they saw in the gay ball while waiting for the drug courier, Kano. This Tondo queer performer is Lilay Magalona, who was born with kyphosis, or hump on her back. She is the breadwinner of her family. Lilay stands four feet two inches tall and lives with her family of eight members under the Raxa Bago bridge. Their homestead hangs above the stinking murky waters of Canal dela Reina. She is a street vendor by day peddling homemade sweetened rice cakes with coconut shavings and a trans-performer by night lip-synching and dancing to Madonna's greatest hits—"Like a Virgin," "Material Girl," "Borderline," "Into the Groove," etc. Through her, Bernal exposes transness and disability as modalities of intersectional disenfranchisements of queer bodies under an ableist totalitarian regime.

If space and subjectivity are coconstitutive, Tondo's heterotopic spaces enable the *bakla* to negotiate and transform its hypermasculine space into a locus of spectacle through the *mujeran* or the *wagwagan* during the martial law period. Usually held in basketball courts, school grounds, town plazas, or streets blocked off from traffic, the *mujeran* or *wagwagan* is a sociocultural event much anticipated by Tondo denizens subsisting under the shadows of authoritarianism. Its high entertainment value draws sizable crowds from the neighborhood. *Mujeran* came from the Spanish loanword *mujer*, meaning "woman" or "female," thus signaling an event for inscribing *bakla* femininity in the public spaces of the community.

The Tagalog word synonymous with the drag ball is *wagwagan*, meaning to "shake," as in wiggle, waggle, and jiggle. It also suggests getting rid of something as superfluous as guilt and shame in a predominantly Catholic environment where *kabaklaan* is viewed as immoral. Dance, music, speech, pageantry, impersonation, and drama of everyday existence are the ingredients of queer spectacle that binds the *bakla* community. Queer balls build relations of solidarity. They instill an attitude of thanksgiving for daily survival and celebrate empowerment through a queer-affirming presence. As a social event, the gay ball is a young gay's initiation to the transgender community and queer culture of the city. Intergenerational gaps are bridged by the *mujeran* as the young initiates are welcomed by their gay sisters, queer mothers, trans aunts, and fairy godmothers to the very challenging life of the *kabaklaan*. The longing to belong, to be cared for, to be accepted, ends when queer kinship begins.

This ritualistic community building is necessary in ensuring gay survival against the systemic aggression and oppressive practices of a heteropatriarchal society. The canivalesque spirit of the *mujeran* allows the *bakla* to perform her identity through the multiple appropriations of femaleness inscripted in the heterotopic spaces of the *mujeran*. In Bakhtinian terms, what the straight men do when they playfully cross-dress or cross gender lines is to produce and emphasize the negative pole of the canivalesque, that is, when inversion becomes caricature or parody. With the *bakla*, gender performativity during the *mujeran* becomes the radical ambivalence between the negative and positive poles—so crucial to the subversive and creative valence of carnivalesque, so delicately sustained and underlined by the *bakla* in queer urbanism. The *bakla* femininity is never a parody. It is rooted from their psychosexual inversion emanating from their feminine selves.

During the martial law period (1972–1981), the *mujeran* would begin at 7:00 in the evening and end at 11:45, before the curfew would toll the knell of parting day. When the siren sounds, the *bakla* amazingly cross over walls in high-heeled shoes, dexterously roll under parked jeepneys, and miraculously scamper toward the nearest house where they can find temporary refuge. When caught by patrolling members of Metrocom (Metropolitan Command) or the Philippine Constabulary (PC), they are brought to Camp Crame to diffidently pull weeds in their elegant gowns. Some are ordered to repeatedly sing the Philippine national anthem and other popular songs till the wee hours of the morning. Others are asked to personally minister to their impounding policemen and their cohorts as maid, masseuse, and mistress of sexual pleasures. These *mujeristas* go home the morning after, a picture of abjection—ravaged, ragged, and exhausted; as the *bakla* is stripped of magic and mystery, she becomes an ugly representation of pathetic buffoonery and comic wretchedness by military state discipline.

The pleasure and excitement brought about by the ephemeral spatial-temporal coordinates of the *mujeran* disappears in time as the queer social body is subjected to disciplinary punishment and military violence intended to reform queer corporeality through prohibition, behavioral modification, and punitive intervention (Foucault 1977). The political economy of time is deemed important in the capitalist neocolonial economy of the Marcosian regime, where the human body is supervised and disciplined to maximize labor productivity. Curfew hours are imposed not only to regulate movement, instill obedience, and impose law and order, but also to ensure that the queer *cyborgian* instrumentality of techno-industrial production is trained for self-regulation and self-enslavement to capitalism (Haraway cited in Schneider 2005).

Disciplinary sanctions, no matter how petty and trivial, visibly illustrate both the macro- and microphysics of coercive power inherent in the militarized institutions acting as domestic and national supervisors. Therefore, the docile bodies of the *bakla*, I argue, are the consequences of the regime of blood, beauty, and brutality. Queer bodies are disciplined, sanitized, and gentrified for the state's economic exploitation and political necessity in the national sex tourism industry, beauty trade, and the messy informal economy. A concrete example of this are the business girls or transgender pleasure-providers who roam the sin cities of Angeles, Olongapo, and Baguio. They would go back to their base of operation in the capital city of Manila whenever they would be flushed out of their sex camps near the U.S. military installations in the Philippines.

In this regard, the *bakla* creates a spectacle of identity during the *mujeran*. In doing so, the flamboyantly cross-gendering *bakla* opens a space to accommodate her queer sexuality. Gilda Gimenez, adjudged Ms. Gay Manila in the 1960s, recalls the gay ball, or *mujeran*, of the martial law period. She said:

> The *mujeran* starts early in those days. We'll start putting on make-up at 5 o'clock PM. By 6:30, one of us will go out to look at the sky to check whether it will rain or not. If there are stars in the sky, we will attend the *mujeran*. The *mujeran* before cannot compare to gay parties now. Firstly, the gays before are properly dressed, which means preparing one's accessories, costumes, shoes, bags, make-up, gowns, ahead of time, etc. Secondly, there were lots of men attending gay parties in the past, so you don't beg anybody to dance with you. Those were happy festive times. But we scamper to different directions when the siren sounds at 11:30 P.M. (Gilda Gimenez in an interview with the author, Tondo, Manila, February 10, 2002)

During the martial law period, gay fantasies were actualized even in policed spaces of the archipelago, where queer presence transformed rigid structures to accommodate *kabaklaan*. It should be noted also that the *bakla* communities were conveniently courted by the administration candidates for votes during snap elections. Likewise, they were used in other government campaign sorties for entertainment value to attract large crowds during election rallies.

Absent from this film are the torture, aggression, and punishment directly imposed upon *bakla* subjects during the martial law regime.[10] Helena de Bourbon recounts an anecdote of how they were rounded up by the military when they were trying to beat the curfew after attending *mujeran* in Tondo. Helena remembers:

> We were caught by military men at the corner of Moriones and Juan Luna St. We were shoved inside a six by six military truck. I was with Janet Kennedy, Violeta de Jesus and Amalia Javier. We all came from a *mujeran* in Dagupan St., when we were rounded up. We were all

brought to Camp Crame and we were forced to tidy up the place and pull grass till our hands begin to hurt. Imagine we were fully made up and we were in our sequined gowns the night before. We perspired a lot while pulling the weeds. And we were released the following day at 10 o'clock in the morning. We had to ask money from strangers to cover our transport from Quezon City to Tondo, so we can go home inasmuch as the arresting officers took away all our money. In the jeepney, the other passengers were staring at us because we look so wasted—wig in disarray, the make-up has melted, the gown, a total disaster. (Helena de Bourbon in an interview with the author, Tondo, Manila, April 15, 2002)

The *bakla* body is the most conspicuous signifier of alterity and otherness. The *bakla* is a marked social subject with a feminine *loob*, or interiority, and a masculine *labas*, or exteriority, where lack of congruence and harmony becomes signifier of grotesque absurdity. No wonder most of the *bakla* trying to harmonize the inward and the outward cross-dress, take birth control pills to feminize their bodies, and resort to cheap medical procedures to correct and heal the cleavage between interiority and exteriority.

Queer pageantries are showcases of feminine ideals where the body become the commodity embodying the values of respectability, responsibility, and decorum of the upper class. The *bakla* appropriate the glitz and glamour through an ephemeral self-transformation (Cannell 1999). They assume the names of their favorite local and Hollywood celebrities, fashion models, and socialites, showcase their best apparels, and exude grace and gentility in the *mujeran*. As artifice of desirability, these gays perform the spectacle of respectability within the ambit of excess, extravagance, and exaggeration. They are dismissed as vulgar, diversionary, mundane, superficial, or *puro arte* (whimsical and capricious) by those *outside* the "shared and dynamic performative practice" of evanescent cultural life (Burns 2013, 89).

Spaces of struggles and spectacular survivals are located in the theater of everyday life, where these *bakla* confront actual personal, economic, and social adversities during the regime of beauty and brutality. Before they are dolled up for the *mujeran* and beauty pageants, some of them had to experience shaming as they were forced to strip naked during *saturation drives* or *zonings* in the crowded streets of Tondo. Others have buried their *bakla* friends who lost all hopes of coexisting with homophobic members of their family and society before attending the *mujeran* in the evening. A lot of the *bakla* become drug dependents taking in high dosage of cough syrups, downers, uppers, and pills of every kind to escape the harsh and bitter realities of *bakla* life. A good number of them engage in back-breaking toils during the day to support extended families. Business girls who are frequent attendees of the *mujeran* are victims of police brutality and harassment when they are unable to remit grease money to police officers while working in the flesh trade. But in spite of these adversities in the city, they find in each other an accepting and affirming queer family—friends and elders who understand their queer dispositions and an embracing community where they can be free, happy, and gay.

These conditions of possibility reside in the *bakla*'s vulnerability and everyday radical resistance and refusal. The disruptive incommensurability of the *bakla*'s beautiful existence and wayward lives is encoded in the *mujeran* and in *lamyerda*. These queered spaces become the avenue for the flourishing of radical hope—a consequential dream, a grounded wishful thinking, an aspiration to generate positive and productive courses of action amid the banality of oppression, injustice, and inequality. These queer lives under constant surveillance and discipline occasion what Ashon Crawley describes as the politics and aesthetics of *otherwise*, a flight from the present, a refusal of violence and violations. It is an inexhaustible plenitude of possibilities, an imaginative pursuit of justice and equity, a disruptive performance of *or else* (Crawley 2017).

Such is their radical hope, the courage to *live life well* amid life's constant clobbering, unavoidable destruction, and inevitable persecutions in the hands of bigots and intolerant, self-righteous hypocrites (Lear 2006). Jose Esteban Muñoz, in talking about the *then and there* of *queer futurity*, states that "queerness is about futurity and hope. That is to say that queerness is always in the horizon" (2009, 11). It is a touchstone of hopeful anticipation, an astonished contemplation away from the enveloping darkness in life toward the unbearable lightness of educated dreams and aspirations, a specter of a new and better world to come.

## Making Sense of the City

Manila, the Ever Faithful and Loyal City of Miguel Lopez de Legaspi's colonial imaginary, is one of the Tropical City Beautiful Projects of urban planner Daniel H. Burnham, architect of U.S. Imperial Modernity in the Pacific. As a colonial invention, the city reproduces a network of imperial relations—patriarchal, neocolonial, migrant, and capitalist. Its infrastructures of intimacies and logistics of "sexual desire and its government are profoundly entangled in bio-, necro-, and geopolitics" (Cowen 2014, 223). Manila is an ecology of disaster, debris, detritus, a duress of imperial subjugations strategically carpet-bombed during the Pacific War by the United States (Stoller 2016, 2013). Moreover, it was left in shambles and rubble by the fleeing members of the Japanese Imperial Army, who upon orders of Tokyo started a systematic rampage in the city that killed a lot of innocent civilians and destroyed urban infrastructures.

Manila is currently one of the world's most densely populated cities, with 42,857 people per square kilometer ratio. It ranked sixth as one of the most-dangerous cities on the planet, with no less than the President Duterte unconscionably perpetrating scores of human rights violations in the metropolis. Moreover, Manila ranked among the lowest (94 out of 102) in the IMD Smart City Index of 2019 conducted by the International Institute for Management and the Singapore University of Technology. It performed below average in regard to health and safety, mobility, activities, opportunities, and governance based on the Manila denizen's perception of the scope and impact of the economic, technological, and humane aspects of the smart urban development.

Manila is an insomniac, a city that never sleeps.[11] It is made up of marginal characters that come out from their culturally closeted existence and cruise the city—mapping and liberating city streets and alleys. It is a night city—queer and colorful as the people who inhabit it, subverting the artificial, genteel illuminations of the city. Ironically, the hidden lives of non-gender-conforming subjects have been revealed in the film *Manila by Night*, exemplified by Manay Sharon and her friends who cruise the streets of Manila with much aplomb and impunity. Their fluid identities, flamboyant bodies, and spectacular sexualities are flexible, adjusting to the vicissitudes of life. Together with other marginalized denizens of night in the city, they try to escape the pernicious cycle of despair, depravity, and destitution by forming supportive communities so they can cope with the forces that seek to decimate the disposable, dispensable, and dysfunctional (un(re)productive) *cityzenry*.

*City after Dark* begins and ends with movement. Day or night, the city stirs and stimulates. The queered spaces of the city disappear at the break of dawn as light dissolves these ephemeral spaces of *kabaklaan*, only to be reborn after the sun has set. These nocturnal creatures, marginalized and oppressed by the light, will again roam the dark and decadent city, kicking and screaming, as all faggots do—celebrating their recovered voice and visibility in a patriarchal society that has silenced, condemned, and consigned them to darkness. Their well-wrought metamorphosis by day finds transcendental completion by night.

Behind the *bakla*'s makeup, wigs, bust pads, hip pads, pantyhose, and other appurtenances of transformation, dwells a strong spirit—scintillating, infectious, illustrious—as our local languages frame our indigenous ideas of beauty that really matter—*marikit* (gorgeous), *maringal* (majestic and elegant), *marilag* (magnificent), and *maningning* (scintillating)—inward qualities nurtured by living countless years of grace under pressure. Their inward lights shine brightly in the dark city. As metaphors of visibility, the *mujeran* and *lamyerdahan* reveal the hidden lives of the courageous *bakla*, cloaked in violence, enveloped in oppression, wrapped in poverty, and restrained by

the institutional norms during the regime of blood, beauty, and brutality—
yet in spite of these travails, the magnanimity of their souls radiates ribbons
of queer luminosity.

## NOTES

Note: A part of this essay, "Decadent Desire and Darkness: Mapping Gay Manila of the
Marcos Regime," from Ishmael Bernal's "City after Dark," appeared in the journal *Manila
Selected Papers of the Annual Manila Studies Conference*, Mary Svetlana T. Camacho and
Lorelei D.C. De Viana, eds. (Manila: Manila Studies Association, 2014). I would like to
thank Dr. Bernardita Reyes Churchill for the permission to include it here.

1. Baroque style of writing is heap-up. Ornate. Flamboyant. Infused with so many
details, it gives birth to long kilometric lines and sentences. Western critics, who have
been trained to say things directly and using economy of words are quick to find fault in
this kind of writing. For them, it is verbose, prolix, and, thus, belaboring. Such style of
writing is a product of culture. The verbal flourish of the Castilian tongue, the rhythmic
and incantatory cadence of Tagalog hospitably gave rise to this style. Nick Joaquin, our
foremost master of this baroque sensibility, would write a sentence joined by semicolons,
spread throughout an entire page. Though writing *from* English, he forged the language
to accommodate the historical and cultural milieu. Transnational feminist scholars
Richa Nagar and Amanda Lock Swarr, talking about accessibility and accountability
to the subjects we are writing about, reminded us that "we argue for a transnational
feminist praxis that is critically aware of its own **historical, geographical,** and political
locations, even as it is invested in alliances that are created and sustained through deeply
dialogic and critically self-reflexive processes of knowledge production and dissemination" (2010, 3; underscoring supplied). See Nagar and Lock Swarr, "Introduction."

2. Tondo is one of the oldest and poorest districts of Manila and also the most densely
populated area of the metropolis. References to *Tundun*, the old Tagalog name of Tondo,
can be seen in the Laguna Copper Plate Inscription dated 900AD. Tondo gave birth to
national heroes Andres Bonifacio and Emilio Jacinto. Tondo is home to National Artists
Francisco Arcellana (literature), Atang dela Rama (theater), Amado V. Hernandez (literature), Cesar Legaspi (visual art), Levi Celerio (music), and Rolando Tinio (theater).
Furthermore, Tondo played a significant role in Philippine history. It was the site of sub-
versions. The Battle of Bangkusay, a naval battle waged by indigenous chieftain Rajah
Sulayman and Tarik Sulayman of Macabebe, Pampanga, against the Spanish conquis-
tadors, led by Miguel Lopez de Legaspi, occurred on June 3, 1571, in Tondo. Also, it
was the site of the Tondo Conspiracy (Revolt of the Lakan: 1587–1578), an uprising led
by the Maharlikas (noblemen) against the Spanish colonial government. Meanwhile, La
Liga Filipina, a secret reformist, revolutionary organization was founded by national hero
Dr. Jose Rizal at Ylaya Street on July 3, 1892. Then Andres Bonifacio's Kataastaasang
Kagalanggalangang Katipunan ng mga Anak ng Bayan (KKK) was established on July
7, 1892, in Azcarraga Street, Tondo. In addition, The Templo de Trabajo, Tondo, was the
birthplace of the Communist Party of the Philippines (Partido Komunista ng Pilipinas,
August 26, 1930). What's more, Tondo was the venue for the first labor uprising during
the Spanish Colonial Period led by women cigar factor workers during the term of Governor General Jose Basco y Vargas (1778–1787). The first Labor Day celebration took place
at Plaza de Moriones, on May 1, 1903. Additionally, during the martial law period, Tondo
was also the setting of the first major labor strike (1975) at the La Tondeña Incorporada,
a distillery plant at Velasquez Street. See Ira and Medina, *Streets of Manila*.

3. To track the various improvisations, virtuosity, and inventiveness of slum dwellers in pursuing happiness despite their despicable situation in the metropolis, see Pasco, "*Eudaimonia* in the Margins." A more detailed account of how the informal settlers cope with the vicissitudes of life in the urban jungle is provided in Jocano, *Slum as a Way of Life*.

4. President Ferdinand E. Marcos signed Proclamation 1081 putting the Philippines under the state of martial law on September 21, 1973. The announcement was made on September 23, 1972. Marcos justified the declaration by citing the growing unrest in both urban areas and the countryside, radical student activism, and the perceived threat of communist takeover as the reasons behind the militarized rule. Political enemies were imprisoned, unlawful arrests of people who offended Marcos and his cronies were made and their private properties confiscated, and political dissidents were imprisoned, raped, tortured, and summarily executed. Task Force Detainees of the Philippines estimated that there were at least 3,275 extrajudicial killings (Amnesty International Report 1975), 35,00 documented tortures, 77 desaparecidos (disappeared), and 70,000 incarcerations. Marcos lifted martial law on January 17, 1981, through Proclamation 2045. Marcos's regime of blood, beauty, and brutality continued until February 1986. For a more detailed look at this atrocious moment in Philippine political history, read Robles, *Marcos Martial Law*.

5. *Aswang* is an all-embracing term to describe shape-shifting, flesh-eating monsters in Philippine folklores. It includes ghouls, vampires, viscera suckers, and were-beasts (dogs, pigs, cats, and other animals).

6. The title *Insigne y Siempre Leal Ciudad*, or "Famous and Ever Faithful City," was bestowed to Manila by King Philip II in 1574 after it was proclaimed the capital of the new Spanish colony by Miguel Lopez de Legaspi. The more poetic title *Noble y Siempre Leal* was adapted later. See Nick Joaquin's popular history for young Manileños, titled, *Manila, My Manila*, commissioned by former city Mayor Gemiliano Lopez.

7. Neferti Xina Tadiar's brilliant critique of the sexual economies during the martial law period is found in *Fantasy Production: Sexual Economies and Other Philippine Consequences for the New World Order*. Tadiar points out the aggressive sex tourism campaign abroad during the Marcos regime that enlivened the flesh trade in the country. Further, she argues that the U.S.-Philippine relation is a gendered filiation where the U.S. empire flexes his hypermasculinity over the colony (Philippines), which he emasculates, effeminizes, and commodifies. This uneven romance between the United States and the Philippines has transformed the colony to a status of a prostitute of the United States.

8. See Neferti Tadiar's "Metropolitan Dreams" in *Fantasy Production*, 77–112.

9. See Baytan, "Looking for the Divine." I would like to thank Prof. Baytan for alerting me regarding the queer nuances of the film.

10. Absence leaves a trace, according to Jacques Derrida. He states that "the mark of the absence of a presence, an already absent present, or lack at the origin that is the condition of thought and experience" (Derrida 2016). See Derrida, Spivak, and Butler, *Of Grammatology*.

11. For an interesting discussion on the trope of darkness in the film, see Tolentino, *Paghahanap sa Virtual na Identidad*.

## BIBLIOGRAPHY

Bachelard, Gaston. *The Poetics of Space*. Translated by Maria Jolas. Foreword by Mark Z. Danielewski. Introduction by Richard Kearney. New York: Penguin Books, 2014. Boston: Beacon, 1969.

Bakhtin, Mikhail. *Rabelais and His World*. Bloomington: Indiana University Press, 1987.

Baytan, Ronald. "Looking for the Divine: The City of Sin and Bernal's *Manila by Night*." In *Spirituality and the Filipino Film*, edited by Clodualdo del Mundo, 62–85. Manila: Communications Foundation for Asia, 2010.

Benedicto, Bobby. *Under Bright Lights: Gay Manila and the Global Scene*. Minneapolis: University of Minnesota Press, 2014.

Benjamin, Walter. *Illuminations: Essays and Reflections*. Edited and with an Introduction by Hannah Arendt. Translated by Harry Zohn. Boston and New York: Mariner Books, 2019.

Berlant, Lauren. "The Commons: Infrastructure for Troubling Times." *Society and Space: Environment and Planning* 34, no. 3 (2016): 393–419.

Betsky, Aaron. *Queer Space: Architecture and Same-Sex Desire*. New York: William Morrow, 1997.

Burns, Lucy Mae S. P. *Puro Arte: Filipinos on the Stages of Empire*. New York and London: New York University Press, 2013.

Cannell, Fenella. *Power and Intimacy in the Christian Philippines*. Quezon City: Ateneo de Manila University Press, 1999.

Careri, Francesco. *Walkscapes: Walking as an Aesthetic Practice*. Aimes, Gainsville, Lemgo, and Rome: Culicidae Architectural Press, 2002.

Cowen, Deborah. *The Deadly Life of Logistics: Mapping Violence in Global Trade*. Minneapolis: University of Minnesota Press, 2014.

Crawley, Ashon. *Black Pentecostal Breath: Aesthetics of Possibility*. New Yok: Fordham University Press, 2017.

Cresswell, Tim. *Place: A Short Introduction*. London: Blackwell, 2004.

de Certeau, Michel. *The Practice of Everyday Life*. Translated by Steven Rendall. Berkeley, Los Angeles, and London: University of California Press, 1984.

DeLoughrey, Elizabeth. *Routes and Roots: Navigating Caribbean and Pacific Island Literatures*. Honolulu: University of Hawai'i Press, 2007.

Derrida, Jacques. *Archive Fever: A Freudian Impression*. Translated by Eric Prenowitz. Chicago and London: University of Chicago Press, 1995.

Derrida, Jacques, Gayatri Spivak, and Judith Butler. *Of Grammatology*. Baltimore: Johns Hopkins University Press, 2016.

Devilles, Gary. "Sensing and Seeing Metro Manila." In *Making Sense of the City: Public Spaces in the Philippines*, edited by Remon Barbaza, 145–180. Quezon City: Ateneo de Manila University Press, 2019.

Diaz, Robert. "The Limits of Bakla and Gay: Feminist Readings of My Husband's Lover, Vice Ganda and Charice Pempengco." *Signs: Journal of Women in Culture and Society* 40, no. 3 (2015): 721–774.

———. "Queer Love and Urban Intimacies in Martial Law Manila." *PLARIDEL: A Philippine Journal of Communication, Media and Society* 9, no. 2 (2012): 1–19.

Elkin, Lauren. *Flaneuse: Women Walk the City in Paris, New York, Tokyo, Venice, and London*. New York: Farrar, Straus and Giroux, 2016.

Elsaesser, Thomas. *New German Cinema: A History*. New Brunswick, NJ: Rutgers University Press, 1989.

Eng, David, Judith Halberstam, and Jose Esteban Muñoz, eds. "What's Queer about Queer Studies Now?" *Social Text* 23, no. 3–4 (2005): 1–18.

Foucault, Michel. *Discipline and Punish: The Birth of the Prison*. Translated by Alan Sheridan. New York: Vintage Books, 1977.

Garcia, J. Neil C. *Performing the Self: Occasional Prose.* Quezon City: University of the Philippines Press, 2003.

———. *Slip/pages: Essays in Philippine Gay Criticism.* Manila: DLSU Press, 1998.

Georgis, Dina. *The Better Story: Queer Affects from the Middle East.* New York: State University of New York Press, 2013.

Gozlan, Oren. *Transexuality and the Art of Transitioning.* London and New York: Routledge, 2015.

Halberstam, Jack. *Wild Things: The Disorder of Desire.* Durham and London: Duke University Press, 2020.

Halberstam, Judith. *In a Queer Time and Place: Transgender Bodies, Subcultural Lives.* New York: New York University Press, 2005.

Hartman, Saidiya. *Wayward Lives, Beautiful Experiments: Intimate Histories of Social Upheavals.* New York and London: W. W. Norton, 2019.

Ira, Luning, and Isagani Medina. *Streets of Manila.* Manila: GCF Books, 1977.

Iveson, Kurt. "Cities within the City: Do-It-Yourself Urbanism and the Right to City." *International Journal of Urban and Regional Research* 37, no. 3 (2013): 941–956.

Jabareen, Yosef. "Do It Yourself' as an Informal Mode of Space Production: Conceptualizing Informality." *Journal of Urbanism* 7, no. 4 (2014): 414–428.

Joaquin, Nick. *Manila, My Manila: A History for the Young.* Manila: City of Manila, 1990.

Jocano, F. Landa. *Slum as a Way of Life: A Study of Coping Behavior in an Urban Environment.* Quezon City: Punlad Research House, 2002.

Laing, Olivia. *The Lonely City: Adventures in the Art of Being Alone.* New York: Picador, 2016.

Lear, Jonathan. *Radical Hope: Ethics in the Face of Cultural Devastation.* Massachusetts and London: Harvard University Press, 2006.

Lefebvre, Henri. *Rhythmanalysis: Space, Time, and Everyday Practice.* London and New York: Bloomsbury, 2013.

———. "The Right to the City." In *Writings on the Cities: Henri Lefebvre,* edited by E. Kofman and E. Lebas, 147–159. Oxford: Blackwell, 1996.

Lumbera, Bienvenido. *Revaluation: Essays on Philippine Literature, Cinema and Popular Culture.* Manila: University of Santo Tomas Publishing, 1997.

Lynch, Kevin. *The Image of the City.* Cambridge and London: MIT Press, 1960.

Manalansan, Martin IV. *Global Divas: Filipino Gaymen in the Diaspora.* Durham and London: Duke University Press, 2003.

———. "The 'Stuff' of Archives: Mess Migration, and Queer Lives." *Radical History Review* 120 (2014): 94–107.

Miraftab, Faranak. *Global Heartland: Displaced Labor, Transnational Lives and Local Placemaking.* Bloomington and Indianapolis: Indiana University Press, 2016.

Muñoz, Jose Esteban. *Cruising Utopia: The Then and There of Queer Futurity.* New York And London: New York University Press, 2009.

———. "Ephemera as Evidence: Introductory Notes to Queer Acts." *Women and Performance: A Journal of Feminist Theory* 8, no. 2 (1996): 5–16.

Nagar, Richa, and Amanda Lock Swarr. "Introduction." In *Critical Transnational Feminist Praxis,* 1–20. New York: SUNY Press, 2010.

Nancy, Jean Luc. *The Sense of the World.* Minneapolis: University of Minnesota Press, 1997.

Oswin, Natalie. "Critical Geography and the Use of Sexuality: Deconstructing Queer Space." *Progress in Human Geography* 32, no. 1 (2008): 89–103.

Pasco, Marc Oliver. "*Eudaimonia* in the Margins: Negotiating Ways to Flourish in Urban Slum Dwellings." In *Making Sense of the City: Public Spaces in the Philippines*, edited by Remmon Barbasa, 121–144. Quezon City: ADMU Press, 2019.

Ranciere, Jacques. *Aesthetics and Its Discontent*. Cambridge: Polity, 2009.

Report of an Amnesty International Mission to The Republic of the Philippines: 22 November–5 December 1975. London: Amnesty International Publications, 1976.

Robles, Raissa. *Marcos Martial Law, Never Again: A Brief History of Torture and Atrocity Under the New Society*. Quezon City: Filipinos for a Better Philippines, 2016.

Schneider, Joseph. *Donna Haraway: Live Theory*. New York: Continuum, 2005.

Scott, Joan. "The Evidence of Experience." *Lesbian and Gay Studies Reader* 17, no. 4 (1993): 773–797.

Soja, Edward. "History: Geography: Modernity." In *The Cultural Studies Reader*, edited by Simon During. London and New York: Routledge, 1993.

Spivak, Gayatri. *An Aesthetic Education in the Era of Globalization*. Cambridge and London: Harvard University Press, 2012.

Springgay, Stephanie, and Sarah Truman. *Walking Methodologies in a More-than-Human World: WalkingLab*. London and New York: Routledge, 2018.

Stoller, Ann Laura. *Duress: Imperial Durabilities in Our Times*. Durham and London: Duke University Press, 2016.

———, ed. *Imperial Debris: On Ruins and Ruination*. Durham and London: Duke University Press, 2013.

Tadiar, Neferti Xina. *Fantasy Production: Sexual Economies and Other Philippine Consequences for the New World Order*. Quezon City: Ateneo de Manila University Press, 2004.

Tolentino, Roland. *Paghahanap sa Virtual na Identidad*. Pasig: Anvil Publishing, 2004.

Torres-Yu, Rosario, rev. ed. *Bayan at Lipunan: Ang Kritisismo ni Bienvenido Lumbera*. Manila: University of Santo Tomas Publishing, 2005.

Tuan, Yi-Fu. *Space and Place: The Perspectives of Experience*. Minneapolis: University of Minnesota Press, 1977.

Tuck, Eve and Marcia McKenzie. *Place in Research: Theory, Methodology, and Methods*. London and New York: Routledge, 2015.

Wise, Edwin. *Manila, City of Islands: A Social and Historical Inquiry into the Built Forms and Urban Experience of an Archipelagic City*. Quezon City: ADMU Press, 2019.

# This Is Our City

*Manila, Popular Music, and the Translocal*

CHRISTINE BACAREZA BALANCE

"This Is Our City" is the first single from Taken by Cars' 2011 album *Dualist*.[1] Its music video, directed by Quark Henares, opens with a brief musical intro and multiple boxes of time-lapse shots of Metro Manila. They evoke the city's frenetic energy and a sense of motion. Once the song "kicks in," we get a wide-angle shot of the band performing on an Intramuros building's rooftop, the Pasig River and modern skyscrapers in the background. Decked out in modern versions of Filipiniana, Taken by Cars' (TbC) lead singer, Sarah Marco, and bassist, Isa Garcia, don *baro't saya* while Bryce Zialcita (lead guitar), Derek "Siopao" Chua (rhythm guitar), and Bryan Kong (drums) don *barong tagalogs* and updated *camisa de chino* with handkerchiefs. Just as the video's architecture and environment illustrate Manila as a city of palimpsests, so, too, does the TbC's attire visually narrate historical mashups and layering. TbC's music might seem "out of time" with the histories and traditions of the Walled City, as their electrified rock sounds clash with the landmark's assumed soundtrack of traditional music (read, acoustic, Spanish-era classical à la *rondalla*). Upon closer consideration, however, the music video directs us to remember that even "traditional music" once fought on the battlefield of modernity. As with other moments in Filipino popular musical history, the contemporary Manila indie rock scene—through its songs, music videos, people, and venues—prove the city of Manila is an always-already translocal place.

The lyrics of "This Is Our City," as sung by Marco, are at times incomprehensible and suggestive, leading the listener toward a "sense" of their meaning rather than a straightforward narrative. The repeated refrain "This is our city"—the song's lyrical hook and anchor—structures its meaning. By evoking "the city," the song's remaining lyrics oscillate between urban life's figurations of hope—"let this be our day / and the thoughts will come / lost in the vibe / that overflows in our veins"—and despair—"why think about the boy / who doesn't even care / lost in this life / between this road and nowhere." The lyrical moments leading up to the song's anthemic refrain— "the sun comes up / at night we say / this is our city"—help us move toward Manila's nightlife as a site for possibility and reflection.

Alongside meanings generated by its music video, when performed live by TbC in venues outside of Manila—namely, Baguio and Los Angeles— "This Is Our City" empowers audiences to take up the anthem for themselves.[2] "Our city" shifts in metaphor, from their visions or memories of the archipelagic capital to the urban centers they currently call home. This opportunity for diverse and divergent meanings is characteristic of popular music's particular import. Whether as music video or live performance, TbC's song evidences Pinoy indie rock as object and approach, one that resounds Manila as a place of translocality.

The translocal is a concept that shifts attention away from the nation-state, focuses on the (im)mobilities of different migrations (both human and otherwise), challenges dichotomies of geographical concepts, and takes an actor-focused approach to the production of place, society, and culture. Centering its analysis on social actors/actual people, the "translocal" requires that we understand social spaces and scales are "not given a priori but rather socially produced, simultaneously fluid and fixed, and fundamentally relational."[3] Here, it is *people* and their activities that constitute and define places such as Manila. By focusing on them, we understand that Manila is not solely a physical place (parameters, geographical locations, etc.), but one constituted by people who inhabit it for various periods of time: those who are native to and remember various iterations of Manila and, while, at the same time, they who "talk, speculate, and fantasize about (other) certain places"; those who travel to and inhabit the city for various lengths of time, bringing with them preconceived notions of Manila as well as goods, ideas, and styles that further redefine what the city means.[4] It is also formed by media outlets who broadcast and advertise the city's meaning to the world, nation, and itself, both through self-assertive and subconscious statements of "Manila-ness" as well as comparative gestures to other places within and outside the nation-state.

When we imagine Manila as a translocal place, we denaturalize notions of the "local," ones put forth by the colonizing discourses of multiculturalism—a model that fetishizes and rewards cultural "Other-ness"—and cultural imperialism—a model that upholds the West as "origin" and the East as derivative. When we resound Manila as a translocal place, we both create and employ a figuration of the city as a site of artistic production, interactions, exchanges, and improvisation. This, in turn, underscores Manila as a trans-locality, a "place where mobile subjects are locally grounded."[5] While Pinoy indie rock's musicians and fans maintain various forms of bodily copresence in Manila, they are also connected to other places—cities and towns across the Philippines and the globe—through media technologies, the exchange and distribution of musical objects, and as mobile individuals themselves.

The translocal articulates "global and local dynamics in specific locali-ties," like Manila, while at the same time, grounding "deterritorialized con-cepts of movement and flow" back into the local context.[6] This is to say, we can consider concepts such as "cultural imperialism" and "neoliberalism," but we must pay attention to the ways in which these concepts manifest locally, bringing to the fore how local traditions and individuals work within and against these structures. In turn, it is imperative for us never to forget that the local itself is simultaneously shaped by its relationship to the nation, the region, the global. Again, these interactions do not simply take place in the abstract but instead are produced by people, both big and small, who live or have lived in Manila, who "talk, speculate, and fantasize" about Manila, who connect with Manila—as place, idea, or collection of people—from other places along various scales of network.[7] For me and for this essay, this net-work takes shape both within a network of musical places within the Philip-pine nation as well as those across a broader Filipino diaspora.

Since its founding as a Spanish colonial city in 1571, Manila, according to D. R. M. Irving, "was the world's first global city." "A crucial entrepôt," as Flynn and Giraldez earlier wrote, Manila "link[ed] substantial, direct, and continuous trade between America and Asia for the first time in history."[8] This essay briefly traces histories of translocality and Pinoy popular music scenes showing that these scenes were also shaped by the dominant media/technologies of each historical period (writing, albums/tapes/CDs, radio, TV/film). By doing so, I hope to shift the focus from discourses of cultural imperialism/national music to a larger network of musical influences, col-laborators, fans/audiences, touring/traveling musicians, and former members permanently settled in other cities/countries.

## Manila: In the World and of the World

There are those who might argue that this turn to the "translocal" is a recent phenomenon, aided and abetted by modern technologies such as television, film, the internet, and digital media. In this formulation, the longer histories of music-making and popular culture in the Philippines (and, therefore, what is categorized as authentically "Filipino") remain untouched by outside in-fluence. Yet, as various musicologists and historians have shown us, for as long as music has been part of Philippine culture, the translocal has taken shape through the *musical technologies*—from sheet music to circuits of musical performances, from LP/album recordings to radio, and everything since those times—as well as the *participatory cultures* of performance, reception, and distribution of their respective times. The forms and styles of these exchanges are precisely shaped by and characterize the place of Manila.

As musicologist D. R. M. Irving so eloquently details in *Colonial Counterpoint*, the place of Manila itself was always-already translocal—constituted by its inhabitants as well as the migrants and travelers, from across the region and the globe, who contributed to its life and society. Irving writes:

> Due to its provision of a reliable maritime connection between Asia and the Americas, and by virtue of its strategic location close to China, early modern Manila attracted a diverse body of migrants seeking to trade, conquer, and proselytize. A concatenation of mercantile interests, political ambitions, and evangelistic enterprises facilitated and propelled the local exchange of people, ideas, and commodities. Manila was, essentially, a microcosm of the world.[9]

Here we see the value of Manila, constituted by its geographical location, as an early modern place shaped by trade, colonialism, and religious crusades. These factors simultaneously consider Manila's place within the Philippine nation, the early modern region of Southeast Asia, as well as the global system of Spanish colonialism. Irving goes on to further note:

> At the same time as it emerged as an important international entrepôt, however, Manila remained an integral part of the Spanish imperial network. From the perspective of Spain, the Philippine colony was an essential frontier in the expansion of commerce and religion, in a fight for control of the Pacific Ocean, and in the creation of a seaborne empire that spanned from Iberia to Asia via the Americas.[10]

Along with fulfilling these colonial aspirations, the place of Manila in the mid- to early sixteenth century also held cultural meaning as a "major center of European print culture in East and Southeast Asia," from 1593 when the first books were printed there until the beginning of the early 1800s when the city's three presses were run by the Dominicans, Jesuits, and Franciscans. The city's religious culture was further solidified by the physical places of "Manila's walled city center, Intramuros" that included "convents and churches of six major religious orders, the cathedral, the palaces of the governor and archbishop, schools, hospitals, colleges and universities," making it, as Irving notes, "truly the 'Rome of the Far East.'"[11]

Music historian Fritz Schenker also helps us think through and about Manila in a preimperial and regional mode. Listening to the archival materials left behind by "colonial Asia's jazz age" with an anthropological intent, Schenker works to undo the narratives of jazz latitude set by a U.S.-centric viewpoint exemplified by Burnett Hershey's "around the world tour" essay. As Schenker points out:

> In his article, Hershey imagines a singular world of jazz, a global coherence created by a musical force that "follows the flag" of U.S. military and economic power. The entire world, he proposes, was subsumed within this all-consuming tendency.[12]

As a discourse, jazz latitude tells a story that at once gives overriding power to the "informal" aspects of U.S. empire (as it "remake[s] the world in the image of American culture") while, at the same time, "willfully ignores the myriad musical influences that informed the creation of music that has become a national representation of the U.S."[13] Therefore, jazz latitude enacts a form of cultural imperialism, narrating America's soft power as all-encompassing, and also enacts discursive power as U.S.-based and American critics, journalists, and scholars continue, to this day, believing and propagating the narrative itself. By listening to a detail of Hershey's 1922 article—the "passing observation" of the "presence of Filipino jazz musicians performing throughout colonial Asia"—Schenker argues against the jazz latitude by presenting an alternative history of global popular music told from the vantage point of colonial Asia. By centering and following these Filipino jazz musicians, as well as Manila-based popular songwriters and professional dance partners (*balerinas*), Schenker observes that Filipinos became so familiar with Western musical practices under Spanish rule that by the end of the nineteenth century, these musicians were renowned as performers of European and American musical traditions. In the era after World War I, the numbers of Filipino jazz musicians increased to meet the demand for dance bands across colonial Asia "from Bombay to Tokyo." Rather than simply understanding this as the effect of a dominant U.S. pop culture machine, Schenker's work prompts us to rethink jazz as a dominant and global industry with Filipinos as a class of musical laborers (what Stephanie Ng would later call "overseas performing artists") whose migrations and movements helped to create an "empire of syncopation."[14]

By listening to "the world depicted in the archives," Schenker argues, current-day historians and listeners are required to listen against "national and colonial boundaries" of place and temporality so that we may instead hear the archive's sounding of "global enmeshment, movement, and immobility" during this historical time period.[15] Listening to the archive from

Hershey's "shipboard perspective," we come to understand Filipino jazz musicians' movements "along the Asian littoral" "as part of a vast, interconnected web in which Manila serves as a central node."[16] As Schenker argues, it is important to note this interconnected web was itself set up by imperial forces and practices. They were not simply global in an organic fashion but instead human-made and therefore "riddled with instability, ambiguity, and disorder." This, in turn, requires we attend to imperial cultures in the Philippines and greater region of Southeast Asia that were not American.

Finally, it is important to underscore that these movements and this interconnected web functioned alongside the history of "Pinoy jazz" and "jazz in the Philippines" but do not tell the complete story of either phenomenon's development.[17] However, these stories of Filipino musicians during colonial Asia's jazz age are historical precedents of Manila's translocality. As we see in Fritz Schenker's as well as Lee Watkins' writings, Manila was a critical node in the regional development of colonial Asia's jazz age culture. It served as the launching point not only for these traveling musicians but also their songwriting musical peers and female dancing partners, people who—along with traveling albums, sheet music, and fan cultures—developed the participatory culture of jazz in and from the Philippines. Hearing these earlier histories of Manila's translocality, ones that appear before even America's "arrival," we must reckon with the port city as a node along broader regional, transnational, and imperial networks. And, importantly, Schenker's work "depict[s] Manila as a critical node in an intra- and inter-imperial entertainment circuit where Filipinos emerged as primary laborers in a vast jazz economy."[18]

## The Participatory Culture of Pinoy Indie

There are those who would argue that popular music is simply the aftereffects of the U.S. empire and colonialism in the hands of elite-led media companies and conglomerates. Popular music and other forms of media colonize the minds of the young, miseducating the Filipino along the way. And while these effects cannot be denied, it limits our understanding of popular music and its political and cultural potential.

Popular music is not just the products and objects of music (LPs, CDs, songs, film soundtracks, etc.). It does not solely reference the music industry (although, of course, that industry has played a big role in distribution). Popular music also references the worlds made, the scenes produced through music's making, listening, and sharing. These include musicians, roadies, promoters, DJs, club owners, writers/journalists, film and music video makers, fans, and even passive listeners. And, it should be noted, scene members often do not occupy just one of these roles. Instead, in Manila's indie rock scene, filmmakers DJ and play in bands, journalists/writers and musicians also own and manage clubs, and almost everyone is a music fan. Fan culture then can be understood as not merely consumptive but as a productive consumption, one where songs and performances inspire and prompt further music, writing, gathering, and so forth. With a broadened awareness that popular music is a participatory culture that shapes and is shaped by translocality, we can focus simultaneously on diverse aspects of a musician's identity—understanding them as fans, promoters, businesspeople who reference other places in the Philippines and beyond in different ways. Understanding popular music as a culture of participation, we turn our attention to record stores, radio stations, and bars and clubs as local hubs of national and international exchanges. Understanding popular music as a culture of participation, we must reckon with the multidirectional flows of translocality—as local (Manila) forms are shaped by musical objects, styles, ideas, and people from other places, as Manila forms travel to shape other scenes within the archipelago and beyond.

Translocality requires an actor-focused approach to place and culture. For the rest of this section, I want to look more closely at forms of musical exchange that took place right at the "dawning" of the internet age and greatly influenced today's Manila indie music scene. Doing so, we witness a historical moment of "convergence culture," at a transformative moment between analog and digital, distributive to social/viral media, and when young people transition from exchanges *with* intimates (family members and close friends) to exchanges *made* intimate through shared interests, namely, music. These stories offer us a portal for thinking through earlier translocal exchanges as the conditions of possibility for a Manila indie music scene.

Raymund Marasigan is a Filipino rock musician and record producer. Best known as the drummer and songwriter (along with Ely Buendia) of the Eraserheads, since the group's disbanding, Marasigan has also performed as the front man of Sandwich, keyboard/synths for Pedicab and Assembly Generals, and drums for Cambio and Basement Lung and is the mastermind behind Squid 9 and Gaijin. As a record producer, songwriter, current podcast host, and audience member, Marasigan has consistently worked to promote new bands and musical acts in Manila's indie rock scene. A prominent figure in the Manila scene for more than thirty years, Marasigan himself hails from the town/municipality of Candelaria, located in the western part of the Quezon province about 108 kilometers (or 67 miles) from Manila. He does not hide this fact, as he recently noted in an interview for the Filipinas Heritage Library's *Muni-Muni Stories* podcast.[19] Instead, he displays his provincial roots and pride in the titles of a Sandwich song and Basement Lung's first album (both entitled "Candelaria"), with the latter band's members made up of friends and family members either originally from or who currently live in the province. In these ways, Marasigan, like Filipino pop musicians before him such as Joey Ayala, Pilita Corrales, and Freddie Aguilar, remind the Manila scene that not all its musical icons (and therefore influences) originate from the capital city. In these ways, they remind us that Manila remains connected to other locales within the Philippines, one node within a translocal network across the country.

Listening closely to Marasigan and other Manila indie scene members' stories of musical exchanges while growing up, connecting them to similar stories in earlier popular musical decades, both evidence and emphasize the translocal nature of Manila's music scenes.[20] Here, translocality is made evident by the impact travelers, visitors, and ex-pats have made and continue to make upon Manila's music and culture. They brought with them not only ideas but also popular musical goods that shaped Pinoy indie rock music. In previous conversations with Marasigan, he has shared stories about U.S.-based family members who, on their trips "back home" to the Philippines, would bring and leave behind "new wave" tapes from the United States—the Cure, Echo & the Bunnymen, and the like. This music, Marasigan shared, greatly influenced songs he later wrote.

Growing up as the youngest in her family and in the late 1980s, writer/ director Marie Jamora learned much about American and British pop music from her older siblings.[21] "Super new wavers," they would watch the latest Brit-pop music videos on *Video Hit Parade* and other shows on local Manila TV networks. When her parents would travel to the United States and Europe for work, Jamora would put in *pasalubong* (gift) requests, which benefited not only her but also the larger family:

My father, he worked for KLM Airlines as a doctor—my parents are both doctors. My dad would get these free flights to Europe and the States, so my family would fly there, buy records from the States or Europe, and then we had a great record collection.[22]

Here, we see the process of translocal and musical exchange taking place within the nuclear family kinship structure, between traveling Manileño parents and their children as opposed to the extended family exchanges of Marasigan's youth. It is worthwhile to note the class differences that allow for different types of gifts—those requested and those "left behind." With neither Marasigan nor Jamora yet officially part of a musical "scene," there was no immediate "payoff" for their musical exchanges, purchases, and investments. Instead, the family record collection served as a makeshift musical library and domestic education whose artistic yield was not apparent until many years later.

As she grew older and more interested in pop music, Marie began writing articles on local bands, including Sandwich and the Eraserheads, pub-

lishing them on the PhilMusic website. Through the PhilMusic email list-
serv, she met Seattle-based Filipino American Johann Fernandez, and they
arranged, between themselves, an informal "CD/tape of the month club" or
musical pen pal system. As Jamora remembers, Fernandez proposed:

> "Hey, I will give you American music, if you will send me Filipino
> music." So, I would buy him the new Wolfgang, the new Razorback,
> whatever. And then, in return, he would ship me *CMJ* music month-
> ly which, I never [had read] . . . that was the best magazine. Because
> of him, I heard Versus for the first time [o]n a cassette tape. Because
> he made me a sampler. And then, from the sampler, he would say,
> "What music do you like from here?" Because he had the actual CDs.
> And, from then on, I liked Superchunk . . . so then he would buy me
> the actual CDs and ship them.[23]

Through mixtapes and a blend of email and (snail) mail, Jamora and Fernandez participated in user-driven practices characteristic of fandom and its
cultures. Based upon their shared interests and tastes, they curated and created
media through which to share their musical knowledge and passions through
improvised and unofficial means. These took place alongside more official
means of CD and tape purchases directly from the record companies or bands.
These creations and exchanges were precursors to the Spotify playlists, music
video sharing on Facebook or YouTube, and uploading of mixes to SoundCloud
of our contemporary musical time. Rather than romanticize the "humanity"
of predigital or early internet days, Jamora and Fernandez's relationship of
exchange directs our attention toward the translocal as lived out through earlier forms of "remote intimacy."[24] Through dialogue and transnational exchange, Jamora and Fernandez curated and shared their versions and visions
of "American music" and "Filipino music," connecting Manila, as a place and
idea, to Seattle as two nodes along Filipino America's translocal network.

Therefore, translocality functions not only through the movement and
migration of people but also by the circulation of goods and ideas. Translocal thinkers such as Oakes and Schein "expand their analytical focus beyond
the limits of the nation-state by focusing on various other dimensions of
border transgressions and on socio-spatial configurations beyond those in-
duced by human migration."[25] While Jamora's and Marasigan's stories of musical exchange with family and strangers speak to transgressing beyond the
Philippine nation-state's borders, in Manila's musical history, other socio-
spatial configurations—built environments that shape social life along with
the ways that locals construct meaning in their everyday lives—emerge. One
such place of sociospatial configuration for musicians growing up prior to the
twenty-first century has been the record store.

In the 1980s, A to Z Records served as a translocal hub for musicians and musical recordings. Owned by music writer Tony Maghiram and located in Manila's Santa Mesa district, A to Z also functioned as a lending library and community center. Offering a community board where bands would list "want ads" for new members as well as post flyers for upcoming gigs, the record store was also infamous for its low-cost cassette tape dubbing services. As Peter Manuel reminds us, unlike vinyl records, cassette tapes are "cheaper, more durable and more portable," a "two-way medium which can record as well as play."[26] Through this dubbing service, A to Z Records provided local musicians affordable access to anything in the store—both classic and more recent Filipino, U.S., and European rock and pop acts. As Sandwich guitarist Diego Castillo reminisced, "You would buy your own little cassette, you'd tell them what you wanted, and they would tape it for you, all for a small fee (something along the lines of ten pesos or today's equivalent of twenty-five cents)."[27] Store patrons were also allowed access to and could buy Xeroxed copies of any album's liner notes, an often overlooked and disappearing genre of musical knowledge that provided artist biographies, musical context, and song lyrics.[28] As California-based musician/festival organizer and former Marikina-based punk rocker Jesse Gonzales recalls, in the early days of his first band:

> Sometimes, we'd want to play a cover of a song by the Descendents but then, we can't figure out the lyrics. We'd be like, "Alright, let's go to A to Z." And then we'd be like, "Boss, *paki-hiram nang* lyrics," and we'd copy it.[29]

In this way, the translocal hub of A to Z Records served as a place where musicians and fans alike could build their musical knowledge—for personal or professional gain—in cheap and affordable ways. With dubbed cassette copies and Xeroxed liner notes, this generation of musicians would go on to make their own music and musical scenes. Here, the "built environment" and sociospatial configuration of the record store is a place of not simply passive consumption but instead consumption that spurs further musical production. Through the informal structures of musical learning A to Z Records enabled, a generation of indie musicians developed. They did so through a translocal hub, a local place where the material flow of goods and the symbolic flow of ideas, knowledge, and styles from other places attracted and gathered local musicians, shaping how they would make future musical meaning. Here, we see the ways that a musical venue often assumed to be a place for upper-class consumption transforms in the service of the popular, the *masa*.

As a form of broadcast technology, radio also functions in a translocal register. While radio has brought individual listeners together, through niche or national audiences, it has also crafted a type of listening that "emphasize[d] the 'worlds between our ears.'" Like early versions of television broadcast, "radio technology and its effectiveness (or aura) are predicated upon a 'sense of liveness.'"[30] This sense is mainly performed by radio's disc jockeys, announcers, and show hosts. At the same time, this sense of liveness also speaks to how listeners turn to specific musical formats (on various radio stations) to access a particular mood or feeling, one to complement or carry them through their daily lives. As Theodor Adorno warns us, radio's political danger lies in its ability to be managed and wielded by corporate interests and the powers that be. In colonial societies, this would lie in the colonizer's ability to manage and wield radio in their own interest.

Yet, as the work of Elizabeth Enriquez shows us, we can approach the history of radio in the Philippines in two ways. The first is with a focus on "the express intent of the colonial administration to employ radio as one of the means to Americanize the Filipino consciousness." They did so through the American music they played on air, the American radio program formats they imported, and the hiring of American broadcasters who spoke English and "made Filipino audiences familiar with American values and concerns." The second is by looking at it "to understand how Filipinos appropriated an alien cultural practice, took it as their own, used it, explored it and converted it for their own purposes." In the early years of radio, this was done by the local Filipinos "who joined the roster of singers, musicians, and announcers" and "while trained to sing and play American music and to broadcast it in English, inserted local material into the programming."[31]

First hitting the airwaves in 1987, NU107 radio station soon became known for its role in developing and strengthening the local Pinoy classic and indie rock scenes. Bought by banker Atom Henares, the radio station's arrival coincided with an executive order by then-President Corazon Aquino requiring all radio stations to play at least three original Pilipino musical compositions an hour. With its tagline "Home of New Rock," throughout the 1990s, NU107 featured both American grunge and alternative bands (such as Pearl Jam, Soundgarden, and Nirvana) as well as local and then-emerging Pinoy indie rock bands such as the Eraserheads, Wolfgang, the Youth, Rivermaya, and others. Its regular weekly show *In the Raw* featured demos and DIY recordings by local and unsigned bands, helping to develop the burgeoning Manila indie rock scene. Its annual NU107 Rock Awards celebrated Pinoy rock legends and honored each year's best rock talents, creating a sense of legacy among and excitement about all forms of Pinoy rock—from punk to classic to indie. And, later, its local (weekly) radio show *Not Radio* brought to a Manila listening audience the diverse sounds of indie and pop rock as well as cultivated their relationship to a much-beloved DJ and musician, Myrene "Maps" Academia.

At the very start of the 1990s, Academia had completed her undergraduate degree in mass communications at the University of the Philippines,

Diliman, and decided to join NU107 as simply a newscaster. The radio station was relatively new at the time (about two years old), and one of her college friends, who was already a DJ there, encouraged her: "Hey, Myrene, you might want to join up din as a newscaster." Counterintuitively, Academia decided to apply because she was "really afraid of being up there on the mic." Despite her communications degree, she was "absolutely terrified." So, she thought to herself, "Okay, this is it. I might as well do it."[32]

While working as a newscaster, she met and worked with Kathy Ilagan (whose on-air name was Roxy). Determined to become a disc jockey, Kathy jumped at the opportunity to take a "graveyard" slot when the station's owners transitioned to twenty-four-hour programming on the weekends. With NU107's paid subscription to Century 21—a service that compiled the latest singles and top hits for each musical genre onto CDs directly delivered to radio stations—Academia and other emerging radio jockeys were able to hear the latest music at a faster rate than if it had been accessed via major record labels' Philippine affiliates. At the same time, she supplemented the subscription service with her own "self-made" expertise in alternative and new wave music. She would grab monthly copies of CMJ magazine ("at 7 US dollars a pop") that not only included news and articles on the latest bands but also would have CD samplers included. As she recalls, "Lucky for us, one of our ex-jocks was a flight attendant! So it worked out that way. You put up your own network, then you meet people and then they can send you stuff. It was great!"[33] In 1993, she started hosting her own show, Not Radio, on Saturday nights at 9:00 P.M.

Academia dubbed the show Not Radio both because she was not so adept at radio "plugs"—short messages said on-air to create interest in a song or product—and because the show did not focus on one musical genre, instead playing music not featured on other radio shows or stations. Not Radio allowed Academia the freedom to "learn" her craft on the air and, at the same time, the freedom to share new music with listeners who otherwise would not have the means to access it. She recalls:

> So, I got my show . . . and then, the station manager . . . his name was Chris . . . goes, "Oh yeah, I'll go ahead and give you Saturday night at 9 [P.M.]." And he didn't have any block timers yet or any regularly scheduled shows, at that time. It was music all the way. So, Saturday night at 9, it was pretty free, so he gave me that. So, I really did not get my plug together . . . and my first few CDs were like, "Uh uhuh . . . Nine Inch Nails' first album." And then I got Ministry . . . it was like a mix talaga. And that's why I named it Not Radio din kasi it was parang na wala. I wouldn't be forced to just play one sort of thing. I'd just have to play stuff that wasn't on the regular playlist. Or that

wasn't being played on other stations. Basically, I was allowed to play more things as long as it was newer stuff or stuff you didn't hear otherwise . . . [*Parang* stuff you couldn't hear.]

*Parang*, if I were a kid and I didn't have any friends from the States or I couldn't afford to buy the music magazines . . . or the CDs . . . what chance would I have of listening to new stuff? So *yun lang yan* . . . this is what I wanted to do [to let them know] "This is what's out there." To give the kids a choice *lang* . . . *kasi* you might be more inclined or . . . "Oh, I'd rather listen to this *pala*."[34]

Academia soon found herself at the helm of one of the most adored radio shows among the Manila indie rock scene of the 1990s. What made it so popular among the generation's listeners and burgeoning musicians was precisely the fact it became associated with their first time hearing soon-to-be-favorite Philippine and American indie rock acts. She would go on to become NU107's musical director as well as to play in the scene's most popular bands. And while she made her mark on the translocal media form of radio, like many Manila youth who grew up in the years following martial law and on the cusp of internet and digital technologies' beginning, Academia also depended upon other translocal and analog media forms for her "makeshift education" in popular music—first hearing Echo & the Bunnymen's "Killing Moon" on a friend's mixtape (most likely concocted from A to Z's recording system), reading and learning about U.S. and European rock bands through *Rolling Stone*, *Spin*, and *Sassy* magazine back issues, and about Filipino musicians and bands and Western pop song structure through *Jingle* magazine and the AM and FM shows like DWXB and 99.5 RT she listened to on her "*lola*'s little mono cassette player with the radio on it."

## Closing Time

Like many other music venues in Manila and across the globe, Route 196—an intimate venue with a dive bar feel located on Katipunan ("Kati") Avenue near Quezon City's university belt—has had to permanently close its doors amid the global COVID pandemic. Started as a restaurant called Border Grill in the mid-2000s, by 2007, its original owners "decided one night to invite their musician friends to play, despite having no sound system."[35] Based on the success of this event, they changed their business strategy, and, by the 2010s, the venue was being run by local musicians, event organizers and promoters, band managers, and a chef. Its location—close to the University of Philippines, Ateneo de Manila, and other "Katips" colleges and universities—created a pipeline for rising musical artists and young audiences. Its "technical difficulties"—no parking, tight audience and performance space, music venue in a residential area—lent Route an air of authenticity while filtering out "true" musicians and fans (i.e., those who cared enough to endure such things). These conditions perhaps best speak to the venue's sense of "Manila-ness" and its translocality as Route 196 was "not given a priori but rather socially produced, simultaneously fluid and fixed, and fundamentally relational."[36]

Like many other music venues in Manila, those who closed during or even before the city's lockdown, the stories, memories, look, and feel of Route 196 remains archived in music videos and indie films, as well as the online Instagram and Facebook accounts of musicians, fans, promoters, and the venue itself.[37] Route 196's official Facebook account, in fact, still houses its seven-hour-long farewell gig, a digital and musical testament to the small bar and *tugtugan* (or music hub).[38] At the same time, Route 196 remains housed in the hearts and minds of all those who have performed and watched shows there these past decades. Through evenings spent at Route 196, I have connected with "Manila" through its musical scene—the bands I have seen perform, the events celebrated, the friends I have made and reunited with in packed shows or hanging outside in the summer nighttime heat. They include not only local Manila musicians, writers, and artists but also those visiting from the United States and Europe. In this way, Route 196 as *tugtugan* connected Manila's musicians and audiences with visiting people and, at the same time, to other cities along the indie music network. At Route 196, I felt a deep connection to Manila's local indie music scene as someone who has experienced "same same but different" venues in San Francisco, L.A., New York, and Austin, Texas. At those gigs and on those evenings, I did not think or feel or listen on the level of the "national" Instead, I made those connections across the globe and at the level of the local.

Diasporic Filipinos across the globe make similar types of connections. One need only think of provincial town fiestas and college alumni groups as their own translocal nodes of community. "Manila," as this collection's editors instruct us, "is not a strictly bounded geographic place within a particular latitude but rather is constructed through affective evocations echoed in unexpected places and times . . . [they] resonate in the fleeting moments of atmospheric recognition, jolting déjà vu, and surprising intimate connections in otherwise foreign spaces."[39] The "nostalgia tours and gigs" of Filipino popular musicians, their own forms of translocal events and "affective evocations," connect immigrants and U.S.-born alike, in Los Angeles, New York, Dubai, and London, with the musical scenes of their youth in Manila and other Philippine cities. Watching their favorite bands live often invokes memories of college days as well as moments after graduation (and before their immigration stateside). Songs from the 1990s, 1980s, and even prior take folks back to the places, ideas, and people of Manila as well as their youth. This phenomenon holds true for native Mañilenos as it does for us Filipino Americans who remember, but differently, the city's venues, scene, people, and energy. As the United States slowly emerges from the COVID pandemic of these past eighteen months while the Philippines still struggles with rising numbers and uneven rates of vaccination, we hold onto our dreams of Manila, Cebu, Baguio, and other Philippine cities while remaining acutely aware of the stark contrast between nations. We listen to the songs of the past and follow our favorite artists and bands, who continue to write and share new songs, podcast episodes, and even online concerts every week. We wait for the day we can physically return to Manila, a city like many others, that will resound differently, having survived.

## NOTES

1. A Filipino indie rock band comprised of Sarah Marco (vocals), Bryce Zialcita (lead guitar), Derek "Siopao" Chua (rhythm guitar), Isa Garcia (bass), and Bryan Kong (drums), Taken by Cars (or TbC, as they are commonly referred to) have garnered a dedicated following of fans locally as well as abroad. With their electro-dance, new wave sound and songs mainly sung in English, TbC's music has translated well to audiences within the Asia/Pacific region and the United States. In 2011, they appeared on TIME Asia magazine's list of "Five New Bands to Watch" and, one year later, made history as the first Filipino band to play at the internationally recognized South by Southwest (SXSW) music festival in Austin, Texas. These events are noteworthy considering that when the band first started in 1998 (while its members were still in high school), its biggest goal was to play at SaGuijo Café, a Makati-based music venue central to Manila's indie rock scene.

2. Taken by Cars' performances in Baguio (Excursion Tour) and Los Angeles (Mr. T's).

3. Greiner and Sakdapolrak, "Translocality" 380.

4. Sun, "The Leaving of Anhui," 240.

5. Greiner and Sakdapolrak, "Translocality" 380.

6. Smith, Transnational Urbanism, 211.

7. Sun, "The Leaving of Anhui," 240.

8. Irving, Colonial Counterpoint, 9.

9. Ibid., 19.

10. Ibid., 19.

11. Ibid., 27.

12. Schenker, "Empire of Syncopation," 3.

13. Ibid., 3–4.

14. Schenker, "Empire of Syncopation," and Ng, "Performing the 'Filipino'"

15. "Forced to listen against the 'postcolonial roman[tic]' narratives of resistance and 'overcoming' in order to instead hear the 'dialectic of resistance and complicity.'" Schenker, "Empire of Syncopation," 17.

16. Ibid., 17.

17. Quirino, Pinoy Jazz Traditions.

18. Schenker, "Empire of Syncopation," 28. Through the dissemination of U.S. popular song, "leisure industry and commercial music market" of the time were reshaped and led to a "new jazz economy." As Schenker's work highlights, Filipino laborers sought to profit from this new economy's promises. His work, as well as Stephanie Ng's, works to

highlight the economic impulses of musical culture and therefore works against "romantic" notions of culture as merely resistance, abstract and/or discursive.

19. Raymund's episode of Muni-Muni Stories (https://podcasts.apple.com/us/podcast/muni-muni-stories-ep-8-raymund-marasigan-betamax/id1533091254?i=1000506076907).

20. Ascona, "Pinoy Punk."

21. Born and raised in Manila, Marie Jamora's work has included music videos, commercials, short and feature-length films, as well as television shows filmed both in the Philippines as well the United States (where she currently resides). Along with her filmmaking skills, Marie is also the drummer for indie bands Blast Ople and Boldstar. Through her work on music videos and her feature-length film *Ang Nawawala* (What Isn't There), Jamora has brought together her love for films, storytelling, and music.

22. Jamora, personal interview.

23. Jamora, personal interview.

24. Jennifer Terry defined it as the "transmission of sentiments through designed uses and creative appropriations of telemediating devices"; see also Tongson, *Relocations*.

25. Greiner and Sakdapolrak, "Translocality" 378.

26. "Most important, mass production of cassettes is incomparably easier and cheaper than pressing records, thus enabling diverse lower-income groups to enjoy access to both production as well as consumption of recorded music." Manuel, *Cassette Culture*, 28–29.

27. Castillo, personal interview.

28. Brooks, *Liner Notes for the Revolution*.

29. Gonzales, personal interview.

30. Enriquez, Appropriation of Colonial Broadcasting, 6–7.

31. Ibid., 6–18.

32. Academia, personal interview.

33. Alamazan, Castillo, and Bodegon-Hikino, "The Many Lives of Myrene Academia."

34. Academia, personal interview.

35. Guevara and Goño, "Saying Goodbye to Home."

36. Greiner and Sakdapolrak, "Translocality," 380.

37. From Jasmine Trice's introduction to *City of Screens: Imagining Audiences in Manila's Alternative Film Culture* and its discussion of *Rakenrol* DVD extra interview with Diego Castillo and Quark Henares discussing the film as archiving these former venues.

38. "One for the Road: Route 196 Farewell & Fundraising Show," Facebook, September 12, 2020, https://www.facebook.com/Route196Rocks/.

39. Manalansan, Tolentino, Diaz, "Manila in the World."

## BIBLIOGRAPHY

Academia, Myrene. Personal interview, July 2009.
Almazan, Isa, Camille Castillo and Kara Bodegon-Hikino. "The Many Lives of Myrene Academia." Bandwagon Asia, March 30, 2019, https://www.bandwagon.asia/articles/myrene-academia-interview-sandwich-imago-duster-nu-107
Ascona, Albert. "Pinoy Punk." *Rogue*, June 2, 2008.
Brooks, Daphne. *Liner Notes for the Revolution: The Intellectual Life of Black Feminist Sound*. Cambridge: MA, Harvard University Press, 2021.
Castillo, Diego. Personal interview, June 2009.
Enriquez, Elizabeth. *Appropriation of Colonial Broadcasting: a History of Early Radio in the Philippines, 1922–1946*, Quezon City: University of Philippines Press, 2009.

Filipinas Heritage Library/OPM Archive, producers. "Raimund Marasigan: Betamax." *Muni-Muni Stories*, Season 1, Episode 8, January 21, 2021, https://podcasts.apple.com /us/podcast/muni-muni-stories-ep-8-raymund-marasigan-betamax/id1533091254?i =1000506076907.

Gonzales, Jesse. Personal interview, October 2011.

Greiner, Clemens, and Patrick Sakdapolrak. "Translocality: Concepts, Applications and Emerging Research Perspectives." *Geography Compass* 7, no. 5 (2013): 373–384.

Guevara, Renzo, and Alexandra Goño. "Saying Goodbye to Home: A Farewell to Route 196." Rappler, September 11, 2020, https://www.rappler.com/entertainment/music /route-196-closure.

Irving, D. R. M. *Colonial Counterpoint: Music in Early Modern Manila*. York: Oxford University Press, 2010.

Jamora, Marie. Personal interview, June 2009.

Manuel, Peter. *Cassette Culture: Popular Music & Technology in North India*. Chicago: University of Chicago Press, 1993.

Ng, Stephanie. "Performing the 'Filipino' at the Crossroads: Filipino Bands in Five-Star Hotels throughout Asia." *Modern Drama* 48, no. 2 (May 2005): 272–296.

Oakes, Time, and Louisa Schein, eds. *Translocal China: Linkages, Identities and Re-Imagining of Space*. New York: Routledge Press, 2006.

Quirino, Richie. *Pinoy Jazz Traditions*. Pasig City, Philippines: Anvil Publishing, 2004.

Schenker, Frederick. "Empire of Syncopation: Music, Race, and Labor in Colonial Asia's Jazz Age." Ph.D. diss., University of Wisconsin-Madison, 2016.

Smith, M. P. *Transnational Urbanism: Locating Globalization*. Malden, Massachusetts: Blackwell Publishers, 2001.

Sun, W. "The Leaving of Anhui: The Southward Journey toward the Knowledge Class." In *Translocal China Linkages, Identities, and the Reimaging of Space*, edited by T. Oakes and L. Schein, 238–262. New York: Routledge, 2006.

Taken by Cars. "'This Is Our City': Official Music Video." YouTube. Uploaded by Party Bear Productions, May 28, 2011, https://www.youtube.com/watch?v=Ymxz8VVrQNg.

Terry, Jennifer. "Proposal: Remote Intimacy," an application for the University of California Humanities Research Institute (UCHRI) working group seminar on "Queer Locations: Race, Space and Sexuality" (Winter/Spring 2004), 2.

Tongson, Karen. *Relocations: Queer Suburban Imaginaries*. New York: New York University Press, 2011.

Trice, Jasmine. *City of Screens: Imagining Audiences in Manila's Alternative Film Culture*. Durham, NC: Duke University Press, 2021.

# Nodes of a City Labyrinth

John B. Labella

I n F. H. Batacan's police procedural *Smaller and Smaller Circles*, two Jesuits help lawmen track a faceless killer who dumps his victims in a massive land-fill.[1] The victims are boys from a nearby slum in Quezon City, one of the Metro Manila's urban cores. The novel is set in 1997, a time before the Payatas dumpsite was closed and its surrounding barrio rehabilitated. The killer mutilates the boys, leaving their bodies in the trash. The police neglect the gruesome murder cases because the victims belong to the masses, whom Zygmunt Bauman says are treated as "wasted humans."[2] When the killings' frequency stirs a media frenzy, the National Bureau of Investigation finds itself inadequate to the task of profiling the cases. Officials call on the ex-pertise of Jesuits priests Gus Saenz and Jerome Lucero, respectively, a foren-sic anthropologist and a clinical psychologist. They struggle to convince the bureau that a serial killer is on the loose. And so determined to stop the body count, they traverse the megacity, going back and forth from a university that caters to elites. They move across diverse locales, mapping places bounded by class lines, informally set up but firmly maintained, until the killer is found.

This summary, based on the 2015 expanded edition, calls attention to the novel's compelling strangeness: the disjunction between Metro Manila and the police procedural's generic traits. The genre, after all, holds a certain will to modernity. That will is fundamental to its plot structure—hence its constant turn to evidentiary science, as Ernst Bloch observes.[3] The logic Bloch highlights in detective fiction seems incompatible with a city whose tumult the rich and poor share unevenly. The signs of such tumult—slums, traffic, and sudden floods—define the scope of my study on Batacan's attention to class tensions and urban geography. What compels me in her work is its use of detective fiction's methodic will not as mere counterforce to a labyrinthine mess. At stake in her use of the procedural, rather, is the chance to parse Manila's city image and the class-driven arrangements that are part of the urban problem.

Tied to evidentiary science in the police procedural is its attention to place details. It must, as Gary Hausladen points out, "get the geography and its sense of place right."[4] And it must begin at the crime scene, a fracture in culturally organized space. *Smaller and Smaller Circles* brings these conventions to the point of excess, suggesting a rupture more brutal than what occurs in the modern spaces often identified with detection. With a dead boy in the rubbish, the landfill in the novel shatters the wholesale belief in modernity's power to organize urban space and to secure the flourishing of all its humans. The barrio on the metro's northeastern edge disrupts the city image and the nation's self-figuration as a node of global flows.

At the end of the 1990s, Payatas gained notoriety even beyond the Philippines. Engineers in the West, studying the perils of landfill construction, record that "since 1996, the metro-Manila area generated an average of a little more than 6,000 tons of trash per day. About 1,500 to 1,800 tons of trash per day were placed at the 18-hectare landfill."[5] Payatas made headlines in July 2000, when about three hundred people living on parts of the landfill were buried alive in a landslide caused by monsoon rains.[6] The slum nonetheless kept growing around the wasteland. Edson Cabalfin recalls that in 2013 the dumpsite fringes hosted approximately 117,000 people.[7]

In the shadow of this history, Batacan provokes at least two questions about the city: What spatial trends and contradictions in Metro Manila does she make evident? If sociopolitical and ecological processes interact to compose place, how does the novel's figuration of place register the unhinging effects of worldwide restructuring? These questions stem from the fact that such restructuring has destabilized local homogeneity. I use the term *place* here as a concept tied to notions of scale—cartographic size as well as the modeling of levels for spatial observation or analysis, giving rise to expressive meanings of a location.[8] Such meanings are grounded on practices and geographic features that sites activate or inhibit.

Replying to the questions posed, the close readings I offer highlight the way Batacan narrates Manila's disarray. Its perplexity for Batacan is, ironically, an outcome of its global aspirations. Central to her novel is an urban-geographical motif in the city image: hypernodality. Within the regional scale, a city is itself a node. Nodality is part of its character in that a city is where routes, as well as labor and capital flows, intersect, manifesting all kinds of accumulation. Within the city scale, according to Kevin Lynch, nodes are interludes in movement, as typified by transport hubs.[9] The emergence of surplus informal nodes, however, results in the spillover of nodal functions on other city elements, generating hypernodality. Reflecting on this condition, Batacan helps city theorists and literary urbanists respond to Jennifer Robinson's call to rectify "an analysis of urban modernity, which places some cities, and not others, in a privileged relationship to concepts of the urban."[10] The search for a fictive serial killer in Batacan's metro tracks its nodality and its modern social vectors.

## City as Labyrinth

There is no denying the sprawl that has altered the Philippine's capital. As the sociologist Manuel Caoili notes, the city looks "haphazard"[11] in its development. It is dense with human surplus, and its service capacities, overburdened. Focusing on transport, Neferti Tadiar proposes that Manila's "labyrinthine, megapolitan fortress of foreclosure" is a legacy of colonial wars and the dictatorship under Ferdinand Marcos.[12] The risk of entrapment confronts all users of Manila's urban space: locals, travelers, repatriated critics engaging the city labyrinth gamely or grimly. Taking up the native city dwellers' lot, Batacan suggests that local perception is far from homogeneous in relation to Manila's dark histories. Narration is set up mainly from the Jesuit investigators' point of view. Professors at an elite university and members of a religious order with global scope, they access spaces inside and outside the nation. But these agile few are not the city's sole custodians of meaning. Narration also plays host to the murderer's voice. Batacan clusters her chapters into sections divided by shards of the killer's interiority. There are, moreover, sections focalized by an opportunistic female journalist; by squatters mourning their lost children; and by an odious detective driven to move up the bureaucratic ladder. These multiple points of view lay bare a semantic labyrinth underpinning city sense and locating different coordinates in the so-called fortress.[13] Those in Manila—local by necessity, dreaming of another city within it—also shape it with their aspirations for just, civil lives.

Is it sheer optimism to say that ordinary citizens respond meaningfully to urban perplexity? That is what Batacan invites readers to consider by offering imaginary access into ordinary urban practitioners' experiences, jostling over the shaping of their city. It sheds light on the "forms of habitation," which, as Martin Manalansan observes, "signify the very instability of a worldly urban landscape and the continuously shifting terrain of people, desires, and material goods and meanings."[14] That instability, it must be added, demands seeing through state policy or its encrustation in the landscape and looking at the spatial interactions of urban dwellers. What must be avoided in examining a polynucleated city is downplaying the relationship between Manila's human geography and the city's impermanence. As with a crime scene, the circling "moves inward to the center."[15] Reading Batacan's police procedural offers the advantage not just of imitating abstract logic but also of making human interactions with places legible and changeable. Through an imaginary exercise in detection, specific conflicts in locales—and among locals—yield clues to general urban processes.

## Detection and Place

Place carries "determinative force" in the detective genre.[16] Its narrative logic passes through place, through geographic details that lend themselves to causal and metonymic signification. Early in the twentieth century, G. K. Chesterton, author of the Father Brown series, defended it as a popular genre "in which is expressed some sense of the poetry of modern life." The genre is hospitable to figurations not only of places in general but of urban landscapes. It cultivates in readers an analytical stance toward the built environment. "Every brick has as human a hieroglyph," writes Chesterton. "Every slate on the roof is as educational a document as if it were a slate covered with addition and subtraction sums."[17] Tracking a criminal and gathering proof of culpability subject the cityscape to the trial of its legibility and, as Chesterton suggests, its assimilability to logic. Through sites of crime, geography in detective fiction becomes a repository of urban perplexity anatomized at the level of the locale.

Closer to the slum Batacan portrays, what Bloch calls "the pathos of evidentiary minutiae" makes detective fiction speak to questions of justice.[18] The rise of the genre coincides with the emergence of fair trial in juridical procedure. "No doubt, evidence can also mislead," Bloch writes. "However, it *is* more civilized than torture and suspenseful in a different way."[19] Suspense in the detective story not only has to do with time required by seeking evidence and making connections. The pathos of gathering holds the archaic pleasure borne with the expectation of justice in a world of routine economic mess and tangled bureaucracy.

Manila's city image is the outcome of peremptory solutions to its spatial mess. A city image, as Lynch defines it, is the representation of urban places in the minds of its dwellers and visitors.[20] And Manila's city image repels the promise of urban life instead of evoking it. Tadiar observes that in this city, state response to global restructuring has resulted "in the dense space-time of its congested flows" and in "the thick noise of its own crisis-managed convolution of social fluencies."[21] The subscription to the order demanded by global restructuring ends up adding to, instead of minimizing, the metro's politico-spatial intricoes. This irony comes into relief in Batacan's work, wherein an epistemological minotaur haunts the city image and its misman-aged processes. Collusion in law enforcement and corrupt churchmen, inepti-tude, and secrecy impede whatever rationality the metro holds. These routine institutional hindrances reflect the convolution of the city image in the novel.

By contrast, the private investigators in *Smaller and Smaller Circles* con-figure the city image with a defamiliarizing view. These imaginary characters disclose, to borrow Slavoj Žižek's phrase, "the meaning that appears through the false appearance itself."[22] With their sharp recall of place details and empa-thy for the poor, their estranging gaze supplements what state responses to urban crises lack. One passage focalized by Saenz illustrates such estrangement:

> After the rain, life—earth, foliage, frogs—momentarily reclaims human
> attention from those things which are not life. Everything else—the
> cars, the buildings, the dingy shop signs and crumbling waiting sheds,
> the garlands of electric wiring that line the streets, the rusting metal
> and concrete and plastic that jut out singly or in masses to stab the city
> air—everything recedes int a damp and quiet dullness. The dead
> things know their place. (S73)

Saenz clears the haze of routine sensing, numbed not only within state bu-reaucracy but also among those who daily endure the shocks of Manila's per-plexity. The description contrasts urban iconography to glimpses of ecologi-cal, pastoral reprieve. Interestingly, what gathers up the cityscape is the phrase "dead things," urbanism colored by noir.[23] The "rusting metal" and "plastic," which detective science sees with its mind's eye, lead the reader back to the scene in the novel's prologue, the dumpsite where a mutilated corpse is un-earthed. For all the lyricism that rain bestows on the metro, what Saenz lo-cates—through a sum of city metonyms—is a labyrinth where trash and the signs of murder rupture organized space.

## Entering the Labyrinth

*Smaller and Smaller Circles* indeed starts with the labyrinth as a motif—two kinds of it, respectively, in the fragmentary exergue and in the prologue. The first portrays crazed interiority, while the second, set in Payatas, narrates how the first dead boy is found. In the exergue, the labyrinth is subjective, narrated in the first-person point of view; the killer's voice breaks the fourth wall as the reader enters the novel. This instance of fragmented speech is also the first in a series of italicized passages marking the novel's divisions; a maimed voice serially cuts up the body proper of the narrative. The ex-ergue conveys the pain of madness in spatial terms: "It's hard," the killer says, "to concentrate on what's going on around me, on what I'm doing."

Batacan depicts madness as an extreme kind of inwardness whose movement reaches no psychical center. Then comes the somatization of that lack:
"I can't breathe right; my hands and feet are cold. My head hurts" (S3).
Mental anguish restricts the killer's perception of an exterior world, reducing the sense of embodiment to bare limits, to breath and touch. Reading
the novel, thus, first involves passing through a psychical labyrinth, a con-
stricted headspace without axis.

Found in the prologue, the second kind of labyrinth is olfactory. Children at the dumpsite lead the parish priest Emil to a corpse half-buried in
the garbage: "His fear grows with each step. It tastes like rust, feels gritty like
dirt in his mouth." While its language of smell turns an exterior setting into
an enclosure, the feeling associated traditionally with the mythic labyrinth
saturates the passage.[24] Batacan goes to describe the landfill:

> The stench from the sea of garbage around them is overpowering. It
> rained last night, and now that the sun is out, the dump site is steam-
> ing. Awful vapors rising lazily with the heat: wet paper and rot and
> excrement mixing in a soup of odors around them, above them. (S5)

Narration in this passage registers the unrepresentable with its constraint on
seeing. As the landfill—described as a "sea"—exceeds the scale of human
vision, what Douglas Porteous calls the "smellscape" takes over the routine
modes of delimitation. Presupposed in smell is "distance from source" or
proximity to it. "Smells environ," Porteous writes. "They penetrate the body
and permeate the immediate environment."[25] Odor in Batacan's prologue
exerts tremendous force on the way Payatas is felt and imagined. Unlike sight,
smell in the text is not repeatable in the sensorium of reading no matter how
susceptible or observant the reader may be. And yet for the characters in the
scene—Emil tasting fear "like dirt"—the gap between the observer and
the observed closes. The labyrinth emerges through affects and through the
environing, penetrating smellscape of the dumpsite.

Entombment, fear of the monstrous, and oblivion conjure the maze even
where it seems to have no physical walls. But it is disorientation above all
that makes the landfill a strange sort of labyrinth. It is a node that inscribes
a biopolitical caesura in urban dwelling and reinstalls the mythic in the modern. While collapsing the distance between the observer and the observed,
this node tends to conflate the living and the dead. Lynch defines nodes as
"the strategic foci into which the observer can enter, typically either junctions
of paths, or concentrations of some characteristic."[26] The landfill is a node
into which things flow only to die, breaking off from urban circulations.
And yet as things disintegrate there, their effluvia tend to erode the line

between castoffs and the people who enter the wasteland.[27] Humans and dead things never quite know their place in a landfill. The plot point setting Batacan's police procedural into motion—the discovery of a corpse scarcely buried in trash, the mutilated body of a boy from the slums[28]—makes the landfill's peculiar nodality irreversibly clear. And so it seems no accident that this olfactory labyrinth recurs in Batacan's novel.

## The Labyrinth's Insistence

Three other instances linking smell and entrapment, monstrosity and disorientation, are worth analyzing. The first example occurs near the conclusion, when Saenz tussles with the psychopath (S328). The second is a dream sequence involving the other Jesuit protagonist, Lucero, and his nightmare about Payatas (S21). With the journalist Joanna Bonifacio as its focalizer, the third example is a description of the landfill at night, the crime scene involving another mutilated child (S167). In all three cases, Batacan downplays the language of sight. The labyrinth is insistent but, recalling other literary mazes, is evoked through disorientation rather than through the representation of a physical enclosure.

The first example, a scene leading to the climax, may be examined briefly. The protagonist enters a van, a mobile clinic, where the boys are murdered: "In the darkness, it seems to Saenz as though some massive, sinister creature has caught hold of the clinic, wrapping it in a grotesque, unbreakable embrace" (S328–329). Alluding to the minotaur in classical myth, Batacan takes up the tropological work of olfaction: permeating the van is "a fishy, rusty sort of smell, and Saenz quickly realizes that it is the smell of blood, and the smell of blood is starting to go bad" (S333). Batacan seems deliberately to minimize any visual reference to the labyrinth, precluding the kind of cognitive separation that the language of sight affords.

The second case, found early in the novel, is a dream foreshadowing the climax. In the dream, the Jesuit clinical psychologist Lucero hears a child crying out and struggles to rescue him: "He starts running, first this way, then that, slipping in the mud and the slime, losing first one slipper, then the other, leaving deep, gouged tracks where his feet slide" (S21). The dreamer moves as if through multiple twists and turns, redolent of the multicursal labyrinth. Batacan goes on to narrate Lucero's disorientation on the same page:

And again he stumbles in the mud and the garbage, legs failing him, arms failing him, and then the hand on his shoulder, rough and hard, shoving him down. He can smell the muck—warm, moist, sweet with rot—as his face is pushed into it. (S21)

Odor dreamt is not common, and so in Lucero's nightmare, it feels doubly strange. Putrescence environs him as he dreams of being murdered: "Always the rock first and then the blade, sharp and slim and cold" (S21). He feels the ground about to swallow him, a detail recalling bits of the prologue. The landfill does not have to collapse to feel tomblike. Being enclosed in the smell of rot, experiencing death by garbage, is surely a kind of haunting. But exactly what has taken hold of the clinical psychologist in this dark urban tale?

Haunting Lucero is not just the memory of the dead—nor is it simply the killer's anonymity. The nightmare, rather, foreshortens the city image from the vantage of the uncanny, in Schelling's sense of the term: "All things are called uncanny that should have remained secret, hidden, latent, but have come to light."[29] Lucero's nightmare cathects the landfill as a site that, excluded from representations of space flows, corrodes the distinction between exposure and secrecy, above and below, inside and outside. Scraps and ruins, things offtrack from circulation, come to a full stop at the landfill. While an exorbitant signification defines the place, such meaning is also based on the decomposition of both objects and social value. This uncanny spatial logic comes to the fore when readers set Lucero's nightmare alongside the real, historical district of Payatas. A journalist reporting for *Harper's Magazine* in 2006 describes the landfill this way: "Unlike the gray muck of the mountain's sides, the summit is a riot of torn-open, primary-colored plastic bags in festive profusion, like a Mardi Gras parade hit by a cluster bomb."[30] This excess in signification, however, only amplifies the need to displace the landfill from the metro's projected image.

Manila urbanites represent Payatas—its slum and dumpsite—as a place that does not belong to the modern.[31] Writing about other abject landscapes, Michael Pinches recalls that in 1976, "whitewashed fences were erected along roadways through Manila in order to hide the most visible of the city's numerous squatter settlements."[32] No sooner do slums form part of the city image than global dreams bar them from it. In fact, as Pinches rightly argues, squatters "are integral to the process of modernization in the Philippines because they are integral to the processes of commodification: of labor, land, and construction."[33] Lucero's nightmare about a voice issuing from garbage salvages the knowledge that Manileños downplay. Payatas marks the loss of the symbolic and economic value of people alongside the waste that production and circulation incur. Putting objects into circulation, urban flows hazard their continuance as its castoffs accumulate elsewhere. Dumpsites and slums are the outcome of this contradiction, forming a knot of rejected knowledge, discarded things, and disavowed communities.

This contradictory logic consigns both squatters and dumpsite to oblivion only because they stick out as nodes. Lynch identifies one type of node with the junction, a terminus where roads come to a break or mark the start of other transport channels. Another type of node pertains to the qualitative element of the break itself: its "thematic concentration." The park exemplifies such a node. A break that features "no transfer point at all,"[34] it creates a gap in movement even when it is not directly linked to transport channels. Its chief purpose is to suspend human movement or to punctuate it altogether. Although linked to citywide circulations, the condition of a landfill is terminal. It may be even more precise to classify the dumpsite as an absolute node. Unique among other types of the strict node, it is the nether opposite of a verdant city park.

## Trashed Nodality

The dumpsite resembles the park but not quite. While things in the park recreate urban dwelling, discarded stuff constitute the landfill as a pure gap, as stasis so concentrated it seethes. Things are dumped when, though once caught in the haze of our longing for commodities, they are stripped of imaginary life. Scavenging in this sense is a practice intervening at a place where matter can neither be broken down further nor be retrieved wholesale from death.[35] The problem that urban culture has with denizens of landfills is its rivalry with their kind of materialism, grasping stuff in terms of its inanimate thereness. To scavenge is to recognize in things their resistance to what the city wishes them to be, selfsame and immutable. Pure objectivity falling away from human relevance is intolerable to capital and capitals, hence its banishment. The city desires no traffic with things drained of mystique.

The uncanniness of waste points to the labyrinth's third iteration. The journalist Joanna Bonifacio and her cameraman rush to the landfill after another body turns up. Leaving the site, she "struggles to maintain her balance, her natural revulsion for dirt forcing her to concentrate intensely on her path" (S167). Once more the labyrinth emerges through disorientation. More intriguing is the portrayal of disorientation two pages prior, which deserves quoting at length because it recalls Lucero's nightmare. Batacan writes of the journalists at the crime scene:

They quickly discover how difficult it is to get up the mound of trash. Every foothold is precarious, every step a struggle for balance atop the shifting garbage and sliding mud. And yet they're only at the fringes of the landfill. At the very center, the mass will, in theory, be even more unstable: loose garbage on the surface, layers and layers of compacted, rotting garbage in the middle and, at the bottom, a pool of filthy leachate, combining the fluids that have oozed and fermented from the garbage and the rainwater that passes through it. Now Joanna understands why the most effective trash pickers are children and

> small teenagers: the lightness of their bodies allows them to tread
> nimbly over this treacherous landscape. (S165)

As the imaginary labyrinth rises, language shifts from the realistic to the
hyperreal. Payatas is perceived through the journalists' televisual eye. Framed
in that gaze, the landfill seems more freakish than Lucero's dreamscape. Notwithstanding the allusion to dancers in ancient rites of initiation linked to
the maze,[36] Joanna recognizes the potential breakdown of a biopolitical limit.
She sees the landfill as a precarious surface where pickers and leachate appear
to merge. At Payatas, Metro Manila's northeastern edge, this surface barely
separates objects drained of worth and subjects assigned the lowest level in
the hierarchy of urban valuation.

Ostensibly as recompense for lost sociospatial meaning, the scene focalized by the journalist mobilizes a varied surplus of idioms. It enacts what
geographer Mitch Rose calls "the totality of possible performances immanent" in a place, "the constitutive potential of an unfolding labyrinth."[37] Bolstering its realism, the narration mixes the linguistic registers of geology,
engineering, and toxicology. The idiom of waste classification, moreover,
intersects an abbreviated sociology on the practice of employing children as
scavengers.

What these mixed registers precipitate is an instant of clarity: "Now Joanna understands." Part of that clarity, that objective cognition, is the un-
earthing of a discursive, technocratic maze used conventionally to make chaotic urban byproducts seem manageable. With surplus acts of language, a
performative labyrinth is called upon to stanch the crisis in meaning produced
by the city itself. But such acts only seep back to their objective correlative, "a
pool of filthy leachate." The excess of idioms supplements the loss experienced
as rot, at the place where humans become things and where things take on the
traits of partial subjects. Persons, objects, and language itself all run up against
the threat of termination. And it is in this particular sense that the landfill
subsists as an anti-park, the most nodal of pure nodes.

## Wasted Personhood

The reporter comes to grasp absolute thingness as antihuman, inscribing
in the scene an implicitly secular perception of mythic traces. "Traditionally the labyrinth," writes Karsten Harries, "describes a condition through
which the hero must pass if he is to gain access to the true center, the true
light."[38] Where the secular prevails, however, the labyrinth no longer carries
mythic hope. Batacan's critical intervention is to bring sentimental affect to
its brutal end with the image of slum children eking out survival despite
harsh odds—and failing. Only agile heroes elude monsters in the nether-

world. Though child scavengers move "nimbly over this treacherous land-scape," it does swallow some of them. The image condenses what Saskia Sassen calls "a new organizing logic" operating globally, whose "predatory dynamics" is altering the "systemic character of poverty and downward mobility."[39] Batacan embeds a landscape of downward mobility in a plot about bureaucratic indifference toward modern forms of sacrificial violence. Descending on "the limit of human misery" inhabited by ragpickers, to quote Benjamin,[40] representatives of secular order find out just how even the nimble cannot survive being trashed.

Trash pickers move among what the philosopher Francois Dagognet calls "wreckage." With its classification of five kinds, here I focus on two, relevant to Batacan's work: "stercoral" objects and "detritus or rubbish." Paraphrasing Dagognet, Anne Lovell identifies the stercoral with "feces, dung, that which is decomposed and rotten." And rubbish is "that which is no longer clearly recognizable because it is fermenting, inconsistent, amorphous."[41] Barred from the upcycling's afterlife, stercoral objects and detritus glut Lucero's fitful sleep. Odors of "muck," as Batacan writes, permeate his nightmare as he follows the disembodied voices of dead children. In the scene focalized by the journalists, on the other hand, the living move through stercoral waste, crossing a landscape where dead objects can kill.

For Batacan, as for Bauman and Sassen, the mobility of trashed subjects is resolutely katabatic. It drags down persons; kids who labor amid wreckage experience a kind of death well before any serial killer can strike. And when their lives fall to predation, justice, too, drags. Batacan depicts the poor as wholly expendable, eliciting almost no tears in the eyes of the state. The Jesuit investigators are extrajudicial actors, and only they truly mourn trashed humanity. This detail seems ironic when read alongside Bauman, who writes: "Overpopulation is but one side-effect of the emergent global civilization bent on the production and disposal of waste."[42] Traditionalist societies are slow to address overpopulation as a reproductive problem. In Philippine slums, according to Felipe Jocano, the use of condoms, though available, tends to be ignored: "If you pause to put it in place, the children may wake up and see you."[43] Cramped dwellings create a vicious cycle. Lack of residential planning for the urban poor compounds the ineffectual policies for mitigating population density.

Bauman uses the phrase "human waste" to name the destitute mass as "unintended and unplanned 'collateral casualties' of economic progress."[44] Wasted personhood results from modernity's inability to transfer unwanted surplus in the same way as in colonial eras. With nowhere else to go, "wasted humans" are tethered loosely to the city by informal economies or by the casualized job market. They live in the cracks of global modernity as "waste products which it can neither reassimilate nor annihilate." Neither inside nor outside, they are not assigned the value of positive surplus, of necessity or use. As the metro strains its service capacities, "the line separating a transient incapacitation from the peremptory and final consignment to waste tends to be blurred and no longer legible."[45] Persons dislodged from circuits of production and labor—but kept nearby as a reserve labor force—become human waste. And the gaps where wasted humanity settles become places of intense rivalry and precariousness.

## City of Nodes

Upon reckoning with human waste, what is gained by a stylized tale of urban brutality? This question recalls the problems stated at the outset, rephrased here as follows: What aspects of the city image does Batacan bring to light? How does her work help readers map the local registers of worldwide restructuring? Framed with the fictive scenario of serial violence, Metro Manila presents itself as an ordinary city where global modernity's toxic consequences break through ordinariness itself. Vulnerable citizens of an inordinately nodal city risk being trapped in its convolutions. Their mobility deteriorates in both physical and economic terms. At this juncture, retracing the metro's patterns and tensions, it seems apt to revisit the provenance of the trope recurrent in *Smaller and Smaller Circles*.

"One of the most persistent and powerful literary metaphors is that of the city labyrinth," writes Werner Senn.[46] Although this trope has circulated since antiquity, its iteration across different periods is as varied as it is ambivalent. The labyrinth, Borgeaud says, is "the place of disguised truth," an earthly prelude to the city of spirit. It is also "the road which leads from life to death and from death to life."[47] As a spiritual trope, it refers to both death and renewal. Similarly, Franco Rella regards the city as "site of perdition and salvation, disorder and order." But although the city is the labyrinth's origin, the labyrinth is also "its transformation from a place of loss to a place of knowledge."[48] Nowhere is this ambivalence or duplicity more pronounced than in the setting Batacan's characters regard with deep anxiety. In fact, an area of Payatas where the landfill collapsed held a neighborhood called Lupang Pangako, "Promised Land."[49] The contradiction seems unremarkable. What begs to be thought, however, is how this contradiction and the loss it carries originate in the metro's desperate yearning for itself, its global dreams on warp speed, blind to rubbish and abjection in its trail.

## Against Hypernodality

Batacan confronts the duplicity that scholars attribute to the city labyrinth. When her spatial critique frames the landfill as a crime scene, its signs re-

quiring interpretation, the quest for truth gets a reboot. Her imaginary de-
tectives view the city image from one of its anti-parks—portraying it such as
it is from below. What these characters disclose is the strangeness interior
to urban modernity but often severed from its imagining. They reveal a city
whose nodality is an unwanted effect of its earnest attempts to take part in
worldwide restructuring. The nodality characterizing landfills and slums,
however, differs from a prior definition of the city as node in the regional
scale, as Lynch writes: "When conceiving the environment at a national or
international level, then the whole city itself may become a node."[50] The spatial pattern evident in Batacan's work, however, has to do with the unan-
ticipated proliferation of nodes *within* the urban scale. The labyrinth that is
Manila is the outcome of intensified production and circulation, processes
that also necessitate the remaindering of persons, the trashing of the mass.

Seen from the wreck of Promised Land, a spatial trend in Manila may now
be drawn with precision. *Smaller and Smaller Circles* detects a condition
wherein the nodes of the city multiply unchecked along its channels, dominate them, and muddle its image. Hypernodality names that condition. It
names the fact that in Metro Manila, nodal functions encroach on other
urban elements so much so that the balance between transitional pauses and
mobility falls apart. It is not just the case that consumerist enclaves breed
parochialism, but rather that the elements of the city image tend to become
nodes. Batacan's ekphrastic passages, her descriptions of the urban, comment on the vexations in a polycentric city that tends to reproduce nodes
everywhere at once. Suspended transitions ascribed to the node disturb the
functions of the city's other elements—paths, landmarks, edges. The city
suffers hypernodality as an effect of reactive solutions to overpopulation and
to global streamlining run amok. An analog to hypernodality is coagula-
tion, a deadening glut of urban flows. Landfills and slums for this reason are
never far apart—and never too distant—from sprawling capitals.[51] Both places
belong to the global city despite being cast out from its imagination. They
are the distended versions of the node idealized in circulations operating on
a worldwide scale.

What my account forwards is not the conservative notion that globalization ruins communities. The idea, rather, is that incursions of nodality
across Manila's districts flow from the deterritorialization that streamlining
generates. Jeremy Seabrook defines the slum as "a refuge for people displaced
by erosion, cyclones, floods, famine, or that more recent generator of insecurity, development."[52] Manila's global aspirations within the past decade or
so have contributed, ironically, to the decay of its mobility. This assessment
can be reframed by characterizing slums and distended nodes benignly as
"integral parts of the metropolis just like office towers, apartment buildings,
hotels and banks."[53] And yet even an urbanist sympathetic to growth cites

"civic jingoism" as a factor in the urban problem.[54] That perplexity is clear to Batacan, who links hypernodality to urban violence in a section about a channel passing through the Payatas area. Commonwealth Avenue intersects two other major paths linking northern residential projects, business districts, and the southern urban core in old Manila. The novel's investigation bureau chief describes this glutted channel:

> "Life is cheap in that part of the city. Just yesterday, a market vendor was stabbed to death in a fight at Litex. He took up a prime selling spot on the roadside that somebody else wanted." Litex Road, along Commonwealth Avenue and not far from the dumpsite, has a teeming flea and wet market whose vendors spill over onto the avenue, sometimes occupying two to three lanes and hindering the flow of traffic. "Between the lack of policing skills and the sheer volume of criminal activity that goes on there—the drugs, the rival gangs, the rapes, the random violence . . ." The director lifts up both hands in a gesture of resignation. (S35)

The metro simply has too many formal and informal nodes. At these sites, interactions between hubs of modernization and its gaps produce spatial conflict across the urban network, particularly where human surplus occurs. The wet market's primary users whom Batacan describes come from the interstitial communities around and between the middle-class subdivisions in the district. Its growth is the result of both real estate development and the influx of squatters.[55] The *tiangge*, as the wet market is called in Tagalog, is a nondestination in the eyes of private commuters. Sourcing needs from other parts of the metro, private commuters pass through the district, and that is the extent of their interaction with the market. They regard it as an obstruction: "vendors spill over onto the avenue," stalling movement but upholding no clear scope of terminal functions. The wet market, as well as its primary users, seems to benefit from this lack of delimitation. It functions as a node for disfranchised motility.[56]

Out of bounds at the intersection with Commonwealth Avenue, Litex Road breeds not just ungainly modes of striving and commerce but also violence. The paths themselves, road versus avenue, come to evoke the difference between commuters with cars and users of public transport. Saenz sums up the problem when he admits confusion in sorting out "the complex interactions between power, poverty, and crime in this city" (S67). Once more, it is Bauman who sheds light on the urban dwellers Batacan describes: "In a society of consumers, they are 'flawed consumers'—people lacking the money that would allow them to stretch the capacity of the consumer market."[57] Clashes at the Litex node itself are indeed class driven, but so is the city government's apparent lack of interest to organize the junction's mixed uses and to forestall the brutality there. Like life in the slums and death in the nearby landfill, consumption on Litex Road is mostly that of the poor. The kind of shoppers and sellers who gather at the *tiangge* seems irrelevant to the free market and so seems to have little purchase with local administration.

## Traffic with Pain

Sectors of dwelling express the standardization of mass workers and its levels.[58] Because transport is vital to these sectors, paths are also subject to levels of policing and upkeep. In the case of Manila traffic, militarized infrastructure is the state reaction to urban perplexity. It regulates space, according to Tadiar, with "ramparts and barricades protecting the free movement of a globally aspiring propertied class."[59] Batacan likewise collocates police neglect with unequal development. In another scene at the bureau, the director scolds a fame-hungry detective for bungling the investigation and for his class politics: "Is it because you think the victims themselves are unimportant?" the chief asks (S48). The confrontation indexes the striations in the shaping and management of Metro Manila. Paths and nodes made up of "unimportant" citizens are *mis*policed in ways that repeat the ongoing history of inequity and violence.[60] State neglect to keep vulnerable constituencies safe—from either crime or extrajudicial killing—coincides with the wild, ineffectual attempts to mediate between clashing mobilities.

To live in a striated city is to be at home with segregation. Batacan shows the clash of mobilities further through the characterization of the serial killer. An only son of poor parents and a recipient of financial aid in boyhood, he carries the burden of having been molested by an adult in school. His parents kept the abuse secret for fear of ruining his chance to escape poverty. His earliest memories of self-consolidation and motility are thus of wounding. And the persistence of his psychic wound into manhood is deeply tied to the social history of nonpersons gleaning what few advantages can be had from a system that devalues them. Although as an adult the killer gains bourgeois status, his modicum of upward mobility gives no reparation beyond an incessant wish for self-making warped by its own logic of self-defacement.

Serial killing is clearly a metaphor, but of what? The murderer compensates himself for traumatic loss by taking individualism to a toxic extreme.[61] Bearing such thwarted psychical transition and secreting a mental sort of leachate, his interiority is hypernodal. His headspace is so choked with pain and the wish to flee it that he seeks to void any intersubjective link to others in whom he discerns repudiated identifications. Driving the serial killer are failed attempts to cut off from knowledge his vulnerability and powerlessness. This repetition harks back to the resentment that grids a segregated metro, the rivalry between main beneficiaries of space flows and bearers of trashed motility. Serial killing in Manila not only configures the interior residue of external convolutions—trash, crowded channels, slums. It is also a trope for the violent wish to be set apart from places that make the hyper-nodal condition all too known. Read through this figure, the significance of the kill site, a van streamlined for the delivery of humanitarian goods, requires no further comment in the space of this essay.

## Path Seizures

Whereas in past forms, the edge formed a decisive terminus, nodality now teems throughout the polynucleated city. Incorporating places forcibly into flows ends up disengaging them from those circuits. Illustrating the problem are Batacan's anecdotes of the ordinary commute. Recall Saenz earlier surveying urban decay: "the cars, the buildings, the dingy shop signs and crumbling waiting sheds" (S73). Pedestrians resentful of state policies that ignore their spatial needs—for shelter as for ample sidewalks—take lawlessness as a given, and their seizure of path functions in turn generates tension with private commuters. Another anecdote features Lucero driving from the idyllic Jesuit campus in the north to an urban core in the south, Makati, the central business district surrounded by rich enclaves. Traffic along the north-south axis of Epifanio de los Santos Avenue stalls movement:

> There are patches of EDSA, the metropolis's main highway, where all vehicles are at a complete standstill, and there is little for him to do but gaze at the fading orange-and-lavender light of the setting sun reflected in the dingy glass windows of the buildings that line the avenue. And then in certain stretches the bottleneck clears, and the vehicles spill forward like beans from a jar, accelerating with a mad, pent-up energy, racing to claim every available space. He has lost count of how many times he has almost been sideswiped by other vehicles trying to squeeze past him. The completed flyovers are absolutely no help in easing the traffic situation, and neither, as far as he can tell, is the Metro Rail Transit. (S127)

Though losing count, Lucero intuits that the number of vehicles in motion exceeds highway capacity. He does not need Samuel Schwartz to remind him that every "car above that critical number on the streets results in fewer total miles traveled."[62] The avenue becomes a zone of friction, making even a priest go ape: Lucero "pounds on the horn with the heel of his palm, like many other irate motorists" (S127). As mobility degrades, scale and texture alter; cars roll "like beans from a jar," and the triumphs of construction look "dingy." It is as if the Jesuit were pierced by a line from Hopkins, viewing a landscape "bleared, smeared, with toil."[63]

While the priest mourns urban traces of postlapsarian loss, the highway represents a different kind of grief for pedestrians. For them, it is rarely about spiritual trial. Major channels quite literally present close calls with death. Batacan addresses this predicament toward the end of her novel in a set of brief portraits about parents whose children were murdered. Binang is one of them. Before her boy's death, she gave up her son and had him raised in Payatas. Her mourning takes a strange turn as she ponders the odds of survival for people like her and her son. The following scene occurs after the police inform her of her son's disappearance:

> Binang looks in the mirror, absentmindedly twirling a strand of hair around a finger, and wonders where her young self went. Fifty-four. How many times in the last two decades had she doubted that she would make it this far? So many possibilities. An accident while crossing the highway after years of dodging murderous passenger jeepneys. A fire sweeping through the neighborhood, densely packed with wooden shanties. (S242)

Piercing the mother's grief is deep regret. She mulls over her failure to pass on the simple lessons of being a pedestrian. This implication darkens, however, when regret pivots toward the dead, the boy imagined as someone unable to learn street-smart lessons on his own. More than the idea of self-cannibalization in grief, a commonplace in psychoanalytical reading, what is worth underscoring in Binang's recrimination is its implied path. It moves from herself to her son, then to jeepneys, but it stops short of considering the infrastructure that pits the mobility of the carless against that of machines.

According to Michael Sorkin, the rights of passage are now codified in similar ways everywhere: "Slower vehicles yield to faster ones and pedestrians to all."[64] Transport machines pose a risk to walkers. And promoting pedestrian safety is the justification given for global traffic policy. What policy takes for granted, however, is the reification at work in the standardization of city paths and their uses. Standardization generates hierarchies of mobility, at once favoring machines and depriviledging persons. "The automobile system seeks invariably," Sorkin rightly argues, "to exclude other modes that might come into conflict with it."[65] The codification of the rights of passage operates on the assumption of speed. The solution to the problem of urban mobility is to subordinate the bodily scale to the scale of the path network. The alternative to speed that Sorkin proposes is deceleration, which putatively strikes a "balance between the predictable and the unexpected, in order to produce the largest number of accidental discursive events."[66]

Guided by this principle, what urban governance must supply is a path system that downplays "unimpeded flow and favors concrete exchange."[67] Constituting democratic traffic as Sorkin envisions it are, apparently, the conversations that can arise in as many ruptures and crowds as possible.

## From Flows to Flooding

But Manila is not Disneyland, Sorkin's heuristic model of the deceleration principle. The movements of a leisure mass for whom deceleration is ideal are not the same as the spatial and transport needs of a working mass rushing to or from work. Sorkin's system of balance presupposes a network with levels of planning spread evenly across the city, which alternately meets the need for speed when it arises and responds to the need for slowing down when pedestrian safety is at stake. In short, as Schwartz tersely puts it: "To have gridlock, you first need to have a grid."[68] There are cities whose public spaces have been rationalized to such degree as to favor speed over demotic forms of movement. Conflict in these cities indeed contributes to "deliberation and marks the vigor of difference within culture."[69] But as Jennifer Robinson argues, "The spatiality of the city does not lend itself to a progressive or linear historicism, in which one urban outcome or one temporality (the new) can do the analytical service for the urban in general."[70]

Sorkin's account, as a matter of fact, begins with heavy traffic in India. The transposition of vehicular glut there onto the idealization of deceleration elsewhere renders his account susceptible to the tendency in globalization studies to treat "places outside the Anglo-American heartland as sources of data rather than as sites for theorization in their own right."[71] But city life is not the same everywhere. The tight integration between capacious nodes and freeways does not exist in Manila infrastructure. Traffic is not equally responsive to cars and pedestrians, as in Batacan's description of "the noontime crowd at the junction of Tandang Sora and the highway" (S246). The experience of deceleration at ground level does not result in democratic exchange. Instead, it provokes hostility between ambulant and vehicular kinds of movements, as well as among the ranks of drivers and the pedestrian mass.

Regarded as an antidote to Disneyland, Manila traffic can look sublime. What this experience of the metro presupposes is detachment, the vision of locals with time enough to contemplate flows or of visitors who treat Manila as leisure space. Such is the case with the priest Saenz in his study at the university campus. Taking a break from analyzing photos of child mutilation, he lifts his gaze toward "the normal flow of everyday life along Katipunan Avenue bordering the campus: the jeepneys, the school buses, the private cars ferrying their human cargo to and from their destinations in the city"

(S38). But the normality of this demotic scene indicating levels of mobility is temporary. Later in the novel, Batacan notes how the monsoon weather wreaks havoc on the very avenue Saenz contemplates:

> A tropical storm has brought heavy rains to Metro Manila and other parts of Luzon. Quezon City is a commuter's nightmare, with floods hitting waist-high levels in certain areas, and creeks have overflowed all over the city. Many streets are impassable, and traffic is snarled nearly everywhere. The road outside the university is packed with vehicles. (S205)

This scene is focalized by Jerome and Saenz, and it is still from the university campus that the priests view the city's sudden transformation into a flood zone. Gridlock holds scarcely any threat to the priests. A few lines down the page, they "wait at the laboratory for the traffic to ease before heading off to personal errands" (S205). But ordinary citizens find deceleration far from enabling. They suffer when flooding reproduces the conditions of the landfill as an absolute node along the transport channels.

Wreckage flowing back to the urban path network is no hyperbole. What precipitates this socioecological return of the repressed? Greg Bankoff describes Manila as "a vast urbanised drainage basin that experiences frequent inundations from overflowing rivers and storm waters."[72] Worsened by climate change, the monsoon dredges up the megacity's trash. Typhoon Ondoy in 2009 is a case in point. Surveying its aftermath, Emma Porio writes of respondents who "complained that floodwaters would carry garbage to where they lived and clog up the nearby drainage channels." Poor households also reported "toilets blocked and overflowing with waste and large worms."[73] What scavengers at Payatas experience does happen beyond the proscribed limits of the dumpsite. Batacan's account of flooding, constellated with other motifs, once more begs the question of hypernodality as a spatial trend, the incursion of nodal functions on city paths due to uneven infrastructure and botched urban governance. Just as the hypernode is a by-product of intense circulations, so is leachate subjectivity a trace not merely of wasted persons but of an aspirational class politics savagely directed against them and their modes of dwelling. As Neil Brenner and Roger Keil observe, "While geographical proximities among cities and their inhabitants have increased, social distancing inside cities and across networks has often increased dramatically."[74] The condition wherein space flows breed human waste calls for more engagement in thought and action. Manila may well be a labyrinth of trashed urbanism. But for all that, it is also a city worth taking pains to change, to free, and not to flee.

NOTES

1. Batacan, *Smaller and Smaller Circles*. Before the revised, expanded 2015 Soho edition published in New York, the novel was first published in the Philippines; see *Smaller and Smaller Circles* (Quezon City: University of the Philippines Press, 2002). The Soho edition was adapted into a film directed by Raya Martin in 2017. For this study, I use the 2015 Soho edition, hereafter cited as S with the page number. Caveat lector, spoilers ahead.
2. Bauman, *Wasted Lives*, 70.
3. Bloch, "A Philosophical View of the Detective Novel," 33–34.
4. Hausladen, "Where Bodies Lie: Sense of Place and Police Procedurals," 46.
5. Merry and Fritz, "Reconnaissance of the July 10, 2000, Payatas Landfill Failure," 100.
6. Davis, *Planet of Slums*, 124.
7. Cabalfin, "The Politics of Nation in the Urban Form," 159.
8. Sayre, "Scale," 97–100. See also McCann, "The Urban as an Object of Study in Global Cities Literatures," 74–77.
9. Lynch, *The Image of the City*, 72–76.
10. Robinson, "The Urban Now," 661. The direction Robinson advocates entails "a spatially exteriorized and historically dispersed understanding of the emergence of specific urban forms" (666). While hypernodality may be found in developing cities, reading Batacan to account for its emergence in Manila is the contribution I wish to make.
11. Caoili, *The Origins of Metropolitan Manila*, 132.
12. Tadiar, "Metropolitan Life and Uncivil Death," 316. Tadiar uses Caoili's adjective: "They are part of a more general, if haphazard, strategy of social disciplinary action." On the dictator, Tadiar writes, "Marcos garrisoned the metropolis not only with soldiers and police but also with spectacular modern public works designed to appeal to the economic and cultural sensibilities of his international political clientele and paid for with funds looted from coffers filled with foreign loans and foreign aid" (318).
13. Batacan differs slightly from Tadiar, who writes, "Against the clustering that both resulted from and aggravated urban congestion, a metropolitan policy of facilitating and 'freeing' movement, of streamlining flows, now prevails. This modus operandi, which helps to realize dreams of flow, mobility, and circulation, encourages ever more parochial forms of locality, such as the deterritorialized locality of global culture." The examples Tadiar cites are "shopping centers, office buildings, and individual homes and the outdoor spaces of private subdivisions and inner-city neighborhoods" as examples of parochialism encouraged by institutional calculation. See Tadiar, "Metropolitan Life and Uncivil Death," 317. What Batacan narrates are streamlining's unintended effects—effects that, contra metropolitan policy, manifest as crowding along channels, flash floods, and informal clusters like slums and wet markets.
14. Manalansan, "Queer Worldings," 577.
15. DuPre, *Homicide Investigation Field Guide*, 125–126. There are four basic search patterns—parallel, grid, zone, and inward spiral. Batacan's title alludes to the fourth. Another textbook calls it the "circle or spiral search," moving from the margins to the center and then reversing the process. See Gardner and Krouskup, *Practical Crime Scene Processing and Investigation*, 89–90.
16. Schmid, "From the Locked Room to the Globe," 8.
17. Chesterton, "A Defence of Detective Stories," 282.
18. Bloch, "A Philosophical View of the Detective Novel," 40.
19. Ibid., 34.
20. Lynch, *The Image of the City*, 46–51.

21. Tadiar, "Metropolitan Life and Uncivil Death," 320.

22. Žižek, "The Detective and the Analyst," 37.

23. Singling out Batacan as one of the Philippines' exemplary crime fiction writers, Hagedorn uses the term *crime fiction* interchangeably with *noir*. Without defining noir, she sketches its "essentials," namely, "alienated and desperate characters, terse dialogue, sudden violence, betrayals left and right." See Hagedorn, *Manila Noir*, 13. Noir in my understanding refers to literary or cinematic representations of "elaborate, stylized brutality." It is "an anti-genre that reveals the dark side of savage capitalism." This definition comes from Naremore, "American Film Noir," 19–20.

24. The labyrinth strikes fear because it leads to a subterranean prison, a monster, oblivion, a tomb. For an excavation of these ancient connotations, see Borgeaud, "The Open Entrance to the Close Palace of the King," 1–27.

25. Porteous, "Smellscape," 91. Reporting on Payatas, a journalist corroborates my reading. The journalist writes, "In the tropical heat the smell of rot and smoke is everywhere; it seeps into the pores and clings to the back of your throat." See Power, "The Magic Mountain," 60.

26. Lynch, *The Image of the City*, 72.

27. Though Payatas denizens are not homeless street people, Anne Lovell makes a relevant observation about people living near trash. They bear the burden of "a representation of self that must account for the materiality of garbage and the cast-off and for their proximity to it." They "perceive themselves as social outcasts in a complex urban structure." See Lovell, "Hoarders and Scrapers," 328–330.

28. Payatas bears a history of violence. Recalling fieldwork in 1987, an ethnographer writes, "Unidentified dead bodies in plastic bags are discarded into the settlement." See Parnell, "The Composite State," 152. A journalist also recalls that Payatas "became infamous as a body dump during the gang wars that raged across the city's slum districts, fought out with spears, machetes, poison arrows, and homemade guns called *sumpok*." See Power, "The Magic Mountain," 58.

29. Quoted in Vidler, "The Mask and the Labyrinth," 56.

30. Power, "The Magic Mountain," 62.

31. Cabalfin, "The Politics of Nation in the Urban Form," 166.

32. Pinches, "Modernisation and the Quest for Modernity," 14.

33. Ibid., 24.

34. Lynch, *The Image of the City*, 74–78.

35. Baudelaire writes of the ragpicker who "collects and catalogues everything that the great city has cast off, everything it has lost, and discarded, and broken." Quoted in Benjamin, *The Arcades Project*, 349.

36. Borgeaud, "The Open Entrance to the Close Palace of the King," 21.

37. Rose, "Landscape and Labyrinths," 463.

38. Harries, "Nietzsche's Labyrinths," 39.

39. Sassen, "Expelled," 199–200.

40. Benjamin writes of Baudelaire: "The ragpicker fascinated his epoch. The eyes of the first investigators of pauperism were fixed on him with the mute question: Where does the limit of human misery lie?" Benjamin, "The Paris of the Second Empire in Baudelaire," 54.

41. Lovell, "Hoarders and Scrapers," 323.

42. Bauman, *Wasted Lives*, 41.

43. Jocano, *Slum as a Way of Life*, 69. Jocano presents other factors. Having more children "has a functional value—economic support, emotional security, social prestige, and

fulfillment of parenthood" (65). There is also an economic gambit: "teaching the child how to earn a living and how to be an effective contributor to the family larder" (95).

44. Bauman, *Wasted Lives*, 39.

45. Ibid., 70–71.

46. Senn, "The Labyrinth Image in Verbal Art," 223.

47. Borgeaud, "The Open Entrance to the Close Palace of the King," 19–21.

48. Rella, "Eros and Polemos," 32–36.

49. Power, "The Magic Mountain," 65. On the same page, Power reports that after returning to the spot where the landslide buried Lupang Pangako, residents were forced to leave because of "restive ghosts rattling their windows, knocking pots over in the kitchen, visiting nightmares into fitful attempts at sleep."

50. Bauman, *Wasted Lives*, 72.

51. See Davis, *Planet of Slums*, 47. His list of landfill slums here include "Quarantina outside Beirut, Hillat Kusha outside Khartoum, Santa Cruz Meyehualco in Mexico City, the former Smoky Mountain in Manila, or the huge Dhapa dump and slum on the fringe of Kolkata." Smokey Mountain is another squatter community, now ostensibly rehabilitated, about twenty-five kilometers southwest of Payatas.

52. Quoted in ibid., 121.

53. Berner and Korff, "Globalization and Local Resistance," 210.

54. Molotch, "The City as a Growth Machine," 315.

55. For a history on slums in Quezon City, see Pante, *A Capital City at the Margins*, 222–233.

56. *Motility* is a sociological term for analyzing the links between changes in social position and corresponding types of physical movement. Understood as such, it holds value as an asset. See Kaufmann, Bergman, and Joye, "Motility," 745–756.

57. Bauman, *Wasted Lives*, 39.

58. Castells, *City, Class, and Power*, 753.

59. Tadiar, "Metropolitan Life and Uncivil Death," 316. Infrastructure, she also contends, aims "to discipline the unruly movements of public commuting masses and ensure the unimpeded mobility of private motorists."

60. Marcosian state violence was in fact used in Batacan's residential *locus dolenti*. Lawmen with assault rifles in 1985 fought "squatters in Barangay Payatas in a violent demolition that left 2,000 squatter families homeless." See Pante, *A Capital City at the Margins*, 231.

61. Castells observes in the urban "a segmenting of interests in terms of individual aspirations, which, in spatial terms, is translated into the dispersion of individual residences." See Castells, *City, Class, and Power*, 27. Prefiguring his idea is that of mental "reserve" in Simmel, "The Metropolis and Mental Life," 15.

62. Schwartz, *Streetsmart*, 204.

63. Hopkins, "God's Grandeur," 139.

64. Sorkin, "Traffic in Democracy," 297.

65. Ibid., 307.

66. Ibid., 302.

67. Ibid., 310.

68. Schwartz, *Streetsmart*, 156.

69. Ibid., 302.

70. Robinson, "The Urban Now," 671.

71. Parnell and Robinson, "(Re)theorizing Cities from the Global South," 596.

72. Bankoff, "Constructing Vulnerability," 227.

73. Porio, "Life along Manila's Flooding Rivers," 261–263.
74. Brenner and Keil, "From Global Cities to Globalized Urbanization," 607.

## BIBLIOGRAPHY

Bankoff, Greg, "Constructing Vulnerability: The Historical, Natural and Social Generation of Flooding in Metropolitan Manila." *Disasters* 27, no. 3 (2003): 224–238.
Batacan, F. H. *Smaller and Smaller Circles*. Quezon City: University of the Philippines Press, 2002.
———. *Smaller and Smaller Circles*. New York: Soho Crime, 2015.
Bauman, Zygmunt. *Wasted Lives: Modernity and its Outcasts*. Cambridge: Polity Press, 2004.
Benjamin, Walter. *The Arcades Project*. Translated by Howard Eiland and Kevin McLaughlin. Cambridge: Belknap Press of Harvard University Press, 2006.
———. "The Paris of the Second Empire in Baudelaire." In *The Writer of Modern Life*, edited by Michael Jennings. Cambridge: Belknap Press of Harvard University Press, 2006.
Berner, Erhard, and Rüdiger Korff, "Globalization and Local Resistance: The Creation of Localities in Manila and Bangkok." *International Journal of Urban and Regional Research* 19, no. 2 (1995): 208–222.
Bloch, Ernst. "A Philosophical View of the Detective Novel." *Discourse* 2 (Summer 1980): 32–52.
Borgeaud, Philippe. "The Open Entrance to the Close Palace of the King: The Greek Labyrinth in Context." *History of Religions* 14, no. 1 (August 1974): 1–27.
Brenner, Neil, and Roger Keil. "From Global Cities to Globalized Urbanization." In *The City Reader*, edited by Richard LeGates and Frederic Stout, 600–608. New York: Routledge, 2011.
Cabalfin, Edson. "The Politics of Nation in the Urban Form of Informal Settlements in Quezon City, Philippines." In *Reading the Architecture of the Underprivileged Classes: A Perspective on the Protests and Upheavals in Our Cities*, edited by Nnamdi Elleh, 153–170. Farnham: Ashgate Publishing Limited, 2014.
Caoili, Manuel A. *The Origins of Metropolitan Manila: A Political and Social Analysis*. Quezon City: University of the Philippines Press, 1999.
Castells, Manuel. *City, Class, and Power*. Translated by Elizabeth Lebas. New York: Macmillan Press, 1978.
Chesterton, G. K. "A Defence of Detective Stories." In *On Lying in Bed and Other Essays.*, edited by Alberto Manguel, 281–284. Calgary: Bayeux Arts, 2000.
Davis, Mike. *Planet of Slums*. London: Verso, 2006.
DuPre, D'Michelle P. *Homicide Investigation Field Guide*. Kidlington: Academic Press, 2013.
Gardner, Ross M., and Donna R. Krouskup. *Practical Crime Scene Processing and Investigation, Third Edition*. Boca Raton: CRC Press, 2019.
Hagedorn, Jessica. *Manila Noir*. Mandaluyong: Anvil, 2013.
Harries, Karsten. "Nietzsche's Labyrinths: Variations on an Ancient Theme." In *Nietzsche and "An Architecture of Our Minds,"* edited by Alexandre Kostka and Irving Wohlfarth, 35–52. Los Angeles: Getty Research Institute for the History of Art and the Humanities, 1999.
Hausladen, Gary. "Where Bodies Lie: Sense of Place and Police Procedurals." *Journal of Cultural Geography* 16, no. 1 (1996): 45–63.

Hopkins, Gerard Manley. "God's Grandeur." In *The Poetical Works of Gerard Manley Hopkins*, edited by Norman H. Mackenzie, 139. Oxford: Clarendon Press, 1990.

Jocano, Felipe L. *Slum as a Way of Life: A Study of Coping Behavior in an Urban Environment*. Revised ed. Quezon City: PUNLAD Research House, 2002.

Kaufmann, Vincent, Manfred Max Bergman, and Dominique Joye. "Motility: Mobility as Capital." *International Journal of Urban and Regional Research* 28, no. 4 (December 2004): 745–756.

Lovell, Anne. "Hoarders and Scrapers: Madness and the Social Person in the Interstices of the City." In *Subjectivity: Ethnographic Investigations*, edited by Joao Biehl, Byron Good, and Arthur Kleinman, 315–340. Berkeley: University of California Press, 2007.

Lynch, Kevin. *The Image of the City*. Cambridge: Technology Press and Harvard University, 1960.

Manalansan IV, Martin. "Queer Worldings: The Messy Art of Being Global in Manila and New York." *Antipode* 47, no. 3 (2015): 566–579.

McCann, Eugene J. "The Urban as an Object of Study in Global Cities Literatures: Representational Practices and Conceptions of Place and Scale." In *Geographies of Power: Placing Scale*, edited by Andrew Herod and Melissa Wright, 61–84. Malden: Blackwell Publishing, 2009.

Merry, Scott M., Edward Kavazanjian Jr., and Wolfgang U. Fritz. "Reconnaissance of the July 10, 2000, Payatas Landfill Failure." *Journal of Performance of Constructed Facilities* 19, no. 2 (May 2005): 100–107.

Molotch, Harvey. "The City as a Growth Machine: Toward a Political Economy of Place." *American Journal of Sociology* 82, no. 2 (September 1976): 309–332.

Naremore, James. "American Film Noir: The History of an Idea." *Film Quarterly* 49, no. 2 (Winter 1995–1996): 12–28.

Pante, Michael. *A Capital City at the Margins: Quezon City and Urbanization in the Twentieth-Century Philippines*. Quezon City: Ateneo de Manila University Press, 2019.

Parnell, Phillip C. "The Composite State: The Poor and the Nation in Manila." In *Ethnography in Unstable Places: Everyday Lives in the Contexts of Dramatic Change*, edited by Carol J. Greenhouse, Elizabeth Mertz, and Kay B. Warren, 146–177. Durham: Duke University Press, 2002.

Parnell, Susan, and Jennifer Robinson. "(Re)theorizing Cities from the Global South: Looking Beyond Neoliberalism." *Urban Geography* 33, no. 4 (2012): 593–617.

Pinches, Michael. "Modernisation and the Quest for Modernity: Architectural Form, Squatter Settlements, and the New Society." In *Cultural Identity and Urban Change in Southeast Asia: Interpretive Essays*, edited by Marc Askew and William S. Logan, 13–42. Geelong: Deaking University Press, 1994.

Porio, Emma. "Life along Manila's Flooding Rivers." In *The Environments of the Poor in Southeast Asia, East Asia, and the Pacific*, edited by Aris Ananta, Armin Bauer, and Myo Thant, 256–270. Singapore: Asian Development Bank and Institute of Southeast Asian Studies, 2013.

Porteous, J. Douglas. "Smellscape." In *The Smell Culture Reader*, edited by Jim Drobnick, 89–106. Oxford: Berg, 2006.

Power, Matthew. "The Magic Mountain: Trickle-down Economics in a Philippine Garbage Dump." *Harper's Magazine* (December 2006): 57–68.

Rella, Franco. "Eros and Polemos: The Poetics of the Labyrinth." *Assemblage* 3 (July 1987): 30–37.

Robinson, Jennifer. "The Urban Now: Theorising Cities beyond the New." *European Journal of Cultural Studies* 16, no. 6 (2013): 659–677.

Rose, Mitch. "Landscape and Labyrinths." *Geoforum* 33 (2002): 455–467.

Sassen, Saskia. "Expelled: Humans in Capitalism's Deepening Crisis." *Journal of World-Systems Research* 19, no. 2 (Summer 2013): 198–200.

Sayre, Nathan. "Scale." In *A Companion to Environmental Geography*, edited by Noel Castree, Daniel Demerritt, Doama Liverman, and Bruce Rhoads, 95–108. Malden: Blackwell, 2009.

Schmid, David. "From the Locked Room to the Globe: Space in Crime Fiction." In *Cross-cultural Connections in Crime Fictions*, edited by Vivien Miller and Helen Oakley, 7–23. New York: Palgrave Macmillan, 2012.

Schwartz, Samuel. *Streetsmart: The Rise of Cities and the Fall of Cars*. New York: Public Affairs, 2015.

Senn, Werner. "The Labyrinth Image in Verbal Art: Sign, Symbol, Icon?" *Word & Image* 2, no. 3 (July–September 1986): 219–230.

Simmel, Georg. "The Metropolis and Mental Life." In *The Blackwell City Reader*, edited by Gary Bridge and Sophie Watson, 11–19. Oxford: Wiley-Blackwell, 2002.

Sorkin, Michael. "Traffic in Democracy." In *Cities in Transition: Power, Environment, Society*, edited by Wowo Ding, Arie Graafland, and Andong Lu. Rotterdam, 297–313: Nai010 Uitgevers, 2015.

Tadiar, Neferti. "Metropolitan Life and Uncivil Death." *PMLA* 122, no. 1 (2007): 316–320.

Vidler, Anthony. "The Mask and the Labyrinth: Nietzsche and the (Uncanny) Space of Decadence." In *Nietzsche and "An Architecture of Our Minds,"* edited by Alexandre Kostka and Irving Wohlfarth. Los Angeles: Getty Research Institute for the History of Art and the Humanities, 1999, 53–63.

Žižek, Slavoj. "The Detective and the Analyst." *Literature and Psychology* 36, no. 4 (1990): 27–46.

# Of Demolitions and Dispossession

*The Everyday Violence of Metro Manila's Growth Politics*

FAITH R. KARES

We are now considered a rising tiger by the World Bank: the brightest spark, according to the Institute of Chartered Accountants in England and Wales, among other accolades that allude to the transformation that is sweeping our nation. From the prudent expenditure of funds to the effective collection of taxes; from infrastructure development to the transparent conduct of business that generates jobs, our message to the world could not be clearer: The Philippines is ready to ride the tides of progress.
—FORMER PHILIPPINES PRESIDENT BENIGNO AQUINO III ("FOURTH STATE OF THE NATION")

Instead of helping the poor, the government actually makes us poorer with what they do. . . . They only take notice of us during election time anyway, when they need our votes. When we approached them [for help] they didn't recognize us. . . . The government only takes notice of us when they need us. What about us poor people? Instead of being helped by the government, we sink further into poverty.
—ELNORA, METRO MANILA RESIDENT

In his fourth State of the Nation Address (SONA) in 2013, former Philippines President Benigno "Noynoy" Aquino III heralded the country's significant economic growth, indexed by a combination of credit upgrades, strong peso, record-high stock market index, as well as gross international reserves (GIR) and foreign investments. Observers and analysts have attributed this massive economic growth to what became the cornerstone of Noynoy's presidency—public-private partnerships (PPPs), widely known among Filipinos as "three Ps." The official transcript generated by the state and its private partners, celebrating unhampered and economic growth "for all," stood in stark contrast to narratives circulated among Metro Manila's urban poor concerning the lived realities of such "progress"; since 2010, when former president Aquino III first introduced three Ps as his development plan, an unprecedented number of demolitions and forced relocations have trans-pired alongside the country's economic growth.

This chapter closely examines the discursive frames with which the state and its partners under the Aquino III administration introduced and justified specific strategies for growth and development. It then attends to the ways in which these policies heightened brutal demolition processes in the service of beautification for the few by offering counternarratives provided by work-ing poor Filipinos working in Metro Manila, the urban hub of the Philippines. Over the course of conducting deep-immersion, ethnographic research be-tween 2007 and 2013 among Metro Manila's working poor, I observed the ways in which government-sponsored urban development and beautification ef-forts to stimulate economic growth through commercial and foreign invest-ment resulted in the often-violent removal of street vendors and poor city residents.

In what follows, I examine how the onslaught of demolitions in the Phil-ippines reflects global neoliberal processes as well as is the result of a long history of failed agrarian reform. I therefore analyze the implementation of neoliberal policies in the Philippines against the backdrop of the country's land policies and argue that public-private partnerships replaced structural adjustment programs (SAPs) as the dominant mode of neoliberal restruc-turing in the Global South. Finally, drawing on Metro Manila–based obser-vations and interviews, I demonstrate the manner in which members of the marginalized majority experience the "fantasies of the few" through wide-spread housing demolition and violent displacement and relocation efforts. In so doing, I answer geographer Andre Ortega's call for "projects that un-cover processes of 'accumulation by dispossession,'" which is needed more than ever "as Philippine real estate continues to boom and new developments are built, a seemingly doxic euphoria" (2012, 1138).

## History of Neoliberal Restructuring in the Philippines

The real estate boom—and the concomitant intensified rate and pace of de-molitions and displacement—in the Philippines reflects global political-eco-nomic shifts characterized by neoliberalism, "an intellectual/political stance that presumes that capitalist trade 'liberalization'—the end of all state regu-lations on business, and indeed, the end of all state-run business—will lead inevitably to market-growth and, *ceteris paribus*, to optimal social ends" (di Leonardo 2008, 5–7; see also Harvey 2004, 2). Scholars from an array of dis-ciplines have long shed light on how aspects of privatization, deregulation, and trade liberalization—central tenets of neoliberal ideology—shape gov-ernance and democratic participation and processes (see Carrier and West 2009; Tsing 2005). Ethnographic studies have been especially important in bringing to the fore the actual workings and on-the-ground effects of neo-liberalization, specifically processes of accumulation by dispossession. By accumulation by dispossession, Marxist geographer David Harvey means:

> the continuation and proliferation of accumulating practices that Marx had treated as 'primitive' or 'original' during the rise of capitalism. These include the commodification and privatization of land and the forceful expulsion of peasant populations (as in Mexico and India in recent times); conversion of various forms of property rights to the commons; commodification of labor power and the suppression of alternative (indigenous) forms of production and consumption. (2004, 145)

He notes that the state, "with its monopoly of violence and definitions of legality, plays a crucial role in both backing and promoting these processes" (2006, 43). Accumulation by dispossession helps us account for the extreme volatility and stratifications produced in neoliberal development processes.

Within the Philippines context, neoliberal restructuring "has been transacted through strategic engagement of the national government with the 'unholy trinity' of the World Bank, International Monetary Fund (IMF) and World Trade Organization (WTO)" (Ortega 2012, 1152; see also Peet 2009). SAPs have saddled the country with exorbitant debt as well as siphoned public sectors into private enterprises. Political analyst Walden Bello and his colleagues relate that "structural adjustment in the Philippines, which was initiated in 1980, sought—at least at the rhetorical level—to achieve greater efficiency through thoroughgoing liberalization, deregulation, and privatization." They go on:

> Growth and development were to be byproducts of efficiency in the narrow sense of reducing the unit cost of the output of productive activity. Adjustment was not, however, divorced from conjunctural needs: among the immediate problems it was meant to address was to gain the foreign exchange to service the Philippines' burgeoning foreign debt via greater export orientation. (2005, 12)

Thus, as presidents from former dictator Ferdinand Marcos to Noynoy's predecessors (including his own mother, Corazon Aquino) prioritized debt repayment, they also starved the country of the capital necessary to develop its domestic manufacturing and agricultural industries. With limited employment prospects and government brokerage of cheap labor to the world,

Filipinos have sought greener pastures abroad—17 percent of the country's working-age population goes abroad in search of work (Whaley 2013, B34; see also Rodriguez 2010). Such mass exodus is not unique to the Philippines but, rather, reflects a wider pattern of labor migration from the Global South to the Global North as people flee the ravages of SAPs and various forms of state devolution and privatization.

Under the leadership of former president Aquino III, public-private partnerships effectively replaced SAPs as the Philippine government's central strategy for economic growth and infrastructure development. In the Executive Summary of its 2004 report on public-private partnerships, the International Monetary Fund (IMF), in consultation with the World Bank and Inter-American Development Bank, opens:

> Public-private partnerships (PPPs) involve private sector supply of infrastructure assets and services that have traditionally been provided by the government. An infusion of private capital and management can ease fiscal constraints on infrastructure investment and increase efficiency. (2013, 3)

In keeping with the report's rationale for public-private partnerships, Aquino's administration cited a lack of government funding for substantive infrastructure and development programs and was able to develop three Ps as *the* signal feature of the country's plan for growth. Aquino entered office in 2010 touting three Ps in his first SONA as the cure-all for the country's financial and social woes:

> We have so many needs: from education, health, military, police, and more. Our funds will not be enough to meet them. No matter how massive the deficit is that may keep us from paying for this list of needs, I am heartened because many have already expressed renewed interest and confidence in the Philippines. Our solution: public-private partnerships.

It is important to note here that as the president defended three Ps as the only viable option for infrastructure and development by citing a lack of government funds, the 2013 pork barrel scandal revealed the widespread corruption among the country's politicians (including President Aquino himself) and the manner in which they regularly pocketed funds dedicated to public projects (Ellao, November 15, 2013; see also Salamat 2013).

Now while the privatization of public assets has always been vital to neoliberal projects, privatization under the rubric of public-private partnerships did not merely reflect a new approach to implementing neoliberal policies but, rather, marked a distinctive shift in governance. Harvey notes that:

> the preferred form of governance is that of 'public private partnership' in which state and key business interests collaborate closely together to coordinate their activities around the aim of enhancing capital accumulation. The result is that the regulated get to write the rules of regulation while 'public' decision-making becomes ever more opaque. (2006, 27)

With the passage of three Ps, the Aquino administration prioritized the needs of real estate developers and private investors—at the expense of land reform and distribution to the Philippine poor majority—all the while making assurances that every Filipino would benefit; in his July 2010 first SONA, President Aquino avowed, "From these public-private partnerships (PPPs), our economy will grow and *every Filipino will be a beneficiary* [my emphasis]." President Aquino maintained this stance in his 2013 SONA, where he referred to the country's "inclusive growth—this all-encompassing progress" as "the principle that drives every initiative, every action, and every decision of your government. The only ones who will be left behind are those who chose not to venture onwards with us, simply because they did not seize the opportunity."

Aquino was so convinced of the power of privatization to transform the Philippine economy that immediately after announcing three Ps as the centerpiece of his administration's economic development plan, he held a summit dedicated to three Ps, which explored investment opportunities, profiles of ongoing and potential three Ps in the Philippines, as well as more general policy, regulatory, and legal concerns in developing the infrastructure sector in the Philippines. In the same year, the Aquino administration developed the Public Private Partnership Center of the Philippines under Executive Order No. 8, accelerating the financing, construction, and operation of government infrastructure projects. Philippines news source ABS-CBN covered Executive Secretary Paquito N. Ochoa's declaration at the center's launch: "This executive order is just the first of many steps this administration will take to provide our people with the infrastructure they need, the infrastructure required to make our country more attractive to investors" (2013).

And growth certainly arrived—albeit not the inclusive growth to which Aquino had referred. Certainly, "the construction sector ... grew by 14.1% in Q1–Q3 2012 from a contraction of 11.9% in the same period in 2011" (IBON Foundation 2013a, 6–7). But while the construction of infrastructure can support economic growth, especially if the construction develops national industries such as textiles and steel, growth in the construction sector "is not because of supporting industrialization but only based on the boom in construction of facilities for the foreign capital-intensive and export-oriented BPO sector, in particular, the building of more office spaces, and to a certain extent, residential units" (Ibid.).

What's more, the growth in corporate profits outpaced growth in workers' wages, where "the average daily basic pay in agriculture for example increased by only 4% in 2010–2011, but the estimated daily net income of top 1,000 corporations in agriculture went up by 821 percent" (Ibid.). In this manner, however, Vice President Jejomar Binay was prescient in his optimism for the investors who stood to benefit from the country's real estate boom. Presenting at the sixth annual Philippines Real Estate Festival (PREF) in 2012, Binay declared that the "biggest opportunity [for investment] lies in housing." Indeed, while the Aquino III administration did not make good on its promise for equitable distribution of wealth generated by three Ps, it certainly fulfilled its pledge to provide new real estate opportunities for foreign investors (Samaniego 2012).

## History of Agrarian Reform

It is the country's long history of failed agrarian policy that has paved the way for lucrative foreign investment opportunities. Activist and scholar Arundhati Roy points out that "the battle for land lies at the heart of the 'development' debate" (2009, 6). The contemporary struggle for land between the landed and landless has its roots in Spanish colonialism (see Guerrero 1970). Before Spanish occupation (1521–1898), Filipinos owned land communally. With Spanish rule, however, the concept of private ownership through land titling replaced the collective ownership. Colonial authorities concentrated land control and ownership in the hands of Spanish friars, military officials, and already-established landed elite through hacienda and *encomienda* legal systems instituted by Spanish colonial authorities (IBON Foundation 2006, 136). With the transfer of Spanish to American colonial rule, the Philippines saw the country's first attempts at agrarian reform. Yet, while laws were passed, actual land redistribution failed. As well, it was precisely through the enactment of these laws that American investors obtained large tracts of land, thereby exacerbating the preexisting problem of landlessness among the Filipino peasantry.[1]

To date, the most promising of all Philippine land reforms remains unfulfilled. With the 1988 enactment of Republic Act (RA) 6657, also known as the Comprehensive Agrarian Reform Program (CARP), under the guidance of former president Corazon Aquino, the landless were hopeful for the equitable distribution of land as well as sharing of economic growth. "Under

Occupy National Housing Authority (NHA) encampment, organized by national urban poor association KADAMAY, Quezon City, November 21, 2011. (From the author.)

the program, distribution of land was combined with a variety of support services, and human resources, and institutional development or social infrastructure building and strengthening" (Alternate Forum for Research in Mindanao 2005, 12). Significant loopholes in the CARP, however, undermine provisions for redistribution and instead enable former landowners to benefit far more from the program than the workers themselves.

Under President Aquino III's administration, land reform came to a standstill, slowing down in 2012. Not so coincidentally, the slowdown delayed the redistribution of land from Hacienda Luisita, which is owned by the former president's family. Based on the monthly average of land redistribution of the post-Marcos administrations, Noynoy's government distributed land the least (Ellao, January 25, 2013). This fact was unsurprising to many of my urban poor respondents. As Bing, a local community organizer and anti-eviction activist, explained, "The idle land use by the urban poor . . . the government gets these lands and sells it to the big capitalists like Ayala, Lopez, Conjuanco." These capitalists to whom Bing referred remain among the most powerful and wealthy families in the Philippines (Conjuanco being the family or maiden name of President Aquino's mother and former president Corazon Aquino). They own banks and popular shopping centers and manage key enterprises such as sugar. For my respondents, three Ps enabled the state to sanction and essentially legalize corporate land grabbing. Bing added, sardonically, "*Yan, yun mga first priority ng government, no* [They are the government's first priority, right]?"

## Progress and Privatization for Poor Metro Manila Residents

An overwhelming number of working poor Metro Manila residents were emphatic that three Ps served the interests of the country's elite and foreign investors. Jojie works as a full-time activist and community organizer for a grassroots urban poor neighborhood organization, which focuses especially on housing issues. Born in Leyte, Jojie moved to Metro Manila in 1989, changing residences all over Quezon City as he searched for work. He recalled:

> *Simula noong 1994 pa naging aktibista ako after ng mawalan ako ng trabaho, nagsara yung pabrika. Eh nag-full time na akong aktibista sa isang urban poor sector* [It was in 1994 when I first became an activist, right after I lost my job when the factory closed down. So I decided to be a full-time activist in the urban poor sector].

He described:

> *Sa office, eh di madali akong nakakatulong doon sa mga problema ng mga maralita sa usapin partikular sa paninirahan, anumang tipo ng usapin. Kung ito man ay pumapasok doon sa CMP o ito man ay dinedemolish ng walang relokasyon. O ito ay dinedemolish at ipinapasok sa mga programa ng pabahay na sinusuportahan ng mga pribadong negosyante o korporasyon* [In the office, I was able to help the poor out through all sorts of issues. Whether it falls under the CMP, if they were demolished without relocation, or if they were entered under housing programs funded by individuals or corporations].

CMP refers to the Community Mortgage Program, a mortgage-financing program, which allows government-approved community associations (CAs) to purchase land under the rubric of community mortgage. But a report by the Urban Poor Resource Center of the Philippines (UPRCP) points out that:

> even at supposedly the lowest average monthly amortization among government housing programs, however, many families under CMP projects struggle to maintain payments due to lack of income. This puts pressure upon the CA, which is responsible for repayment of the community loan; in these cases, the CA may move to 'substitute' recalcitrant members with other prospective beneficiaries who can shoulder their share. (2011, 5)

The CMP has thus earned its nickname "Collecting Money from the Poor" among urban poor activists and critics of the program, and I address this specifically and more extensively in my other articles.

Graffiti on the wall outside the National Housing Authority offices, November 8, 2011. (From the author.)

As Jojie related his thoughts on the government's role in displacing the poor to make way for private investors, he added firmly, "*Kaya ito ginagawa lang itong NHA, sa tingin ko ginagawa lang itong parang broker* [NHA seems to function as a broker to the private sectors wanting to do business in government]." I remembered the rally I had attended the two weeks prior to our interview. Protesters had sprayed red paint on the wall surrounding the National Housing Authority (NHA) compound to draw attention to the agency's illegal and inhumane demolitions, which had overwhelmingly displaced the poor while serving the interests of key real estate investors, such as Ayala Enterprises.

While he sat across from me at a table in McDonald's in Quezon City, Jojie was adamant that I understand the Noynoy's real aims regarding three Ps. As he stirred powdered creamer into his morning coffee, he shook his head:

*Ang tingin niya kasi doon uunlad ang Pilipinas sa pakikipagtulungan sa mga pribadong negosyante. Ang interes kasi ng mga pribado sa ilalim ng PPP, hindi sila nagiisip kung paano nila seserbisyuhan ang mamamayan kung hindi ang kanilang itatayo niyan ay kung paano sila kikita o paano sila tutubo* [He thinks that he can make the country progress through its partnership with the private sector. But the interest of the private sector under PPP would not be about thinking ways to provide better service to the population—instead anything they build is meant to earn them profits].

He elaborated further:

*Eh di naglilipana na ngayon halos ang kalakhan ng mga eskwelahang kontrolado ng gobyerno binabalak isapribado. Yung mga ospital wala ka nang makita ngayon na government-owned and -controlled na ospital. Yung tubig, yung kuryente inasa sa pribado. Paano uunlad ang bayan? Paano uunlad ang mamamayan sa ilalim ng PPP? Ito'y nakikita ng gobyerno na ito raw yung madaling solusyon para umunlad ang gobyerno gawa ng wala raw gagastusin, pribado ang magpupundar. Pero yung income o yung tubo nito saan mapupunta? "Magbabayad," daw. Magbabayad lang ang negosyante na siyang nagkontrol ng isang negosyo ng buwis sa negosyo. Pero yung tubo noon hindi napupunta sa gobyerno nasa pribado. Sa kalagayan na yan, patuloy lang na malulugmok ang kalagayan ng mga mamamayan* [They're planning on privatizing public schools all over the place. There are hardly any government-owned and -controlled hospitals anymore. Water, electricity, they're all run by private corporations. How do you expect the country to develop? How will the people thrive under the PPP? The government sees PPP as the quickest solution for the country to progress because they say, this way, the state doesn't have to spend anything, the private sector would come up with the investment. But where would the income or profit go? "They'll pay," they say. The investor who controls the business would pay taxes. But the profits wouldn't go to the government, it would go to the investors. This way, the people's situation would only get worse].

Even before the inception of three Ps, as urban planning and policy development scholar Gavin Shatkin, drawing on 2003 data from the National Statistics Office, points out:

foreign direct investment and export-oriented industrial development have been highly concentrated in Metro Manila and its surrounding region, with Metro Manila and the Southern Tagalog region to its immediate south accounting for about 70% of the country's employment in medium to large manufacturing firms. (2009, 385–386)

In this manner, the city has not merely been affected by economic development and growth policies but, rather, reflects the very machinations of the country's growth and, consequently, uneven geographical development and corresponding social stratification (see Logan and Molotch 1987). Hence, the urban hub of the Philippines is the "paradigmatic global city" to which geographer Neil Smith refers, as the cityscape is "marked by extreme bifurcation of wealth and poverty, dramatic realignment of class relations, and dependence on new streams of immigrant labor" (2002, 430). And three Ps have exacerbated these preexisting divisions—former president Aquino III's premonition that every Filipino would become a beneficiary has not been realized, and the "progress" of which he has spoken has come at a price. A report produced by Urban Poor Associates (UPA), an independent eviction watchdog, notes that the year 2012 had the highest documented number of cases since UPA started monitoring in 1992. In this same year, "81 percent of evictions were illegal; almost none had certificates of compliance" (2012, 3).

An interview with Bing, another respondent, reverberated Jojie's concerns. In the middle of speaking, Bing switched over from Tagalog to Taglish to ensure that I took in the magnitude of his statement. He said gravely, "The genuine face, *yung mukha ng* [the face of] public-private partnerships, is a massive demolition." His companion Nobo provided an affirmative nod: "*Hindi maganda yung* public-private partnership [It's not good, this public-private partnership]." Elaborating on perceptions among the poor of the president's intentions, Bing continued,

> *Ang tingin lang natin dito no, di ginagamit nya itong mga ganitong klaseng issues para bumango sya sa mamamayan para sabihin nya sa mamamayan na merong ginagawa ang gobyerno para sa mga mahi-hirap sa usapin ng pabahay. Pero ang totoo nga, nakikita natin na ang mga programang ito ay nagluluwal lamang ng mga pagsasamantala sa anyo ng negosyo. Na ang programang pabahay ay hindi libre bagkus ito ay negosyo dahil ito ay pinagkakatiwala nya mismo sa mga priba-dong korporasyon* [We look at this as him using these kinds of issues so he would look good to the people, so he could tell the people that the government is doing something for the poor in terms of housing. But we see that this program only led to exploitation in the guise of business—that the housing program had become a business venture because it is being entrusted to private corporations].

Toward the end of my ethnographic study (most notably between 2010 and 2013), as my respondents struggled to protect their homes from the on-slaught of demolitions throughout the city, I observed new and shiny developments springing up everywhere—from the hyper-urbanized "the Fort" district in Taguig to Eastwood's "cyberpark" boasting luxury retailers. New shopping centers and condominiums peppered the C5 highway and Katipu-nan Avenue in Quezon City, overlooking the Miriam College, University of Philippines Diliman, and Ateneo de Manila University campuses. Men in polo shirts and beige khakis and women with rebonded (straightened) hair, fuchsia lipstick, and heels regularly approached me in Mandaluyong City's

SM Mega Mall and Tri-Noma (Triangle North of Manila), Quezon City's premier shopping center. These smiling sales agents eagerly offered me glossy informational pamphlets, outlining the merits of new developments such as "Blue Residences," where one could "live like a star." Promises of "glitz and glamour" crowded brochure covers, and the latest subdivision developments such as "the Ranch" boasted "hobby farms" where prospective new homeowners can cultivate their own crops "for fun."

Meanwhile, at the same time local elite and foreign investors clamored for development, poor Filipinos fled from and struggled with managing the consequences of it. Such economic growth schemes in the form of "redevelopment and infrastructure development has left to a large amount of dislocation of low-income households" (Shatkin 2009, 386–387). Former President Aquino III has portrayed demolitions as state-sponsored efforts to protect its citizenry: "We are already fulfilling our goal to remove from harm's way those who crammed themselves into high-risk areas of the city. After all, I do not think anyone will disagree with us when we say the current situation cannot be allowed to persist" (2013). He proceeded to cite the general welfare clause (Article 2, Section 5) in the Philippines Constitution: "The maintenance of peace and order, the protection of life, liberty and property, and the promotion of the general welfare are essential for the enjoyment by all the people of the blessings of democracy" (Ibid.). Continuing in this fourth State of the Nation Address, Noynoy further detailed:

Here we have proven that the Filipino listens to reason. If it is clear that compassion is your bedrock principle, then we will be more eager to work with you. Before roofs were dismantled, before walls were demolished, we explained how we came to our decision: better housing, access to public transport, and, for the diligent, no shortage of opportunities to earn. We made it clear that we wanted to provide a refuge to those who were high-risk and most in need. . . . After a batch of informal settlers was moved to the relocation site, they urged their former neighbors: Join us. It is safer here. This year, our priority is to relocate more than 19,4000 families living along Metro Manila's major waterways. (Ibid.)

But, for the majority of my interlocutors, the notion that the government has their best interests at heart and that every Filipino will reap the benefits three Ps has always been *buladas*, or empty talk. Ortega relates that "over the years, neoliberal policies have been legitimized and framed around efforts to build a 'globally competitive' nation by attracting foreign investments and by promoting entrepreneurialism, which will in turn provide much-needed jobs" (2012, 1125). But foreign direct investment (FDI) as a job creation strategy has not generated more jobs. One of the most recent decades (2001–2010) was the worst in the history of recorded unemployment in the Philippines (IBON Foundation 2012). And unemployment numbers during Aquino III's presidency were dismal: the unemployment rate of 10.9 percent "bolsters the longest sustained record-high unemployment in the country's history" (IBON Foundation 2013b). All of my respondents constantly struggled with making ends meet and managing the significant droughts of employment between contracts:

> Under Philippine labor law firms do not have the same obligations to provide benefits to contract employees, and are also freed from constraints posed by regulations regarding provision of proof of just cause for dismissal of permanent employees. . . . One study found that 43% of wage and salary employees are contractual. (Shatkin 2012, 387)

Shoring up a good business climate for investors and removing regulatory mechanisms have been key features of the state's development plan. Three Ps were thus part of a long-standing tradition of national progress at the expense of the poor. For instance, when Republic Act 7279, also known as the Urban Development and Housing Act (UDHA), a policy aimed to help the poor, was first signed into law on March 24, 1992, by former president Corazon Aquino, opponents suspected it would only legalize demolitions and land grabbing. Aimed at "uplift[ing] the condition of the underprivileged and homeless citizens in urban areas and in resettlement areas by making available to them decent housing at affordable cost, basic services, and employment opportunities," the act sought "to provide for the rational use and development of urban land in order to bring about access to land and housing by the underprivileged." Further, UDHA made explicit the extent to which the state would grant the private sector and NGOs incentives to invest their resources.

That said, land grabbing has been rampant not despite but, rather, *because* of particular government policies. Many of my respondents noted the spike in demolitions after the 1992 passage of the UDHA—in narratives of migration, "*Dinedemolish kami* [We were demolished]" was a common utterance among the majority of my working poor respondents. And, more pointedly, placing blame squarely on the shoulders of the perpetrator, one of my respondents, Elnora, explained, "*Eh, kinuha na ng gobyerno ang tinitirikan namin* [Eh, the government took the land we were settled on]," adding that it had erected a new office building in the place of her family's previous residence. After the NHA demolished their home in Quezon City in 1997, Elnora and her family moved to Caloocan City, toward the outskirts of Metro Manila and farther away from employment prospects. When I asked Elnora if the

NHA provided any relocation assistance, she was aghast: "*Hindi kami inintindi* [They didn't care about us]." Gesturing to her surrounding environment, the small house in which we sat and she and her family rented, she continued:

> *Hanggang three years lang tapos demolish na naman. Eh paano naman kaming mahihirap, palagi na lang kaming palipat-lipat kung saan kami itatapon. Para kaming mga basura, kung saan lang kami itapon* [We can only stay here three years, then they'll demolish us again. What happens to poor people then? They keep transferring us from one place to another. . . . We're just like garbage, they throw us anywhere].

A cab driver's statement echoed in my ears: "If you're poor, you have no place in this world." Another respondent, Gina, conveyed a similar sentiment, relating the state of chronic insecurity she experienced:

> *Kasi kumbaga pag-aari ka ng government mo, yung tinitirhan mo pag-aari ka dun. Pwede kang pwedeng sabihin nila daanin na lang sa sunog para mapaalis yung mga tao. Yun din po ang isang ano . . . kasi kadalasan ganoon po ang ginagawa ng mga malalaking kumpanya. Daanin na lang po sa dahas para mapaalis ang tao. . . . Para automatic na maalis na yung mga tao, para wala nang balikan yung mga tao. Ganun na lang po ang ginagawa nila. Hindi nap o sila tumingin sa mga tao na para walang matirahan . . . para mapaalis nila ang mga tao, sunugin na lang po. Kaya kawawa po yung taong mahihirap. Dun na po sa kalye natutulog. Kasi wala na pong matirahan eh. Hindi kagaya dito na walang magpapaalis* [It's like your government owns you, so your government owns where you live as well. They can just start fires to drive people out; that's what big companies usually do. They'll use this kind of violence to chase people away, to make sure they get out and have nothing to return to. They don't care if the people have nowhere to live . . . they just want to make sure people leave so they start fires. That's why people end up sleeping on the streets. There's nowhere left to live in. It's not like here, where nobody asks us to leave].

The violent demolitions experienced by poor Filipinos struggling to live and work in Metro Manila reflect the expulsion of what Philippine studies scholar Neferti Xina M. Tadiar terms "excess," which she defines as:

> the by-products of maldevelopment and mismanagement, to what is designated as informal production, that is, people who engage in activities recognized as nonproductive, unregulated and, hence, il-

legitimate according to the standards of the national economy. It is to this surplus population, which engages in 'unconventional' forms of livelihood, and its own by-products that the chaos of the street is attributed. (2004, 81)

Further, Tadiar's depiction of the state's urban renewal and sanitization processes as "bulimic" is a useful metaphor with which to flesh out the state's accumulation by dispossession processes and, more broadly, the contradictions of capital. It enables us to consider the government's fundamentally contradictory approach to the poor. On the one hand, in its efforts to attract potential investors, the state relies upon poor Filipino bodies. On the other hand, however, large-scale demolitions and forced relocation projects suggest the state's disdain for the very bodies on which its development initiatives based on cheap labor have been contingent. In effect, the bodies on which the economy relies and is built are excluded from full belonging or participation; they are valued only insofar as they continue to provide labor without demanding the right to housing. Social scientist Erhard Berner explicates that:

the proliferation of squatting, implying a large-scale violation of [property] rights, can no longer be seen as a temporary anomaly that will disappear in the course of development. We have to be aware that the role of squatter colonies is fundamental rather than marginal: the metropolitan economy is heavily subsidized by their existence, and cannot function—much less be competitive—without this subsidy. (2000, 57; see also Aldrich and Sandhu 1995, 20)

Herein lies another contradiction endemic to the state's development plan: to participate in the workforce, many Filipinos face the possibility of violent demolition as they struggle to remain within the city limits. Shatkin observed:

In the Metro Manila case, the Philippine government has undermined its own efforts in the areas of housing, transportation and economic development by fostering a condition of such pervasive insecurity of employment that households face fundamental contradictions between stability of land tenure and stability of job tenure. (2009, 406)

Local community organizer and anti-eviction activist Bing made this point most clearly:

*Kung wala kang trabaho eh di mahirap yung ano mo, yung situation mo kasi wala ka talagang pwedeng ano, wala kang pwedeng magawa kung nag uusap ka sa usapin ng bahay. Wala kang trabaho. Papano ka ngayon uupa ng bahay?. . . Kaya yung mga taong walang trabaho na majority ng papulasyon ng National Capital Region ay walang trabaho. Kaya nandun sila sa kalagayan na nasa squatter area, nasa urban poor, informal settler, yun. Sila ngayon yung prone to demolish* [If you have no job then your situation is difficult because you can do nothing in terms of housing. If you have no job how can you rent a house? . . . The majority of the people in the National Capital Region don't have a job—that why they are squatters, urban poor, informal settlers. They are the ones prone to demolition].

Yet, after the state has demolished people's homes and moved them to relocation sites, many of my respondents have found themselves worse off. Bing explained that relocation often made people's lives "more miserable." As we sat on the front stoop of his Quezon City house, we surveyed a street vendor down the street selling green mango with *bagoong*, or shrimp paste, and a neighbor across the way selling pastel-colored ice candy out of a small white Styrofoam cooler. Several houses on Bing's block exhibited *sari-sari* stores, offering anything from Smart and Globe phone load, colorful sachets of Palmolive shampoo and conditioner, to cigarettes, eggs, small C2-brand iced tea bottles as well as bags of ice. "*Dito nga sila kahit papano sumusurvive lang eh* [Here, at least they survive]." He explained that those struggling to survive are *diskarte* because, while they "try to find the means," they are not engaged in what the state would consider formal or desirable employment. As Tess, another respondent, put it, "*Kagaya namin, mahirap lang din kami diba? Pero tayo gumagawa tayo ng paraan para mabuhay* [We are poor, you know? But we do what we need to do to survive]." Indeed, the Metro Manila poor have become "managers of complex asset portfolios" (Moser 1998, 5; see also Berner 2000, 555–556), albeit not of their own choosing.

Despite government portrayal of aggregate growth as a public good, ethnographic detail indicates otherwise. First, respondents experienced *increased* insecurity and instability (often in the form of demolitions and forced relocation) with the country's economic growth. Second, the state rarely provided a relocation allowance to those displaced by demolitions. As twenty-one-year-old Malen, whose family was displaced from their Estero, Quezon City, residence in 2010 due to an MMDA road-widening project, explained:

*Wala silang* relocation [assistance], ma'am. *Kaya yung mga ibang id-edemolish doon, hindi umaalis kasi wala silang mabigay na tulong hindi nila binibigyan ng* relocation *yung mga gigibain nila kaya hindi umaalis* [They did not provide relocation [assistance], ma'am. That's why some people don't leave even if they've been demolished, because they don't relocate the people whose homes they destroy].

In fact, frequently government relocation packages included food packs of five to six kilos of rice, sardines, and maybe corned beef or noodles, but rarely significant financial relocation assistance (Urban Poor Associates 2012, 5–22). That said, the majority of my respondents were surprised by my question concerning government support after the demolition; lack of assistance was commonplace and expected.

And third, *if* families were "lucky enough" to obtain relocation assistance from the state, nongovernmental organizations (NGOs), or church groups, the site was very far from the city and employment. Respondents described significant disruption in conducting their "daily round," or manner in which they manage their daily life. In their book *Urban Fortunes: The Political Economy of Place*, coauthors John Logan and Harry Molotch expound:

> Defining a daily round is gradually accomplished as residents learn about needed facilities, their exact locations and offerings, and how taking advantage of one can be efficiently integrated into a routine that includes taking advantage of others. Routes and timings have to be carefully worked in a routine that includes taking advantage of others. Routes and timings have to be carefully worked out to achieve maximum benefits. The development of an effective array of goods and services within reach of residence is a fragile accomplishment; its disruption, either by the loss of one of the elements or by the loss of the residential starting place, can exact a severe penalty. (1987, 104)

For Malen, her experience living in her former residence Estero, a Quezon City waterway and what the government labeled a "danger area," was *masaya* (fun or happy). She continued:

> *Masaya kasi laro-laro kami tapos...yung tambay.... Tapos kapag may mga piyesta dun, sayaw-sayaw kami. Ganun. May* dance group *ako dati noong bata ako.... Kaya masaya noon* [It was fun because we would play and hang out. Whenever there was a fiesta we would go and dance. I had a dance group when I was young, and that's what made me happy].

She reflected:

> *Noong lumipat na kami sa Montalban, siyempre wala pa akong mga* friends *na bago.... Parang naninibago ako sa lugar.... Tinatamad akong mag-aral, tinatamad akong mag-aral* [When we transferred to Montalban I had no friends.... It felt strange being in a new environment. I had no drive to study].

In this way, the demolition and subsequent displacement experienced by Malen had a tremendous impact on her education and the informal support networks upon which she depended.

Now, certainly, many of those who relocated acknowledged the extent to which their new house was an improvement from their previous residence—on some level, it represented a new level of security. Malen communicated that:

*Kung pinaayos namin yun tapos dinemolish, sayang ang ano,* expenses *na inano namin. Eh ngayon nagkaroon kami ng sariling bahay sa Montalban. Doon na lang namin pinaayos yung bahay namin. Pinagawa namin, pina-ano, ganun-ganon. Tapos okay naman ngayon. Kaya nga yun nga lang malayo* [If we constructed that house beautifully, one day a demolition team could just smash it into pieces and that would be a waste of money. But now we can renovate and beautify our own house here in Montalban. The only thing is that it's far].

Nevertheless respondents also related the hardship facing them as a result of the demolition(s) that displaced them and subsequent relocation. Bing pointed out, drawing on his extensive experience working as an urban poor housing advocate:

*Sa unang tingin mo maganda. Pero kung iisipin mo pa rin naman kasi, aanuhin mu naman yang maganda yung bahay mo kung wala ka namang makakain, di ba? Papano mo maimemaintain din yung bahay mo* [It looks good at first glance. But if you think about it, what will you do with a beautiful house if you have nothing to eat, right? How can you maintain your house]?

Tess and her family moved to a neighborhood in Montalban in 2010 with the assistance of their church after the MMDA demolished their home in Quezon City to make way for a road-widening project. While grateful to the church for their new house, which was big compared to their previous residence, she expressed frustration:

*Malayo kasi* ma'am *ano eh hindi pa siya gaano ka-*urban *yung area. Hindi pa ganoon nadedevelop kasi ano talaga ito eh* province. *Dati kasi ito nung hindi pa tinatayuan ng gobyerno ng pabahay . . . ano yung mga palayan, bundok ganyan. So wala talaga siyang wala ka talagang makukuhang trabaho dito depende kung dito ka na talaga nabuhay* [It's just far from my current job. The relocation area is far from being an urban area. It's not really developed—it really is a province,

Tess pointing out the vast farmland outside her family's new relocation site, November 17, 2011. (From the author.)

you know? This used to be a rice field, a mountain. You'll find it difficult searching for work here unless you are born here].

She continued emphatically, "*So hindi naman porket ililipat ka sa isang lugar, bahay lang kailangan mo. . . . Siyempre kailangan mo ng hanapbuhay* [We don't need just a house—we also need a livelihood . . . that's why you'll hear housing beneficiaries selling their houses to other people because of this. You can't even get a sideline job here]." To emphasize the distance, her sister Malen added, "*Maglalakbay pa po ng isa't kalahating oras* [We need to travel one and a half hours to get to the nearest hospital]." Tess jumped in, "*Oo! Papaano kapag emergency? Papaano mamatay ka na lang dyan* [Yes! What if it's an emergency? You're gonna die here]."

Like the sisters Tess and Malen, Rhea, another respondent, had similar struggles concerning employment, as well as demolitions and displacement—lots of moving either within the city and/or between the city and province. Originally from Bicol, Rhea moved to Metro Manila in search of employment. After meeting her husband in the city and the birth of their first child, Rhea moved back to Bicol in hopes of finding permanent work and starting a life there with her husband and new child. She quickly added,

"*Bumalik kami sa Bicol. Pero* after a year, *balik na naman kami dito sa Manila tapos balik naman kami doon* [We went home to Bicol. But after a year, we were back in Manila, back to where we were]." They moved back and forth for several years because it was difficult to find work:

> *Hanggang noong ano marami na nga sila . . . kasi minsan kapag uuwi kami dito, maiiwan yung ibang anak doon. Nagdesisyon kami na pumirme na dito. . . . Tapos nag-*demolish *doon* [That continued until we had more children. Sometimes when we went back to Manila, some of our children remained behind in Bicol. Finally we decided to stay put here. Then there was a demolition].

Sponsored by the NHA, the demolition made way for new office space. While the NHA partnered with Philippines-based NGO *Gawad Kalinga* ("to give care") to procure housing for Rhea and her family, at the time of our interview, she had yet to receive any paperwork indicating lease or ownership. In this vein, as the new concrete house provided a sense of security (e.g., it could withstand heavy rains during typhoon season), it also introduced more insecurity. Rhea confided, "*Mahirap kasi ano parang lagi kang nangangamba na . . . kasi temporary* [It's hard because it's like you're always worrying . . . because it's only temporary]." And, similar to Tess, Rhea was discouraged concerning the dearth of employment opportunities in the remote village to which she and her family had relocated. Put bluntly, she weighed in, "*Yung* livelihood, *hindi nagfu-*function *dito sa lugar na ito eh* [The livelihood program doesn't work in this place]."

Respondents thus continued to work in the city even if government-sponsored demolitions had pushed them to the outskirts of Metro Manila. The majority of them bemoaned the high *pamasahe*, or fare—round-trip fare could cost more than a third of daily wages. Nevertheless, many developed creative ways to circumvent the long and expensive commute. Malen described:

> *Papa ko, stay-in siya sa trabaho.* Thursday at Sunday *lang siya umuuwi para tipid sa pamasahe. Kasi Quezon Ave siya malayo din kung Montalban uuwian. Eh sa amin naman hindi pwedeng mag-stay in kasi hindi pwede dyang matulog* [My dad, he stays at his work. He goes home only Thursdays and Sundays to save money for transportation because he works on Quezon Avenue, which is far from home. But me, I don't stay because I'm not allowed to sleep in the salon].

The manner in which workers have managed their marginality and dispossession might be aptly termed what Smith refers to as "desperate resilience." As he puts it:

Extraordinarily, chaotic and arduous commutes have not yet led to an economic breakdown; the impulses of economic productions—and, especially, the need to have workers turn up at the workplace—have taken precedence over any constraints emanating front the conditions of social reproduction. The rigors of almost unbearable commuting have not yet compromised economic production. Instead, they have elicited a "desperate resilience" and been absorbed amidst the wider social breakdown that Katz (forthcoming) calls "disintegrating developments." (2002, 436)

Six days a week, Malen caught a tricycle to a jeepney, transferring to a bus in the CBD (central business district) of her province, then again to a different jeepney. Winding down mountains and narrow roads, she passed through Tandang Sora, then got onto the C-5 highway, also known as CP Garcia Avenue, on which she would remain until her final stop on Katipunan Avenue. The entire trip took her anywhere from two and a half to three and a half hours, depending on traffic. On a daily basis, Malen faced the heat, heavy smog emanating from jeepneys sitting in traffic, and cramped seating with no complaint. When I described my commute from Marikina City upon arrival to her house in Montalban, Malen nodded solemnly, "*Malayo* [It's far]."

An overwhelming number of respondents slept at their workplaces or were "bed spacers," renting a bed in hopes of saving money and to avoid commuting daily. Urban poor neighborhood organizer Jojie explained the circumstances he faced as a result of the demolition he and his family experienced:

*Tapos ang tinitirahan kong bahay noon na-demolish. Tapos lumipat ako sa Payatas natabunan ng basura. Tapos lumipat na ako ng Montalban. Doon naging organizer na ako . . . dito sa office namin. Ang problema malayo. Gagastos kang ng 70 to 100 pesos sa isang araw. Dahilan naman sa volunteer ako, ang ginagawa ko sa office ako tumitira. Once or twice a month saka ako umuuwi sa pamilya. Sa office, eh di madali akong nakakatulong doon sa mga problema ng mga maralita sa usapin partikular sa paninirahan, anumang tipo ng usapin . . . Totoong sakripisyo ang ginagawa namin. Hindi mo matatawag na sweldo ang natatanggap mong allowance kahit sa pansarili ko ay kulang. Tumatanggap ako ng allowance, 1000 kung meron sa isang buwan. Kaya yun din ang isang dahilan paano ako makakaipon ng pauntiunti para pagdating ng panibagong unang linggo ng buwan, saka lang ako uuwi. Yung isang libo na yun babawasan ko pa ng pamashe, yun ang ibibigay ko sa pamilya ko* [The first house I lived in got demolished. So I transferred to Payatas, where my house collapsed under an avalanche of garbage. After that incident I became an organizer in our office here. The problem is that the office is far. I would have to spend around 70 to 100 pesos per day. Since I'm a volunteer, I decided to live here in the office. I go home to see my family once or twice a month. Here, it's easy for me to help the poor with housing issues, or any other issues, really . . . you can say that it's a sacrifice doing this work. You can't really call what I'm getting a salary, it's not even enough for me. I would only receive a thousand pesos every month. I can save a little bit of it, so at the first week of the month I can go home. I take out my fare from that a thousand and give whatever's left to my family].

Such efforts to manage or offset the expensive commute, however, often created repercussions for family time. Ester's husband worked in construction in Taguig, where he received 350 pesos per day. But his round-trip fare was 120 pesos. As a he result, he would come home to Caloocan City once a week, every Saturday evening. Then he would leave again Sunday night. Ester explained:

*Family day namin iyon. Nag-chuchurch kami, namamasyal. . . . Bonding namin na matutulog kami lahat. Manunuod kami. Iyon lang iyong time naming . . . mahirap kasi—dati kasi araw-araw umuuwi siya. Kailan lang naman siya nagstay kasi mahirap nga ang pamasahe. . . . Noong magstay siya doon, parang hindi kami sanay na wala. Sinasanay na lang namin, wala naman akong baby. Pero noong maliliit sila hanggang lumaki sila . . . inaalagaan niya na everyday* [Sunday is our family day. We go to church and go out for walks. We make sleeping time bonding time. We watch movies. He used to come home every day. But recently he has to live at work because the fare costs too much. When he started doing that it took us a while to get used to him not being here. But we endure, at least now we don't have a baby. But he used to look after our children from when they were small].

Another respondent, Jean, who worked as a nail technician in Quezon City, also traveled home once a week to spend time with her daughter, who she left in the care of her mother in their house in Rizal Province, outside the city limits. During the week, she stayed in a boarding house near her employment. She expressed guilt about being away from her daughter but shrugged, "What am I supposed to do?"

Another theme that emerged among interviews with my respondents was the difficulty they faced regarding water and electricity. Some had limited access. Others had to pay an exorbitant amount to obtain these services. In the case of Malen and Tess, they had neither water nor electricity connections despite living in their new house for a year. For electricity, they "borrowed" from their neighbors. In terms of water, Malen explained that they fetched it from the neighborhood water pump. "*Wala kami noong gripo-gripo ganun. . . . Ang tubig namin per drum-drum* [We have no faucet yet. . . . The water we have now is stored in big containers]." Her sister Tess clarified that they were still waiting to receive their own water meter. And while it was rather inconvenient to wake up early and line up to fetch water before work or, if they were able, to find someone to do it for them, at least it was much cheaper than what they were expecting to pay with the installation of their water meter. Exclaimed Tess, "Thrice *siguro ang presyo kasi kung may sarili kang metro ng tubig* [The rate is thrice the price if you have your own water meter]."

## Conclusion

Toward the final leg of my research in Metro Manila, former president Aquino III boasted in his third State of the Nation Address, "Isn't it great to be a Filipino living in these times?" Here I have highlighted the incongruence between how neoliberal policies are drafted and how they have been experienced in Metro Manila. As government officials and local elites in the Philippines framed the benefits of three Ps as indiscriminate, ethnographic detail reveals otherwise. Key Marxist geographers such as Neil Smith and David Harvey, among many others, have elucidated the contradictions of capital, most notably theorizing accumulation by dispossession processes. Here, however, in drawing on my own observations and interviews, I bring to the fore the manifestations of public-private partnerships in a specific context and the *particular* ways in which working poor people experience and mitigate the devastation of uneven geographical development and ancillary accumulation by dispossession processes.

What's more, I demonstrate the extent to which neoliberal restructuring took on a new form in the Philippines under Noynoy's leadership. Urban renewal processes under neoliberal governance, dating back to the Marcos dictatorship era, involved either the concealment or expulsion of the poor and their activities. Since then, beautification projects such as Metro Gwapo: Urban Facelift aimed to sanitize public space through the often-violent removal of street vendors as well as informal settlers in attempts to shore up foreign investment. But the advent of Noynoy's three Ps signals a noteworthy shift in how the Philippine government came to legitimate present-day demolitions and the displacement of the poor. Whereas previous administrations framed demolitions as the removal of the "urban blight" impeding its efforts to shore up an attractive business climate, in recent years, it has rationalized demolitions as a necessary prerequisite for the progress from which all will benefit. But the poor have borne an inordinate amount of the burden, absorbing the majority of the government's risky business ventures and partnerships with private investors. Moreover, in this alphabet soup of macro-adjustment in the Philippines, as three Ps supplant SAPs, it is imperative to consider the broader implications of such a transition. Only by bringing ethnographic detail to bear on theories of uneven geographical development will we be able to both illuminate the extent to which this shift in neoliberal restructuring reflects a new era of neoliberal governance as well as reveal the social actors who benefit from such "progressive" development policies.

## NOTES

Acknowledgment: This piece is dedicated to Karletz "Lito" Badion, who dedicated his life to fighting for Metro Manila's urban poor. Funding for this research was provided by the National Science Foundation.

1. The Philippines-based not-for-profit research institute IBON Foundation has published extensive studies showing that it was during this period that the seeds for growing peasant unrest were planted. Also, Philippine scholar and activist Jose Maria Sison has argued that "the illusion of land reform is also conjured by the formal conversion of a few hundreds of thousands of rice and corn tenants into so-called leaseholders who remain tenants in areas where there is yet no armed peasant movements. . . . The system has been devised as a counterinsurgency measure." See Sison and de Lima, *Philippine Economy and Politics*, 36.

## BIBLIOGRAPHY

ABS-CBN News. "Aquino Issues EO 8 Creating Public-Private Partnership Center." *ABS-CBN News*, September 12, 2012.

Aldrich, Brian C., and Ravinder S. Sandhu, eds. *Housing the Urban Poor: Policy and Practice in Developing Countries*. London: Zed Books, 1995.

Alternative Forum for Research in Mindanao (AFRIM). "Where Does the Road Lead To?" In *Mindanao Focus Report*. Davao City: Alternative Forum for Research in Mindanao, 2005.

Aquino, Benigno. "First State of the Nation Address." Session Hall of the House of Representatives, Batasang Pambansa Complex, Quezon City, Philippines, July 26, 2010.

———. "Fourth State of the Nation Address." Session Hall of the House of Representatives, Batasang Pambansa Complex, Quezon City, Philippines, July 22, 2013.

———. "Third State of the Nation Address." Session Hall of the House of Representatives, Batasang Pambansa Complex, Quezon City, Philippines, July 23, 2012.

Bello, Walden, et al. *The Anti-Development State: The Political Economy of Permanent Crisis in the Philippines*. London: Zed Books, 2005.

Berner, Erhard. "Poverty Alleviation and the Eviction of the Poorest: Towards Urban Land Reform in the Philippines." *International Journal of Urban and Regional Research* 24, no. 3 (2000): 554–566.

Binay, Jejomar. "Address." Philippines Real Estate Festival (PREF), World Trade Center, Pasay City, Philippines, July 26–28, 2012.

Bing. Personal interview. February 9, 2012.

Carrier, James G., and Paige West, eds. *Virtualism, Governance and Practice: Vision and Execution in Environmental Conservation.* Oxford: Berghahn Books, 2009.

di Leonardo, Micaela. "Introduction." In *New Landscapes of Inequality: Neoliberalism and the Erosion of Democracy in America,* edited by Jane L. Collins, Micaela di Leonardo, and Brett Williams, 3–19. Santa Fe: School for Advanced Research Press, 2008.

Ellao, Janess Ann J. "Tens of Thousands Gather Vs. Pork Barrel as Aquino Gov't Skirts the Issue." *Bulatlat News,* August 28, 2013.

———. "26 Years After Mendiola Massacre, Farmers Still Fight for Genuine Land Reform." *Bulatlat News,* January 25, 2013.

Elnora. Personal interview. May 9, 2012.

Ester. Personal interview. January 26, 2012.

Gina. Personal interview. November 17, 2011.

Guerrero, Amado. *Philippine Society and Revolution.* Quezon City: Aklat ng Bayan, 1970.

Harvey, David. *A Brief History of Neoliberalism.* Oxford: Oxford University Press, 2004.

———. *Spaces of Global Capitalism: Toward a Theory of Uneven Geographical Development.* London: Verso, 2006.

IBON Foundation. *IBON Economic and Political Briefing.* Quezon City: IBON Foundation, January 10–11, 2013a.

———. "Neoliberal Offensive: Impact on Agrarian Reform in the Philippines." In *Neoliberal Subversion of Agrarian Reform.* Ujjaini Halim, ed. Quezon City: Asia-Pacific Research Network, 2006, 59–141.

———. "Philippine Report to UN: No Improvement in Economic Rights Situation in PH." *IBON News,* May 18, 2012: n.p.

———. "Rising Joblessness and Increasing Poor-Quality Work Refute Inclusive Growth." *IBON News,* September 11, 2013b: n.p.

IMF. *Public-Private Partnerships.* International Monetary Fund, March 12, 2004: n.p., December 8, 2013.

Jean. Personal interview. February 1, 2012.

Jojie. Personal interview. January 25, 2011.

Logan, John R., and Harry L. Molotch. *Urban Fortunes: The Political Economy of Place.* Berkeley: University of California Press, 1987.

Malen. Personal interview. November 17, 2011.

Moser, Caroline O. N. "The Asset Vulnerability Framework: Reassessing Urban Poverty Reduction Strategies." *World Development* 26, no. 1 (1998): 1–19.

Nobo. Personal interview. February 9, 2012.

Ortega, Arnisson Andre C. "*Desakota* and Beyond: Neoliberal Production of Suburban Space in Manila's Fringe." *Urban Geography* 33, no. 8 (2012): 1118–1143.

Peet, Richard. *Unholy Trinity: The IMF, World Bank and WTO.* 2nd ed. London: Zed Books, 2009.

RA 7279 UDHA. March 24, 1992.

Rhea. Personal interview. May 9, 2012.

Rodriguez, Robyn. *Migrants for Export: How the Philippine State Brokers Labor to the World.* Minneapolis: University of Minnesota Press, 2010.

Roy, Arundhati. *Field Notes on Democracy.* Chicago: Haymarket Books, 2009.

Salamat, Marya. "Aquino Deserves 'Pork Barrel King' Tag-KMU." *Bulatlat News,* October 3, 2013.

Samaniego, Theresa S. "Inspired Real Estate Success." Business Section, *Philippine Daily Inquirer,* May 4, 2012, n.p.

Shatkin, Gavin. "The Geography of Insecurity: Spatial Change and the Flexibilization of Labor in Metro Manila." *Journal of Urban Affairs* 31, no. 4 (2009): 381–408.

Sison, Jose Maria, and Julieta de Lima. *Philippine Economy and Politics.* Quezon City: Aklat ng Bayan, 1998.

Smith, Neal. "New Globalism, New Urbanism: Gentrification as Global Urban Strategy." *Antipode* 34, no. 3 (2002): 427–450.

Tadiar, Neferti Xina M. "Metropolitan Dreams." In *Fantasy-Production: Sexual Economies and Other Philippine Consequences for the New World Order,* 77–112. Quezon City: Ateneo de Manila University Press, 2004.

Tess. Personal interview. November 17, 2011.

Tsing, Anna Lowenhaupt. *Friction: An Ethnography of Global Connection.* Princeton: Princeton University Press, 2005.

Urban Poor Associates (UPA). *Eviction Monitoring.* Quezon City: Urban Poor Associates, 2012.

Urban Poor Resource Center of the Philippines (UPRCP). *UPRC Update: Urban Poor Data and Analysis.* Quezon City: Urban Poor Research Center of the Philippines, October 2011.

Whaley, Floyd. "As Some Filipinos Gain, Poverty Tightens Its Grip." *New York Times,* June 20, 2013, B4.

# Recalling to Sitio San Roque

*Countermapping Urban Spaces in Quezon City*

VANESSA BANTA

Against a backdrop of lush urban greenery, we first see the now-ubiqui-
tous map icon and Sitio San Roque in bold red. Yet before we can even
begin to settle, the camera pans immediately to its right, past the busy
highway and the sound of a motorcycle zooming by—a sound that tells us we
are indeed in Quezon City, Manila. Then, the real Sitio San Roque appears in
the frame. In the foreground are Yumi and Jawi, dressed in matching baby-
pink hazmat suits and bright-blue face masks and with their thermometers
in hand. Oozing pink, fun, and resplendence against the backdrop of gray,
Yumi and Jawi strike poses à la Charlie's Angels and issue us, the viewers, a
welcoming greeting. What is supposed to follow is a serious and sobering
look into the life conditions of those who still currently live in Sitio San Roque
under President Rodrigo Duterte's "enhanced community quarantine" during COVID-19. But before that, Jawi backs up and falls to the ground. A
moment of laughter before the grim.

This piece marks a return to Sitio San Roque. A few years ago, collaborators and I conducted a performance countermapping project together with
some residents of Sitio San Roque. Drawing from the power of art and performance to provide different means to apprehend, reimagine, and engage
with the community,[1] our countermapping project took on two main objectives. First, we used art installations and performances to contest what we
believed constituted the dominant visual archive of urban "informal settlements" like Sitio San Roque. At that time, we believed that the visual archive
of San Roque only reflected the unjust turning of residents' indignant pro-

test and resistance into dissidence and unlawfulness, with the poor and the homeless of Sitio San Roque cast as perpetrators rather than casualty in what some have called an "urban battle zone" at the heart of Quezon City. Considered as the last standing impediment for a massive development project in Quezon City, San Roque, in fact, has had to withstand numerous kinds of tactical attacks to break up the community and finally displace them from their homes. Therefore, we presented visual art, mixed media, and performances based on interviews with residents and local activists from Sitio San Roque. This was primarily to render visible the everyday lives of the urban poor in Manila whose stories of displacement remain understudied.[2]

Second, we aimed to explore through countermapping and performance how we could reconnect spaces, reestablish relationships, and forge new alliances. Critical research on Manila have thus far rightly examined the processes through which the Philippine state has created and continues to create urban fantasies of highways, high-rise condominiums, and mega shopping centers as evidence of economic development.[3] Dominant in accounts is the state's influence on a kind of urban development that is based on dreams of "beautification," thus causing the erasure of what is considered mere urban blight and the destruction of so-called "squatter" communities.[4] However, as of late, a few scholars have also argued that this aesthetic vision is not as centralized in the heads of state and local government heads alone. Rather, it is shared as reflected in the numerous public-private partnerships responsible for urban change that is heavily skewed to the interests of the Metro Manila elite. Building on analyses that focus on the numerous exclusions and segregations that these partnerships have engendered,[5] our aim was to use performance/countermapping as a way to initiate the creation of a new space wherein people, separated by spatial and social distance, could forge new relational ways of being. The goal was therefore not simply to change people's perceptions about San Roque. It was to bring them into a stronger alliance with residents of San Roque in their struggle to keep their homes, families, and lives in their community.

In this chapter, I foreground the ways in which performance and countermapping may be used as a tool to work toward rewriting dominant urban scripts that have long excluded the working class and the urban poor in Manila. Although I describe the night of the performance with some detail, the intention is not to evaluate the performance for its aesthetic merits. Nor is it to argue that true and perfect alliance was achieved through this single performance alone. Rather, I draw our attention to key moments of our collaborative, creative process wherein empathy and solidarity did not emerge as immediately as we had hoped. These critical moments lay bare some of the underlying tensions and possibilities that come with putting to work what the editors refer to as the "dialogic nature of beauty and brutality" as lens to view, apprehend, and engage with Manila. Despite the messy, uncomfortable, and even antagonistic feelings this work might produce, however, I argue that performance bears the potential to create and solidify concrete praxis, specifically oriented to the struggles of Sitio San Roque and other urban poor.

## Placing the Performance

Quezon City, the most populated city in all of Metro Manila, as it is often told, was born out of the "Quezonian dream" of the first Commonwealth president of the Philippines, Manuel L. Quezon. The city's glorious beginnings are attributed to the creative and visionary leadership of the first president. In addition to envisioning Quezon City as the seat of the national government, Quezon had grand economic plans for the city. The local government's historical records tell the story of the "benevolent" Quezon, who intended to build a "working man's paradise" for employees and laborers in 1939 to address what would be the "population explosion" problem of crowded Manila. However, Quezon's vision of a "dignified concentration of human life, aspirations, endeavors and achievements," composed of both the rich and poor, never truly materialized. Because the price of land in Quezon City was far too high for the minimum wage workers, Quezon City would essentially become more of a suburb for middle-class professionals and government workers from Manila who became the actual beneficiaries of the government's housing projects, superior roads, and other transport services.[6]

Seventy years after Quezon's pronouncement of his vision, the local government and private corporations would continue to invoke a similar urban developmental model for a "productive" and "self-contained" Quezon City. This is made possible through the creation of the 250-hectare Quezon City Central Business District (QC-CBD). With five distinct commercial, residential, and recreational districts, the QC-CBD is expected to maximize the city's "large parcels of land" and thus harness the area's economic potential. In 2009, Ayala Land, the real estate arm of one of the nation's biggest conglomerates, the Philippine National Housing Authority, and the Quezon City local government forged a joint agreement. Through this public-private partnership, Ayala Land would invest PHP 65 billion pesos over a period of ten years to build Vertis North, a twenty-nine-hectare premier, mixed-use business district composed of offices, retail spaces, a hotel, and residential buildings. Vertis North is the biggest investment of Ayala Land, to be built exactly on the land where Sitio San Roque currently sits. Thus, to turn what the government has been calling "idle land" into "productive use," Ayala Land, the NHA, and the local government must clear all of Sitio San Roque, a community that is home to fifteen thousand families of "informal settlers."

The violence that accompanies this spatial clearing must never be under-estimated.[7] In fact, a few of our students sought to perform the direct violence experienced by San Roque residents either through their choreographed dance pieces or performance art. The project itself as a whole, however, was also concerned with how these urban development visions imposed what Ghertner terms "grid of norms."[8] Similar to what he observed in Delhi, the local government and private developers have worked in tandem to disseminate a powerful aesthetic vision of Quezon City as simultaneously beautiful *and* economically productive over the years. For example, from the comfortable movie theater seat of Trinoma Mall (short for Triangle North of Manila), a large shopping mall owned by Ayala Land that sits on the twenty-hectare land beside Sitio San Roque, one is always made to view its various Ayala advertisements: gone are the heavy traffic, never-ending lines for public transport, and shanties for the homeless of Quezon City. Instead, in these fantastical depictions, urban dwellers move with ease from one shiny Ayala development to the next and through pristine landscapes of posh concrete and greenery. "There's room for everyone" to work hard, move, and expand, according to one advertisement. Ghertner argues in his work that there is more at stake to this kind of "aesthetic governmentality." In addition to marking the distinctions between beautiful spaces and those that are deplorable, it also produces the subjects who share in this aesthetic urban vision. One Ayala commercial even makes explicit use of art in its attempt to shape the ideal Manila resident. One commercial features young Filipino visual artists working on artwork, which were later placed together to form one bigger canvas forming "PILIPINAS" in large, blocked letters. Here, the commercial unfolds a new urban dramaturgy from which a new Manila urban dweller is set to arise—a young, hip, and creative denizen who commits to "build the nation" one Ayala development at a time. Thus, part of our concern too was the teachers, students, and other members of our university who share the same Quezon City space with San Roque residents. In other words, we aimed for the project to be a means through which we could reflect upon our own understandings of space—have we begun to see San Roque as reprehensible space due to its nonconformity to the city's established norm of beauty, development, and productivity?

If the roles of the local government and the private developer are more apparent, the role of our university is less so. Since the University of the Philippines was moved to its current location north of San Roque in 1937, the university has always been imbricated in the local government's plan for the city to become the "center of gravity" of business and commercial activity. Specifically, as the acknowledged "epicenter" of the Knowledge Community District of the QC-CBD, UP serves as an important nodal point for business more generally.[9] Aside from major businesses being developed close to the university, UP has also opened its own doors to major corporations for profit due to diminishing public funding for tertiary education. To "increase their self-financing capacity,"[10] UP has also initiated its own income-generation programs such as increased tuition, the privatization of food and other services, and the leasing of its "idle" land to Ayala. Despite protests by residents of San Roque and several student activists from UP,[11] Ayala Land went ahead in building UP-Ayala TechnoHub, an "economic zone" that converted UP land to cater to local and foreign outsourcing companies. In 2013, Ayala Land built another commercial complex called U.P. Town Center on the other side of campus, which was heavily advertised as an "industry and academic collaboration" and as the "first and only university town center." What made U.P. Town Center distinct from UP-Ayala TechnoHub is its blatant claims to "support for the needs of the community" by providing an interactive space "conducive to free expression, skills development and discourse."[12] This mission, according to Ayala, reflects the university's goals to foster the minds of the country.

Lest all these be read as simply an encroachment of business, reading the fine print reveals the university's use of similar rhetoric once employed by Quezon. According to the most recent development plans of the university, economic development for the UP community will depend on successful enclosure and containment of UP space. In the next few years, UP aims to secure all land titles and assets of the university to accelerate their commercialization.[13] However, according to the plan, this also means that "academic zones" must be "defined and protected from illegal occupants."[14] Although there also have been pronouncements about the administration "working with the community" and how residents will be "treated with sensitivity, compassion and social justice,"[15] UP officials have always remained silent on how their plans to relocate the many residents of the thirteen communities considered as informal settlements on campus will be implemented.[16] What is certain, however, is that there will be thirteen communities in total that will join Sitio San Roque on the list of areas to be demolished and then "developed" as part of the Quezon City Central Business Development Plan.

Here, I highlighted the ways in which a dominant visual regime of urban development has made its way through and across local government institutions, private developers and even our public university. This visual regime, we believed, does not merely serve as underlying logic for the violent demolitions of "informal" communities, it also shapes people's understanding of and, hence, their movements and relations within that space. Therefore, although we can perhaps assume a shared feeling of frustration and exhaustion that comes with living and working in QC, we would be remiss not to acknowledge that others may find themselves subscribing to the same aesthetic vision that excludes the urban poor. Given the specific context of our neoliberalizing university, for example, we also had to reckon with the fact that some of our students are being pulled more strongly into the commercial spaces of Ayala and away from the lived struggles and concerns of San Roque and other informal communities that surround our campus. Some of our students—future architects, urban planners, geographers, and artists—though not explicitly in support of violent demolitions by the state, shared very early on their consternations regarding San Roque's resistance. These students outrightly viewed the community's resistance to demolitions and relocations as baseless rejection of state-led and private developer–sponsored acts of benevolence.

## Confronting Urban Tensions

The tensions, limitations, and challenges in participatory mapping projects have been the subject of many scholarly works in the field of critical cartography. While most works affirm the power of maps to counter and to make geographies concealed by the dominant hegemonic maps visible, serious concern also has been expressed that maps as *objects* reinscribe colonial exclusions or reinforce neoliberal governance policies.[17] Sletto (2015) suggests that theories of performativity provide ways to go beyond the paradox formed by "apparent contradiction between emancipatory goals (through visibilization) and cartographic violence (through erasure) of counter-mapping."[18] For Sletto, this theoretical turn enables a more processual understanding of *how* maps are brought into being through context-specific mechanisms that involve "embodied, social and technical" practices of cartographers, participants and institutions.[19] If we take the view that maps are practices and are "always mappings,"[20] then close attunement to a map's "unfolding life" will not only reveal how its meanings are being debated, challenged, and negotiated.[21] It could also lead to the expansion of the scope of any cartographic analysis or practice beyond the making of maps and into other practices such as the reading or the "audiencing" of maps as constitutive of the "continuum" of participation and map-making.[22]

Directing our attention to the relational components of the *process* of mapmaking also brings us closer to the work of feminist cartographers and geographers who continue to argue for the inclusion of bodies and emotions as constitutive to spaces that are mapped.[23] In this body of scholarly literature, emotions are given the due recognition as "socio-spatial mediation and articulation rather than as entirely interiorized subjective mental states."[24] Urban geographers in particular shed light on the different and complex affective practices of place-making of city residents including youth, the poor, and the homeless; these scholars demonstrate that while we can trace the city inhabitants' movements in and between their "assigned" spaces, they also rewrite and remake alternate spaces of city living.[25] Scholar Till, for example, in his retheorization of postcolonial cities as "wounded," argues that the city inhabitants' affective practices of mourning, memory work, and care enact a kind of "active citizenship" toward creating a more socially just city.[26]

Our project is understandable within these two literatures, but also pushes the notion of performativity and mapping further by explicitly bringing mapping into performance and by unpacking the many challenges of the making of this performance/map. The difficulties we encountered in bringing our students to San Roque and "requiring" their participation, also their "feelings of resistance" to listen, encounter, and join the urban poor residents of San Roque, drove us to explore how countermapping performances could serve as spaces for "dialogic empathy."[27] Reflecting upon these challenges is necessary if we wish to guard against facile claims of "co-feeling" with the communities we work with.

## In Place, Together

Entitled *Lugar: Counter-Mapping Mega Manila*, the performance that we created in collaboration with the residents of San Roque sought to first and foremost challenge the prevailing image of San Roque. Site plans and flat illustrations of mega constructions, along with shiny advertisements for the upcoming "developments" in the area, conceal the violent destruction of the many homes that remain in San Rogue and are vital to the lives of these residents. At the same time, official maps enshroud San Roque as a terrain of poverty, illegality, or irrational rebellions and of urban degradation. Through a mix of documentary methods such as surveys, audio and video recordings, photography, and one-on-one and group interviews, we gathered narratives that contest these dominant depictions of the place and people of San Roque. Selected transcripts were then transformed to short performances and installations presented for one night in March 2013 in an exhibit in the small black box theater inside the University of the Philippines. That night, residents of San Roque arrived on our campus to be part of the audience. With them were our students, their friends, and other members of the UP community; most of the university community had not set foot inside San Roque.

To countermap the space of San Roque and our university, our major objective was to dislodge the stable position of the Cartesian viewing subject who tends to view San Roque and its residents as a complete, knowable whole inside the theater and out. This meant destabilizing the very strong foundations of the university theater department in Western modern dramatic techniques by doing away with the figure of the sole playwright, often tasked with writing a dramatic text with a beginning, a middle, and an end. Also,

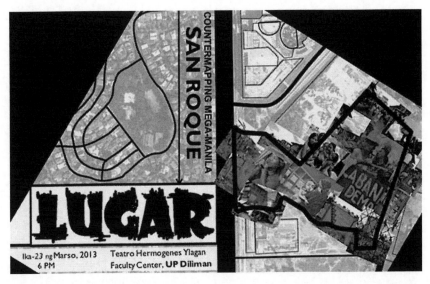

*Lugar: Countermapping Mega-Manila* poster. (Photo courtesy of Arnisson Ortega. Used with permission.)

efforts were made not to privilege one resident's story over another through typical action-driven plots wherein characters get locked in a narrative and telos that end up reproducing hegemonic ideologies.[28] More importantly, we explored how we could use performance itself to expose the perceptual practices of our audience. In other words, by presenting both beauty and brutality together in their entangled mess, we wanted to challenge our students to reflect upon how those two categories inflect their own thinking, judgment, and thus engagement with San Roque and its residents.

We ensured that the first few moments spent inside the performance space engendered a crucial disorientation and deterritorialization. Countering expectations that there will be a "play" or stories to be told in this performance, audience members were asked to remain standing in order to view different installations as prelude. These installations were meant to construct new viewing arrangements that unhinged the stable positions of the observer, the middle-class spectator, and the observed, San Roque, the informal settlement and the community living there. The installations were meant to present the different ways San Roque is made to "appear" or "disappear" and then, in turn, argue for a different apparatus for "seeing" and "knowing" San Roque.[29] For example, a simple setup recalls the shiny real estate development booths often located in malls that positions San Roque as one that hinders economic development. The spectators become the main target for the sales tactics of a student-actor distributing pamphlets featuring prime sites included in Quezon City. From this standpoint, San Roque becomes a

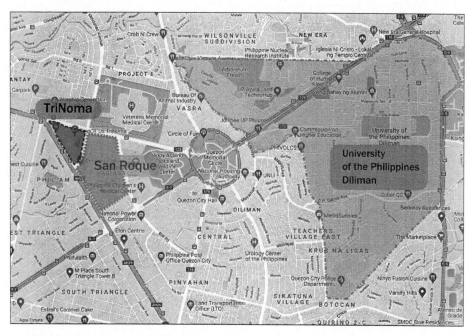

Bringing San Roque and University of the Philippines together. (Map prepared by author.)

stand-in for other sites that will need to be removed for the completion of this large-scale development. Disturbing the "market appeal" of this setup, however, is the short roughly edited video we prepared from downloaded images of San Roque from Google Earth. From this perspective of the all-seeing eye of the satellite of the Philippines, then to Metro Manila, the viewer then sees a zoomed image of a much bigger San Roque when it still had not experienced the numerous demolitions. The incomplete accounting of the visuals of San Roque's transformation through the years is set against the vivid recording of Nanay Inday, a strong community leader. In this recorded interview, Nanay Inday uses the same downloaded image of San Roque and points out the areas demolished and not reflected in the image. Through this intentional overlap of the silenced histories of San Roque with images taken from Google Earth, we hoped to retrieve the multidimensionality of San Roque that these flattened illustrations fail to capture.

Through another installation, we wished to direct the inward gaze of a spectator toward his/her position in relation to the site of San Roque. On a hand-drawn map placed on the floor, participants were asked to mark their points of activity within and around the area of San Roque. For residents of San Roque, this meant identifying and seeing their activities and movements in the area—San Roque as more than a place of residence but also a place of

Drawing the map of San Roque in the KADAMAY office in San Roque. (Photo courtesy of Arnisson Ortega. Used with permission.)

social and religious activities and a source of their livelihood. Opposition to the demolition and promised relocation by the government to a remote area thus is not to resist only the destruction of the homes they built but of the severance from the lives they built in the area. Based on our own students' reflections in class, we expected a crowd comprised of students who not only have never been to San Roque but may also deliberately avoid it, and so we asked nonresidents to mark their points of activity in or around the community on the hand-drawn visual rendition of the community by the residents. Through the colorful markings of everyday paths and activities by teachers, students, and residents, this countermap showed the many routes, flows, and paths that connect the university to San Roque and illustrate a shared space between them.

After several minutes upon entering the black box theater, further destabilization continued as a voice summoned the scattered audience to cohere in the middle of the space after making their way in and out of the installations. The coming together of bodies began the series of performances that followed. Although we were certain that we could rely on performance's power to provoke a feeling or a thought that may not have otherwise arisen, some preliminary discussions with my students centered around the relation between how we make bodies move in the theater in order to make them move outside of it. If not protest now, how do we unleash another type of "social

A performance piece by an undergraduate theater major from the University of the Philippines, Diliman. (Photo courtesy of Jomel Reyes. Used with permission.)

kinesthetic" in the interim?[30] One theatrical experiment was to activate what Bleeker calls "perceptual systems" that involve "seeing" through a "process of bodily response and investigation, measuring, exploring through sight and hearing, as well as through proprioception and kinesthetic."[31] One objective was to jolt the audience into seeing and moving with others. With no spoken instructions where to go, the audience were asked to respond to a shift in lights, sound, and the movement of another body. Without a narrative guide or set choreography, the audience had to make their way to different spots of the space to listen to an unnamed activist sing a song, watch projected video art pieces and monologues, and stand witness to moving bodies in the theater space. Thus, while being confronted with bits and pieces about San Roque, these theatrical prompts were intended to initiate kinaesthetic responses from the audience in their pursuit to understand San Roque better. We will not go as far as to assert that this experiment produced empathy in its kinaesthetic mode. Rather, we maintain that it is precisely in between the interrupted and incomplete movement of this moment that we must strategize around how we must further build upon the possible diverse kinaesthetic empathies felt by the viewers to collectively move for San Roque.

While in the process of conceptualizing the short performance pieces, some undergraduate students expressed their difficulties, especially in light

Nanay Inday participates in a performance piece. (Photo courtesy of Jomel Reyes. Used with permission.)

of expected responses of friends, in breaking away from representing San Rogue through tropes of the poor's "suffering." A few graduate students seconded this thought, also reflecting on their own viewing habits of not wanting to watch the poor's suffering on TV. One student asserted that the "middle-class person" who is in "social denial" will be "turned off" by presentations of such suffering and display of poverty.[32] Encouraged to think about the body and its relation to the state and capital's enactments and performances of power instead,[33] a few performances that night attempted to show that the supposed "middle class" is not in any way protected or exempted from such enactments of state power. A choreographed piece by one theater student began with comical music playing in the background. A figure who could have been a stand-in for a politician, city planner, or urban developer enters the stage and begins to move around the bodies first seen by the audience in calm repose. He throws around the unmarked but live bodies, contorting and then reconfiguring their positions—at first, putting them together, then separating one from the other and parodying the almost random and farcical movement and displacement of bodies in the city. The outdoor performance that followed was by Boyet, a performance artist and cultural worker. After leading the audience members outside of the black box theater, Boyet asked several members to paint his face, which, according to the artist, familiarizes himself to the audience as opposed to alienating him. He then asked the volunteers to be his coperformers and stand inside his rope-lined demarcated square just outside the black box theater. At first, this produced laughter and amusement for the audience members, but it was not long after that Boyet's intentions were made clearer. Masked as another unnamed power figure, the performance artist repeatedly made lines and demarcations, thus limiting the space that could be occupied and inhabited. As volunteers were displaced one by one or in groups, we see that the piece was an interrogation of any sense of security in land and tenure for both resident and nonresident of San Roque in their shared space of Metro Manila.

In sum, the mix of installations and performance pieces during our performance event was intended to operationalize what theater scholar Roxworthy calls "critical empathy" in the context of San Roque and the University of the Philippines.[34] Roxworthy carefully considers the critique of empathy in her review and analysis of performance projects that depict the experiences of Japanese American internees in the United States. According to her, some works that claim to be immersive and interactive end up erasing racial violence and colonialist histories when empathy is "peddled" so that spectators identify with the "assimiliationist" racialized other in the United States. Roxworthy, however, does not foreclose the possibility of mobilizing critical empathy in performance and argues that by destabilizing the mise-en-scène, for example, we can "disallow easy empathy." Although Roxworthy centers this argument on the "thing-power" of objects on stage and their role in critical empathy, we took on her challenge to initiate performative experiments that disallow easy empathy. Playing around with the usual "affective structures" of performance, for example, creates "jarring" and "ponderous" effects. In our own work, the compendium of short performance pieces and installations sought to surround the spectator with fragmented life narratives, unseat them from their stable positions as observer, and generate feelings of dislocation and displacement (though partial and fleeting) in the theater.

## Feeling Our Way Through

Empathy has been part of wider discussions regarding the crucial role of emotions in social justice movements.[35] At the same time, we take note of the serious critique of how empathy reifies the privileged position of the one who empathizes by endowing them with the capacity of co-feeling.[36] The statements of UP administration, for example, demonstrate how empathy could easily become an "affective capacity" susceptible to appropriation by market-oriented logics to validate more palatable tactics of displacement and dispossession. Responding to these critiques, I would like to exercise a different

emotional reflexivity[37] and suspend reflecting on our capacities as researchers to empathize with our research participants or the success of the project
in producing empathetic subjects. I keep my focus on the address of a few
community organizers of KADAMAY (*Kalipunan ng Damayang Mahihirap*)[38]
and their allies during the tense and uncertain space of the postshow discussion, as they make crucial interventions in the usual circuit of empathy examined by scholars. For one, their presence within this space makes more
evident the multidirectionality of performance where empathy should not
be conceived as a sole and isolated exchange from spectator to performer or
aesthetic object. Cummings argues that it is only through considering this
dynamism and multidirectionality that we could begin cultivating "dialogic
empathy" and engaging in constant dialogue wherein we discuss "how to do
empathy well."[39] Also, a focus on these "moment-to moment" engagements"[40]
open up ways to work toward decolonizing empathy in critical scholarship
wherein we look at alternate spaces, the margins, or even occasions during
which empathy fails in order to examine how it might be put to work differently.[41] I also see this as an effort to extend discussions about the radical potential of the "zones of encounter" between our audience, mostly comprised
of the middle class and the poor.[42] Thus, in what follows, I recount these moments as a way to reflect upon the role of academics and others in both creating spaces of contact and ensuring empathy is sustained and channeled to
concrete actions that forge paths of resistance, in this case for both UP and
San Roque.

As soon as the low lights came up in the black box theater after the last
outdoor performance of the night, the crowd gathered, not knowing what
would happen next. At that moment, right after the performance, empathy
was hardly the glue that congealed into a truly shared space. Breaking the
silence was Yumi, a young organizer and resident of San Roque, who addressed
the crowd gathered to talk about the economic development that will displace
many residents and remove them from good sources of livelihood. Yumi,
though "trained" by numerous experiences to speak in rallies and mobilizations, showed signs of worry and frustration in speaking to the very quiet
crowd of students and young professionals and, almost in a desperate attempt to appeal to the emotions of the audience, asserted:

We [Yumi, students, and other nonresidents] are lucky that we are
able to get an education; there are professionals like you. You are
lucky that you are able to study without worrying about anything. I
wish that despite that, when you pass by "squatter areas," I wish you
could also think about the conditions of the residents inside it every
day. The employed are very lucky.

Nanay Inday, Yumi, and another resident address our students during the postshow discussion. (Photo courtesy of Jomel Reyes. Used with permission.)

Yumi's address to the crowd revealed not only the complex negotiations of class difference between the educated and the unemployed poor in the room, but it also reminded us that engaged contact should never be taken for granted and must be continuously generated. Especially for those who make their way out of campus to go home or to go to the commercial centers, they would definitely pass by San Roque to get to the main lines of transit. And yet San Roque has remained invisible and inaccessible to them because of the many ways Ayala has tried to conceal San Roque from public view. Yumi, definitely not trying to evoke pity, was in her own way trying to evoke empathy. Yumi was asking the crowd to look at San Roque quite differently from what they were used to doing when they passed by the "informal settlement" areas.

Most residents and community members of KADAMAY attest to difficulties in addressing the dwindling numbers of residents who attend protests and participate in barricades they have set up through the years. Some reasons for this within San Roque include disappointment over personal conflicts within the group or "activist fatigue," wherein some residents have started to doubt the group's plan of resistance. Dhel, another community activist, draws this comparison. If the urban poor experiences this, we can assume that there is even a bigger hurdle for the middle class. For Dhel, spatial distance between the two groups grows, as does the social distance, and media images about San Roque's dissidence or Ayala's glitzy plans of urban developments become ingrained. Moreover, if we recall the statements of the human rights commissioner in the beginning of this chapter and the spectacles of Quezon City government and the UP administration, their empathetic performances of "understanding" the poor are only extended until what are perceived as violent, rebellious acts on the part of the residents occur. Some hesitate to extend their support when invitations are issued to join putting barricades around the area, fight the police or demolition teams, or march toward the mayor's office. For Dhel, the middle class must be pulled in and steered into the direction of San Roque.

The particularity of countermapping through performance is that the space of performance brought different communities into the same space for a moment in time. Aside from the use of performance space itself as a place to meet, we saw the project and the practice of performance making to find—and even create—more strategic places in which everyone could encounter each other. Dhel remembers that in the past, he was able to enter the university and classrooms to talk to students and ask for their support. "We would just go in because that's UP before." Now, in addition to the expense of commuting from San Roque to UP, he said security guards do not allow them to enter. After the performance, Dhel thanked us. "You could just speak for us sometimes," he asserted and challenged us to take their issue to the "middle forces" in the ways we could. Thus, after the performance, conversations continued as to how we could help with bringing San Roque to the university. This might happen through inclusion of the project or other urban issues in our syllabi or by supporting San Roque residents gaining access to university spaces, offices, and venues for meetings, events, and film screenings. Yumi and Dhel made clear at the performance talkback that establishing proximity and contact do matter to them, but asking us to speak for them does not signify that the empathic process even for us, scholars and researchers, is already complete, therefore making us the perfect spokesperson for San Roque. The task is two pronged in this case: One, we still need to be thinking of ways of how to materially contribute to the struggles of San Roque by making use of our privileges in the university. But, at the same time, creating spaces of encounter from within and around the university are to view our own institution as a "dense site" wherein we could examine what Elwood, Lawson, and Nowak call "relational place making." For these scholars, how the middle class enact poverty politics has serious implications for us in understanding how class boundaries are reproduced. But, within these sites, we could "disrupt dominant narratives of poverty that can lead to more reflexive interactions, sowing seeds for cross-class alliance."[43] Hence, part of the task of countermapping is to open up critical discussions about middle-classness and poverty within our classrooms and beyond and to implore other academics to do the same.

A tense impasse was felt inside the performance space after Yumi, Nanay Inday, and Richard, another young resident of San Roque who inspired one of the monologues of the night, delivered impassioned accounts of injustice. Another urban planning student questioned the residents about the basis of their claims and their refusal of the government's plans for relocation. For this student, despite her own visits to San Roque and discussions in the classroom, with "no clear demands" to government, resistance is not only futile, but also it is simply groundless and illogical. A response from a resident brought an insufficient and, perhaps worse, only temporary clarification. The demand is clear, yet alternatives are uncertain, unknown even. Paolo and Boyet, both cultural workers, activists, and two of the performers that night, had this to say in response to this student. Paolo, a nonresident of San Roque who at the time was working for a different activist organization, stated:

> The poor are defenseless against the chorus of the government and big businesses. Yet, there will be an opportunity for us to shake the foundations laid out by the strong partnership between the government and the big corporations, especially when professors, urban planners, scientists, and students speak and share their analyses as to why our laws, policies, and programs by the government do not serve the poor. It's a big thing, if this will come from our architects and engineers. It's a totally different thing if they will not only help expose the truth, but also help the poor with their knowledge.

Paolo in his response contends that what is clear is the power of partnerships between the state and big, private corporations and the resistance we need to wage against it. For Paolo, what needs exposing and illumination are the state laws, policies, and programs that continue to keep residents in poverty. Boyet addresses the impression of "groundless" resistance by suggesting a more active alternative response:

> If there is a question about alternatives, if not a relocation, suing the government or a return to the countryside, then we need to study it then. How much do we need to pay rent if the minimum [wage] is not even more than 400 pesos a day? We, who are in the middle class, a big part of that are the educated. You can make a big contribution.

Paolo and Boyet, for example, help us reflect more on how Pedwell defines empathy as the "giving up of the empathic desire for cultural mastery or psychic transparency."[44] Rather, for Pedwell, empathy is a "giving in" to what is "foreign" and not as easily comprehensible. Paolo and Boyet's response to the audience was not an appeal for a deeper identification with the subject position of the poor as prerequisite for *more* empathy. However, they were strong provocations to "give up" their unfounded assumptions by appealing to the student, architect, urban planner in them, help with their knowledge, study the issue, and proffer solutions.

Indeed, the failure to attain a concluding emotional "dramatic" climax to the performance and the uncertain outcomes of Boyet and Paolo's address impel us to consider how much more work is required for empathy to move beyond its "perspective taking potential." While Cummings encourages us to cultivate dialogic empathy in *all* stages of performance (including after-show talks), our experience with our Q&A after the show pushes us to think further on how we could help create different pathways for our students based on careful attunement to our own interactions with them. This is how we hope to create empathic routes into San Roque from our campus even beyond performance. Boyet offered one critique of our project that same night. For Boyet, we missed the simple yet important task of putting a sign-up sheet with name, affiliation, and contact number for our small audience: our students, colleagues, artists, performers, geographers, urban planners, architects, the educated, the middle class. He told us that we cannot expect our students to know what is next, nor should we take for granted whatever was felt or seen that night. If not San Roque, Boyet said, there are *other* communities that will need the help of the students. "How are we to know where and how we could lead these students?" he asked. The first step, for Boyet, is not to treat the audience as a faceless and already empathetic crowd. Paying attention to the affective dimension of countermapping would require a steady process of leading our students to specific points of inquiry and walking together with them as the needs of the group of activists and residents in San Roque also change.

Nevertheless, we are wary of and vigilant against merely being comfortable conduits of "immersion trips" to San Roque, which, according to one ally we interviewed, "only adds to the burden of residents and activists to host students and teachers" with no concrete gains for the residents or the movement they are building. Thus, although these trips or visits may indeed increase the number of students who come to San Roque, we realize that the time and effort spent doing so could instead be used to establish stronger relations with the students and colleagues who have expressed some interest in learning and practicing what it might mean to be in true solidarity with San Roque residents. The "middle-class allies," the architects or urban planners that Boyet and Paulo refer to in their statements, for example, will be able to help with their knowledge and expertise directly in the group's ongoing political campaigns. Academics and other researchers could contribute in helping organizations like KADAMAY distinguish their claims and methods of practice from other NGOs and other community-based organizations that offer short-term solutions that further entrench the poor in systems that oppress them.[45] It is also through our relationships with them that we could lead them somewhere *else*. While some students or colleagues may not be able to help San Roque directly, potential formed relationships through performance may activate them in other spaces. How do we encourage urban planners, for example, to take up these issues in their workplaces or institutional spaces as forms of resistance to the growing privatization of urban planning and development in Manila?[46] Akin to the colorful dots on the map discussed earlier, we need to encourage and challenge others to take up their critical positions in relation to San Roque, the University of the Philippines, Quezon City, and other places in Manila.

## Circuiting Back

As a way to conclude, here is one last performance from that night in 2013. In one corner of the room of the performance space sat a video installation. Two small, old television sets were playing videos on loop in a setup made to look like Nanay Inday's living room, where our students once gathered to hear her tell her story. One video showed several clips of news TV coverage of the demolitions in San Roque over the years. The other video showed my collaborator, Andre and I reading together a letter handed to him during one of his trips to Montalban, a site of relocation for displaced residents. In this letter, seventy-five residents signed to seek justice and report the violent destruction of their homes. At the end, they pleaded for a news team to visit their area, but no one came. We now recall this letter from the United States and Canada, miles away from San Roque, Montalban, Quezon City, and Manila.

In this chapter, I argued for the need to consider the role of empathy specifically in projects that attempt to explore the productive synergy between performance and countermapping. By situating our project within the spatial context of San Roque and the University of the Philippines and critically examining the challenges that we faced as a group of students and teachers who aimed to connect with a community such as San Roque, I discussed how empathy *hardly* emerges as something that could be possessed by the middle-class spectator. I highlighted the interventions of community activists instead to underscore the need to strategize around creating concrete channels that lead into specific activities that ensure dialogic empathy, continuous involvement, and active participation. In other words, performance countermapping does not only expose the dominant aesthetic (and thus possibly also violent) lens through which one views San Roque, performance also helps create new and embodied itineraries[47] to engage with it differently and help in the struggle of residents to keep their homes and place in Quezon City.

*Lugar* was not conceived to be simply a one-off event. Rather, we hoped it would ignite other performance countermapping projects that hold on to a vision of performance similar to that outlined by Houston and Pulido: performance as a "dialectical operative" that puts into motion practices that simultaneously change everyday material life and enact many different kinds of "imaginative work."[48] Since 2013, *Lugar* is only one of the many events, artistic projects, and other initiatives that have been created for and alongside the work of Save San Roque Alliance—a group composed of academics, architects, and other professionals, also formed in 2013. This alliance has helped craft a counterproposal for a development strategy "on-site" San Roque, one that presses for on-site mass housing, social services, and education for its many residents rather than massive displacement. Currently, its Facebook page is replete with visual documentation of its many activities, including the work of many artists, performers, illustrators, and graphic artists contributing their work and proceeds to San Roque. These photos and images, instead of erasing what has been previously perceived as deplorable, render them in unity with the beauty of life, growth, and collectively defined "development" now being cultivated in San Roque. Most importantly, Nanay Inday and Yumi, as in the video this chapter began with, engage in performance themselves, performances that are recorded, archived, and circulated. Poetry, song, and satire are and will always be part of their repertoires of resistance. These performances tenaciously hang on despite the ongoing onslaught of violence, of San Roque graffiti being torn down by military forces, of long-enduring state abandonment of life. These performances, therefore, require our renewed and escalated attention, thought, and action.

## NOTES

Note: "Empathic Projections: Performance and Countermapping of Sitio San Roque, Quezon City, and University of the Philippines," by Vanessa Banta, originally published in *GeoHumanities* November 17, 2021, by Taylor & Francis. Reprinted by permission of Taylor & Francis, http://www.tandfonline.com/.

1. Pinder, "Arts of Urban Exploration"; Guazon, "Creative Mediations of the City."
2. Choi, "Metro Manila through the Gentrification Lens."
3. Tadiar, *Fantasy Production*.
4. Lico, *Edifice Complex*; Benedicto, "The Queer Afterlife," 581.
5. Garrido, "How Interspersion Affects Class Relations"; Garrido, "The Sense of Place."
6. Pante, "Quezon's City."
7. Ortega, "Exposing Necroburbia."
8. Ghertner, "Calculating without Numbers," 199.
9. "Comprehensive Land Use Plan 2011–2025," 30.
10. Ramon Guillermo, "Rationalizing Failures," 129.
11. Quijano, "Maralita Ng North Triangle."
12. "U.P. Town Center."
13. "University of the Philippines Strategic Plan 2011–2017."

14. Ibid., 24.

15. Ibid., 25.

16. Oblino, "13 Na Pook Sa Loob Ng UP."

17. Wainwright and Bryan, "Cartography, Territory, Property"; Hodgson and Schroeder, "Dilemmas of Counter-Mapping."

18. Sletto, "Inclusions, erasures and emergences in an indigenous landscape," 926; see also Sletto, "We Drew What We Imagined."

19. Kitchin and Dodge, "Rethinking Maps," 335.

20. Ibid.

21. Kitchin, Gleeson and Dodge, "Unfolding Mapping Practices," 484.

22. Allen et al., "Can Participatory Mapping Activate Spatial and Political Practices," 264.

23. Kwan, "Affecting Geospatial Technologies."

24. Davidson, Bondi, and Smith, *Emotional Geographies*, 3.

25. Smith, Ibáñez, and Herrera, "The Importance of Context"; Duff, "On the Role of Affect and Practice"; Cloke, May, and Johnsen, "Performativity and Affect."

26. Till, "Wounded Cities," 13.

27. Here, I use Cummings' (2016) concept of dialogic empathy.

28. Lehmann, *Postdramatic Theatre*.

29. Bleeker, *"Visuality in the Theatre,"* 9.

30. Martin, "Toward a Kinesthetics of Protest," 796.

31. Bleeker, *Visuality in the Theatre*, 175.

32. Student's personal essay; Also, see Ong's "Witnessing Distant and Proximal Suffering."

33. wa Thiong'o, "Enactments of Power," 30.

34. Roxworthy, "Revitalizing Japanese American Internment," 99.

35. Wright, "Justice and the Geographies of Moral Protest."

36. Pedwell, "Affective (Self-) Transformations."

37. Brown and Pickerill, "Space for Emotion"; Evans, "Feeling My Way."

38. Translation: "National Alliance of Filipino Poor."

39. Cummings, *"Empathy as Dialogue in Theatre and Performance,"* 6 and 17.

40. Ibid., 20.

41. Pedwell, "Affect at the Margins"; Gunew, "Subaltern Empathy."

42. Lawson and Elwood, "Encountering Poverty," 213.

43. Elwood, Lawson, and Nowak, "Middle-Class Poverty Politics," 140.

44. Pedwell, "Decolonising Empathy," 20.

45. Hutchison, "The 'Disallowed' Political Participation of Manila's Urban Poor"; Kares, "Practicing 'Enlightened Capitalism'"; Shatkin, "Working with the Community."

46. Shatkin, "The City and the Bottom Line."

47. Roy, "Slumdog Cities."

48. Houston and Pulido, "The Work of Performativity," 402.

## BIBLIOGRAPHY

Allen, Adriana, Rita Lambert, Alexandre Apsan Frediani, and Tatiana Ome. "Can Participatory Mapping Activate Spatial and Political Practices? Mapping Popular Resistance and Dwelling Practices in Bogotá Eastern Hills." *Area* 47, no. 3 (2015): 261–271, https://doi.org/10.1111/area.12187.

Benedicto, Bobby. "The Queer Afterlife of the Postcolonial City: (Trans)Gender Performance and the War of Beautification." *Antipode* 47, no. 3 (2015): 580–597, https://doi.org/10.1111/anti.12101.

Bleeker, Maaike. *Visuality in the Theatre: The Locus of Looking.* New York: Palgrave Macmillan, 2008.

Brown, Gavin, and Jenny Pickerill. "Space for Emotion in the Spaces of Activism." *Emotion, Space and Society* 2 (2009): 24–35, https://doi.org/10.1016/j.emospa.2009.03.004.

Choi, Narae. "Metro Manila through the Gentrification Lens: Disparities in Urban Planning and Displacement Risks." *Urban Studies* 53, no. 3 (2016): 577–592, https://doi.org/10.1177/0042098014543032.

Cloke, Paul, Jon May, and Sarah Johnsen. "Performativity and Affect in the Homeless City." *Environment and Planning D: Society and Space* 26, no. 2 (2008): 241–263, https://doi.org/10.1068/d84j.

"Comprehensive Land Use Plan 2011–2025." Quezon City, 2011.

Cummings, Lindsay B. *Empathy as Dialogue in Theatre and Performance.* UK: Palgrave Macmillan, 2016.

Davidson, Joyce, Liz Bondi, and Mick Smith, eds. *Emotional Geographies.* Aldershot, U.K.: Ashgate, 2005.

Duff, Cameron. "On the Role of Affect and Practice in the Production of Place." *Environment and Planning D: Society and Space* 28, no. 5 (October 1, 2010): 881–895, https://doi.org/10.1068/d16209.

Elwood, Sarah, Victoria Lawson, and Samuel Nowak. "Middle-Class Poverty Politics: Making Place, Making People." *Annals of the Association of American Geographers* 105, no. 1 (2015): 123–143, https://doi.org/10.1080/00045608.2014.968945.

Evans, Monica. "Feeling My Way: Emotions and Empathy in Geographic Research with Fathers in Valparaíso, Chile on JSTOR." *Area* 44, no. 4 (2012): 503–509, https://www-jstor-org.ezproxy.library.ubc.ca/stable/23358206?pq-origsite=summon&seq=1#metadata_info_tab_contents.

Garrido, Marco. "How Interspersion Affects Class Relations." *International Journal of Urban and Regional Research* 42, no. 3 (May 1, 2018): 442–460, https://doi.org/10.1111/1468-2427.12632.

———. "The Sense of Place behind Segregating Practices the Sense of Place behind Segregating Practices: An Ethnographic Approach to the Symbolic Partitioning of Metro Manila." *Social Forces* 91, no. 4 (2013): 1343–1362, https://doi.org/10.1093/sf/sot039.

Ghertner, D. Asher. "Calculating without Numbers: Aesthetic Governmentality in Delhi's Slums." *Economy and Society* 39, no. 2 (2010): 185–217, https://doi.org/10.1080/03085141003620147.

Guazon, Tessa Maria. "Creative Mediations of the City: Contemporary Public Art as Compass of Metro Manila's Urban Conditions." *International Journal of Urban and Regional Research* 37, no. 3 (May 1, 2013): 864–878, https://doi.org/10.1111/j.1468-2427.2013.01211.x.

Guillermo, Ramon. "Rationalizing Failures: The Philippine Government in the Education Sector." In *Mula Tore Patungong Palengke: Neoliberal Education in the Philippines.* Edited by Bienvenido Lumbera, Ramon Guillermo, and Arnold Alamon. Quezon City: IBON Philippines, 2007, 127–137.

Gunew, Sneja. "Subaltern Empathy: Beyond European Categories in Affect Theory." *Concentric: Literary and Cultural Studies* 35, no. 1 (2009): 11–30, https://doi.org/10.6240/CONCENTRIC.LIT.200903_35(1).0002.

Hawkins, Harriet. "Geography and Art. An Expanding Field: Site, the Body and Practice." *Progress in Human Geography* 37, no. 1 (2012): 52–71, https://journals-sagepub-com .ezproxy.library.ubc.ca/doi/pdf/10.1177/0309132512442865.

Hodgson, Dorothy L., and Richard A. Schroeder. "Dilemmas of Counter-Mapping Community Resources in Tanzania." *Development and Change* 33, no. 1 (2002): 79–100, https://doi.org/10.1111/1467-7660.00241.

Houston, Donna, and Laura Pulido. "The Work of Performativity: Staging Social Justice at the University of Southern California." *Environment and Planning D: Society and Space* 20, no. 4 (2002): 401–424, https://doi.org/10.1068/d344.

Hutchison, Jane. "The 'Disallowed' Political Participation of Manila's Urban Poor." *Democratization* 14, no. 5 (2007): 853–872, https://doi.org/10.1080/13510340701635696.

Kares, Faith R. "Practicing 'Enlightened Capitalism': 'Fil-Am' Heroes, NGO Activism and the Reconstitution of Class Difference in the Philippines." *Philippine Studies: Historical and Ethnographic Viewpoints* 62, no. 2 (2014): 175–204.

Kitchin, Rob, and Martin Dodge. "Rethinking Maps." *Progress in Human Geography* 31, no. 3 (2007): 331–344, https://search-proquest-com.ezproxy.library.ubc.ca/docview /230731893?pq-origsite=summon&accountid=14656.

Kitchin, Rob, Justin Gleeson, and Martin Dodge. "Unfolding Mapping Practices: A New Epistemology for Cartography." *Transactions of the Institute of British Geographers* 38, no. 3 (2013): 480–496, https://doi.org/10.1111/j.1475-5661.2012.00540.x.

Kwan, Mei-Po. "Affecting Geospatial Technologies: Toward a Feminist Politics of Emotion*." *Professional Geographer* 59, no. 1 (2007): 22–34, https://doi.org/10.1111/j.1467 -9272.2007.00588.x.

Lawson, Victoria, and Sarah Elwood. "Encountering Poverty: Space, Class, and Poverty Politics." *Antipode* 46, no. 1 (January 2014): 209–228, https://doi.org/10.1111/anti.12030.

Lehmann, Hans-Thies. *Postdramatic Theatre.* New York: Routledge, 2006.

Lico, Gerard. *Edifice Complex: Power, Myth and Marcos State Architecture.* Quezon City: Ateneo de Manila University Press, 2003.

Martin, Randy. "Toward a Kinesthetics of Protest." *Social Identities* 12, no. 6 (2006): 791–801, https://doi.org/10.1080/13504630601030990.

Oblino, Diana. "13 Na Pook Sa Loob Ng UP, Maapektuhan Ng Demolisyon." Manila Today, 2017.

Ong, Jonathan Corpus. "Witnessing Distant and Proximal Suffering within a Zone of Danger: Lay Moralities of Media Audiences in the Philippines." *International Communication Gazette* 77, no. 7 (November 1, 2015): 607–621, https://doi.org/10.1177 /1748048515601555.

Ortega, Arnisson Andre C. "Exposing Necroburbia: Suburban Relocation, Necropolitics, and Violent Geographies in Manila." *Antipode* 52, no. 4 (2020): 1175–1195, https://doi .org/10.1111/anti.12629.

Pante, Michael D. "Quezon's City: Corruption and Contradiction in Manila's Prewar Suburbia, 1935–1941." *Journal of Southeast Asian Studies* 48, no. 1 (2017): 91–112, https:// doi.org/10.1017/S0022463416000497.

Pedwell, Carolyn. "Affect at the Margins: Alternative Empathies in a Small Place." *Emotion, Space and Society* 8, no. 1 (2013): 18–26, https://doi.org/10.1016/j.emospa.2012 .07.001.

———. "Affective (Self-) Transformations: Empathy, Neoliberalism and International Development." *Feminist Theory* 13, no. 2 (2012): 163–179, https://doi.org/10.1177/1464 700112442644.

――――. "Decolonising Empathy: Thinking Affect Transnationally." *Samyukta: A Journal of Women's Studies* 16, no. 1 (2016): 27–49.

Pinder, David. "Arts of Urban Exploration." *Cultural Geographies* 12, no. 4 (2005): 383–411, https://doi.org/10.1191/1474474005eu347oa.

Quijano, Ilang-Ilang. "Maralita Ng North Triangle, Binato Ng Putik Ang Technohub Ni Ayala." Pinoy Weekly, 2011, https://pinoyweekly.org/2011/08/video-maralita-north-triangle-binato-putik-ayala-technohu/.

Roxworthy, Emily. "Revitalizing Japanese American Internment: Critical Empathy and Role-Play in the Musical 'Allegiance' and the Video Game 'Drama in the Delta.'" *Theatre Journal* 66, no. 1 (2014): 93–115.

Roy, Ananya. "Slumdog Cities: Rethinking Subaltern Urbanism." *International Journal of Urban and Regional Research* 35, no. 2 (2011): 223–261, https://doi.org/10.1111/j.1468-2427.2011.01051.x.

Shatkin, Gavin. "The City and the Bottom Line: Urban Megaprojects and the Privatization of Planning in Southeast Asia." *Environment and Planning A: Economy and Space* 40, no. 2 (February 1, 2008): 383–401, https://doi.org/10.1068/a38439.

――――. "Working with the Community: Dilemmas in Radical Planning in Metro Manila, the Philippines." *Planning Theory and Practice* 3, no. 3 (2002): 301–317, https://doi.org/10.1080/1464935022000019545.

Sletto, Bjørn Ingmunn. "Inclusions, Erasures and Emergences in an Indigenous Landscape: Participatory Cartographies and the Makings of Affective Place in the Sierra de Perijá, Venezuela." *Environment and Planning D: Society and Space*, 33, no. 5 (2015): 925–944. https://doi.org/10.1177/0263775815604927.

――――. "We Drew What We Imagined: Participatory Mapping, Performance, and the Arts of Landscape Making." *Current Anthropology* 50, no. 4 (August 2009): 443–476, https://doi.org/10.1086/593704.

Smith, Derek A., Alicia Ibáñez, and Francisco Herrera. "The Importance of Context: Assessing the Benefits and Limitations of Participatory Mapping for Empowering Indigenous Communities in the Comarca Ngäbe-Buglé, Panama." *Cartographica: The International Journal for Geographic Information and Geovisualization* 52, no. 1 (2017): 49–62, https://muse-jhu-edu.ezproxy.library.ubc.ca/article/652030.

Tadiar, Neferti. *Fantasy Production: Sexual Economies and Other Philippine Consequences for the New World Order.* Hong Kong: Hong Kong University Press, 2004, https://muse.jhu.edu/book/5612.

Till, Karen E. "Wounded Cities: Memory-Work and a Place-Based Ethics of Care." *Political Geography* 31, no. 1 (2012): 3–14, https://doi.org/10.1016/j.polgeo.2011.10.008.

"University of the Philippines Strategic Plan 2011–2017." Quezon City, 2012.

"U.P. Town Center: An Industry and Academic Collaboration." WheninManila.Com, 2014.

wa Thiong'o, Ngugi. "Enactments of Power: The Politics of Performance Space." *Drama Review* 41, no. 3 (1997): 30, https://doi.org/10.2307/1146606.

Wainwright, Joel, and Joe Bryan. "Cartography, Territory, Property: Postcolonial Reflections on Indigenous Counter-Mapping in Nicaragua and Belize." *Cultural Geographies* 16, no. 1 (2009): 153–178, https://doi.org/10.1177/1474474008101515.

Wright, Melissa W. "Justice and the Geographies of Moral Protest: Reflections from Mexico." *Environment and Planning D: Society and Space* 27, no. 2 (2009): 216–233, https://doi.org/10.1068/d6708.

# Infrastructural Futures

*Arroyo's Philippines in a Technological Frame*

PAUL NADAL

## "First World in Twenty Years"

In times of crisis, amid worldwide social upheavals and financial intensification, timetables of the future proliferate as so many prophecies purportedly designed to address the plight of those living under conditions of disposability. In recent Philippine history, one particular projection materialized itself: namely, President Gloria Macapagal-Arroyo's vision of First World development in twenty years.[1] Spawned by the meltdown of speculative markets that culminated in the global finance crisis of 2008, as well as the seemingly perennial national crisis of the Philippines, in which over a third of its ninety-one-million population live with hunger; three thousand exit daily in search for employment overseas; and hundreds of labor organizers, activists, and journalists are abducted and murdered, which make the Philippines, apart from Iraq, in 2010, the deadliest country for reporters—Arroyo's projection of First Worldom sought to capture the imagination and dreams of an entire nation.[2] Yet Arroyo's prophecy of First Worldom also sprung at a time of apparent economic growth in the form of four successive years (2004–2007) of rising gross domestic product (GDP)[3] at rates not seen since the 1970s and even rivaling those generated by neighboring Southeast-Asian economies.[4] Crescendoing around the latter half of her second term, Arroyo's rhetoric of "First World in twenty years" imparted a set of social and economic initiatives that aligned itself to the United Nations Millennium Development Goals of reducing global poverty in half by 2015. At the center of those initiatives was Arroyo's citation of infrastructure building as a key instrument in ameliorating poverty and achieving the Philippines' First World status.

Thus, poised before a resurgent nation in the wake of a world economy in turmoil, Arroyo declared the following at her 2009 State of the Nation Address (SONA):

> The story of the Philippines in 2008 is that the country weathered a succession of global crises in fuel, in food, then in finance and finally the economy in a global recession. . . . The state of our nation is a strong economy. Good news for our people, bad news for our critics.
>
> I did not become President to be popular. To work, to lead, to protect and preserve our country, our people, that is why I became President. When my father left the Presidency, we were second to Japan. I want our Republic to be ready for the First World in twenty years.[5]

Arroyo's speech is significant for the way in which it registers a certain economic imperative that is also a temporal exigency. The future here is figured as the prospect of economic progress that would synchronize the Philippines's pace of development with the industrialized nations of the Global North, thereby delivering the nation and its people from the sundry crises that seem to abound. In this way did Arroyo's speech embody a certain messianism, whose prophetic force sought to arrest the time of the nation by positing a future end toward which Filipinos everywhere would be propelled and enjoined to bring about at the new millennium. At her farewell speech, broadcasted nationally on June 23, 2010, Arroyo waxed confidently the achievements of her two-term, nine-year presidency (2001–2010) as follows:

> Nine years ago I came to presidency at the time of great turmoil in our nation. I accepted the challenge to the office when it was thrust upon me. At that time our country was reeling from political intrigue and a distressed economy. We set to work to reform our economy and invest in our people. . . . We needed new and better roads, bridges, ports and a "technology backbone" to attract new businesses and investors to create new jobs. Through hard work, determination, and a clear plan of action, we helped achieve many of these objectives. As a result we have had thirty-seven quarters of uninterrupted economic growth even against the head winds of a major global recession.[6]

Arroyo's self-congratulating valediction of unprecedented growth is supported by the legions of infrastructure projects she credits to the work of her government. According to Arroyo, the Philippines under her term has entered an infrastructural age. So central was infrastructure to her administration's development platform that Department of Public Works and High-ways Secretary Victor Domingo made the claim that Arroyo has built "more bridges and roads than the combined infrastructure projects of former presidents Joseph Estrada, Fidel Ramos, and Cory Aquino."[7] As Arroyo herself boasted, contrary to evidence of actual underinvestment:[8] "We have built more and better infrastructure, including those started by others but left unfinished" (2009 SONA). From the view of Arroyo's Malacañang Palace, the 47,773 kilometers of roads and 289,944 lineal meters of bridges ostensibly built and repaired are taken as the objective correlatives of the nation's peregrination to First World modernity.[9] As one economist put it: "The story of our infrastructure is the story of our economy."[10]

The purpose of this essay is to probe into the rhetoric of infrastructure underlying the development programs during Arroyo's presidency, a rhetoric that persists in the present regime of Marcos-Duterte alliance. I am interested in how a concept of infrastructure came to delimit the referential field of public discourse around futural visions of millennial development. While infrastructure is nothing new to the social and economic history of Philippine development,[11] what is distinctive about its deployment by Arroyo is its peculiar yoking to a First Worlding imaginary. Infrastructure—and the value of technological modernity it came to signify—became both the sign of Arroyo's futurism and the very form through which its prophesied contents were disclosed. Drawing on empirical sources, the first half of the essay conceptualizes Arroyo's infrastructural futures as technologies of apprehending the time of the nation, which I suggest can be analyzed as a certain technological enframing of Philippine social forms to neoliberal globalization. The second half reflects on what is distorted and altogether vanished from Arroyo's infrastructural messianism. Through a reading of a Tagalog poem by activist-poet Joi Barrios, I examine the link between the drive toward infrastructure and the spike of extrajudicial killings during Arroyo's presidency. What kind of future-making is Arroyo's dream of "First World in twenty years"? How and why is First Worldom the imagined future? What is the meaning of change, progress, and political democracy in this context? The essay concludes by counterposing the technicist messianism of millennial development with other, more poetic ways of conceiving the present. Implicit throughout is the question, Why, in what so many viewed as the most corrupt government since the authoritarian regime of Ferdinand Marcos, was there no "People Power Revolution," no "EDSA IV"?

## The Case for Infrastructure

In the last months of her administration, facing the lowest of approval ratings and continued allegations of election fraud, corruption, and human rights violations from national and international organizations alike, Macapagal-Arroyo, or "GMA," set out on an aggressive "information dissemination project,"[12] spending millions of pesos on various media outlets in an effort to cast a more positive light on her almost decade-long, crisis-ridden administration.[13] Let us return to her June 2010 farewell speech and consider how Arroyo frames the idea of progress and its image of the future:

> Look around you in our cities, as you drive by the office towers that have changed the skylines. Look around you in our provinces, as you drive along the roads, bridges, and Ro-Ro ports where we have made massive investments. *This is the face of change.* Eighty-five percent of our people now have access to PhilHealth insurance. Over a hundred thousand new classrooms have been built and 9 million jobs have been created. We developed the call center industry almost from scratch. Today there are 500,000 call center and BPO [Business Processing Outsourcing] jobs when only 5,000 existed when I took office, yet these accomplishments are merely part of the continuum of history.

If the legacy of Fidel Ramos's presidency (1992–1998) is marked by his public-works campaign of Philippines 2000, the intensive liberalization, privatization, and deregulation of the national economy toward the goal of making the Republic a newly industrializing country by the new millennium,[14] Arroyo's is what we might describe as the infrastructural, technological enframing of Philippine millennial development. The aim: *"mapabilang ang Pilipinas sa mayayamang bansa sa loob ng dalawampung taon"* ["to count the Philippines among the rich nations within twenty years"] (2007 SONA). Motivated by the aspiration to achieve a "world-class" economy, Arroyo has made infrastructure investments the centerpiece of her administration's strategy for staving off the threat of recession and for relaunching the nation's economy. Her infrastructure speak gained her the epithet "Infrastructure Icon," a twenty-first century recapitulation of the "edifice complex" of Imelda Marcos.[15]

We can distinguish two aspects of the use of *infrastructure* at the outset: first as capital, second as trope. As a form of capital, infrastructure is seen as an investment that will yield positive returns to the extent that it enlarges a country's technological and human capacities, in turn stimulating the inflow of money and increasing production. As trope, infrastructure bears the entelechy of First World modernity, and, thus, lack of it would mean retaining the opprobrium of Third World subalternity. Importantly, the benchmark of First Worldom is not necessarily the United States, but increasingly post-Crash Singapore and Malaysia, the Philippines' hyperdeveloping

ASEAN neighbors, signaling a broader shift since the 1970s from a U.S.- to an Asian-centered driven capitalist world system. Reminiscent of Malaysia's *Wawasan* 2020 ("Vision 2020"), former prime minister Mahathir Moham- ad's vision of Malaysian development,[16] Arroyo's "First World in twenty years" projects itself as the rhetorical soundbite for her administration's mil- lenarianism.

In 2005, the World Bank assessed the needs of infrastructure in the Philippines as follows:

> The overall state of infrastructure in the country has not kept up with rapid population growth and urbanization, and has emerged as a key impediment to the Philippines' economic competitiveness. Compet- itiveness rankings underscore the importance of infrastructure to the Philippines' investment climate. The country slid to 52 (from 49) in the 2004 *World Competitiveness Yearbook*, with its infrastructure ranking slipping to 59 from 56 (out of 60 countries). In 2004, the World Economic Forum ranked the country 89 out of 102 countries for overall infrastructure quality—well below both Indonesia (51) and Vietnam (76).[17]

Accordingly, the World Bank, then and now, prescribes large fiscal adjust- ments to the Philippines' national budget in order to raise infrastructure spending.[18] By increasing its spending on infrastructure, the Philippines is said to benefit from the modernization of its technological capacities, thereby giving the national economy the edge it needs to make itself more competi- tive for private and foreign investments.[19] Infrastructure thus obtains a tal- ismanic value: the construction of roads, bridges, tunnels, airports, skyways, power plants, and technological centers is posited as a means of attracting inflows of foreign investment capital. The notion of infrastructure as beget- ting capital became the centerpiece of Arroyo's infrastructure-driven de- velopment, which her administration touted as the financial instrumental- ity to tide over the 2008 global finance crisis and to win the "War on Poverty" (*"Laban sa Kahirapan"*).

By integrating the seven thousand islands of the archipelago, infrastruc- ture building is said to increase the inflow of much-needed capital into key economic sectors, from agriculture, tourism, service, and manufacture—a process of capitalist integration Neferti X. M. Tadiar has theorized as "city everywhere." As one of Arroyo's slogans puts it: "More connectivity means more progress for the Filipino." Within this frame, the rural and urban poor become sites *of* and *for* capital, that is, "poverty capital," wherein spaces of impoverishment are transformed as a "subprime frontier where develop- ment capital and finance capital merge and collaborate such that new subjects of development are identified and new territories of investment are opened up and consolidated."[20] Yet, not surprisingly, poverty levels rose even as the national economy grew, indicating a development program marginalizing the interests of the already pauperized Filipino masses and benefiting only the privileged and the multinationals.[21] In spite of purported efforts to reverse conditions of poverty, "the proportion of the population deemed poor rose from 31.3 percent in 2000 to 33 percent in 2006 despite the increase in GDP per capita of about 2.7 percent a year during the same period."[22]

The claim that Arroyo has built more infrastructure than past administrations is contradicted by the fact that actual government expenditures as percentage of GDP reached historic low levels during her presidency.[23] Where infrastructure projects were undertaken, they were mired by a structure of management and financing characterized by heavy borrowings, lack of transparency, poor governance, and corruption.[24] Financing largely depended on the procurement of foreign loans from the IMF, World Bank, and Asian Development Bank, as well as bilateral agreements with the U.K., United States, Japan, China, Austria, Germany, and Australia, to name only a few. These loans gave the impression of prodigious money coming in from the outside, while surreptitiously increasing the government's already bloated debt holdings.[25] With ever-widening loans, galloping national deficits, and a dysfunctional tax bureau,[26] Arroyo became, at the time of her presidency, *the largest debtor among post-Marcos presidents.* The nation's public debt more than doubled from an already precarious P2.2 trillion in 2000 to an unsustainable P4.7 trillion in 2010.[27] To put it in the words of one credit analyst, Arroyo's Philippines is "living on borrowed time."[28] As new loans were secured to fund artificially inflated projects, fiscal policy shifted toward repaying these debts. As a result, national revenue atrophied as more than a third of the government's budget went into servicing interest payments, gutting much-needed public funds for social services, health, and public education.[29] Worse still, Arroyo's urban planning experiments were carried out by a deeply entrenched cartel network involving government officials, lawmakers, and contractors, who formed a nefarious system of pork barrel graft, bribery, and fixed bidding, in which favored firms won contracts and elite politicians gained cash advances.[30]

Behind the opacity of bureaucratic and politico-economic technocracy, what we can, bit by bit, piece together is the following situation: insofar as infrastructure spending continues to be underwritten by debt and pushed primarily by the interests of finance speculation and of maximizing market efficiency, Arroyo's program cannot be said to bring about the democratizing goal of providing freer access to resources and greater mobility and well-being to the Filipino citizenry. Rather, in its materialization under untenable conditions of debt, it appears as a scheme to accelerate the country's integration to neoliberal globalization, without scarcely any interrogation of its assumptions and operations. Who bears the costs of living on this borrowed time?

## Infrastructure as Technological Enframing

Arroyo describes her ascent to presidency as both an accidental coincidence and a historical necessity. "It was thrust upon me," as she is often heard saying, a destining she attributes to the forces of history and the people's democratic will, as played out in 2001's EDSA People Power II, a popular mass uprising that overthrew President Joseph "Erap" Estrada (1998–2000). "Looking back," Arroyo says, "rather than shirk from the onerous task, I rolled up my sleeves—determined to turn the Philippines around."[31] Arroyo fashions herself as the messiah, the national redeemer and savior of the Filipino people from the crisis that is them and their nation. As captured in the slogan, "*Ako ang simula ng pagbabago* [I am the start of change]," Filipinos are called upon to direct their energies toward realizing the seeds of their president's work, to actualize out of present crises her dream of Philippine First World modernity.[32]

Arroyo's messianism consists of an enframing the time of the nation, binding it toward a predetermined path of salvation via capitalist accumulation on grounds of social and economic development, even survivability. I want to suggest that the act of sovereignty behind the technological enframing of time issues from an authoritarian will masking itself as a messianic power, one which authorizes a future ideal toward which the nation is to aspire. The messianism is a form of time disciplining, in which time is measured as having an appropriable value only insofar as it can be ordered and strategically invested within market calculations. Enframing the time of the nation to a predetermined system of valuing disciplines the temporalities of social life by incorporating the necessarily heterogeneous aspirations of Philippine society within a reified singularity. That is, it aims to channel the temporal manifold of the nation within what Partha Chatterjee, following Walter Benjamin, calls the empty homogeneous time of global capital.[33] In this respect, Arroyo's messianism is a prophetic force whose projections of an infrastructural future to come contains not only an idea of development but also the meliorist ethos of delivering the *now* into modernity's teleology of universal history.

All this is to insist that at stake in infrastructure is the future—its possibility, meaning, and shape. In times of crisis, Arroyo's "predatory"[34] state mitigates national feelings of uncertainty by furnishing timelines for whom built infrastructure serves as physical, durable monuments of change. Hence, the future is monumentalized, spatialized, foreclosed, made concrete. We might even say that Arroyo's messianism has the consequence of "killing" time. It "kills" time inasmuch as the constitutive exposure of the now to the future—to the happening or coming of that which is not always known in advance—or, indeed, cannot be known in advance—is preemptively apprehended as something that can be anticipated and rationally calculated. To enframe the future in this way "is to deprive the future of its explosiveness . . . to annex the future as a new area for investment."[35] The future that is supposed to come unexpectedly and as surprise comes now as a plan, a fixed timeline to follow—an ordering of nation-time from the outside whose genealogy stretches back to the ten-year schedule to independence under the Tydings-McDuffie Act of 1934. Such foreclosures of the future effaces what Jacques Derrida calls "the pure eventfulness of the event" or "the coming of the to-come"[36] (which I suggest in the concluding section as taking the figure of the disappeared in contemporary Philippine politics). To call into question this technological enframing is to call into question a political order that would seek to contain, but cannot fully capture, the manifold time of Philippine social and political life. As we shall see, critique here will have something to do with the theme of life and death to the extent that the project of crafting the future, which continues to be the business of contemporary global capital, produces normative frames by which certain times and lives are considered worthwhile and others jettisoned as mere epiphenomena, superfluous, redundant, and so "disposable."

Arroyo's messianism "kills" time not only in the figurative sense. It "kills" also in the most dangerously literal. Infrastructural futures of Philippine First World development have in fact proven deadly, with state terrorism and extrajudicial killings as the political strategies through which Arroyo's regime consolidates itself by eliminating threats to her government. In 2002, Arroyo established *Oplan Bantay Laya* (Operation Freedom Watch), a counterinsurgency campaign to root out communist guerrilla rebels and persons suspected of belonging to the National Democratic Front, the Communist Party of the Philippines, and the New People's Army—declared enemies of the state and designated by the United States as terrorist groups. Since its establishment, more than 1,200 political killings and forced disappearances of labor organizers, journalists, peasant leaders, progressive officials, activists, students, church personnel, and everyday civilians have occurred.[37] Arroyo has in fact failed to account for these killings and abductions. Amid triumphalist claims of a stronger democratic republic, we might ask what remains of the conditions of democratic existence, including critical public discourse and civil engagement, in the face of such lethal human rights violations. These killings point to an ongoing war being waged by the state against the very people it claims to serve and protect. As the people are imperiled, so are their democratic institutions undermined, as indicated by the wave of political tribulations, which the following list can only partially limn:

> An uprising by the urban poor that nearly breached the walls of the presidential palace on May Day 2001; a botched military mutiny in July 2003; corruption scandals involving the first family; allegations of presidential involvement in fixing the 2004 elections; a failed coup-attempt-cum-popular-uprising in February 2006 that led to the declaration of emergency rule; concerted attacks on the press; an alarming spike in extrajudicial killings; impeachment attempts in 2005, 2006, and 2007; two major bribery scandals in late 2007, one involving the chief election officer and the other, brazen cash pay-outs from the Palace to congresspersons and governors; and a November 2007 bombing at the House of Representatives that killed a notorious warlord congressman from Mindanao.[38]

Under intensified conditions counterinsurgency, de facto anti-dissent policy, and evisceration of people power, what of the infrastructural futures that loom before the Philippines? These futures, indeed, have become hegemonic ways of framing the time of the nation. To frame means to delimit and confine an object within an apportioned representational space, which involves excluding that which is outside the space of the frame.[39] The systemic repression of activists and journalists points to what is violently excluded: the radical futures and communitarian desires that struggle for other, more viable forms of world-making—fallouts of Arroyo's new image of infrastructural modernity. The power of infrastructure is therefore not only the power to engender profits and bridges, but also the power to wage war and terror. It is in this respect that Arroyo's development apparatus, whose prognostications of progress are projected onto the sensuous, material frameworks of built infrastructure, can be understood as a temporal constriction of a genuine democracy to come. With its attendant military apparatus that threatens to disarm conditions of critique and popular sovereignty, Arroyo's regime of infrastructure development cannot be said to be democratic. It proves, rather, inimical to democracy itself.

I have tried to suggest that the politics of time around Arroyo's infrastructural futures technologically enframes nation-time so to render amenable the heterotemporalities of Philippine social life to market metrics. The saving power of Arroyo's messianism lies in its self-presentation as the desire to catapult the Philippine nation into First World modernity, which supposedly would bring salvation to the country not only by its position in the world market but also by its emplotment in world history. Insofar as it is predicated on this instrumental technological enframing of time, Arroyo's infrastructure development annihilates other modes of historical making and ways of imagining the future. Armed with the extrajudicial means and paramilitary force to erase opposition to her government, Arroyo's authoritarian messianism can be read as forcibly suppressing the "weak" messianic power of which Walter Benjamin spoke of in his "Theses on the Philosophy of History" (1940).[40] According to Benjamin, it is not the Messiah with a proper name that moves history; it is, rather, a messianism without presence—without a proper name. The present bears within it, and is generated by, this weak messianic power: the nonevincible forces of past generations that infuse the now with meaning and purpose. It is a notion of present time as the once promised future of those who came before. This weak messianic power bequeaths to people the "gift of time,"[41] and with it the twofold responsibility of remembering present and past injustices and bringing about the unfulfilled hopes of those who have passed.

## Futures Past to Come

In her collection of poetry, *Bulaklak sa Tubig: Mga Tula ng Pag-ibig at Himagsik (Flowers in Water: Poems on Love and Revolt)*, Joi Barrios engages in a politics of time that extends this messianic power of the present by conceiving of political action as the poetic act of loving, remembering, and struggling. In her poem, *"Litanya ng Paghahanap* [Litany of the Seeker]", Barrios opens by introducing a poetic persona who "Patches together evidence [*Pinagtatagpi ang mga ebidensiya*]" / "Threads together stories [*Pinagdudugtong ang mga salaysay*]" / "To present to the court [*Idinudulog sa hukuman*]" the claims of the wounded and the disappeared.[42] As suggested by the stressed plsoives drummed in the original Tagalog, *"Litanya,"* like many of the poems in her collection, is born out of a cumulative indignation in the wake of a public war to which it defiantly calls into question. In particular, the poem bears witness to the phenomenon of enforced disappearances linked to Arroyo's counterinsurgency campaigns. Enclosed is a dedication to the families of Karen Empeño and Sherlyn Cadapan, students of the University of the Philippines; Leonilo Arado and Luisa Dominado, campaigners for worker's and women's rights; and activist Jonas Burgos, all of whom remain, at the time of the writing of this essay, missing.

In inscribing the memory of their struggles, Barrios's exemplifies an aesthetic practice of giving poetic presence to Benjamin's notion of the weak messianic power of history. The poem asks: What does it mean to search for the missing—even those whom one does not directly know and those whom one may ultimately never know? To search for the missing is conceived here not only as an act of representational recuperation or historical restitution, a rallying cry to resurface the abducted (though certainly it is that as well). Clutched by an immeasurable sense of human loss, the poem also disposes the reader to relate to the disappeared in terms of a radical, ethical responsiveness. I say radical because it is unconditional and without end. At the heart of the poem lies this radical conception of political responsibility, which signifies the act of searching as the poetic activity of unleashing the past's unfulfilled hopes as well as the people's world-making potentials that have been violently extinguished under present infrastructural enframings. It is toward these uncounted, unredeemed experiences—figures of *futures past to come*—that Barrios writes of a communal self searching for the *desaparecidos*.

> *At tatanggapin ng aking puso,*
> *Siyang nawawala*
> *Siyang hinahanap*
> *Siyang minamahal*

> [And my heart will admit
> What it has sought,
> Those who are missing,
> The beloved]
> . . . . . . . . . .
> *Hinahanap ko*
> *Siyang nawawala,*
> *Pagkat ako ay ina,*
> *ako ay anak, ako ay asawa,*
> *ako ay kapatid; ako ay kasama.*
> *Ako'y nagmamahal*
> *kaya't kumakapit*
> *sa kaynipis na hibla*
> *ng nagdurugtong sa aming pag-asa.*

> [I seek out
> The disappeared,
> For I am mother,
> I am child, I am wife
> I am sister; I am comrade.
> I love even now
> Holding fast to the
> Delicate threads
> Which bind us, tethered
> To this hope.]

For Barrios, to search for the disappeared is to extend the ethics of mourning by engaging in the empathetic act of calling and listening. The poem not only tenders the claims of the disappeared but paradoxically signifies their absence as having claiming power. The disappeared possess an agency that is without full presence. The poem is thus less an elegy than an impassioned exhortation to struggle in concert with forces that lie outside the field of the visible—a field, which as we have seen in the foregoing analysis has been foreclosed by a technological enframing through built infrastructure. Unlike Arroyo's infrastructures whose promise of social connectivity is of a technological kind, Barrios's poem builds upon a different kind of infrastructure whose field of intelligibility extends beyond what is simply near or visible or, as Heidegger would say, present-at-hand. (Marx called it the "supra-sensible" dimension of reality.) As suggested in these lines, searching for the disappeared becomes for Barrios[43] a practice of personal relating that is interminable, cutting across all forms of social belonging and identification: as "mother," "child," "wife," "sister," and "comrade." Thus the one who searches instantiates what we might call an *infrastructural relating and being-with others*. It is infrastructural in the sense that the seeker forges bonds of solidarity that exceed the ethical economy of the same and the familiar. It does so by summoning and giving infrastructural form to the weak messianic power of the people.[44] In contrast to the being-for-others, which characterizes the technicity of Arroyo's infrastructure development, Barrios binds together affective ties for an infrastructural being-with-others, an interminable and ever-present being-with the disappeared.

For Barrios, the disappeared inexhaustibly haunt the present. This haunting, as Resil Mojares has pointed out in his study of Filipino poetics, is a form of desire that is marked by a peculiar temporality: "As a sign of what is amiss, a lack unfulfilled, the shade of something left unfinished, it does not only point to the past but the future . . . not only of something past but *the trace of what one had desired but had not quite accomplished*."[45] To the extent that this haunting can have a claim over us, the present bears within it precisely this "trace," which, like the figure of the ghost, is a paradoxical presence that is without presence or, like the disappeared, without body. As spectral traces of the "missing" (*nawawala*), their being-without-presence does not mean that they are politically inconsequential. Rather, the claims of the disappeared insist on *truths that defy a juridical system that would deny the evidence of things unseen*. Stepping forth as their witness, Barrios's poetic consciousness gives form to these silenced atrocities, voicing a moral outrage in the face of lives injured and lives lost under conditions of state-sponsored violence.

The poetic vocation of searching and giving testimony is, to be sure, awakened by grief and certainly outrage. But here it is also structured around a sense of hope (*pag-asa*), which is bound up with a future whose meaning cannot be posited in advance because it, like the anticipation of full justice for the disappeared, is yet to come. One recalls here the Derridean lesson that there is no democracy without this relation to the nonactual.[46] Just as democracy is never simply present because it is haunted and riven by the temporality of the "to come,"[47] without which democracy would not be open to self-critique or revision, Barrios goads into being a self whose search for the disappeared is compelled by, and engages with, forces that exceed the order of sensible presence. The disappeared demands a way of seeing that looks beyond what comes readily to view as given reality, as though inviting one to imagine what lies beyond the brute facticity of present technological enframings: a building, a bridge, a road. What is more, to search for the missing is thematized in the poem as a form of political responsibility that, like a democracy to come, is incalculable, infinite, and untimely. Indeed, in Barrios's poem, such untimeliness is expressed as an unconditional urgency: "I search / Even if I do not know beginning and end [*simula't hantungan*]." It is a responsibility that is not deferrable precisely because it contains an absolute injunction, which obliges one to act even when the "corpse lays there unrecognizable [*hindi na makilala*]." The disappeared is thus the figure for both the state capture of democracy (democracy in the original sense of the power of the people) and the unfinished project of a democracy to come. To search for the disappeared would mean retrieving both significations, not by recovering some pure past or speculating a calculable future, but by pursuing "what one had desired but had not quite accomplished," here: justice (*katarungan*). The political order to which the poem calls into question is displaced by, and exposed to, the redemptory potential around which the figure of the disappeared spectralizes: glimpses of the not-so-far past that serve as critical resource for another future.

Yet, what does it mean to think of a future redemption based on an infrastructural responsiveness that is unconditionally urgent, without limits, and without the recognizable emplotment of beginning and end? It means to wrench free the times of crises from the exclusionary determinations of what is often precomprehended as either "progress" or "development." In Barrios's poem, the seeker prompts a thinking of the past, present, and future that is nonchronological: to act—*there*, where beginning and end remain unrecognizable. The poetic consciousness calls out to the disappeared because she is compelled by a notion of democratic justice, whose time is at once enduring and without end. Its shape, not a line but a circle: "I seek / The disappeared / As the disappeared / Seeks justice [*Hinahanap ko / Siyang nawawala / At siyang nawawala / Ay naghahanap ng katarungan*]." In "*Litanya*," to search means more than the elementary sense of seeking or revealing that which is sought. It means also the poetical process of bringing-forth, of disclosing words and worlds, which precipitate each and everyone to the demand of critique, if not "regime change," to borrow the language of popular protest.

The contrast I am making here is one between Arroyo's millenarian messianism and Barrios's messianic poetics. The difference lies fundamentally in their temporal structure of feeling and relating to the present and the claims over the future one can make from such a position. As I have suggested in my reading, Barrios's poem strives to bring forth the messianicity of the past in the *poiesis* of searching for those who, in the very present, remain missing, a searching that enlivens political life. In contradistinction, Arroyo's messianism exorcises the messianicity of the past by foisting the present into a terminal future, whose promises of salvation serve only to obfuscate a sovereign order marked by an undemocratic will to crush out such forces. With regard to Arroyo's messianism, we might then say that to the extent that the present is rendered redeemable only on condition that it is linked to a future whose meaning and shape are settled in advance, the sphere of political life becomes foreclosed by a temporal grammar that can be understood in the tense we call *future perfect*: the "I shall have done X." Listen, for instance, to Arroyo's June 2004 inauguration address, which commenced her second term as president: "When I step down six years from now this will have been my legacy: I *shall have created* more than 6 million jobs . . . I *shall have developed* 1 million hectares of land . . . I *shall have balanced* the budget . . . I *shall have supported* the people."[48]

The ruse of development is that it presents itself as the very source of "the gift of time," of issuing forth a ready-made future that will be, whose proleptic form it calls progress. In times of crises, the task at hand is not only to discern which possible futures are most serviceable in given actualities, but also to interrogate the very parameters of the possible itself, indeed, of maintaining the potency of possibility as such. This was also Heidegger's point when, in *Being and Time* (1927), he suggested that "higher than actuality stands *possibility* [Höher als die Wirklichkeit steht die *Möglichkeit*]."[49] What we are grappling here through Barrios's poem is a creative practice of nonpunctual timing that is different from Arroyo's futurism, one that displaces the determination of ends, as well as precomprehended emplotments of "getting there": a poetical reckoning with, and opening of, the nation-time as an interminably "unfinished" project.[50] Against the messianic prophecies of the "it-will-have-been," Barrios's poem is an example of an alternate time practice of bridging ethical engagements. Emboldened by a notion of democracy to come, "*Litanya*" appeals on behalf of the nonpresent(able) by infusing the present with the messianicity of the past and bringing forth the unfulfilled hopes and promises it represents. Thus, as a poetics of *futures past to come*, Barrios's poem voices a revolutionary poetic counterpart to the *future perfect* images of infrastructural modernity produced by Arroyo's technological enframing of Philippine social life and its arrestation of the political present.

This essay has attempted to examine not only how the future of contemporary Philippines is enframed—what conceptual frames are being used and to what ends and effects—but also what is displaced, distorted, and altogether extinguished in technological enframing. Following Jean-Luc Nancy's insight that "what forms a world today is exactly the conjunction of unlimited process of eco-technological enframing and of a vanishing of the possibilities of forms of life,"[51] this essay has also tried to suggest that at the heart of development lies the question of world and the temporal forms in which that world is said to unfold. To frame the question of development in this way has allowed us to put into relief certain determinations and disciplinings of time at work in the very economism of contemporary neoliberal globalization. As demonstrated in the context of Arroyo's presidency, infrastructure-driven development contains a normative claim on economic progress, whose messianic conceit has the effect of saying, "We *ought* to live in *this* order of time," as opposed to another possibility of time and timing, hence, other possibilities of life and living.

Political struggles over practices of development thus become increasingly marked as struggles over the meanings of time, whose articulation in the Philippines is surely but one example of many in the postcolonial Global South. We also have seen how the practical question concerning the future, of the possibility of building a sustainable, livable world, demands another scalar concept of historical change. It would be based neither on instrumental frameworks of positing pregiven means and ends nor in the teleological foreclosures of the "it-will-have-been," from which built infrastructure emerge as their visual, material ballast. Rather, it would draw upon the more difficult to perceive, yet politically decisive, poetic historicity of futures past to come. Reading Barrios's poem, one wagers that the critical sensibility worthy of the question of the future may prove to be the activity of searching for, and responding to, not only the one who may return, but also to those who may never finally arrive: the missing, the disappeared, the dead. Their silent testimonies—all everywhere around us—call us to engage in the interminable search of what continues to "fall away" from the modern technological enframing of time we call global capitalism:[52] the radical possibilities that pass through and shape the time of the now.

## NOTES

1. Arroyo's "First World in twenty years" locution crescendoed around the beginning of the latter half of her second term, with some commentators viewing it as an attempt

to extend her political reach and influence beyond her post as president. See, in particular, "GMA Backtracks on Wage Hike Issue"; "Gloria Rocks as Peso Rolls"; "GMA's 'Enchanted Kingdom'"; "RP Economic Growth to Drift or Take Off?"; "Growth for Whom?"; "Light of Learning"; "GMA Back, Urges Nation to Emulate Malaysia"; "GMA: Prepare for 2010"; and "GMA: Mums the Word." It even appears in the codification of laws, see Executive Orders No. 599 and No. 739.

2. According to the international advocacy group Committee to Protect Journalists, the grisly November 2009 Maguindanao Massacre of thirty-two journalists in the southern town of Ampatuan reinstates the Philippines among the most dangerous countries for reporters and media workers, making the total number killed since 1991 seventy-one with "motive confirmed." For a useful collection of critical essays on the spate of political killings and enforced disappearances allegedly linked to Arroyo's administration, see Raymundo and Tolentino, *Kontra-Gahum*.

3. Percentage growth rates of Philippine GDP are as follows: 6.4 (2004); 5.0 (2005); 5.3 (2006); and 7.1 (2007); sourced from Balisacan et al., "The Philippine Economy and Poverty."

4. A senior economist at the World Bank ascertains the Philippines' success this way: "High GDP growth, reduced public debt, a balance of payment surplus, falling interest rates, recovering financial markets and high remittance levels by overseas Filipino workers have combined to bring about the highest economic growth achieved by the Philippines in twenty years." See World Bank, "RP Registers Highest Growth." Compare World Bank, "Philippines Leads Peers." The 2004–2007 period of accelerated GDP growth, however, was short-lived, with rates sharply falling from 7.1 in 2007 to 3.8 in 2008 and then to 0.9 in 2009, indicating an unstable, unsustainable growth path.

5. Transcripts of President Gloria Macapagal-Arroyo's public speeches, including this July 27, 2009, State of the Nation Address, are archived and available online at www.macapagal.com/gma. Hereafter, State of the Nation Address speeches will be designated in the main text as SONA, followed after the year.

6. This speech is available online at www.macapagal.com/gma, also www.youtube.com/watch?v=MLWubkTCG4E.

7. "PGMA Exceeds Infra Projects of 3 Past Presidents." For critiques of Arroyo's exceptionalism regarding higher spending on infrastructure, see, in particular, "It's GMA, Stupid," and "In the Shadow of Debt."

8. Actual spending on infrastructure ran consistently below 2 percent of GDP during Arroyo's two terms as president. The data on public spending on infrastructure as percentage of GDP are as follows: 1.77 percent (2001); 1.51 percent (2002); 1.41 percent (2003); 1.06 percent (2004); 0.92 percent (2005); 1.52 percent (2006); 1.47 percent (2007); 1.70 percent (2008); and 1.70 percent (2009); sources: Philippine Department of Budget and Management and Senate Economic Planning Office. Comparative figures of total government expenditures on infrastructure as percentage of GDP show that Arroyo has in fact spent considerably less than past administrations: 2.4 percent (Aquino, 1986–1992); 2.7 percent (Ramos, 1993–1998); 2.9 percent (Estrada, 1999–2000); see Diokno, "The Philippines: Fiscal Behavior in Recent History."

9. Under Arroyo's P40 billion Bridge Program (US$870 million), about 1,275 bridges were cited as complete, projects that were financially backed by loan agreements between the Philippine government and the Japan Bank for International Cooperation, World Bank, and the British government's Export Credit Guarantee Department. For our purposes here, there is, of course, a symbolic value behind bridges; see, for example, Fredric Jameson's discussion of the bridge as concept-image in Kidlat Tahimik's 1977 interna-

tionally acclaimed film, *Mababangong Bangungot* (Perfumed Nightmare): "As a 'concept', [the bridge] has something to do with the relationship between cultural stages (Third and First Worlds) . . . between the past and the future, as well, and between confinement and freedom" (1992, 196).

10. "Inferior Infrastructure."

11. A historical antecedent to Arroyo's infrastructuralism is Marcos's architectural beautification of Metro Manila under the regime's New Society campaign, which included the construction of cultural centers, convention halls, and other innumerable projects of urbanization. On how state investments in architecture during the Marcos era became linked with industrial development and urbanization, see Lico, *Edifice Complex*; see also Tadiar, "Manila's New Metropolitan Form," and Rafael, "Patronage, Pornography, and Youth."

12. In addition to full-page advertisements in national newspapers and prime-time TV commercials, Arroyo used P10 million of public funds at the 2010 Philippine Independence Day celebration, a public relations campaign to showcase her administration's achievements with ten parade floats each standing for "budget reform; education for all; automated elections; transportation and digital infrastructure; terminate hostilities with the separatist Moro Islamic Liberation Front and the communist New Peoples Army; heal the wounds of Edsa I, II and III; electricity and water for all; opportunities and livelihood and 10 million jobs; decongestion of Metro Manila; and develop Subic and Clark"; see "GMA Parades Triumphs."

13. See Hutchcroft, "The Arroyo Imbroglio in the Philippines." For the history of oligarchic rule in Philippine state politics to which Arroyo's political career belongs, see Benedict Anderson's characteristically illuminating analysis, "Cacique Democracy in the Philippines."

14. For a concise account of Ramos's financial and trade liberalization, see Bello, *The Anti-Development State*, chapter 3; and Bello, *The Future in the Balance*, 262–265.

15. The title comes from Deputy Presidential Spokesperson Charito Planas quoted in "Palace Scores Lp on Ad."

16. For a succinct analysis of Mahathir's "Vision 2020" as a nation-building development program, see Hilley. *Malaysia: Mahathirism, Hegemony, and the New Opposition*, 19–46.

17. Von Amsberg and Delvoie, *Philippines: Meeting Infrastructure Challenges*, xviii.

18. See note 9 for figures on government expenditure rates on infrastructure.

19. According to the World Competitiveness Yearbook report published by International Institute for Management Development (IMD), the Philippines' overall rankings in infrastructure quality, which are used to indicate a country's competitiveness for capital investments, are as follows: forty-seventh (2002); fifty-sixth (2003); fifty-ninth (2004); fifty-fifth (2005); fifty-sixth (2006); fifty-first (2007); forty-eighth (2008); fifty-sixth (2009); fifty-sixth (2010); and fifty-seventh (2011).

20. Roy, *Poverty Capital*, 30.

21. Despite an average GDP growth rate of 5.3 percent between 2003 and 2006, the number of poor people increased from 23.8 million in 2003 to 27.6 million in 2006; see Asian Development Bank, *Poverty in the Philippines*, 14–15.

22. See Balisacan et al., "The Philippine Economy and Poverty," 4.

23. See Diokno, "Philippine Fiscal Behavior in Recent History." As Diokno writes: "Infrastructure and other capital outlays in percent of GDP declined slightly from 2.6 percent during Marcos's final years to 2.4 percent during the Aquino administration.

It rose to 2.7 percent during the Ramos years and 2.9 percent during the Estrada years, before hitting a historic low of 2.0 percent during the Arroyo administration" (53).

24. See, for instance, "World Bank Lists Sources of Corruption in Philippines."

25. The amounts for combined domestic and foreign debt are as follows (in trillion pesos): 2.2 (2000); 2.4 (2001); 2.8 (2002); 3.4 (2003); 3.8 (2004); 3.9 (2005); 3.8 (2006); 3.7 (2007); 4.2 (2008); 4.4 (2009); and 4.7 (2010). Source: Philippine Bureau of Treasury.

26. The *New York Times* reports: "Tax revenues in the Philippines amount to only 14.5 per cent of gross domestic product, ranking it behind every other nation in Asia but Laos and Cambodia. Last year [2003], according to one bureau official, the bureau collected only $1.6 billion in personal income taxes from less than 2 million individuals in a country with a population of 86.2 million" (August 3, 2004).

27. According to data from Freedom From Debt Coalition (www.fdc.ph), Arroyo's total borrowings and debt services from 2001 to 2009 exceeded the aggregate amount of the past three presidents (1986–2000). For a succinct comparative analysis of fiscal data from Marcos to Arroyo, see also Diokno, "Philippine Fiscal Behavior in Recent History," and the appendices on government fiscal performance and debt financing therein cited.

28. Quote by Agost Benard of the international credit-rating agency Standard & Poor's, from "Mess in Manila."

29. The anomalous decline in debt holdings between 2005 and 2007 (see note 26 above) is often attributed to foreign exchange revaluation adjustments after the weakening of the U.S. dollar against the yen and euro. What it represents is in fact the extraordinary spike in government servicing of external debt, which took the form of automatic appropriations of public funds: in 2005, debt repayment amounted to P679 billion (compared with P274 billion in 2001), representing about 85 percent of the country's then-total revenue.

30. See the revealing report by Aries C. Fufo, which details multilevel cartel activities involving bid manipulation, overpricing of materials, falsification of documents, and tax evasion on projects funded by the Japan Bank for International Cooperation, in "Bidders Spill Names, Modus Operandi in Bid Fixing," ABC-CBN News, February 3, 2009, rp1.abs-cbnnews.com/print/39978; see also "What the Witnesses Said" for excerpts of interviews with anti-corruption investigators of the World Bank on the alleged bidding collusion and fraud behind Arroyo's National Road Improvement and Management Program-1.

31. Arroyo's Speech on Philippine Independence Day, June 12, 2010.

32. See "GMA: We Are on the Right Side of History."

33. See Chatterjee, *The Politics of the Governed*, 5.

34. See Quimpo, "The Philippines."

35. Jameson, *Archaeologies of the Future*, 228.

36. Derrida, *Rogues*, 84.

37. According to reports gathered by the human rights organization Karapatan, the number of victims of extrajudicial and arbitrary execution per annum under Arroyo's government is as follows: 100 (2001); 124 (2002); 130 (2003); 85 (2004); 194 (2005); 235 (2006); 100 (2007); 90 (2008); 130 (2009); and 17 (2010, as of June 30); available at www.karapatan.org/Karapatan-Monitor-AprJun-2010.

38. Hutchcroft, "The Arroyo Imbroglio in the Philippines," 141–142.

39. Compare Butler, *Frames of War*, 8–12: "To call the frame into question is to show that the frame never quite contained the scene it was meant to limn, that something was already outside, which made the very sense of the inside possible, recognizable. The frame never quite determined precisely what it is we see, think, recognize, and appre-

hend. Something exceeds the frame that troubles our sense of reality; in other words, something occurs that does not conform to our established understanding of things" (9).

40. Benjamin, "Theses on the Philosophy of History." The passage reads: "The past carries with it a temporal index by which it is referred to redemption. There is a secret agreement between past generations and the present one . . . Like every generation that preceded us, we have been endowed with a *weak* Messianic power, a power which the past has a claim" (254).

41. The thinking of the messianic politics of time I pursue in the following pages draws from the work of Derrida, especially *Given Time, Specters of Marx*, and *Rogues*. "The gift," as Derrida writes in *Given Time*, "like the event, as event, must remain unforeseeable, but remain so without keeping itself. It must let itself be structured by the aleatory; it must appear chancy or in any case lived as such, apprehended as the intentional correlate of a perception that is absolutely surprised by the encounter with what it perceives, beyond its horizon of anticipation . . . a gift or an event that would be foreseeable, necessary, conditioned, programmed, expected, counted on would not be lived as either a gift or as an event" (122–123).

42. Barrios, *Bulaklak Sa Tubig*, 33–35. Translations have been modified where necessary to better match aspects of the text under discussion. "*Litanya ng Paghahanap* [Litany of the Seeker]": Reprinted with permission of the author.

43. Marx, *Capital: A Critique of Political Economy*, Vol. 1, 145.

44. My reading here draws from the hermeneutics of *kalayaan* (freedom) and millenarian revolt that Reynaldo Clemeña Ileto explicates in his study of late-nineteenth-century Philippine peasant movements, in *Pasyon and Revolution*; it is also inspired by Tadiar's reading of *kapwa* (fellow-being) as a politically enabling mode of relating she describes as syncretic sociability, in *Things Fall Away*, 45–52.

45. Mojares, "Haunting of the Filipino Writer," in *Waiting for Mariang Makiling*, 309–310, my emphasis.

46. As Derrida writes in *Specters of Marx*: "No justice . . . seems possible or thinkable without the principle of some *responsibility*, beyond all living present, within that which disjoins the living present, before the ghosts of those who are not yet born or who are already dead, be they victims of wars, political, or other kinds of violence, nationalist, racist, colonialist, sexist, or other kinds of exterminations, victims of the oppressions of capitalist imperialism or any of the forms of totalitarianism" (xviii).

47. See Derrida's argument in *Rogues*, wherein he characterizes the temporality of the "democracy to come" (*démocratie à venir*) not in terms of a utopian hope or ideal but in terms of the aporetic structure of self-difference or "différence": "Democracy is what it is only in the différance by which it defers itself and differs from itself. It is what it is only by spacing itself beyond being and even beyond ontological difference; it is (without being) equal and proper to itself only insofar as it is inadequate and improper, at the same time behind and ahead of itself . . . interminable in its incompletion beyond all determinate forms of incompletion" (38). I have also benefited from the invaluable remarks on Derrida's concept of democracy to come in Hägglund, *Radical Atheism*, chapter 5.

48. In an interview published by the *Philippine Star* (March 24, 2011), Arroyo confidently recapitulates: "From day one that's what I tried to do—tried to have permanent change in the economy of the Philippines so that it can have our growth sustainable and move into the First World within twenty years."

49. Heidegger, *Being and Time*, 34; Heidegger, *Sein Und Zeit*, 51–52, original emphasis.

50. As Caroline S. Hau writes: "Because our programs of action must always be open to contingency and risk, the act of struggling to transform society, to make and remake community, remains an ethical imperative we cannot afford to ignore, let alone dismiss. This is a way of saying that the nation is irreducibly marked by the imperative toward radical transformation and by its historical and particularized responses to this imperative. The nation is an *unfinished revolution*, and the impossibility of reducing the heterogeneous 'excesses' of the nation to one coherent narrative, far from nullifying the difficult task of critique, makes the task of critique necessary, protracted, unending"; see Hau, *Necessary Fictions*, 281–282, my emphasis.

51. Nancy, *The Creation of the World*, 95.

52. I am indebted to Tadiar's richly suggestive use of this term for inspiring some of these reflections. "Refurbished as well as unreconstructed nationalisms and transnationalisms ... such are the familiar trajectories of world-historical agency in these times, trajectories from which all other manner of human and parahuman lives, pasts, presents, and futures, cultural imaginations, and virtual realities are jettisoned. These things *fall away*, and their barely apprehended importance to our worlds is lost to us, who seek different holds on our immanent futures" (Tadiar, *Things Fall Away*, 3, my emphasis).

## BIBLIOGRAPHY

Amsberg, Joachim von, and Christian Delvoie. *Philippines: Meeting Infrastructure Challenges*. Washington, DC: World Bank Group, 2005.

Anderson, Benedict. "Cacique Democracy in the Philippines." In *The Spectre of Comparisons: Nationalism, Southeast Asia, and the World*, 192–226. London: Verso, 1998.

Asian Development Bank. *Poverty in the Philippines: Causes, Constraints, and Opportunities*. Manila: Asian Development Bank, 2009.

Balisacan, Arsenio, Sharon Piza, Dennis Mapa, Carlos Abad Santos, and Donna Odra. "The Philippine Economy and Poverty During the Global Economic Crisis." *Philippine Review of Economics* 47, no. 1 (2010): 1–37.

Barrios, Joi. *Bulaklak Sa Tubig: Mga Tula Ng Pag-Ibig at Himagsik*. Pasig City: Anvil, 2010.

Bello, Walden. *The Anti-Development State: The Political Economy of Permanent Crisis in the Philippines*. Quezon City: Focus on the Global South, 2004.

———. *The Future in the Balance: Essays on Globalization and Resistance*. Quezon City: University of the Philippines Press, 2001.

———. "In the Shadow of Debt." Focus on the Global South, April 28, 2008, www.focus web.org/node/1363.

Benard, Agost. "Mess in Manila." *Economist*, July 16, 2005.

Benjamin, Walter. "Theses on the Philosophy of History." In *Illuminations*, edited by Hannah Arendt. New York: Shocken Books, 1968.

Butler, Judith. *Frames of War: When Is Life Grievable?* London: Verso, 2009.

Chatterjee, Partha. *The Politics of the Governed: Reflections on Popular Politics in Most of the World*. New York: Columbia University Press, 2004.

Derrida, Jacques. *Given Time. I, Counterfeit Money*. Translated by Peggy Kamuf. Chicago: University of Chicago Press, 1992.

———. *Jacques Derrida, Rogues: Two Essays on Reason*. Translated by Pascale-Anne Brault and Michael Naas. Stanford, CA: Stanford University Press, 2005.

———. *Specters of Marx*. Translated by Peggy Kamuf. London: Verso, 1994.

Diokno, Benjamin E. "Philippine Fiscal Behavior in Recent History." *Philippine Review of Economics* 47, no. 1 (2010): 39–87.

———. "The Philippines: Fiscal Behavior in Recent History." In *AC-UPSE Economic Forum*, 11–58. Quezon City: UP School of Economics, 2008.

"Gloria Rocks as Peso Rolls." *Philippine Daily Inquirer*, November 25, 2005.

"GMA Back, Urges Nation to Emulate Malaysia." *Manila Bulletin*, September 2, 2007.

"GMA Backtracks on Wage Hike Issue." *Philippine Daily Inquirer*, November 8, 2005.

"GMA: Mums the Word." *Philippine Daily Inquirer*, June 21, 2009.

"GMA Parades Triumphs." *Philippine Daily Inquirer*, June 13, 2010.

"GMA: Prepare for 2010." *Philippine Daily Inquirer*, January 30, 2009.

"GMA: We Are on the Right Side of History." *Philippine Daily Inquirer*, April 7, 2006.

"GMA's 'Enchanted Kingdom.'" *Manila Standard*, May 30, 2006.

"Growth for Whom?" *Philippine Daily Inquirer*, December 29, 2006.

Hägglund, Martin. *Radical Atheism: Derrida and the Time of Life*. Stanford, CA: Stanford University Press, 2008.

Hau, Caroline S. *Necessary Fictions: Philippine Literature and the Nation, 1946–1980*. Quezon City: Ateneo de Manila University Press, 2000.

Heidegger, Martin. *Being and Time*. Translated by Joan Stambaugh. Albany: State University of New York Press, 1996.

———. *Sein Und Zeit*, vol. 2. Edited by Friedrich-Wilhelm von Herrmann. Frankfurt: Vittorio Klostermann, 1975 [1927].

Hilley, John. *Malaysia: Mahathirism, Hegemony, and the New Opposition*. London: Zed Books, 2001.

Hutchcroft, Paul D. "The Arroyo Imbroglio in the Philippines." *Journal of Democracy* 19, no. 1 (2008): 141–155.

Ileto, Reynaldo C. *Pasyon and Revolution: Popular Movements in the Philippines, 1840–1910*. Quezon City: Ateneo de Manila University Press, 1979.

"Inferior Infrastructure." *Philippine Daily Inquirer*, January 26, 2004.

"It's GMA, Stupid." *Philippine Daily Inquirer*, February 15, 2010.

Jameson, Fredric. *Archaeologies of the Future: The Desire Called Utopia and Other Science Fictions*. London: Verso, 2005.

———. *The Geopolitical Aesthetic: Cinema and Space in the World System*. Bloomington: Indiana University Press, 1992.

Lico, Gerard. *Edifice Complex: Power, Myth, and Marcos State Architecture*. Quezon City: Ateneo de Manila University Press, 2003.

"Light of Learning." *Philippine Daily Inquirer*, July 31, 2007.

Marx, Karl. *Capital: A Critique of Political Economy*, Vol. 1, translated by Ben Fowkes. New York: Penguin, 1976.

Mojares, Resil B. *Waiting for Mariang Makiling: Essays in Philippine Cultural History*. Quezon City: Ateneo de Manila University Press, 2002.

Nancy, Jean-Luc. *The Creation of the World or Globalization*. Albany, NY: SUNY Press, 2007.

"Palace Scores Lp on Ad, Cites Infrastructure Achievements." *Manila Bulletin*, March 5, 2010.

"PGMA Exceeds Infra Projects of 3 Past Presidents." *Philippine News Agency*, May 26, 2010.

Quimpo, Nathan Gilbert. "The Philippines: Predatory Regime, Growing Authoritarian Features." *Pacific Review* 22, no. 3 (July 2009): 335–353.

Rafael, Vicente L. "Patronage, Pornography, and Youth: Ideology and Spectatorship during the Early Marcos Years." In *White Love and Other Events in Filipino History*, 122–161. Durham, NC: Duke University Press, 2000.

Roy, Ananya. *Poverty Capital: Microfinance and the Making of Development*. New York: Routledge, 2010.

"RP Economic Growth to Drift or Take Off?" *Manila Bulletin*, September 23, 2006.

Tadiar, Neferti X. M. "City Everywhere." *Theory, Culture & Society* 33, no. 7–8 (December 2016): 57–83.

———. "Manila's New Metropolitan Form." *Differences: A Journal of Feminist Cultural Studies* 5, no. 3 (1993): 154–178.

———. *Things Fall Away: Philippine Historical Experience and the Makings of Globalization*. Durham, NC: Duke University Press, 2009.

Tolentino, Rolando B., and Sarah Raymundo, eds. *Kontra-Gahum: Academics against Political Killings*. Quezon City: IBON, 2006.

"What the Witnesses Said." *Manila Times*, February 14, 2009.

World Bank. "Philippines Leads Peers With 7.3 Percent GDP Growth." April 1, 2008, go.worldbank.org/NZLVO8I130.

———. "RP Registers Highest Growth Among Southeast Asian Middle Income Countries." November 15, 2007, go.worldbank.org/8XM1P2RND0.

"World Bank Lists Sources of Corruption in Philippines." *Philippine Daily Inquirer*, April 1, 2008.

# "The Struggle Continues . . ."

*On the Cruel Optimism of LGBT Organizing*

ROLAND SINTOS COLOMA

This chapter advances and extends my previous examination of the political and educational activism of *Ladlad*, the first lesbian, gay, bisexual, and transgender (LGBT) political party in the Philippines and the only existing LGBT political party in the world (Coloma 2013). When *Ladlad* was founded in 2003, its original name was *Ang Lunduyan* ("the center"), but it changed its name to *Ang Ladlad* ("the unfurled") in 2006. In my previous work, I contend that *Ladlad* enacts what I call "parrhesiastic pedagogy": "an oppositional form of teaching by subordinated subjects who assert their freedom to tell truths that counter hegemonic understandings of established discourses." I suggest that *Ladlad* leaders "derive their truths from lived experiences, participatory observations, and thoughtful introspections, and are considered trustworthy due to their courage to take unpopular positions, their honorable backgrounds and reputations, and their consistency in words and actions. Situated in an inferior position in relation to their dominant interlocutors [i.e., the state, church, and general populace], [*Ladlad* as a collective] believe in their moral duty to tell the truth and willingly take the dangerous risk of engendering potentially negative responses" (Coloma 2013, 503–504).

The emergence and development of *Ladlad* as a national political party needs to be understood within a broader LGBT social movement of grassroots organizing and coalition building in the Philippines since the early 1990s (Coloma 2013). *Ladlad* built upon the queer road paved by earlier organizations, such as Babaylan at the University of the Philippines (founded in 1992), the Progressive Organization of Gays (1993), the Womyn Supporting Womyn Center (1994), the Lesbian and Gay Legislative Advocacy Network (1999), the Lesbian Advocates Philippines (1999), the Society of Transsexual Women of the Philippines (2002), and the Rainbow Rights Project (2005). The first Gay March in Asia—now more commonly referred to as Pride March—was held in the Philippines in 1994. In 1999, the country's first LGBT newspaper, *ManilaOut*, was published, and the first LGBT (Pink) film festival was convened. Perhaps it is not too surprising that the LGBT social movement and, in particular, many of the pioneering LGBT cultural, educational, and political organizations began in Metro Manila. The country's capital region is not only the seat of government, but is also the center of arts, culture, entertainment, economy, and education. As a result, it draws a diverse cross section of people from across the country and around the world who are immersed in cultural differences and are keen to organize for equity, fairness, and justice.

In this chapter, I will expand my research on *Ladlad* in three ways—spatially, temporally, and conceptually. First, while my previous analysis primarily focused on Metro Manila, I will attend to the ways in which geographical spaces outside of the capital region need to be seriously considered to gain a fuller perspective of LGBT organizing in the Philippines. For instance, *Ladlad* worked extensively in the provinces to develop regional chapters, build leadership capacity, and garner electoral support. Second, I will track political events since the 2010 election in the Philippines, the time period at which my previous article ended, until 2016 to document key moments that insightfully reveal both the challenges and inroads in LGBT mobilization. I will examine *Ladlad*'s campaign for the 2013 midterm election and the historic victories in the 2016 national election of the first transgender woman in Congress and the president supposedly considered to be the most LGBT-friendly. Third, I will connect my theorizing of *Ladlad*'s parrhesiastic pedagogy to Lauren Berlant's (2011) concept of "cruel optimism," which "names a relation of attachment to compromised conditions of possibility" (24). In this chapter, I aim to understand the central affective mode that compels LGBT leaders and activists to continue pursuing political and educational work in spite, or perhaps because, of ongoing losses—through electoral defeats or through the killing and murder of lesbians, gays, bisexuals, and transgender people.

In her book *Cruel Optimism*, Berlant (2011) argues that people maintain fantasies of the "good life" with attachments to an "object of desire," defined as "a cluster of promises we want someone or something to make to us and make possible for us," which may or may not always feel optimistic (23). These attachments to the good-life fantasy, she suggests, enable individuals to "invest in one's own or the world's continuity" (13) and to persevere in their daily living even if it has become unlivable and untenable. So what happens "when something you desire is actually an obstacle to your flourish-ing" (1)? What if it is harmful or self-destructive or if it constrains your abil-ity to thrive and progress? For Berlant, the relational "affective structure"—instead of the "experience of optimism"—is crucial in analyzing attachments to the good-life fantasy because in cruel optimism, "the very pleasures of being inside a relation have become sustaining regardless of the content of the relation" (2). The National LGBT Conference, held in Cavite on June 3–5, 2011, issued an official statement, which symbolizes the good life common-ly desired by LGBT Filipinos: "For years we, the lesbian, gay, bisexual and transgender (LGBT) groups in the Philippines, have always pushed forward the agenda of equality and respect from mainstream society and have been clamoring for the passage of laws that will protect the rights of all people regardless of sexual orientation and gender identity (SOGI). LGBT groups have held on to the promise and dream of every LGBT person in the Philip-pines: to live a life of dignity and respect, free from discrimination and vio-lence" (Rainbow Rights Project 2011). Note the main objects of desire ar-ticulated in the national statement: "equality and respect from mainstream"; "passage of laws that will protect"; "a life of dignity and respect"; and "free from discrimination and violence." Following Berlant's notion of cruel op-timism, what if these objects of desire become obstacles to LGBT flourish-ing? How do they signify compromised conditions of possibility?

I argue that so long as the terms of LGBT rights and equality remain embedded within mainstream heteronormative standards and values, the goals and pursuit of LGBT organizing will continue to be compromised and will never fully actualize LGBT freedom and liberation. To elaborate on the ways cruel optimism has operated in LGBT organizing, this introduction will be followed by three sections and a conclusion on the continuation of LGBT struggles. The first section will concentrate on *Ladlad*'s third attempt to win a congressional seat in 2013 and what others perceived as compro-mised tactics in the party-list's electoral campaign. The second section will foreground the killing of transwoman Jennifer Laude and the transnational dynamics of government and military agreements that enabled a U.S. ma-rine to get away with murder. The third section will focus on the mainstream-ing of LGBT politics, especially during the 2016 national election, which produced comparatively significant triumphs for the LGBT community. As I analyze these three "moments," I keep the question—On whose terms?—in mind, to which I will return at the end of the chapter.

## Third Time's the Charm?

In 2013, the *Ladlad* party-list staged its third campaign to win at least one elected seat in the House of Representatives in the Philippines. It faced strong resistance during its first two attempts and geared for a promising third run in the national election cycle. During its first attempt in 2007, the Commission on Elections (COMELEC) did not approve *Ladlad*'s registration and accreditation petition because it claimed that *Ladlad* did not meet a requirement to have national membership with official local and regional chapters across the country. During its second attempt in 2010, COMELEC tried, once again, to disqualify *Ladlad* from participating in the election, this time not based on technical stipulation, but rather on moral judgment. Citing the Bible and Koran, the holy texts of the country's two dominant religions of Catholicism and Islam, COMELEC considered *Ladlad* as immoral and a danger to youth. *Ladlad* fought COMELEC's second dismissal by taking its case to the legal system and appealing to the Supreme Court, which ruled, ultimately, in favor of *Ladlad*. However, with the court's official decision coming less than a month prior to the election, *Ladlad* had a very short campaign period. It garnered 114,120 votes, or 0.39 percent of the party-list votes cast nationally, thereby missing the 2 percent threshold to win a congressional seat (Coloma 2013).

Vigilant and undeterred, *Ladlad* launched another valiant campaign for the 2013 midterm election. In June 2011, it unveiled a new logo and slogan. According to its political adviser, Boy Abunda, a popular celebrity known as the "King of Talk" in the Philippines, "We made exciting revisions to the image of *Ladlad* like our new, livelier and compelling butterfly logo. Our new slogan, '*Bukas isip. Bukas puso.*' ['Open mind. Open heart.'], also offers more inclusivity that touches everyone's minds and hearts" (*Ladlad* 2012). The new slogan was a departure from its previous slogan, "*Pantay na karapatan para sa lahat*" ["Equal rights for all"], which seemed to be more explicitly and directly political (Pascual 2012). At *Ladlad*'s national convention in February 2012, the general membership elected five representatives for its 2013 slate (listed in order of votes garnered): Bemz Benedito, Danton Remoto, Germaine Trittle Leonin, Raymond Alikpala, and Wilfredo Villocino. Due to personal reasons, professional commitments, and internal decisions, three of them eventually became the party-list's official congressional nominees: Benedito, a transgender woman who was the *Ladlad* chair and standard bearer during the 2010 national election; Remoto, a gay man who was a *Ladlad* founder, university professor, and news media personality; and Alikpala, a gay man, attorney, and author of *Of God and Men: A Life in the Closet*. *Ladlad*'s political platform remained consistent as the previous election campaign: to refile the anti-discrimination bill to provide equal opportunities in employment, education, and other public arenas regardless of sexual orientation and gender identity and expression; to repeal the anti-vagrancy law that has been used by some police to extort bribes from LGBTs; to set up microfinance and livelihood projects for poor and handicapped LGBTs; and to establish centers for LGBT seniors and for LGBT youth driven out of their homes. In my conversations with Remoto and Benedito prior to the 2013 election, they indicated that *Ladlad* strategically decided not to include same-sex marriage and gender recognition laws in their party-list platform due to concerns with potential controversy and backlash from mainstream voters. Instead, they focused on the urgent necessity and wider impact of the anti-discrimination bill that has been languishing in Congress for years.

*Ladlad* leaders are keenly aware of the complex geographical and class politics that they needed to take into account as they organized nationally beyond the capital region. According to Bemz Benedito, "from our reputation before to be mobilized by LGBT advocates in 'Imperial Manila,' we've maneuvered our movement to the grassroots by creating local chapters in the provinces. . . . [T]he paradigm of *Ladlad* is different compared to other partylist (groups since) we started in the middle class (i.e., the founding members are middle class) going to the grassroots" (Tan 2012). The intensive grassroots outreach and mobilization that *Ladlad* pursued for the 2013 election is vividly captured by the documentary *Out Run: Make Politics Fierce* (2016) by U.S.-based directors S. Leo Chiang and Johnny Symons. The film shows the three *Ladlad* nominees, key coordinators such as Santy Layno and Bhuta Adelante, and other party-list organizers and members campaigning in Metro Manila and traveling to provinces like Abra, Benguet, Cebu, Negros Occidental, and Pangasinan. *Ladlad* leaders and organizers spoke with individuals on the street and in public markets, went door-to-door canvassing, led motorcades, marches, and processions, and held small group meetings to learn about local conditions to make people aware of their political positions and to garner support and votes. Danton Remoto offered a crucial insight into the "personalistic culture" of Philippine politics and elections: "They want to touch your hand. They want to talk to you. . . . Unless they see you, they won't vote for you."

From the vantage point of mainstream politics, *Ladlad* took an unconventional approach to their electoral campaign and organizing. With limited funds and personnel, they extensively used social media, galvanized in beauty salons, and presented at gay pageants. Cheryll Ruth Soriano (2014) analyzed *Ladlad*'s "internet-based campaign strategies, including online narratives and discursive spaces in its website, e-group, and social networking sites" and found that "narratives of discrimination are used to mobilize the sentiments of its membership and move them into solidarity and action" (21, 33). Mark Gevisser (2013) pointed out *Ladlad*'s "unique" strategy of "hitting almost every beauty parlour and Miss Gay pageant in this vast archipelago. In a culture obsessed with adornment and beauty, there are more than enough of both to keep a campaign busy: every neighbourhood hosts at least one annual pageant, and every street in every town seems to have a parlour run by a *bakla*." In the *Out Run* (2016) documentary, a *Ladlad* organizer considered beauty salon owners as potential "brand evangelists" for the party-list. When a reporter asked Benedito, "Why are you concentrating on beauty parlors?" she quickly replied, "Because our constituents are there. We are transforming beauty parlors into our headquarters nationwide." She added, "The *parloristas* are our backbone. These are the nerve-centres of the community and also the place where *bakla* come into contact with the broader community. Every Filipina woman has a *bakla* hairdresser!" (Gevisser 2013). Moreover, *Ladlad* disrupted the common view of gay pageants as sites of ridicule, tawdry spectacle, and low-brow entertainment. Rather, they aimed to resignify these events as spaces of empowerment for marginalized LGBT individuals and communities (*Out Run* 2016). At one beauty pageant competition, a contestant proudly responded during the question-and-answer portion, "I believe that the gay pageant is not to exploit us gays, but in fact it is to uplift us third sex saying that whether you like it or not, we gays are here to stay." As a guest speaker at another pageant, Benedito reminded the audience, "This evening, we entertained you with this contest. But after tonight, I ask you, I urge you, after all the cheering and laughter, please give us back the dignity and respect as human beings." *Ladlad* enacted their political and educational mobilization in unconventional sites, such as social media, beauty salons, and gay pageants, to reach out to their main base of LGBT constituents and allies and to raise awareness to the general populace.

*Ladlad* understood what was at stake in centering the lives and experiences of working-class LGBTs in Metro Manila and in other urban and rural communities in their advocacy. At the beginning of the documentary (*Out Run* 2016), Benedito was chatting with a group of LGBTs about discrimination in poor neighborhoods. After they shared incidents of physical and verbal assaults, Benedito empowered and gave them hope by stating, "Don't let them get away with discriminating against us. Don't let them shame us. When we are in Congress, we can make laws to protect us, so people who abuse us can be punished and held accountable for oppressing us." Bhuta Adelante, a transgender elected ward councillor in Manila who lives in a government tenement, believed in *Ladlad*'s vision for change. She shared that "we have lots of LGBT poor here. If *Ladlad* wins, then they will do something for the benefit of us, poor LGBTs." At an outreach meeting in one of the provinces, a young gay man tearfully confessed, "We're breadwinners of our families . . . I'm a maid. I work in my aunt's house. Even though I'm gay, I am proud because I am helping my brother and hopefully this March, he's going to graduate. . . . Being gay, discrimination is a part of our life. And I think that the *Ladlad* partylist would really help a lot. And if ever, it will really help not only me, but the whole gay community, as well." *Ladlad* focused their grassroots outreach and organizing on the marginalized poor and working-class sector that constitutes the majority of the LGBT community in the Philippines. *Ladlad*'s intersectional approach to politics accounts for the intertwined dynamics of unemployment, labor exploitation, class disenfranchisement, and discrimination based on nonnormative sexual orientation and gender identity and expression. It counters the lifestyles and worldviews of globally mobile, urban bourgeois queers that claim not to be tethered to the mundane realities and concerns of their putatively parochial *bakla* and *parlorista* counterparts.

However, unlike Pia Alonzo Wurtzbach, who won the *Binibining Pilipinas* title after three attempts and was eventually crowned Miss Universe in 2015, the third time was not the charm for *Ladlad* at the May 13, 2013, midterm election. *Ladlad* received 100,958 votes, or 0.37 percent of the party-list votes cast nationally, consequently not attaining the minimum threshold to gain a congressional seat. It is difficult to pinpoint exactly what caused *Ladlad*'s loss and not meeting the positive projections of their leaders and constituents. In my conversations with Benedito, Remoto, and Germaine Trittle Leonin after the election, they highlighted the lack of unity within the fractured LGBT community and the limited financial resources to pursue a national electoral campaign. They were frustrated and dismayed by internal tension and division, individual suspicions of the nominees, discreet agreements with other party-lists, and lack of support from the LGBT community and its allies. Part of the tension and suspicion derived from what others perceived as *Ladlad* leaders "sleeping with the enemy" when they collaborated with mainstream parties and politicians in exchange for financial and material resources for publicity tarpaulins, posters, and handouts. *Out Run* (2016) showcases this complicated dynamic of what Benedito called "playing politics." She believed that "I think there's nothing wrong [with these collaborations] as long as I don't sell out the commitments and advocacies of *Ladlad*." To accrue much-needed funds and mainstream votes, Remoto was resolute in their strategy "to have alliances with local government heads, mayors, governors, congressmen, and to set up new ones." The third nominee, Raymond Alikpala, touted *Ladlad* as ushering "new politics" whereby candidates like him, an openly gay man, would push for laws and initiatives to advance the livelihood and conditions of LGBTs and would not succumb to vote-buying that has become a common and expected practice during election seasons in the Philippines. After losing in the election, Alikpala reflected ruefully on what he deemed to be the grave cost of building alliances and compromising to the mainstream: "We believed that by making political alliances with local politicians, the mainstream voter would vote for *Ladlad*. But that's obviously not what happened. And we didn't even get all LGBTs because many LGBTs were turned off by the fact that we didn't have same-sex marriage on our platform. . . . We were afraid of creating controversies, so we decided 'no talk on same-sex marriage.' It was a mistake. As *Ladlad* leadership, we let Filipinos down."

I would like to suggest another possibility that may have contributed to *Ladlad*'s loss: there was no common enemy or major event that could have coalesced the diverse LGBT constituencies and galvanized the sympathies of their heterosexual allies. In the 2013 election, COMELEC and the Catholic Church did not pose as threats to their accreditation, and *Ladlad* was not disqualified due to technical or moral grounds. In fact, *Ladlad* had three full years to prepare for the election: they clearly articulated their political platform; they brought a power broker as senior adviser; they received endorsements from several politicians and celebrities; they established and developed chapters across the country; and they ran an extensive public relations and outreach campaign. The ingredients seemed to be all present for success. However, without an external antagonist as target and cause for collective action and solidarity, the LGBT community turned their gaze inward and focused on internal differences and frictions that may have been lingering prior to, and may have been exacerbated by, the high-stakes election. Interestingly, *Out Run* (2016) foregrounds the drive to defeat Benny Abante, a conservative Christian preacher and former congressman who organized a gay support group in his district called "*Alyansa ng Ikatlong Lahi ng Distrito Sais*" with "A.I.D.S." as its acronym. The film features Abante as the main antagonist, symbolically standing in for the government, church, and general populace that could tolerate LGBTs but never view them as equals. Despite losing in the national election, *Ladlad* campaign coordinator Bhuta Adelante, who lives in Abante's congressional district, was overjoyed: "We won the battle against Benny Abante. The LGBTs won against the devil."

Ultimately, the loss was most deeply felt by Bemz Benedito. As the partylist's first nominee for the 2010 and 2013 elections, she ran to win. Dubbed as "*Sinta ng Pilipinong LGBT*" ("Beloved by LGBT Filipinos"), she became the face and voice of *Ladlad* and the LGBT political movement in Metro Manila and across the country. She shared with me the heavy weight of responsibility to effectively represent and articulate the issues, needs, and concerns of fellow LGBTs. She received unconditional support from family and friends, and those close to her knew the tremendous personal and professional sacrifices she made. But she was not immune to the hurtful sting of malicious criticisms that questioned her competence, credibility, dignity, and even ability to win. After the 2013 election, she briefly withdrew from the public to recover and then became managing director of Boy Abunda's Make Your *Nanay* [Mother] Proud foundation. Due to two consecutive losses in the national elections, *Ladlad* was not eligible to participate in the 2016 election.

For Benedito, "one or two elections for *Ladlad* doesn't define the movement, doesn't define the journey of the LGBT community. The struggle continues, the journey continues, the fight continues" (*Out Run* 2016).

Embodying cruel optimism, *Ladlad* remains steadfast in its commitment to serving LGBT Filipinos and to the democratic election process and mainstream political representation as avenues for empowerment and advocacy. During the COVID-19 global pandemic, it continues to serve its vulnerable constituents, especially elderly LGBTs who have been abandoned by their families and jobless LGBTs who are struggling in these difficult times, by raising funds and providing food, rice, sanitizers, soap, and masks. Moreover, *Ladlad* did not enter the 2019 midterm election, and COMELEC denied its accreditation for the 2022 elections. What *Ladlad* has done since 2016 is beyond the scope of this chapter and will be the focus of another publication.

## How to Get Away with Murder

Close to midnight on Saturday, October 11, 2014, a transwoman was found dead in a motel bathroom in Olongapo City, her naked body partially covered from the waist down, her neck injured with strangulation marks, and her head slumped in the toilet bowl. She was identified as Jennifer Laude, a twenty-six-year-old Filipina, whose cause of death was reported in the autopsy as "asphyxiation by drowning" (Francisco 2014a). Charged for her murder was Joseph Scott Pemberton, a nineteen-year-old white U.S. marine from Massachusetts who was in the Philippines to participate in naval training exercises. Laude and Pemberton met at the Ambyanz disco bar earlier that evening and then checked into Celzone Lodge, as confirmed by motel cashier Elias Galamos and CCTV security footage. They were accompanied by Laude's friend Barbie, who left them alone when they reached their motel room. Galamos saw Pemberton leaving about thirty minutes after checking in. When Galamos later investigated the room, he found the main door ajar and Laude's lifeless body in the bathroom.

After learning about her sister's death, Marilou Laude with lawyer Harry Roque filed a murder charge against Pemberton, who was stationed in the USS *Peleliu* warship docked at the Subic Bay Port (CNN Philippines Staff December 1, 2015). Seeking custody of Pemberton, a U.S. citizen and military personnel, posed serious legal, diplomatic, and political problems in the Philippines. Complicating matters was the 1999 bilateral Visiting Forces Agreement (VFA) between the Philippines and the United States, which facilitated the return of U.S. troops to the Philippines after the closure of U.S. military bases in 1992. According to the VFA, "the custody of any United States personnel over whom the Philippines is to exercise jurisdiction shall immediately reside with the United States military authorities, if they so request" (U.S. Department of State n.d.). The presence of Pemberton and the U.S. military in the archipelago was concrete manifestation of the VFA as well as the Enhanced Defense Cooperation Agreement (EDCA), signed in April 2014 and hailed by the U.S. National Security Council as "the most significant defense agreement that we have concluded with the Philippines in decades" (Eilperin 2014). EDCA allowed increased U.S. military presence in the Philippines putatively to assist in deterring domestic and global terrorism and to help bolster maritime security capacity in countering Chinese aggression in disputed territories in the South China Sea.

When news broke about Laude's murder, activists—mostly from LGBT, women's, and other progressive leftist groups—called it a "hate crime" (dela Cruz 2014) and raised three central issues in their "Justice for Jennifer" organizing. First, they insisted on the recognition and use of Laude's gender as a transgender woman. They called to task the government, police, media, and public at large for repeatedly referring to Laude as male and using her male name. In an open letter, Risa Hontiveros (2014), chair of the democratic socialist *Akbayan* party-list, wrote: "Jennifer Laude identified as a woman; she was one, and I am happy to call her a fellow woman. It is a fundamental right of any individual to define his or her own gender identity, and no one should experience violence and hatred because of the gender they live in. . . . Jennifer is a woman, and in her death let us not perpetuate the injustice against her by denying her womanhood." Second, they countered accusations of Laude being a prostitute and deceiving Pemberton for not being a "real" woman. According to the police report, Pemberton engaged Laude for "sex service" and then "discovered that his sex partner was . . . gay that prompted him to kill the victim" (Francisco October 16, 2014). The Laude family vehemently denied that she was engaged in sex service or prostitution, especially since she had a fiancée in Germany who provided some financial support. Bemz Benedito pointed out the rampant "blaming the victim syndrome" in public commentaries indicating that Laude deserved such treatment for not disclosing her true status. She stressed that "Laude's identity as a transgender woman does not give anyone the 'license' to kill her" (dela Cruz 2014). Like Benedito, Dindi Tan of the Association of Transgender People insisted that the key issues for the government to address were hate crimes based on sexual orientation and gender identity and the need to pass anti-discrimination and gender recognition bills. She wondered, "How many more Jennifers do we have to lose just for the government to start taking affirmative measures to protect LGBT welfare?" (Francisco October 19, 2014).

Third, in their Justice for Jennifer campaign, activists and organizers raised questions about U.S. imperialism and Philippine sovereignty. They viewed their advocacy not only as a struggle for justice and human rights for the LGBT community in general and a transwoman in particular, but also as resistance against ongoing U.S. military, economic, and cultural domination that continues to exert neocolonial power and control over the Philippines. In their public actions, including street demonstrations, rallies, and prayer vigils in Metro Manila (e.g., University of the Philippines–Diliman and University of Santo Tomas), in cities outside of the capital (e.g., Cebu, Legaspi, and Olongapo), and beyond the Philippines (e.g., Los Angeles, New York, and San Francisco), they invoked the unequal historical and contemporary dynamics between the Philippines and the United States and called upon the Philippine president and other politicians to fight for their people and nation. Their protest signs read: "Uphold Philippine sovereignty"; "Junk VFA"; and "Junk EDCA." They also demanded "US Troops Out Now" to assert and reclaim local control over their land, people, and laws. I maintain that their highly visible and persistent activism and organizing in public spaces and social media, as enactments of cruel optimism, put pressure on the Philippine and U.S. governments and contributed to a more accountable juridical process in prosecuting Pemberton for Laude's death.

Standing behind the juridical protection of the VFA, the U.S. government and military refused to give custody of Pemberton to the Philippine authority. Activists were acutely concerned that a U.S. serviceman would be acquitted, once again, of a crime committed against a Filipina. In November 2005, four U.S. marines—Lance Corporals Daniel Smith, Keith Silkwood, and Dominic Duplantis and Staff Sergeant Chad Carpentier—were charged for the rape of twenty-two-year-old Suzette Nicolas in Subic, another port city about fourteen kilometers away from Olongapo. Although Carpentier, Duplantis, and Silkwood were charged with complicity and later acquitted, in December 2006, Smith was convicted of rape because the victim was "severely intoxicated that night and was deprived of reason to consent to sex and incapable of sensing or fighting off danger" (Fonbuena 2014). However, in 2009, Nicolas recanted her allegations in an affidavit, and Smith was acquitted and released from the U.S. embassy in Manila, where he had been detained. This turn of events led many activists and politicians to surmise that "a backroom deal was worked out to free Smith" and facilitated Nicolas's furtive departure to the United States. Liza Maza, a former member of the Philippine Congress representing the Gabriela Women's Party, asserted that "our government and the U.S. government have colluded in order to get this recantation to get Smith free and also continue with an unequal Visiting Forces Agreement" (Watson 2009). With the Nicolas's case debacle in mind, organizers of the Justice for Jennifer campaign vigilantly demanded the custody of Pemberton and questioned the power of bilateral agreements that undermined the sovereignty of Philippine laws over foreign nationals. Their public campaigns to redress the rape and murder of Filipino women (Nicolas and Laude, respectively) symbolized overt agentic assertions by women's and LGBT groups in their struggles for justice under uneven political conditions.

Two weeks after Laude's death, Pemberton was transferred to a U.S.-guarded compound in Camp Aguinaldo, a Philippine military headquarters in Metro Manila, but he did not appear at preliminary investigation hearings (CNN Philippines Staff December 1, 2015). In December 2014, the Olongapo regional trial court finally issued a warrant of arrest for Pemberton, whose lawyer filed a motion to downgrade the case from murder to homicide. In August 2015, Pemberton took the stand and admitted to receiving oral sex from Laude and to punching and putting her in a chokehold when he found out that she still had male genitalia. He insisted that Laude was unconscious but breathing when he left and that "his acts were all a matter of self-defense" (CNN Philippines Staff August 25, 2015). Pemberton testified, "I felt like I was raped by Laude," and felt "violated and angry" (Talusan 2015). After over eight months of trial hearings, on December 1, 2015, the Olongapo court found Pemberton guilty of homicide in the death of Laude. He was sentenced to six to twelve years of imprisonment and was ordered to pay the equivalent of about USD $100,000 to Laude's family.

Meredith Talusan (2015) astutely points out the "trans panic" defense used by Pemberton's legal team. One of his attorneys claimed that Pemberton was "so repulsed and so disgusted because he did not give consent to allow a man" to perform oral sex on him. Another attorney added that he "only acted in defense of his life and honor." Talusan (2015) offers a convincing analysis of the "failed logic of 'trans panic' criminal defenses":

> By seriously comparing the discovery that a sex partner is trans to being raped, Pemberton's defense team equates the violation Pemberton felt with someone forcing him to have sex against his will. If one were to follow this logic, it would mean that any time someone does not disclose a fact about themselves that would otherwise disqualify them from being another's sexual partner, then the violation would be akin to rape. Such logic not only denies trans women's fundamental identities and attempts to define us as men hiding in women's clothing, but also denies that the reason heterosexual men become attracted to us in the first place is *because* we are women— when men like Pemberton find out we're trans, their attraction runs counter to their erroneous sense of gender essentialism that defines gender purely through a person's genitals. In this way, trans panic is intimately intertwined with a misconstrued sense of gay panic: Pemberton assumed that he had been having homosexual sex against his will, even though Laude was not a man.

We will never know what truly happened on that fateful October evening in 2014. We only know Pemberton's version of the story, and the only way Laude could speak was through the remains of her lifeless body. One particular testimony that received relatively little attention was a forensic expert's statement that the lubricant in a condom wrapper found in the motel room was the same lubricant found on Pemberton's penis and in Laude's anus (Datu 2015). The court verdict made no mention of anal sex, thereby juridically erasing the possible likelihood that he knew that she was a transwoman and they engaged in more than oral sex. Why would the court privilege Pemberton's testimony that he only realized that Laude was transgender after he felt between her legs? Since she was found naked in the bathroom, partially covered from the waist down, why eliminate the probability of penetrative anal sex? Moreover, was the anal sex between them forced or consensual? On the one hand, was the struggle between them a result of Pemberton forcing himself into Laude? Could we consider the possibility of Laude as a victim of rape? On the other hand, if he was aware that she was a transwoman, could we imagine that his initial physical attraction and sexual desire for her may have turned into a horrifyingly deadly "trans panic," as Talusan (2015) suggests?

At the end, what we know is that Pemberton got away with murder: he was found guilty of homicide, considered a less serious offense carrying a lighter sentence. The court ruled that mitigating circumstances, including Laude's nondisclosure of her gender identity to Pemberton and not meeting the legal standards for murder, such as treachery, use of superior force, and cruelty, contributed to its lowering of charge from murder to homicide. After the release of the ruling, *Ladlad*'s Bemz Benedito warned that the court's decision "sets a dangerous implication and precedent to have mitigating circumstance due to the discovery of one's sexual partner's gender identity and expression. This makes us all more vulnerable and easy targets of hate crimes and bigotry related violence" (Placido 2015).

On September 7, 2020, President Rodrigo Duterte pardoned Pemberton, who boarded a U.S. military cargo plane out of the Philippines a week later. Pemberton served almost six years in a private air-conditioned detention unit at the military base Camp Aguinaldo instead of the New Bilibid Prison, where he was originally assigned, which houses more than twenty-six thousand convicted men. Not only was Pemberton charged with a less serious offense and given a lighter sentence, but he subsequently received a full pardon. Many Filipinos viewed the presidential pardon as Duterte's utter disregard of Laude's life and murder and his betrayal of previous support of the LGBT community. Others considered it as a "tool for political leverage rather than justice" within the context of "historic power imbalance between the Philippines and its former colonial ruler" (Redfern 2020). Ultimately, according to Rey Valmores-Salinas of Bahaghari National, the message is clear: "It tells us how, even in our own country, if you are of a particular gender, if you are a transgender woman, your life matters less." Moreover, "if you call for justice for Jennifer, that's never going to happen for so long as the Visiting Forces Agreement stands, . . . for so long as any US soldier stands in Philippine soil" (Redfern 2020).

## The Mainstreaming of LGBT Politics

After the 2010 and 2013 elections and after the death of Jennifer Laude in 2014, various educational, public awareness, and organizing initiatives were launched to address LGBT issues and concerns across the country.[1] For instance, from September 2010 to February 2011, a Rainbow Tour dubbed "EDUC8, LIBER8, CELEBR8" targeted eight colleges and universities in Metro Manila.[2] These free lectures and workshops were aimed to "deepen their understanding of the human rights issues facing the LGBT community in the Philippines (EDUC8)"; to "free themselves from damaging, stereotypical and incorrect notions about LGBT people and culture (LIBER8)"; and to "affirm and respect the inherent dignity of all human beings including themselves (CELEBR8)" (Task Force Pride Philippines 2010). With speakers including Germaine Trittle Leonin of *Ladlad*, Naomi Fontanos of the Society of Transsexual Women of the Philippines, and Rev. Ceejay Agbayani of the Metropolitan Community Church, they covered topics ranging from politics, spirituality, sexuality, and gender identity to human rights and media activism. On June 3–5, 2011, a National LGBT Conference was held in Cavite with the theme of "Forging Unity Towards the Recognition of LGBT Human Rights in the Philippines." Its official statement, representing forty-six LGBT groups across the country, demanded the government to pass laws that protect and promote the rights of LGBT people, including anti-discrimination, gender recognition, and anti-hate crime legislation, and to repeal anti-LGBT policies, such as the Vagrancy Act (Rainbow Rights Project 2011).

On April 21, 2012, the LGBT community gathered in Quezon City Memorial Circle to participate in the Worldwide LGBT Civil Rights March. This multisectoral event, bringing together LGBT, women's, legal, religious, and other advocacy groups, foregrounded call to action on local issues, such as the passage of anti-discrimination and reproductive health bills (Human Rights Online Philippines 2012). After the 2013 election, Ging Cristobal of Lesbian Advocates Philippines and Raymond Alikpala of *Ladlad* facilitated workshops on "Gender, Sexuality, and Human Rights" to police officers in Metro Manila and gave a lecture to the human rights officers of the Philippine National Police. Partly sponsored by the International Gay and Lesbian Human Rights Commission, these workshops and lecture were geared to "challenge the discriminative and patriarchal attitudes and behaviors people have valued and believed in for most of their lives" and "to let go of their prejudices and fears and try to provide space in their hearts for respect for people they find different from them" (Cristobal 2013). In May 2015, U.S.-based Gender Proud founder Geena Rocero provided two-day media training and skills-building seminars to address transgender issues in Cebu, Quezon City, and Vigan. In collaboration with the Human Rights Campaign in the United States and the Association of Transgender People in the Philippines, the seminars' goal was to empower "advocates with lasting skills who will grow from strength to strength because they have been able to tell their stories with confidence using their own voices" (Brodie 2015).

The various educational, public awareness, and organizing initiatives launched by LGBT activists from the early to mid-2010s coincided with the increasing visibility and popularity of LGBT media and entertainment celebrities, such as Boy Abunda, Vice Ganda, and Jake Zyrus, as well as LGBT-themed films and television shows, such as *Bwakaw* (2012), *In My Life* (2009), *My Husband's Lover* (2013), and *The Rich Man's Daughter* (2015). More recently, the BL (Boys Love) television and online streaming series has gained tremendous popularity with LGBT and straight audiences. Inspired by Japanese homoerotic fiction and popularized as a romance drama subgenre in Thailand, the market for narrating same-sex attractions and relationships has produced widely watched series in the Philippines, such as *Gameboys* (2020), *Like in the Movies* (2020), *My Extraordinary* (2020), and *Oh, Mando!* (2020). In his analysis of popular culture as a crucial site to examine the intertwined dynamics of gender, sexuality, and class politics in the Philippines, Robert Diaz (2015) convincingly argues that "queer mediascapes are important conduits for nationalist sentiments, longings, and aspirations" (724). Consequently, queer media both reflects and affects the nation's perspectives on LGBT matters. The mass appeal of LGBT personalities, films, and television shows was also noted by Danton Remoto. In my discussions with Remoto, he considered the political work of *Ladlad* and the cultural work of LGBT-oriented media as converging, but not altogether consciously coordinated efforts to impact mainstream Filipinos and to transform their beliefs and attitudes toward LGBT people. In fact, he wondered what the result of the 2013 election and the fate of the *Ladlad* party-list would have been if popular teleserye like *My Husband's Lover* were shown then or if Jennifer Laude's death had taken place prior to the election. Mindful of the political and cultural influence of media on Filipino consciousness, Remoto, a well-regarded media figure himself, continues his work in broadcast, radio, and print media.

Whereas *Ladlad* was not eligible to run as a party-list for the 2016 national election, other politicians and political parties sought the LGBT vote.

Nowhere was the mainstream solicitation of the LGBT vote more obvious than *KeriBeks* ("Go, Gays" or "Onward, Gays"), allegedly the first National Gay Congress, held at the Smart Araneta Coliseum in Quezon City in August 2015. Convened by Korina Sanchez, a broadcast journalist and the wife of then-presidential candidate Manuel "Mar" Araneta Roxas, *KeriBeks* was putatively "the brainchild of [Sanchez's] several gay friends from the entertainment industry." She said, "I've always wanted to help *bekis* [a slang term for gays] in a bigger way. This event was actually just the beginning of other projects we are thinking of to help empower the LGBTQ community against several forms of discrimination in the areas of employment, education, opportunity and health" (Gomez 2015). Admittedly, a job fair was held on the day of *KeriBeks*, and a follow-up job fair took place at SM North Skydome a couple of months later (Standard Showbitz 2015). Yet what grabbed the media and public attention was the "star-studded production numbers and heartwarming inspirational messages from some of the country's most respected gay icons and leaders" (Gomez 2015). The evening concert featured performances and presentations by well-known actors, singers, and comedians, such as Anne Curtis, Vice Ganda, Martin Nievera, and Maricel Soriano, as well as international pageant winners and transgender beauty queens. In attendance were Roxas and Sanchez, other politicians from then-ruling Liberal party, businesspeople, and thousands of LGBT folks, many of whom came from the provinces and arrived in buses rented and coordinated by Sanchez's team. Although *KeriBeks* did not officially have endorsements from political parties (but garnered several corporate sponsors with ties to the Liberal party), *Ladlad*'s Benedito, Remoto, and Rica Paras were featured at the evening show and shared their perspectives on the LGBT state of affairs in the country.

That *KeriBeks* was a campaign tactic for Mar Roxas's presidential bid was not lost to LGBT leaders and activists, as evinced in their Facebook postings. *Ladlad* party-list's postings on the event referenced Roxas when they wrote "*MARaming salamat sa inyong pagdalo* [Thank you for attending]" to the LGBT participants, with the candidate's nickname "Mar" capitalized. A critical posting by netizen Francisco Cabuena stated: "The #KeriBeks circus reeks of exploitation so typical of the historical deception of marginalized sectors by the ruling class." Naomi Fontanos was more elaborate in her critique: "In a cacique democracy ruled, controlled, and regulated by elites, our beloved LGBTIQ movement, our beloved community, that has borne the weight of gender-based inequity and oppression must rise-up against any form of politics that is not progressive, revolutionary, and liberatory. . . . Always question the motives of politicians and political actors who will only recognize us during election season, but deny our civil, political, economic, social, and cultural rights for the rest of their political careers." Geena Rocero further asked, "If they really want to help our community, what is the long-term plan? If there are job fairs and employment programs, how will they make them happen? Is Mar Roxas ready to say he supports the LGBTIQ community? Will he support the Anti-Discrimination Bill, Same Sex Marriage Law, or Gender Recognition Law?" Shakira Sison (2015) warned the LGBT community to "beware of being used as pawns. Beware of being the face of faux acceptance where personalities with their own motives are happy to party with you but will call your real-life concerns demanding if you even dare ask them about it. . . . Ask them the one important question— 'Do you believe I should have exactly what you have?'"

One of the privileges that heterosexuals enjoy and largely take for granted is the ability to form a union through marriage. The question of same-sex marriage was posed to candidates during the 2016 election season, with only one of the five presidential candidates (Grace Poe), and not a single one of the six vice presidential candidates, giving unequivocal support for same-sex marriage (Shahani 2016; CNN Philippines Staff 2016). Although *Ladlad* was reticent to advocate for same-sex marriage in previous elections, Remoto stated, "We support same sex marriage. This is found in the equal rights provisions of the Constitution that mandates a level playing field for everybody" (Calayag and Gita 2016). When asked about his view on same-sex marriage in February 2016, world boxing champion and Senate candidate Manny Pacquiao believed that gays and lesbians are "worse than animals" ("*mas masahol pa sa hayop*"). A born-again Christian and an elected member of Congress, he said, "It's common sense. Have you seen any animals that are engaged in male to male, or female to female [relations]? Animals then are better (as) they know to distinguish male [from] female" (Calayag and Gita 2016). Even though Pacquiao later apologized while still maintaining his position, several politicians denounced his homophobic remarks. *Ladlad* responded with: "Please do NOT vote for so-called Representative Manny Pacquiao for senator of this land. His anti-LGBT statement betrays a shallow understanding of the issues that are important to the community." Unfortunately, even though Paquiao lost the corporate sponsorship of athletic apparel Nike, he still won one of the twelve Senate seats in May 2016. In December 2020, he was sworn in as president of the ruling PDP-Laban party (Philippine Democratic Party–People's Power), and ran an unsuccessful campaign for the country's presidency in the 2022 election.

During the 2016 national election, the main highlight for the LGBT community in the Philippines and around the world was not Pacquiao and his derogatory comments, but rather the historic victory of Geraldine Roman, the first transgender person elected to the Philippine House of Representatives. Winning the congressional seat for the first district of Bataan, a city over 120 kilometers from Manila, she succeeded her mother who was term limited and her late father who also previously held the post. Educated at elite institutions in the Philippines (Ateneo de Manila elementary and high schools and the University of the Philippines–Diliman), she completed two master's degrees in Spain and worked as a senior editor for the Spanish News Agency. She returned to the Philippines in 2012 to care for her ailing father and decided to carry on her family's resolve for public service. In her victory statement, Roman said, "The politics of bigotry, hatred and discrimination did not triumph. What triumphed was the politics of love, acceptance and respect" (Agence France-Presse 2016). Mindful of how her identity as a transwoman became a cause for vicious ridicule and contempt by political rivals as well as a source of curiosity by the general public, she downplayed her gender identity during and after the election. Preferring to be known as "just another politician who happens to be transgender," she viewed gender as "not an important issue really. The capacity of a person to serve his or her country does not depend on our gender. It depends on what you have in your heart and your desire to serve others" (Pearson 2016). Her campaign platform focused on education, health care, agriculture, transparency in government, and youth (ABS-CBN News 2016).

Roman's political and public relations stance as a candidate considerably differed from that of Erick Habijan, who ran for city council in Marikina, Metro Manila. His campaign slogan of "Bata, Bago, Bakla" ("Young, New, Gay") was refreshingly unique, candid, and unapologetic (Bonalos 2016). The eldest son of educators who has dabbled in "colorful career paths" as a university instructor, television show writer, and even pageant contestant, Habijan was noted for his "bubbly personality" and "fabulously witty campaign" (Dacanay 2016). (He later transitioned to Mela Habijan and became the first Filipina to win Miss Trans Global in September 2020.) The contrasting results of their respective campaigns (Roman won; Habijan lost) point to what I call "a politics of acceptable respectability, whereby those that exercise it can be considered upstanding and hence tolerable individuals, even though they are LGBTs who, in the eyes of the dominant authorities, are considered immoral and abnormal" (Coloma 2013, 507). Educated, poised, worldly, and from a well-connected family, Roman epitomized the tolerable LGBT politician for the mainstream since she did not foreground her (trans) gender identity and did not push for LGBT issues in her election campaign, unlike Habijan, who was explicitly gay in his self-presentation and politics. Roman was deemed a "real" woman since she has been living as a woman for decades, had gender confirmation surgery in the 1990s and is lovingly supported by her family. That she continues to be a Catholic mattered and added to her acceptable respectability: for Roman, being Catholic and transgender are "not irreconcilable." One of the first tweeted photographs announcing her victory showed Roman inside the town church "offer[ing] prayer for her historic win" (ABS-CBN News).

Since her election, Roman has become a more outspoken advocate of LGBT rights and protection. She was coauthor of the SOGIE (Sexual Orientation and Gender Identity or Expression) Equality Bill, which passed in the House of Representatives, but died in the Senate. She was also coauthor of a House bill that would allow couples to enter into a civil partnership regardless if they are of the opposite or of the same sex. Instead of same-sex marriage, she advocates for civil partnership which would provide the same rights, benefits, recognition, and protection to spouses in a marriage.

## The Struggle Continues

In 2016, the populist candidate Rodrigo Roa Duterte won a landslide election victory and became president of the Republic of the Philippines. The country's first president from Mindanao, he was mayor of Davao City for most of the past three decades and is credited for the city's transformation as a safe and orderly area and "an enclave of peace and relative prosperity" with his tough stance against crime, drugs, and corruption (Whaley 2016). Known as "Duterte Harry" after the Hollywood movie *Dirty Harry* character, his solution for civil order was to "fire corrupt officials and detain street thugs. If suspects resist arrest, kill them" (Moss 2016). While critics raised grave concerns about his vigilante attitude, coarse language, and womanizing and misogynistic ways, supporters pointed to his charisma, simplicity, frankness, and solid track record of success as a city mayor. For the LGBT community, support for Duterte may be ambivalent. On the one hand, Duterte was one of the first public figures to defend *Ladlad* when the Commission on Elections ruled the party-list ineligible to run in the 2010 election on moral grounds and led the passage of an anti-discrimination ordinance based on sexual orientation and gender identity in Davao City in 2012. On the other hand, he derisively called his political rival Mar Roxas a "*bayot*" (a Cebuano term for "gay"), accused his vocal critic Antonio Trillanes IV of being gay, and insulted the U.S. Ambassador to the Philippines Philip Goldberg by calling him "a gay son of a bitch" (Umbao 2016). He also claimed that he had "cured" himself from being gay. Moreover, he supports anti-discrimination laws and policies that protect LGBT individuals yet vacillates on the issue of same-sex marriage and civil partnership. Many Filipinos, including those in the LGBT, women's, and other progressive and human rights sectors have raised grave concerns about the extrajudicial killings and, more recently, the anti-terrorism bill. At the Pride March in June 2020, LGBT activists, community members, and allies protested against the draconian bill that is widely considered worse than martial law (Nakpil 2020). It is yet to be determined what the socio-political positions will be of new President Ferdinand "Bongbong" Romualdez Marcos Jr. in regard to LGBT matters.

At the beginning of the chapter, I suggested that Lauren Berlant's (2011) concept of cruel optimism serves as a helpful explanation for the incessant drive that ironically inspires and fosters LGBT organizing in the Philippines. I forwarded cruel optimism as an analytic to help "track the affective attachment to what we call the 'good life,' which is for so many a bad life that wears out the subject who nonetheless, and at the same time, find their conditions of possibility within it" (27). For *Ladlad*, their conditions of possibility resided in the electoral process and winning a rightful seat in the congressional halls of power. For Jennifer Laude's family and supporters, theirs were placed in the judicial system and obtaining justice for her murder. For the LGBT community, theirs were situated in the public sphere and gaining respect, dignity, and protection. Yet all conditions of possibility were and continue to be embedded within mainstream heteronormative discourses that regulate the terms and draw the parameters for legibility and engagement. *Ladlad*'s electoral aspirations were set within mainstream politics, with formal party machineries, political dynasties, regional and sectoral influences, and the hegemonic power of the Catholic Church. The international diplomatic and military relations between the Philippines and the United States, with disturbing questions regarding empire, neocolonialism, and sovereignty, were a significant mediating context in Laude's murder case and court decision. In the 2016 election, the politics of acceptable respectability facilitated the historic congressional victory of a transwoman and a scion from a political family dynasty.

So, following Berlant (2012), "why do people stay with lives, forms, and fantasies of life that don't work?" Admittedly, they work . . . for some, especially for individuals who are deemed bearable and for causes that serve to benefit the mainstream. Yet for the large majority in the LGBT community, the good-life fantasy is a double-edged sword. In her investigation of "practices of democracy, labor, love and intimacy that sustain and diminish us at the same time," Berlant forwards the relevance and utility of queer theory. For her, queer theory's aim is "to seek to open up understanding the relation between conventional patterns of desire and the way they are managed by norms, and to focus on patterns of attachment we hadn't even yet known to notice, patterns in which sexuality and intimacy are enacted in a broad field of social relations that anchor us to life." The good-life fantasy has been defined within mainstream heteronormative terms, primarily for the benefit of individuals, cultures, and structures deemed normal and acceptable. To be/come otherwise seems to be a possible alternative. Trans activist Santy Layno in the documentary *Out Run* (2016) offers both a critique and a seemingly simple yet radical position: "People tell me that 'You should be prim and proper. You should sit like a lady. You should not be [acting] bad if you want people to take you seriously because you are part of *Ladlad*.' And I would always say to them, 'This is exactly what we're fighting for, y'know: to be who you are.'" Hence, the struggle for LGBT freedom and liberation continues.

## NOTES

1. By no means a comprehensive listing of LGBT events in the Philippines, the ones noted in this section primarily highlight key events from 2010 to 2015 where *Ladlad* as an organization or its leaders were involved as well as local events that received international sponsorship and collaboration.

2. The eight colleges and universities were the following: College of Saint Benilde (September 29, 2010); Quezon City Polytechnic University (October 2, 2010); St. Joseph's College (November 19, 2010); University of the Philippines–Los Baños (December 1, 2010); Ateneo Professional Schools (December 3, 2010); University of the Philippines–Diliman (February 10, 2011); Polytechnic University of the Philippines (February 18, 2011); and San Beda College (February 22, 2011).

## BIBLIOGRAPHY

ABS-CBN News. "Get to Know PH's First Transgender Politician." *ABS-CBN News*, May 10, 2016, http://news.abs-cbn.com/halalan2016/lifestyle/05/10/16/get-to-know-phs-first-transgender-politician.

Agence France-Presse. "Transgender Politician Wins Seat in Philippines Parliament." *Guardian*, May 11, 2016, https://www.theguardian.com/world/2016/may/11/transgender-politician-philippines-parliament-geraldine-roman.

Berlant, Lauren. *Cruel Optimism*. Durham, NC: Duke University Press, 2011.

———. "On Her Book *Cruel Optimism*." Rorotoko, June 4, 2012, http://rorotoko.com/interview/20120605_berlant_lauren_on_cruel_optimism/?page=2.

Bonalos, Pia. "Gay Candidate from Marikina Trends Online." *CNN Philippines*, May 11, 2016, http://cnnphilippines.com/videos/2016/05/11/Gay-candidate-from-Marikina-trends-online.html.

Brodie, Kerry. "HRC and Gender Proud Launch Partnership to Raise Transgender Visibility in the Philippines." *Human Rights Campaign*, May 13, 2015, http://www.hrc.org/blog/hrc-and-gender-proud-launch-partnership-to-raise-visibility-of-the-transgen.

Calayag, Keith A., and Ruth Abbey Gita. "Ladlad Hits Pacquiao's View on Same-Sex Union." *Sun Star*, February 16, 2016, http://www.sunstar.com.ph/manila/local-news/2016/02/16/ladlad-hits-pacquiaos-view-same-sex-union-457562.

CNN Philippines Staff. "Pemberton Takes Witness Stand, Admits Choking Laude." *CNN Philippines*, August 25, 2015, http://cnnphilippines.com/news/2015/08/24/joseph-scott-pemberton-choked-filipino-transgender-jennifer-laude.html.

———. "Revisiting the Jennifer Laude Murder Case." *CNN Philippines*, December 1, 2015, http://cnnphilippines.com/news/2015/02/23/Transgender-Jennifer-Laude-murder-case-accused-US-Marine-Joseph-Scott-Pemberton-timeline-verdict.html.

——— "VP Candidates' Stand on Death Penalty for Corrupt, Same-Sex Marriage, and More." *CNN Philippines*, April 11, 2016, http://cnnphilippines.com/news/2016/04/10/vp-debate-vice-president-candidates-stand-on-issues-same-sex-marriage-political-dynasty.html.

Coloma, Roland Sintos. "*Ladlad* and Parrhesiastic Pedagogy: Unfurling LGBT Politics and Education in the Global South." *Curriculum Inquiry* 43, 4 (2013): 483–511.

Cristobal, Ging. "Wanted: Room for Respect." *New Civil Rights Movement*, June 1, 2013, http://www.thenewcivilrightsmovement.com/special-report-philippines-national-police-undergo-lgbt-sensitivity-workshops-part-i/news/2013/06/01/67895.

Dacanay, Aimee. "Erick Habijan, the 'Bakla' who Ran for Marikina Councilor." *Spot.ph*, May 16, 2016, http://www.spot.ph/newsfeatures/the-latest-news-features/66348/interview-erick-habijan-marikina-councilor-a00001-20160516-lfrm2.

Datu, Randy V. "US Expert: Pemberton's Fingerprint on Condom Wrapper." *Rappler*, June 23, 2015, http://www.rappler.com/nation/97212-us-forensic-experts-evidence-pemberton-laude.

dela Cruz, Kathlyn. "Why Murder of Jennifer Laude May Be a Hate Crime." *ABS-CNBnews.com*, October 15, 2014, http://rp3.abs-cbnnews.com/focus/10/15/14/why-murder-jennifer-laude-may-be-hate-crime.

Diaz, Robert. "The Limits of *Bakla* and Gay: Feminist Readings of *My Husband's Lover*, Vice Ganda, and Charice Pempengco." *Signs: Journal of Women in Culture and Society* 40, 3 (2015): 721–745.

Eilperin, Juliet. "U.S., Philippines Reach 10-Year Defense Agreement Amid Rising Tensions." *Washington Post*, April 27, 2014, https://www.washingtonpost.com/world/us-philippines-to-sign-10-year-defense-agreement-amid-rising-tensions/2014/04/27/a04436c0-cddf-11e3-a75e-463587891b57_story.html.

Fonbuena, Carmela. "EDCA, Olongapo Murder, and the Old Case of Daniel Smith." *Rappler*, October 13, 2014, http://www.rappler.com/nation/71871-edca-olongapo-daniel-smith.

Francisco, Katerina. "Killing of Jennifer Laude a 'Hate Crime'—Police Report." *Rappler*, October 16, 2014, http://www.rappler.com/nation/72224-killing-jennifer-laude-police-report.

——. "Transgender Group to Gov't: Pass Laws to Protect LGBT." *Rappler*, October 19, 2014, http://www.rappler.com/nation/72435-govt-laws-protection-transgender-community.

Gevisser, Mark. "Ang Ladlad Party Brings Beauty Parlours and Gay Pageants Out to Vote in Philippines." *Guardian*, May 12, 2013, http://www.theguardian.com/world/2013/may/12/ang-ladlad-philippines-elections-transgender.

Gomez, Chuck. "Korina Is Gay." *Philippine Star*, August 10, 2015, http://www.philstar.com/entertainment/2015/08/10/1486176/korina-gay.

Hontiveros, Risa. "On the Murder of a Fellow Woman." *Akbayan Party-List*, October 16, 2014, https://akbayan.org.ph/news/32-specials/487-on-the-murder-of-a-fellow-woman.

Human Rights Online Philippines. "Statement of the Worldwide LGB Civil Rights March—Manila." April 22, 2012, https://hronlineph.com/2012/04/22/statement-statement-of-the-worldwide-lgbt-civil-rights-march-manila/.

Ladlad. "No More 'Ang' for Ladlad Partylist—Boy Abunda." January 5, 2012, http://ladladpartylist.blogspot.com/2012/01/no-more-ang-for-ladlad-partylist-boy.html.

Moss, Trefor. "Philippine Candidate Splits Voters with 'Dirty Harry' Crime-Fighting Tactics." *Wall Street Journal*, March 20, 2016, http://www.wsj.com/articles/philippine-candidate-splits-voters-with-dirty-harry-crime-fighting-tactics-1458449558.

Nakpil, D. "Pride Protesters Arrested at Rally Against Anti-Terror Bill in Mediola." June 26, 2020, https://cnnphilippines.com/news/2020/6/26/Pride-protest-arrest-Mendiola.html.

*Out Run: Make Politics Fierce*. Directed by S. Leo Chiang and Johnny Symons. San Francisco and Oakland, CA: Walking Irish Films and Persistent Visions, 2016.

Pascual, Patrick King. "Ladlad Adopts New 'Open Mind, Open Heart' Campaign Slogan." VERA Files, April 21, 2012, https://sg.news.yahoo.com/blogs/the-inbox/ladlad-adopts-open-mind-open-heart-campaign-slogan-091949933.html.
Pearson, Michael. "Geraldine Roman: 'Just Another Politician Who Happens to Be Transgender.'" CNN Philippines, May 18, 2016, http://cnnphilippines.com/news/2016/05/18/geraldine-roman-transgender-philippines-interview.html.
Placido, Dharel. "Pemberton Verdict Could Lead to More Abuse vs LGBTs." ABS-CBN News, December 2, 2015, https://news.abs-cbn.com/nation/12/02/15/pemberton-verdict-could-lead-to-more-abuse-vs-lgbts.
Rainbow Rights Project. "2011 National LGBT Conference Statement." https://www.facebook.com/rainbowrightsphilippines/notes.
Redfern, Corinne. "He Killed a Transgender Woman in the Philippines. Why Was He Freed?" New York Times, September 17, 2020, https://www.nytimes.com/2020/09/17/magazine/philippines-marine-pardon-duterte.html.
Shahani, Lila Ramos. "Same-Sex Marriage: Yet Another Election Issue?" Philippine Star, February 29, 2016, http://www.philstar.com/opinion/2016/02/29/1558019/same-sex-marriage-yet-another-election-issue.
Sison, Shakira. "#KeriBeks: Where Gays Are the Latest Political Pawns." Rappler, August 6, 2015, http://www.rappler.com/views/imho/101621-keribeks-gays-latest-political-pawns.
Soriano, Cheryll Ruth Reyes. "Constructing Collectivity in Diversity: Online Political Mobilization of a National LGBT Political Party." Media, Culture & Society 36, 1 (2014): 20–36.
Standard Showbitz. "1st KeriBeks Job Fair at SM North EDSA Skydome." Standard, October 20, 2015, http://manilastandardtoday.com/showbitz/189989/1st-keribeks-job-fair-at-sm-north-edsa-skydome.html.
Talusan, Meredith. "The Failed Logic of 'Trans Panic' Criminal Defenses." BuzzFeed, August 25, 2015, https://www.buzzfeed.com/meredithtalusan/trans-panic-criminal-defense?utm_term=.yeM44eG51W#.rvbMMD79Ym.
Tan, Michael David dela Cruz. "Ladlad for Change." October 1, 2012, http://www.philippine-transgender-movement.com/news/ladlad-partylist/.
Task Force Pride Philippines. "EDUC8, LIBER8, CELEBR8: The 8-Campus Rainbow Tour." Task Force Pride Philippines, 2010, http://taskforcepride.blogspot.com/2010/09/educ8-liber8-celebr8-8-campus-rainbow.html.
Umbao, Ed. "Mayor Duterte's Response to Roxas Statement 'Si Mar, Bayot. 'Di niya kaya." Philippine News, April 7, 2016, http://philnews.ph/2016/04/07/mayor-dutertes-response-to-roxas-statement-si-mar-bayot-di-niya-kaya/.
U.S. Department of State. "12931 Philippines—Agreement Regarding the Treatment of US Armed Forces Visiting the Philippines; Agreement Regarding the Treatment of Philippines Personnel Visiting the US." U.S. Department of State, n.d., http://www.state.gov/s/l/treaty/tias/107752.htm.
Watson, Paul. "Philippine Women's Groups Say There's a Plot to Free U.S. Marine Convicted of Rape." Los Angeles Times, March 19, 2009, http://articles.latimes.com/2009/mar/19/world/fg-philippines-rape19.
Whaley, Floyd. "Welcome to Davao, the Philippine Leader's Town: 'No Smoking, No Crime.'" New York Times, June 16, 2016, http://www.nytimes.com/2016/06/17/world/asia/philippines-davao-duterte.html?_r=0.

# Sociotechnical Infrastructures

*Tracing Gay Socio-Sexual App Socialities in Manila*

PAUL MICHAEL LEONARDO ATIENZA

The introduction of this collection started with descriptions of Manila as a messy, chaotic machine. This is also a good analogy for how gay Filipino men think of their sexual and romantic prospects in Manila. Some claim that the gay scene is too small, while others remark on the mediocre choices available in the city. Citing frustrations from the lack of places to gather and meet, gay Filipino men take to their mobile devices and download geolocative socio-sexual app platforms like Grindr, Tinder, Jack'd, and Blued with hopes of finding an immediate and/or lasting connection.[1] Others rely on social media sites like Facebook and Instagram to tactically deploy likes, follows, and comments to gain attention from their virtual crushes. The gay marketplace for intimate possibilities on mobile digital media may have similar inspirations and objectives in a global scale, but a situated examination of technoscientific developments and its everyday applications sheds light on the asymmetries and inequities concerning access and expertise. It also gives life to multiple worlds of queer desire, longing, and frustration infused with specific sociocultural dynamics and compounded through platform interfaces and communicative practices among its users.

This chapter asks similar questions from Sherry Turkle (2012) to gay men in Manila: "Why do we expect more from technology and less from each other?" She adds, "Insecure in our relationships and anxious about intimacy, we look to technology for ways to be in relationships and protect ourselves from them at the same time" (xii). Constant connectivity has detached people from the trials of face-to-face interaction. We use technology

244 / Paul Michael Leonardo Atienza

to gauge interpersonal relationships with others because they are deemed low risk and readily available. Turkle claims that "in intimacy, new solitudes [emerge]" (19). Connecting and disconnecting in various ways, Filipinos use a multiplicity of digital platforms to generate ecologies of desire in Manila. Situated within its geopolitical realities of labor outsourcing, rapid and unequal industrializing of economies, and the highest HIV infection rates in the world, gay men in Manila find differing strategies of using technologies to connect with each other. As I culled my field notes and memory of the loosely bounded connections that made up contemporary ecologies of Manila, I found that our symbiotic relationship with technologies generate new forms of connection: "in solitude, new intimacies" (Turkle 2012). Analyzing cultural exchanges among gay Filipino men in Manila on mobile digital media platforms, I complicate normative roles of mediation between technology use and identity categories (McNamara and Batalova 2015). Through participant-observation and discourse analysis on gay socio-sexual apps as well as social media platforms in addition to informal interviews about app practices from users in Manila between May 2015 and June 2015, I ask how mobile phone apps change how gay Filipinos communicate desires and generate intimate connections with others. I trace how mobile digital media app users make sense of the technological artifact and the social categories embedded in the design of platform interfaces. Initially, I observed how users establish constructions of their digital selves as commodity to improve their chances of connecting with other users. But what I found compelling were how users in the Philippines reimagine alternative forms of intimacy and sociality both on- and offline. As sociological construction of technology scholars demonstrate, artifacts released to publics will generate situated and unintended user practices (Kline and Pinch 1996).

To answer these questions, I use the concept of sociotechnical infrastructures as an analytical lens to study unequal arrangements and access to complex systems in shaping qualities of social interaction and definitions of attractiveness. These complex systems include transportation infrastructures, access to technological hardware and data storage, along with social differences such as class and gender as forms of power that inform different ideas of aesthetic beauty. My invocation of infrastructure works through feminist ethnographer Ara Wilson's (2016) formulation who extends the concept from Susan Leigh Star. Star (1999) claims that infrastructures are relational and encompass a multitude of components and that only teasing out the calculated moves between actors and networks allows for a more nuanced analysis of complex infrastructures as objects of study. Wilson takes these perspectives from feminist science and technology studies and adds framings from queer studies to the study of infrastructure. She writes, "Understanding how infrastructures enable or hinder intimacy is a conduit to understanding the concrete force of abstract fields of power by allowing us to identify actually existing systems rather than a priori structures" (248). I would also incorporate affective components or structures of feeling that are difficult to articulate through words and text as essential to infrastructure (Williams 1961). I argue that mobile digital media such as geolocative socio-sexual apps, social media, and messaging platforms are part of Manila's infrastructural assemblage. Looking specifically at everyday interactions, language use, beliefs about digital media, and group affiliations makes visible moments of infrastructural failure and breakdown, where its interrelated social, organizational, technical dimensions become more transparent for analysis.

Born from the mixing of imported colonial governance and existing social hierarchies, infrastructures are part of the Global North's ongoing extraction of labor and resources around the world. Discourses tied to novelty, growth, and progress overshadow the ways publics and networks help restore and maintain the fragile ecologies we share. An examination of failures and mistranslations through mobile digital media generate new worldmaking practices that address the entangled realities of queer lives—the everyday survival within the clogged arteries of global flows. My aim is to expand what constitutes Manila's sociotechnical infrastructure through an examination of communication practices on mobile digital media apps geared toward a promise of intimate connection. Short for *application*, apps are software programs on mobile devices like smartphones or tablet computers. Apps are designed to perform specific functions to assist users with multiple tasks. Geolocative socio-sexual apps and social media are part of a system of gateways and portals enmeshed within sociotechnical infrastructures of queer Filipinos in the city.

Manila is shot through with histories of multiple colonizations, national struggles, the political and material excesses of ruling elites, and the limits and possibilities of surviving life one day at a time. I examine the situated configurations of the city's technoscientific networks with its dynamic significations and multivocality animated through the lives of gay Filipino men.[2] I take up the mobilities of technoscience in multiple sites to make visible the instability of translations and to unpack layered complexities among varied attachments that loosely hold enrolled networks situated throughout the planet (Anderson and Adams 2007; Harding 2011; Medina 2011). The overabundance of technoscientific studies within Global North sites erases the ways multiple cultures refigure and translate technoscientific knowledges and fails to recognize other situated forms of technoscience as equally valid. Here, I want to push against formations of proper modern subjectivities and instead emphasize other possibilities between disparate alliances that elaborate on the entanglement of multiple modernities. There is a wide variation of tactics and ways of knowing new media cultures in the Philippines as declared in the aptly titled collection, *Hindi Nangyari Dahil Wala sa Social Media* [It Did Not Happen if It's Not on Social Media] (Tolentino, Gonzales, and Castillo 2021). I encourage us to acknowledge the messiness of interactions, fluid spaces, and the possibilities of carving out new ways of knowing and being based on unequal power relations that keep the local and global entangled with one another.

## Ethnographies of Socio-Sexual Apps in the Philippines: World-Making Possibilities

Recent qualitative studies on gay socio-sexual apps in the Philippines reveal how Filipinos use mobile technologies differently from their intended purpose and function.[3] One study found high school and college-aged men use various applications to learn more about same-sex desire and sexual identity, community practices, and popular gathering spaces (Castañeda 2015). Apps assisted in the social formation of localized hybrid communities based on global gay subcommunity categories. Nathan Rondina's (2013) research in Manila on the gay socio-sexual app Growlr found a growing bear community that uses the technology to advertise dance parties and offline hangouts for gay men who prefer heavier-set frames and hairier bodies.

Communication studies scholar Jonathan Ong's (2017) project with a humanitarian relief organization observed that gay socio-sexual apps like Grindr were themselves sites of cultural exchange. After one of the strongest cyclones ever recorded ravaged through the central region of the Philippines in 2013, a new population of relief workers in the postdisaster area used gay socio-sexual apps to establish intimacies with locals and with each other. As one of Ong's informants stated, "Overnight, my Grindr became the United Nations." Ong determined that the humanitarian workers and the local gay users were using intimacy to deal with the stresses of everyday life. For the international staff, it was a way to soothe long hours working with rebuilding entire material infrastructures from the ground up. For the local gay users, it was an opportunity to meet, feel, and engage with global gay figures. Inequalities persisted in these exchanges. Local gay elites and middle-class men were more likely to use these mobile technologies, but I take away the world-making possibilities enabled through socio-sexual apps even after a horrific catastrophe.

Despite mobile digital platforms providing peer education, resource sharing, and the potential for sexual, romantic, and/or platonic intimacies for gay Filipinos, social obstacles continue. Stigmatization among gay, bisexual, and trans communities in the Philippines persist through lack of proper sexual education, a lack of more positive representation in media, and ongoing social conservatisms toward the greater LGBTQ community from the Catholic Church and other faith-based groups.[4] Media articles often conflate studies and reports about the proliferation of sexually transmitted infections with access to affordable communication technologies. A headline from a 2019 news piece by Agence France-Presse that circulated in several news outlets such as the *Washington Post* and Rappler declared, "WHO Alarmed at STD Spread in the Era of Dating Apps."[5] Yet the official World Health Organization report did not specifically name geolocative socio-sexual apps in the study, although it did recommend priority actions for countries to gather data about risk factors and determinants among its surveillance priorities.[6] The link between transmission and digital platform came from study coauthor Teodora Wi, who asserted the connection in a press response.[7] Wi commented on the potential decline of condom use and how sex was becoming more accessible through the greater accessibility of media technologies. These actions reinforce stigma attached to the LGBTQ community and those people living with HIV. In a 2019 report from the World Health Organization, UNAIDS and the Philippine Health Ministry report that the Philippines recorded the fastest-growing HIV/AIDS epidemic in the Asia-Pacific, with a 200 percent increase between 2010 and 2018.[8] In May 2017 alone, 1,098 new cases of HIV infections were reported in the Philippines, the highest recorded number of cases since 1984, when infections were first reported.[9] Eighty-three percent of new HIV cases occurred among males who have sex with males and transgender women who have sex with males.[10]

Anxieties about sexually transmitted infections are often associated with the growing population of workers supporting the country's business process outsourcing (BPO) industry. As American Studies scholar Jan M. Padios writes about the initial HIV response in the late 2000s, "The alarm about HIV signaled not only a medical concern but also deep anxiety about call centers as sites where deviant bodies put the nation at economic, cultural, and social risk" (2018, 159). I met several gay Filipino men who work in BPO companies who use gay socio-sexual apps not just to meet other users for sex but to imagine different futures of sociality. Their odd working hours and a considerably higher wage compared with other service industries allow greater spending power. As I learned from multiple call center workers, they recognize that they work long hours, so they make the most of their leisure time. Many shared that they would save their salaries to be able to purchase luxury items like top-of-the-line electronics or splurge on late nights in bars and restaurants with top-shelf liquor brands. With the odd work hours of BPO workers, bars and restaurants around these call centers adjust their hours of operation to cater to worker schedules. Happy hour specials start at three o'clock in the early morning during shift turnovers, and twenty-four-hour convenience stores like 7-Eleven and Mini Stop have constant business during breaks throughout the day and night.

Reflecting on socio-sexual app practices of Christian, a BPO worker living in Eastwood City, and Wesley, a young professional who manages a family business in Quezon City, gay socio-sexual apps are gateways away from the daily stresses of life. But app practices here are not just about coping. They are making their own messy worlds (Manalansan 2013) that are emergent, open-ended, and, in some ways, in collaborative survival (Tsing 2015).

## Living on the Edge: Eastwood City

Three days after I arrived in Manila, a scholar from the University of the Philippines invited me to join him at one of the high-rise condominiums in Eastwood City, where he was cat sitting for a friend. They knew about my research interests on gay socio-sexual apps and suggested I check out the app users in that specific area. Towering amid older homes and makeshift settler camps of the urban poor, Eastwood City is a concept space that integrates residential, commercial, business, and entertainment outlets into one complex. Engineered spaces like Eastwood City, coined "edge cities" (Garreau 1991), discursively invoke an unmoored global identity with promises of modernity, security, and leisure. It is part of a regional trend of rapid urbanization in Southeast Asian countries where the proposal of new city spaces are aspirational strategies to create not only new material infrastructures but also a specific type of citizen (Lemos 2010; Shatkin 2005).

Paying attention to the design of infrastructures can illuminate how science, business, and technology advance the logics of authoritative statecraft (Scott 1998). The Philippine state colludes with its industry elites to foster development projects such as grand shopping complexes and edge cities like Eastwood. These edge cities proliferate throughout key metropolitan centers located in the northern and central regions of the country. The naming alone of these complexes invoke the modernist tropes of progress. Bonifacio Global City (BGC) and Ayala Land TechnoHub are two of examples of new edge cities in Manila. In response to the spread of edge cities, Philippine shopping development powerhouse SM Supermalls began to expand its current sites to attract and entice multinational companies to establish business process outsourcing (BPO) centers in its locations. SM Mall of Asia, SM Megamall, and its ultramodern SM Aura Premier are just a few examples of the development craze tied to luring strategies of the Philippine state and its allied business institutions. Whether reclaiming land, paying off landowners, or forcibly removing temporary settlers from prime locations, state and corporate power enabled the rise of Manila's contemporary sociotechnical infrastructures.

With the Philippines overtaking India as the top outsourcing destination for the call center industry, the country's recent college graduates find themselves with alluring opportunities to earn decent starting salaries through multinational BPO centers. According to FT Confidential Research, a *Financial Times* research service, Philippine revenues for 2016 from BPOs could equal the remittances sent from overseas Filipino workers (OFW).[11] One of the largest sources of economic growth in the Philippines, remittances from OFWs are not accruing as quickly, as migrant workers struggle with current employment stagnation in many Global North sites of the Philippine diaspora. A young middle class is rising situated in the greater cosmopolitan region of the Philippine's capital through the prolific BPO industry. With greater spending power, a growing number of Philippine citizens are gaining easier access to consumer technologies. Many own multiple mobile communication devices where they can stay networked wherever they go.

With access and excess, a media and public discourse emerged in the Philippines tying BPO workers to moral depravity. Gay men working in BPOs became symbols of sexual promiscuity tied to the rise in cases of HIV infections in the Philippines.[12] What have been compounding factors to the country's HIV crisis are the combination of poorly funded state public health initiatives, the lack of sexual health education resources, and the strong influence of the Catholic Church that allow for misinformation and cultural silences about sexuality in general. Some Filipinos used media technologies to counter the moral discourse with statements and testimonies from BPO workers. A collective of BPO workers and lobbyists joined forces with an established labor party with hopes of giving more exposure to the rights and needs of the rising call center industry.

Aksyon Magsasaka Partido Tinig ng Masa (AKMA-PTM) is an accredited party-list that ran for a seat in Congress during the 2010 Philippine national elections. Its aims were to safeguard the rights of indigent farmers. Although AKMA is its own party-list, it accepted collaborating with an unofficial candidate organization, the Association of Call Center and BPO Agents of the Philippines (ACCAP). ACCAP was founded in 2007 to address the needs of the fast-growing population of call center and BPO agents in the Philippines. The organization wanted to improve regulations in Philippine call center industry and to make the country more conducive to this type of business. AKMA-PTM and ACCAP together adopted a two-pronged campaign approach: AKMA-PTM would concentrate on the grassroots level in rural regions, while ACCAP would focus on young urban professionals through a solid base in social networking sites and internet campaigning. The coalition disbanded due to ACCAP's failed attempt to attain state recognition, but media materials from the group continued to circulate. These cultural products fought negative public opinions of BPO workers as dirty, reckless, and irresponsible.

One such campaign focused on online testimonials of HIV-positive BPO workers. In one online video, BPO employee Joseph Ryan spoke about how he contracted the virus.[13] Wearing a surgical face mask and a baseball cap, Joseph Ryan sat veiled in shadow as he pleaded for viewers to resist popular public opinion and stereotypes of BPO workers. He added that the BPO industry is helping the Philippine economy. It was fascinating how such a personal narrative was juxtaposed with the ongoing political and economic labor brokerage system that the Philippine state supports (Rodriguez 2010; Guevarra 2009). For Robyn Rodriguez and Anna Guevarra, their examination of the Philippine state strategies of exporting migrant workers commodifies its citizens as a form of development. With BPO companies setting up firm stakes in the country, in conjunction with the slowing down of economies around the world, labor outsourcing as import complicates the sociotechnical infrastructures of contemporary Manila.

## In Solitude, New Intimacies: Christian's Grindr Strategy

For BPO worker Christian, being part of the rising middle class has left him working odd hours. He shares a one-bedroom condominium in Eastwood City with three other coworkers. I met Christian through Grindr while I was sitting in an adjacent condominium with my colleague who was cat sitting for a friend. First available to iPhones in 2009, Grindr is now one of the most widely used gay socio-sexual apps in the world. My colleague insisted we invite Christian over to share wine and perhaps encourage him to join my long-term study. For Christian and his friends, living together in a small space close to work was a better choice than living with their families. Christian's family lived less than fifteen kilometers from Eastwood City, but the stress of dealing with his parent's house rules in addition to managing a commute that would last nearly two hours each way made the cramped condo a space of liberation and freedom. But living in Eastwood City during rising inflation and coupled with a work schedule that keeps him busy from 8:00 PM to 10:00 AM, Christian's social life became difficult to manage. He turns to gay socio-sexual apps in hopes of connecting with local users when he has free time. He invites users to hang out and drink with him and his other condo mates. He tells me that it is cheaper to drink at home, plus you do not have to deal with the attitudes from patrons of gay bars and clubs.

Sometimes sex happens, Christian explained. There is no door between the living room and the bedroom, so they use a sheet as a divider. There is an unspoken understanding when the sheet is drawn across the door, but the condo is so small that they have inadvertently walked in to each other having sex with other guys. Eastwood City has multiple high-rise condominium complexes, each more than thirty stories high. They house local Filipino BPO workers, business workers from other countries with temporary assignments, and tourists staying through space-sharing services like Airbnb. Christian explained that sometimes you see the same people. Sometimes there is not much response. "It would be nice to meet someone for a long-term relationship," Christian shared, "but with my work hours when would we have time to spend with each other? In time, I'm sure it will happen but for now I'm trying to save money, he added. I would like to move up in the company or even transfer to another place close by once I get more experience."

Mobile technologies are leaving people more connected, yet oddly more alone. The good life holds a promise that those who work hard will achieve job security, equality for all, lasting relationships, and a steady social mobility (Berlant 2011). These cruel optimisms are not sustainable, yet people are invested in its ideology. We should look at the present as effects of mediation between these ideological investments in order for us to critically understand how entrenched we are in this injurious cycle. Not until we recognize this state can we devise alternate ways of being in this world. Berlant writes that optimism is a structural feeling, one that an "optimistic attachment is invested in one's own or the world's continuity, but might feel any number of ways," including not optimistic at all (13). Maintaining attachments that sustain the good-life fantasy, no matter how injurious or cruel these attachments may be, allows people to make it through day-to-day life when the day-to-day has become unlivable.

Christian's gay socio-sexual app practice was a form of collaborative survival faced with the precarious nature of his job as a BPO worker. Being at work when most of Manila's residents are asleep makes it difficult to sustain social relationships. The gay socio-sexual app provides Christian with a way to connect with other gay BPO workers in the area. They share similar structured lives. Confined in a location with limited spending options, Christian found a different arrangement of connection and community that works with the constraints of his social and financial realities. Even as people are entrenched in working toward the good life, gay BPO workers find other ways to endure through difficult work-life arrangements. The sociotechnical infrastructures that have brought further material inequalities in greater metropolitan Manila have also generated new forms of intimacy. As Christian demonstrates, people find ways to adapt to new circumstances. In a time of constant interconnection, technologies and people reconfigure each other to survive countless failures and short circuits that are part and parcel of being alive in the present.

## In Solitude, New Intimacies: Wesley's Path and Gay Socio-Sexual App Ecologies

I met Wesley on Scruff.[14] Scruff is one of the most widely downloaded gay socio-sexual apps in the world, with more than eight million users. Through the mobile device's geolocative function, Scruff allows for users to search within their local vicinity or a targeted location around the world. The app also allows for multiple photo uploads for user profiles and other interactive functions that were not available on Grindr during the time I met Wesley. Its users are known to subscribe to gay men who present themselves as guys next door, rugged, and masculine. Wesley was curious about my profile headline, which read, "ResearcherOfApps." Our initial communicative exchange progressed quickly from greetings to sharing of personal information such as age, places of residence, and schools attended. I learned during our text conversation that Wesley works for his family business. He runs and manages domestic service contracts for one of the largest Philippine trade corporations. Business was not what he wanted to do. He had traveled the world and trained as a chef in Europe before returning to the Philippines. He hopes to start his own restaurant someday, but he explained that he needed to help with the family business because his father was getting old. He and his siblings have to start learning the specific duties of the company before their father retires. Wesley's family knows that he is gay, but they do not talk about it or make a big deal about it. He told me that they let him do what he wants as long as he carries out the required work. Later, he invited me to join him for lunch. I replied with affirmation and set up a time the following day.

Wesley texted me when he was getting close to where I was staying. I waited for him outside and saw a new Cadillac Escalade drive up to the house. I received another text telling me to get in the car. Once I entered the passenger side, Wesley seemed nervous. He was smoking. A heavier-set guy, Wesley wore a plain oversized white shirt, Gucci sunglasses, and gray sweatpants. His Louis Vuitton messenger bag rested on the passenger-side floor. I reassured him that I was doing well and that I appreciated him taking time to meet with me. He took me to a new restaurant along Tomas Morato Street, an area in Quezon City known for its eateries. I had told him that I'd prefer Filipino food, and he chose a new spot that specialized in classic recipes presented with a modern aesthetic. We shared several dishes while we talked about gay life in Manila.

It was tough for Wesley to meet other guys for romantic relationships, he said. He blames his size. He told me that he had been working with a trainer and that he had lost a ton of weight. Although romantic relationships were tough to come by, he found plenty of acquaintances through other friends. They often went out to BGC (Bonifacio Global City) or the O Bar (a gay nightclub and cabaret), or they planned short trips to other parts of the country.[15] I asked him if they met on apps like Scruff. He said that he met a few of them through apps like Grindr and Scruff, but most of them through a different app called Path. I had not heard of that app, I replied. He said it was not a gay dating app per se, but more social networking. He directed me to download it and see for myself.

Path is a social network app that launched in 2010 and has since terminated its service in 2018.[16] Based in San Francisco, the company's mission stated that "through technology and design we aim to be a source of happiness, meaning, and connection. We do what we do so that you might be a little closer to what you care about most." It allows its users to share thoughts, images, videos, and links to a maximum of 150 accounts. In early 2014, the company launched a messenger app that works with the media-sharing interface. Wesley explained to me that there are gay Filipino communities using this app to stay connected with one another. He added that gay socio-sexual apps are just for people wanting to find a quick sexual encounter. "There are tons of liars and people who spread negative energies on those things," he said. Although Wesley still used gay socio-sexual apps, he explained that Path was another way of keeping in touch with your close gay friends. Wesley explained that Path users can check in at specific locations, share your current mood through a song or album you are listening to, or stay up to date with your friends' gossip.

Once I completed setting up an account in Path, Wesley shared information on some of his friends and encouraged me to start adding them to my Path list. I thought it would be an excellent way to meet more people that may be interested in joining my long-term study. It took a while to get more interactions on my interface, so Wesley suggested I start liking and leaving comments on other user posts. I should also start posting more photos and check-in statuses so other users would see that I was an active participant. Path's design sets it apart from gay socio-sexual apps. New posts from users populate your wall feed, unlike the static profile photos of gay socio-sexual apps. In time, I started getting notifications of other users liking my posts and updates.

Wesley and I spent most of the day getting to know each other. After lunch, we had coffee and dessert at a nearby Starbucks. He shared his dreams and aspirations. He asked me about my life in the United States and how I became interested in studying anthropology. While we continued to talk, I noticed him on his mobile phone switching quickly between different apps. Replying to messages on one, then checking posts on another, Wesley was connected with his networks. He mentioned offhand that it would be nice to date one of these guys on Path. He was working hard to become more fit—a nod to a global gay conventional aesthetic through biopolitical regimes of self-presentation. We both examined multiple Path users sharing shirtless photos of themselves in the gym, at home, on vacation, or in the shower. These app posts were mixed in with obscure memes, check-ins to local restaurants, bars, or shopping malls, and even rants on friends who stole someone's boyfriend. The information you get from Path users is unlike the seemingly unchanging information on gay socio-sexual apps. Path user information makes it seem that you get to know them more. The ongoing updates and streaming content provide app users with a sense of unfolding intimacy. In conjunction with Path's messenger function, users can engage in one-on-one text conversation that would foster further opportunities to tighten app connections on- and offline.

As we were finishing our coffee, Wesley alerted me that a few of his Path friends wanted to meet up for drinks later that evening at a pub in BGC. He asked me to join, and I eagerly accepted. Wesley mentioned that his four friends all worked in BPO companies but in management or IT positions. He made sure to inform me that they were not call center workers. I have alluded to Wesley's class background in this essay through his material possessions and business position, but this was the first time I noticed him directly provide pointed communication about the value and hierarchy of workers within the BPO industry.

Once we arrived at the bar, introductions were made as each of them smoked their cigarettes. They ordered a whole bottle of Black Label Johnny Walker to share. It was roughly one hundred U.S. dollars for the bottle. Wesley made sure his friends knew about my research objectives, and they were all intrigued. A few of them teased each other about their dating app stories. In between conversations, each checked their mobile phones. They answered messages, checked Facebook, and scrolled through Path postings. Each confirmed that they used gay dating apps, but they were mostly for finding sexual encounters. They met through friends and found they all got along well with one another. They would hang out often after work or during their free times. Sometimes it would be one-on-one lunch dates or smaller configurations of the larger friend circle they share on Path. They affirmed that Path was a better way to stay in contact with close friends. They all added me in on Path and vowed to stay in touch.

## Queer Futures within Sociotechnical Infrastructures

Moving from members-only nightclubs to private parties on the balconies of high-rise luxury condominiums, an elite group of gay Filipino men dream of materializing connections with a global gay network. Bobby Benedicto (2014) delivers a beautifully written account of upper-class gay Manila's aspirations that contribute to a particular form of worlding or "scene-making" through the "shade" of class-based hierarchies. What Benedicto coins "bright lights scene" sought to incorporate them among a gay globality that rubs against the material conditions of Manila as a failed city. This gay globality is itself an assemblage of privileged places, ideologies, and disciplined bodies that invests a particular image.

Benedicto depicts Manila as a city in crisis, one that is negotiating the voracious needs of a global market capitalism seen through its rapid building of luxury high rises and its real problems of abject poverty and overpopulation. The bright lights scene deploys a discursive and imaginative practice of idealized world making to differentiate themselves as proper modern citizens in relation to the messiness and unruly ecologies they reluctantly share. Benedicto writes, "The third-world city here becomes both the drag that weighs the scene down, as it marches forward and outward, and an object of desire itself, a thing that must be transformed in order to fulfill, if partially, the promise of modernity. . . . It is . . . a material complex teeming with objects and spaces that exhibit inertia and that demonstrate a kind of agency themselves" (16). But the daily struggles and triumphs of Christian, Wesley, and the other gay socio-sexual app users I met in Manila somewhat challenge the dire prognosis of Benedicto's bright light scene. I believe the critique of the poor as limiting is a wide practice of performative social aspiration. Although Christian and Wesley may not have the same access as the upper-class gays of the bright lights scene, they cope with the imperfections of the city through the possibilities of digital media platforms. They are able to form casual connections and intimate networks to help pass their mundane struggles. Each have their aspirations for social mobility, yet they fall short of placing blame on the inadequacies of Manila. With mobile digital platforms on hand, Christian and Wesley dream of queer futures enmeshed in the sociotechnical infrastructures of Manila's multiple modernities and emergent local intimacies.[17]

Crisis in its contemporary form becomes abstracted from its multiple, unequal, historical, and contingent sources. Various tools from management and governance through statecraft, corporate media circulation, and the paradoxical relation of space and time across the planet work together to portray crisis as natural, distant, and too large to unpack. Scholars loosely bounded in the interdisciplinary field of science and technology studies (STS) have generated possibilities in teasing out the messy entanglements of global crises. These projects highlight the multiple networks across scale that contribute to or become enrolled in systems of dis/ordering the mutual ecologies we share with all forms of matter in this world. Moving away from suggesting forms of life as properly modern, but instead as multiple, relational, and situated in difference, allows for the further interrogation of our social worlds as constructed assemblages, already an unequal mix of technoscientific components. Attuned to discursive regimes that further obstruct understanding of technoscience to a larger public, the social construction of translation across technoscientific differences is tantamount to moving toward STS's ethical investment toward social change.

For Christian, it was an alternative user practice to gay socio-sexual apps that allowed for other possibilities of connection amid the drive of work productivity situated in edge cities among BPO workers, while Wesley and his friends are using social media platforms to stay connected. These may not be resistant or revolutionary practices against established social norms within communities of gay men in Manila, but they are new possibilities out of the present configurations. Manila's sociotechnical infrastructure works similarly. To understand its intricate connections, we must examine the daily minutiae that complicate system aims and functions.

Seeking intimate connections through mobile technologies is part of contemporary practices of survival amid the precarity of speculative finance, flexible labor contracts, and an expanding gap between rich and poor throughout the world. Amid the rapid decay of our planet are people reconfiguring themselves with the materials available to them. What are the long-term effects to the lived realities of living matter through the onslaught and drive of unequal industrialization? For Christian and his condo mates, they continue to try to make connections no matter how many times connection fails, while Wesley and his friends enjoy social exchange on a platform that does not have the same overt pressure for sexual and romantic intimacies. The instances that lead to intimate gatherings are worth the time and investment that brings them to another day.

## NOTES

1. I borrow the term *socio-sexual app* from Andrew DJ Shield instead of the more vernacular term *dating app* or *hook-up app* to emphasize the multiple social forms of intimacy app users seek. See Shield, *Immigrants on Grindr.*

2. See Pratt, "Arts of the Contact Zone."

3. For a current review of scholarship, see Labor, "Mobile Sexuality."

4. See also Muyargas, Manalastas, and Docena, "The 'I ♡ Lesbian and Gay Rights' Pin." For a regional perspective, see Manalastas et al., "Homonegativity in Southeast Asia."

5. Lavallee, "WHO Alarmed at STD Spread."

6. For published findings from the WHO report, see Taylor and Wi, "Transforming and Integrating STI Surveillance."

7. See Larson, "WHO Alarmed at STD Spread."

8. See Joint United Nations Programme on HIV/AIDS (UNAIDS), *Country Progress Report.*

9. See "Philippines Has Highest HIV Infection Growth Rate in Asia-Pacific."

10. Ibid. See also Department of Health, "Philippines Addresses Rising Trend in New HIV Infections."

11. See Salvosa, "Philippine Remittances." But as of 2021, BPO revenues have not surpassed overseas remittances even with the COVID-19 pandemic. See de Guzman, "BPO Industry Seen Performing Better vs PH Economy."

12. See Padios, "Queering the Call Center."

13. For a snippet of the video, see Corpuz, "Ex-Call Center Agent with HIV Shares Story."

14. I also wrote about Wesley in a separate self-reflexive essay that analyzes how fear and anxiety influences the crafting of ethnographic work. I argue that the ethnographer's own affective and sexual participation during field research complicates the anthropological assumptions regarding power dynamics between the researcher and subject. It also addresses disciplinary conservatisms that continue to influence and police how sexual actions are circulated through forms of academic writing. See Atienza, "Censoring the Sexual Self."

15. For more about Bonifacio Global City, see Lim, "Global City as Place Branding Strategy"; Shatkin, "Colonial Capital, Modernist Capital, Global Capital"; and Kleibert, "News Spaces of Exception."

16. See Moreau, "A Look Back on the Social Networking App Called Path."

17. For more information on how mobile media technologies interact with local intimacies, see Cabañes and Uy-Tioco, *Mobile Media and Social Intimacies in Asia.*

## BIBLIOGRAPHY

Anderson, Warwick. "Introduction: Postcolonial Technoscience." *Social Studies of Science* 32, no. 5/6 (2002): 643–658.

Anderson, Warwick, and Vincanne Adams. "Pramoedya's Chickens: Postcolonial Studies of Technoscience." In *The Handbook of Science and Technology Studies*, 181–204. London: MIT Press, 2007.

Atienza, Paul Michael Leonardo. "Censoring the Sexual Self: Reflections from an Ethnographic Study of Gay Filipinos on Mobile Dating Apps in Manila." *Asia Pacific Journal of Anthropology* 19, no.3 (2018): 231–244.

Benedicto, Bobby. *Under Bright Lights.* Minneapolis: University of Minnesota Press, 2014.

Berlant, Lauren. *Cruel Optimism.* Durham, NC: Duke University Press, 2011.

Cabañes, Jason Vincent A., and Cecilia S. Uy-Tioco, eds. *Mobile Media and Social Intimacies in Asia: Reconfiguring Local Ties and Enacting Global Relationships.* Dordrecht, The Netherlands: Springer Nature, 2020.

Castañeda, Jan Gabriel Melendrez. "Grindring the Self: Young Filipino Gay Men's Exploration of Sexual Identity through a Geo-Social Networking Application." *Philippine Journal of Psychology* 48, no. 1 (2015): 29–58.

Corpuz, Niña. "Ex-Call Center Agent with HIV Shares Story." ABS-CBN News, March 10, 2010, news.abs-cbn.com/lifestyle/03/01/10/ex-call-center-agent-hiv-urges-safe-sex.

de Guzman, Warren. "BPO Industry Seen Performing Better vs PH Economy This Year." ABS-CBN News, November 20, 2020, news.abs-cbn.com/business/11/20/20/ibpap-expects-05-growth-in-revenues-as-ph-economy-likely-to-contract-by-over-55.

Department of Health. "Philippines Addresses Rising Trend in New HIV Infections." https://doh.gov.ph/node/10649.

Garreau, Joel. *Edge City: Life on the New Frontier.* New York: Anchor, 1991.

Guevarra, Anna Romina. *Marketing Dreams, Manufacturing Heroes: The Transnational Labor Brokering of Filipino Workers.* New Brunswick, NJ: Rutgers University Press, 2009.

Haraway, Donna. *The Companion Species Manifesto: Dogs, People, and Significant Otherness.* Vol. 1. Chicago: Prickly Paradigm Press, 2003.

———. "A Cyborg Manifesto: Science, Technology, and Socialist-Feminism in the Late Twentieth Century." In *Simians, Cyborgs, and Women: The Reinvention of Nature*, 149–182. New York: Routledge, 1985.

Harding, Sandra G., ed. *The Postcolonial Science and Technology Studies Reader*. Durham, NC: Duke University Press, 2011.

Joint United Nations Programme on HIV/AIDS (UNAIDS). *Country Progress Report*. Philippines: Global AIDS Monitoring 2019, https://www.unaids.org/sites/default/files/country/documents/PHL_2019_countryreport.pdf.

Kleibert, Jana M. "News Spaces of Exception: Special Economic Zones and Luxury Condominiums in Metro Manila." In *Developmentalist Cities? Interrogating Urban Developmentalism in East Asia*, edited by Jamie Doucette and Bae-Gyoon Park, 110–133. Leiden: Brill, 2019.

Kline, Ronald, and Trevor Pinch. "Users as Agents of Technological Change: The Social Construction of the Automobile in the Rural United States." *Technology and Culture* 37, no. 4 (1996): 763–795.

Labor, Jonalou. "Mobile Sexuality: Presentations of Young Filipinos in Dating Apps." *Plaridel: A Philippine Journal of Communication, Media, and Society* 17, no. 1 (2020): 247–278.

Larson, Nina. "WHO Alarmed at STD Spread in the Era of Dating Apps," Medicalxpress.com, June 6, 2019, https://medicalxpress.com/news/2019-06-alarmed-std-era-dating-apps.html.

Lavallee, Guillaume. "WHO Alarmed at STD Spread in the Era of Dating Apps." Rappler.com, June 7, 2019, www.rappler.com/science/life-health/world-health-organization-alarmed-std-spread-era-of-dating-apps.

Lemos, Andre. "Post—Mass Media Functions, Locative Media, and Informational Territories: New Ways of Thinking about Territory, Place, and Mobility in Contemporary Society." *Space and Culture* 13, no. 4 (2010): 403–420.

Lim, Michael Kho. "Global City as Place Branding Strategy: The Case of Bonifacio Global City (Philippines)." In *Re-Imagining Creative Cities in Twenty-First Century Asia*, edited by Xin Gu, Michael Kho Lim, and Justin O'Connor, 27–39. London: Palgrave Macmillan, 2020.

Manalansan, Martin F. "Queer Worldings: The Messy Art of Being Global in Manila and New York." *Antipode* 47, no. 3 (2013): 566–579.

Manalastas, Eric Julian, Timo Tapani Ojanen, Beatriz A. Torre, Rattanakorn Ratanashevorn, Bryan Choong Chee Hong, Vizla Kumaresan, and Vigneswaran Veeramuthu. "Homonegativity in Southeast Asia: Attitudes toward Lesbians and Gay Men in Indonesia, Malaysia, the Philippines, Singapore, Thailand, and Vietnam." *Asia-Pacific Social Science Review* 17, no. 1 (2017): 25–33.

McNamara, Keith, and Jeanne Batalova, "Filipino Immigrants in the United States." Migration Information Source. July 21, 2015. https://www.migrationpolicy.org/article/filipino-immigrants-united-states-2013.

Medina, Eden. *Cybernetic Revolutionaries: Technology and Politics in Allende's Chile*. Cambridge: MIT Press, 2011.

"Mission Statement." *Path*. Accessed December 4, 2015, https://path.com/about.

Moreau, Elise. "A Look Back on the Social Networking App Called Path." Lifewire.com, July 17, 2020, www.lifewire.com/what-is-path-3486483.

Muyargas, Moniq M., Eric Julian Manalastas, and Pierce S. Docena. "The 'I ♡ Lesbian and Gay Rights' Pin: An Experiential Learning Exercise to Understand Anti-LGBT Stigma." *Philippine Journal of Psychology* 49, no. 2 (2016): 173–188.

Ong, Jonathan Corpus. "Queer Cosmopolitanism in the Disaster Zone: 'My Grindr Became the United Nations.'" *International Communication Gazette* 79, no. 6–7 (2017): 656–673.

Padios, Jan M. "Queering the Call Center." In *A Nation on the Line: Call Centers as Postcolonial Predicaments in the Philippines*, 157–180. Durham, NC: Duke University Press, 2018.

"Philippines Has Highest HIV Infection Growth Rate in Asia-Pacific: U.N." Reuters, August 1, 2017, www.reuters.com/article/us-health-aids-philippines/philippines-has-highest-hiv-infection-growth-rate-in-asia-pacific-u-n-idUSKBN1AH3CW.

Pratt, Mary Louise. "Arts of the Contact Zone." *Profession* (1991): 33–40, http://www.jstor.org/stable/25595469.

Rodriguez, Robyn Magalit. *Migrants for Export: How the Philippine State Brokers Labor to the World*. Minneapolis: University of Minnesota Press, 2010.

Rondina, Nathan. "Bears Gone Wild: Fat Is the New Sexy, Shout Manila's Gay Bears," Coconuts Manila, September 6, 2013, http://manila.coconuts.co/2013/09/06/bear-community-in-metro-manila.

Salvosa, Felipe. "Philippine Remittances: Under Threat." *Financial Times*, July 21, 2015, www.cnbc.com/2015/07/21/philippines-remittances-under-threat.html.

Scott, James C. *Seeing Like a State: How Certain Schemes to Improve the Human Condition Have Failed*. New Haven, CT: Yale University Press, 1998.

Shatkin, Gavin. "The City and the Bottom Line: Urban Megaprojects and the Privatization of Planning in Southeast Asia." *Environment and Planning A* 40, no. 2 (2008): 383–401.

———. "Colonial Capital, Modernist Capital, Global Capital: The Changing Political Symbolism of Urban Space in Metro Manila, the Philippines." *Pacific Affairs* 78, no. 4 (2005): 577–600.

Shield, Andrew D. J. *Immigrants on Grindr: Race, Sexuality and Belonging Online*. Cham, Switzerland: Palgrave Macmillan, 2019.

Star, Susan Leigh. "The Ethnography of Infrastructure." *American Behavioral Scientist* 43, no. 3 (1999): 377–391.

Suchman, Lucy. "Mediations and Their Others." In *Media Technologies: Essays on Communication, Materiality, and Society*, 129–137. Cambridge, MA: MIT Press, 2014.

Taylor, Melanie M., and Teodora Ec Wi. "Transforming and Integrating STI Surveillance to Enhance Global Advocacy and Investment in STI Control." *Journal of the International AIDS Society* 22, S6 (2019): e25361.

Tolentino, Rolando B., Vladimeir B. Gonzales, and Laurence Marvin S. Castillo, eds. *Hindi Nangyari Dahil Wala sa Social Media: Interogasyon ng Kulturang New Media sa Pilipinas*. Quezon City: Ateneo de Manila University Press, 2021.

Traweek, Sharon. *Beamtimes and Lifetimes: The World of High Energy Physicists*. Cambridge, MA: Harvard University Press, 1993.

Tsing, Anna Lowenhaupt. *Friction: An Ethnography of Global Connection*. Princeton, NJ: Princeton University Press, 2005.

———. *The Mushroom at the End of the World: On the Possibility of Life in Capitalist Ruins*. Princeton, NJ: Princeton University Press, 2015.

Turkle, Sherry. *Alone Together: Why We Expect More from Technology and Less from Each Other*. New York: Basic Books, 2012.

Williams, Raymond. *The Long Revolution*. London: Chatto & Windus, 1961.

Wilson, Ara. "The Infrastructure of Intimacy." *Signs: Journal of Women in Culture and Society* 41, no. 2 (2016): 247–280.

# Halimaw

*A Hauntology of Manila in Street Art*

LOUISE JASHIL R. SONIDO

## Points of Departure

Discourses about street art, or the transformation of public spaces into discursive canvases, have been typically concerned with dogmatic examinations of the act as lawful or unlawful behavior, academic musings about the performance as cultural practice or youthful rebellion, or aesthetic debates about the pieces and their validity as "art" or readable texts. Because of these debates and controversies, street art remains constantly under erasure. But while other kinds of writing presumably attempt to protect against death or to "[create] immortality,"[1] street art has come to claim "death" or "erasure" as inherent to its nature, "[grasping] the idea of [its] own mortality."[2]

The question of mortality is particularly poetic in street art that installs literal ghosts of folklore in an urban space. From May to June 2011, street art crew Gerilya (Guerilla) installed the *Halimaw: Filipino Lower Mythology Edition* of their Gawgaw (wheat paste) Sessions, a term the group uses to refer to works that are painted on kraft paper, cut out, and then put up on walls and public spaces using an adhesive mix made of vegetable starch and water. The exhibit, with shortened title *Halimaw*, meaning "monster," was installed in various places in Metro Manila and featured creatures from traditional Filipino lore. "*Ang ideya*," wrote Gerilya in a retrospective social media post of the wheat paste session, "*ay through Street Art, ibalik yung kultura ng mga halimaw, aswang at engkanto sa mga siyudad* [The idea was to bring back the culture of monsters, ghosts, and spirits to the city]."[3]

*Halimaw*'s evocation of folk beliefs in the urban city is a cultural project that participates in placemaking efforts to produce the fast-changing spaces of the city as also spaces of history and memory. The iteration of such a project in an ephemeral medium like street art does not only create ghosts to haunt the urban life that has forgotten it, but *performs* the erasure as an ontological, or "hauntological," imprint of both forgetting and remembering, creating erasure itself as the basis of meaning rather than mere consequence of urban apathy and disregard. Imbricated in the "messianic" postcolonial project of identity-formation in an arguably still neocolonial city caught in the web of U.S. imperialism's global networks of power, *Halimaw* activates the ghosts of forgotten cultural histories as well as the hauntings of the marginal "regions"—that crude and broad category used for all other, and Othered, cities and rural areas in the Philippines outside of "Imperial Manila"—that vex Manila's positioning as the capital city of a disunited Republic.

Ten years since *Halimaw* was installed, this study necessarily contends with its ghosts amid President Rodrigo Duterte's regionalist nationalism and self-proclaimed embodiment of Mindanao's resentment against Imperial Manila. Duterte's 2016 presidential campaign drew heavily from this narrative, not only to secure votes from the margins, but to provide fuel to his discourse toward a federal state system and the most convenient excuse for his controversially course language, "gutter talk," inveterate cursing, and unapologetic political incorrectness in jokes and presidential speeches—apparently, he and his supporters claim, a Bisaya quirk.[4] The invigoration of debates surrounding Manila imperialism brought about by Duterte's "Bisaya advantage"[5] for his presidency now places this study's examination of *Halimaw* in dialogue with such debates, as Gerilya had invoked both the ideological and geographic displacement of these creatures from national imagination when they addressed the pieces to the Pinoy who will see them on the streets "*kahit wala sila sa mga baryo* [even if they are not in the (rural) barrios]."[6]

The haunting of *Halimaw*'s ghosts also become more pronounced and multifold today, as many of these pieces have since been erased. Their sightings persist instead in the archives of Gerilya's social media accounts, in the spectral traces of photographic and video documentation archived by the Gerilya crew themselves.[7] This archive of erasure creates a hauntology of Manila, of Gerilya, and of this very study in the way that Derrida addresses the "scholar of the future" in *Specters of Marx: The State of the Debt, the Work of Mourning and the New International* (1994) as having to "learn it . . . from the ghost . . . by learning not how to make conversation with the ghost but how to talk with him, with her, how to let them speak or how to give them back speech, even if it is in oneself, in the other, in the other in oneself."[8] *Halimaw*, now in conversation with its future in which it exists only spectrally, thus narrativizes urbanism's inheritance of cultural amnesia, the "archival banditry" of documented street art, and the centrality of memory work in our relentless aspirations toward democratic nation-formation.

## *Halimaw*: The Ghosts of Manila

Metropolitan Manila's physical and cultural transformations through the centuries have been shaped largely by its colonial experiences, succinctly summarized in the phrase, "three hundred years in a convent and fifty years in Hollywood." In other words, the city's metamorphoses have been dictated mainly by its most affective historical encounters: the violence of Spanish colonization and the persisting domination of American imperialism. This history frames Manila as a "contact zone," a "space of colonial encounters, the space in which people geographically and historically separated come into contact with each other and establish ongoing relations, usually involving conditions of coercion, radical inequality, and intractable conflict."[9]

Such conflicts are visible in the geographic and architectural features of Manila: its colonial past in the cobblestones of Intramuros and its neocolonial present in the glitter of multinational corporations in Makati and Bonifacio Global City; its narrow streets and wide cars; its sprawling slums and towering shopping malls; its monuments to national heroes, which point to its history as a center of revolutionary resistance time and again;[10] and the predominance of state infrastructures in the city that remain as significations to a problematic democracy: the Malacañang Palace, Camp Aguinaldo and Camp Crame,[11] the Supreme Court, the House of Representatives, the House of Senate, and so forth. Resil Mojares succinctly describes the dominance of Metro Manila as the place

> where power and resources are concentrated in terms of educational and media facilities, the apparatus of cultural policy making, and the instruments for canonical recognition and reward. Here are to be found the headquarters of government cultural agencies, publishing houses and centers of book distribution, prestigious award-giving bodies . . . and—not the least—the nexus in the promotion of a Tagalog-based national language. Here cultural productions take the privileged guise of the *national*, beside which all else is merely *regional, provincial,* or *local.*[12]

Participating in the social production of this fractious urban space, Gerilya's *Halimaw*[13] series consists of several figures from Filipino lower mythology, that strata of mythical creatures that anthropologist Maximo D. Reyes describes in *Creatures of Philippine Lower Mythology* as those who "unlike the higher deities . . . have withdrawn from human concerns and thus are of comparatively little consequence in people's thoughts, beliefs, and actions."[14] The many creatures of *Halimaw* are similarly blasé, occupying odd walls and unremarkable streets all over Manila, like marginal footnotes to city life, more textures than highlights that leap out on passersby only when people pay closer attention. In this playful and whimsical peppering of ordinary city spaces with random mythological creatures, *Halimaw* literally and literarily "allows art to join the living,"[15] reintroducing forgotten cultural beliefs to the hustle and bustle of the city to perform and narrativize their invisibility.

In Quezon City, the *Kapre*, the Filipino counterpart to the European giant, popularly imagined as benign and constantly smoking a cigarette, hangs out by a roadside waiting shed, what perceivably stands for a "crude [home] close to human villages" or a large tree for the kapre's residence in traditional lore.[16] The *Santelmo*, whose name derives from the meteorological phenomenon St. Elmo's fire, a flaming and typically fast-speeding skull believed to be the spirit of a deceased person, chases after passersby and motorcyclists on random walls along the highway. *Nuno* and *Lamanlupa*, preternatural creatures in the shape of old men no taller than two- or three-year-old children, occupy slabs of concrete close to the ground, under which these dwarf-like creatures are believed to reside. *Anito*, or nature spirits, whimsically float on leaves or bicycles all over random walls in Makati City. In Pasig City, another highly urbanized area in Metro Manila, the *Tikbalang*, a humanoid creature known for its speed, with the head and lower torso of a horse and the upper body of a human, canters alongside cars on the cement walls.

The unobtrusive art pieces of *Halimaw*, creatures primarily of whimsy and mischief, create subtle inflections to city life that play out its narrative rather than ask to be spectated as art-on-the-street. They are placed in strategic locations to participate momentarily in the life of urban Manila, as part of the city scene: the *Kapre*, often depicted in stories as a docile tree dweller who, by and large, simply observes people invisibly from his verdant residence, sits in the middle of Kalayaan Avenue and continues this inconspicuous habit, looking on at passersby with a grouchy, furrowed brow. While not a giant in scale, *Halimaw*'s *Kapre* maintains his hulking proportions, one hand holding a massive tobacco cigar and the other on a thinly rolled modern-day cigarette. In history, the kapre came to be depicted with his iconic cigar when the Spanish first introduced it to the islands in the late sixteenth century, leading to its eventual ubiquity with the emergence of the tobacco monopoly that culminated profits mainly from controlling farmers' crops in Luzon and Mindanao.[17] This tangent to colonial history is no longer common knowledge in popular depictions of the kapre, but the contrast of the fat cigar to the narrow cigarette stick that *Halimaw*'s *Kapre* holds in his left hand is

Kapre by a waiting shed on Kalayaan Avenue, Quezon City, 2011. (Photo courtesy of Gerilya.)

certainly a gesture to the historical developments and changes that the Kapre has borne witness to, negotiates, and, the street art insists, remains a part of.

Invoking the same transhistorical sojourning, *Halimaw*'s *Anito* hover, literally, on objects of nature and of nurture: leaves, which stand out garishly against the dirty walls, and a man-made bicycle. As environmental spirits, the *Anito* are guardians of a world changed by rapid urbanization, a city with only 25 percent of forestland left as of 2019, of which 96 percent remained unclassified without security of environmental protection, and only 0.3 percent classified as environmental reserves (national parks, game refuge and bird sanctuaries, wildlife areas).[18] A bustling business district like Makati, widely known for its cement-and-glass commercial areas, is a far cry from the mountains, rocks, and lakes where engkanto and anito traditionally prefer to dwell.[19] This context leaves *Halimaw*'s *Anito* adrift: on their oases of leaves, they brood in fetal positions against the grit and grime of multiple layers of vandals, while one contemplates the new world astride a machine—looking for all the world like a naked man on a bike if viewed outside of the context of the series. Indeed, key to the *Anito* pieces is the visual unity of the three figures, enabling spectators to also recognize how they negotiate differently and unevenly with the strangeness of the city—or perhaps their own strangeness within the city.

The *Tikbalang* forms a lean, sinewy figure in Pasig City as he races along with the speeding cars by a main road. One of the most recognizable creatures of Philippine folklore, the *Tikbalang* is characterized in Gerilya's *Halimaw* by powerful legs and a beautiful, flowing mane and tail. Visually resonant with the Greek centaur or minotaur, the majestic tikbalang is often assumed to have been an influence of Spanish colonization, as the encounter introduced the horse-drawn calesa and European literature to the natives. However, researcher Jordan Clark points out that mentions of the tikbalang in early Philippine writings indicate that they predate Spanish colonization[20] and may even be traced to Hindu cultural exchanges that may have occurred during pre-Hispanic trading and migration encounters with neighboring islands and groups.[21] Notably, pre-Hispanic Philippines is a historical period often understated in Philippine history and only briefly and broadly discussed as "the precolonial," gesturing toward the tendency of dominant historiography to organize Philippine history around the nation's colonial experiences more than local and grassroots narratives. This is certainly in no small part because of the text-based writing system that European education introduced, the "civilized" upgrade from the oral-based literatures and traditions that did, in fact, gesture to the predominance of animist beliefs among the natives that could easily place a horse demon in the indigenous worldview even before the encounter with Spain.[22] Both the tendencies and pitfalls of defaulting to colonial histories are perhaps retraced in *Halimaw*'s

Tikbalang, Pasig City, 2011. (Photo courtesy of Gerilya.)

*Tikbalang*, which contemporizes the humanoid in a comic-book style treatment often perceived as an American aesthetic recognizable in Marvel or DC visual fare. The politically fraught debates of aesthetic mimicry and appropriation in art are not within the purview of this study, but they are secondary to the more important recognition of how the Tikbalang, in effect, plays out the heterogeneity of Philippine history and identity that is particularly pronounced in the urban city and emphasized in Gerilya's cultural agenda. These are points I will return to shortly in the paper.

*Halimaw*'s creatures also connote the violence of Manila in the *Santelmo* and *Nuno*. The santelmo's mythology varies across accounts, but all agree in the santelmo's association with death. The ball of flame is believed to come from the blood of one who died before his time, whether by suicide or violence,[23] and may sometimes be interpreted as an angry soul seeking revenge or a lost soul seeking peace.[24] Yet *Halimaw*'s *Santelmo* are fiery skulls with mouths wide open in apparent mischief, speeding across the walls with their flames billowing out behind them or hovering curiously over street vendors as they go about their daily tasks. The choice to render them with skulls as a universal reference to death makes them easily understandable, and they seem appropriately placed in Quezon City, with its reputation for historically high crime rates due to drug use, homicide, robberies, murders, and a host of other urban crimes. The santelmo's grim origin is thus distinctly

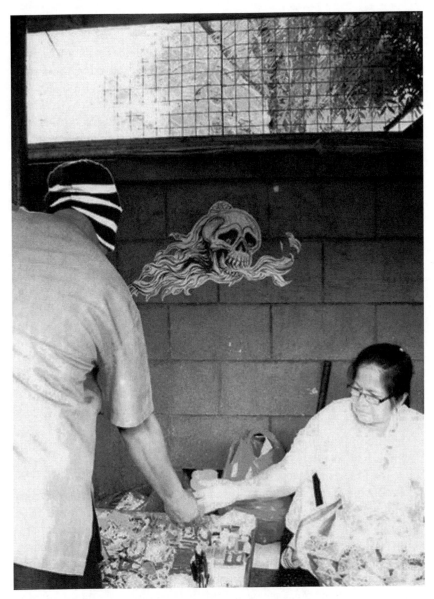

Santelmo, Quezon City, 2011. (Photo courtesy of Gerilya.)

undercut by the silent laughter of *Halimaw*'s *Santelmo*. Their impishness and unruliness results in a dark witticism, a joke on the unsuspecting public: that, here, death observes, surrounds, and laughs at the living; that death is, in fact, quite comfortable in this place. The fact that passersby are often either oblivious or endeared by these amused *Santelmo* only begs the question,

How much normalized violence has made this city home and playground to lost souls?

The proximity of death to citizens becomes particularly stark in light of the casualties of Duterte's drug war that would be witnessed by these walls in the years to come. Five years since the *Santelmo* were first installed 2011, Duterte would win the 2016 presidency, and the war on drugs he had promised during his campaign would commence in thousands of extrajudicial killings of alleged drug users, drug pushers, and drug lords. These executions without due process, euphemized as "deaths under investigation" by unrepentant police,[25] did not take long to evolve into targeted killings of activists, community leaders, and human rights defenders,[26] naturally the most vocal critics of the drug war. Thus, while Duterte has been heavily criticized in the West for legitimizing the killing spree, his drug war has conveniently doubled as a counterinsurgency strategy fulfilling the United States' anti-Communist "civilizing mission" as a particular feature of U.S. imperialism.[27] This has maintained its grip on the nationalist imagination of the neocolonial state and has been enacted in the country through decades of U.S. "military assistance" and "development aid," justifying extrajudicial political killings many years and presidencies before Duterte. In Manila, this normalized violence is made more obscene by the benign face of U.S. imperialism: rampant consumerism manifested in the proliferation of shopping centers, markets, and malls in the palpitating heart of the city—a distillation of decades of American commercial capitalism dominating what constitutes modernity in the neocolonial space. And so, the *Santelmo* pieces literalize how "so much of our public life is littered with the unburied dead. Brutal facts of social misery, abominations past and present, government investigations going nowhere, new scandals replacing old ones, leaders who refuse to be buried, the present reprising the past again and again."[28]

Producing another critique of the violence that Metro Manila witnesses, *Halimaw's Nuno*, the inconspicuous but notoriously crabby mound dweller of Philippine folklore, where he is installed in Mandaluyong, covers up a painted slate of local political leaders, the *kagawad*, or barangay councilors. This makes an eloquent visual pun, as nuno are traditionally also perceived as hoarders of gold and precious stones, "ancient gods gone underground" from whom farmers must ask permission before cultivating their lands and to whom they must pay rent in the form of sacrificial offerings.[29] However, *Halimaw's Nuno's* hand is outstretched, its expression ambivalent, mimicking a beggar asking for alms on the sidewalk. It is a convincing act for an old man standing as tall as a three-year-old child,[30] and it may be only a wily trick on unwitting passersby, but in a city that has paved over soil mounds and anthills, the *Nuno* is nonetheless homeless and displaced. Amid Manila's sprawling slums, his poverty becomes all too familiar; in the face of

Manananggal and Kaputol, 2011. (Photos courtesy of Gerilya.)

cultural heritage and folk history, his reduction to a beggar in the large city is pitiful and bleak.

Malevolent spirits are perhaps more familiar to city dwellers, as Manila does not lack for urban legends of haunted streets and restless ghosts. It is perhaps proportionate to the brutal city's familiarity with malevolence. A variety of *aswang*, a term that covers a broad category of malevolent spirits including vampires, ghouls, and witches, also haunts the city in *Halimaw*. A *Tiyanak*,[31] a vampiric baby and in various accounts an abandoned child and a monstrosity born of a human and a demon, or a baby that had died without being baptized, cries and salivates blood on a vandal-covered wall, edited by an unknown hand to have a demon's horns in permanent ink. *Manananggal*, a self-segmenting ghoul that can sever her upper body from her lower half, also known as a viscera sucker, which preys on human entrails and the fetuses of pregnant mothers,[32] hovers over the city on an overpass, its *Kaputol*, meaning "other half," tucked away in some patch of grassy area around the metro. The demon *Batibat*, or Bangungot, known to give sleeping people nightmares by riding or embracing them, often, although not always, resulting in a victim's death by suffocation,[33] grins naughtily, its heavy flesh billowing, on a cement wall. A *White Lady*, one of many ghosts of dead women who haunt places where they are said to have been betrayed and/or violently killed, glows, luminescent in white, in a shadowy corner.

Aswang are typically more strongly linked to places outside of the capital city, more normalized in the lore of places like Sorsogon in the southern tip of Luzon and Capiz in Western Visayas.[34] Largely, therefore, they remain outside of the realm of the modern, the sophisticated, and Westernized Manila, where "quality education" in the top schools of the country is governed by either liberal rationalism or Catholic conservatism, both of which historically have rejected aswang as fantasy or heresy at worst, literary metaphor at best. Among the lettered city folk, stories of aswang are often dismissed as merely superstitious or sentimentally *makaluma* ("old-fashioned; archaic"). Even Gerilya's note on how *Halimaw* hopes to "rekindle" these tales of the supernatural "*kahit wala . . . sa mga baryo* [even outside the barrio]"[35] points to their association with the provincial and precolonial. This twofold othering of the aswang displaces them in both space and time, rejecting them from the sophistication of the new and modern world.

Yet the contradiction of Philippine modernity is precisely that the present remains contemporaneous with its indigenous and precolonial "past." In fact, aswang feature vividly in many popular media, most recognizably in the incessant rollout of *Shake, Rattle & Roll* comedy-horror films that have been bringing malevolent spirits to the silver screen since 1984, with the fifteenth and most recent film released in 2014. They also feature strongly in emergent speculative fiction,[36] have inspired thirty-seven volumes of PSI-COM's massively popular pocketbook anthologies *True Philippine Ghost Stories* to date, and even preoccupy news specials during Halloween or All Saints' Day in that unique brand of TV journalism that can only be described as reportage on "our own marvelous real."[37] As recognizable characters in Philippine life, aswang are familiar and easily aestheticized, for as in the Latin America that Kumkum Sangari describes in *The Politics of the Possible* (1990), "here the strange is commonplace, and always was commonplace."[38]

The various aswang of *Halimaw* present this contemporaneity with an art style distinctly reminiscent of Western comic books while remaining distinctly indigenous, familiar, and Pinoy; the effect reboots these characters into a bid for belonging in the Westernized city and the metropolitan urbanite's modern imagination. Their haunting of the city's walls is a haunting by Othered regions excluded from the imperialist imagination of the nation; at the same time, it is an insistence on the city as a more marvelous reality than what rational modern education permits. This marvelous realism "displaces the established categories, questions certain Western myths of 'progress' and 'modernization,' asserts another realm of (pre-industrial) possibility, acknowledges that perceptions are relative, but historically determined."[39] In this way, the haunting of *Halimaw*'s aswang performs the "precolonial" as a past that remains conversant with the present and imaginatively (re)possesses the imperial city by reminding it of its own ruralism.

Gerilya's *Halimaw* series is part of the postcolonial fixation on identity-formation and the tireless project of imaging, or imagining, the nation, as it strives to write alternativities in the very spaces created by the excesses of hegemonic imperialist cultures. Amid the noise and rush of a metropolitan city, where dementia can set in too quickly, the ghosts of *Halimaw* have the valuable role of taking us by surprise, forcing us into a pause, and demanding a second look. The monsters of Manila emerge out of the collusion between the spectral presence of its imperialist traumas in the modern features of the metro and what may now be read as the inscription and activation of a folk-indigenous Filipino consciousness through street art.

*Halimaw*'s hauntology of Manila, with its urbane seductions and egregious excesses, thus dovetails with Resil Mojares's iteration of what haunts the Filipino writer or artist:

> This haunting, this hauntedness is a problem of soul. . . . To be visited by a spirit, touched by the spectral presence of absence; to catch the miasmic whiff of the unburied dead, the traces of what has been silenced and forgotten—haunting is a metaphor for what drives the vocation of writers and the practice of writing. It is also an eloquent sign of our social malaise as Filipinos, symptom of the profound affliction of a nation not quite conscious of itself.[40]

This problem of soul is the hauntology of Manila. The cast of *Halimaw*, in imbricating themselves as characters in the life of the city, even as they obsolesce and disintegrate in their "commitment to ephemerality," disquiets Manila's metropolitan spaces and performs the haunting of a perpetually deferred Filipino identity, or what Derrida calls a "messianic" impulse—in Jonathan Joseph's paraphrase, a "spectral anticipation of the future, a waiting inspired by a deferred spirit or a promise of a spirit to come. . . . The messianic entails the promise of a future to come and, in hope, it entails a desire for emancipation from the present."[41]

## The Specter's Specters: *Halimaw* in the Archives

In the future that has come to Gerilya's *Halimaw* series, this study is forced to examine only the traces of its ghosts, as they had since been erased from the city walls. This is made possible by their spectralized presence in digital photography, documented and archived by the Gerilya crew themselves. Indeed, since the group was first formed in 2008, they have religiously documented their works in both anticipation of and resistance to their transience. This impulse to record and document ephemeral art is not new; for many street artists, "photographing . . . their pieces, together with other technological resources, is . . . an essential part of their work, assuming the role of *memory technologies, communication technologies,* and *narrative and representative technologies.*"[42] According to Ágata Dourado Sequeira:

> Photography appears as a way of preserving the street art interven-
> tion, as an image record that surpasses its ephemeral nature. Sec-
> ondly, photography appears, for some street artists, as a key aspect
> of their street art practice, as way of learning and sharing new tech-
> niques. In this sense, it also allows for new sociabilities to take place
> between street artists, or between them and street art enthusiasts.
> Thirdly, photography constitutes itself as a way of observing the re-
> actions of the passers-by, in the sense the act of someone casually
> finding a street art piece and then photographing it and putting it
> online can be a way of appreciating the artwork.[43]

Photography, in spectralizing the real, destabilizes notions of "ephemerality," "erasure," and even "public space" as images are uprooted from their
actual conditions of existence and yet are retained as visible, such that they
are at any given time both present and absent, real and not-real—"a trace
that marks the present with its absence in advance."[44] Certainly, this translation from physically present art to digitally spectral art inevitably ruptures
meaning, as it does away with certain indissociable aspects of street art:
"localization, eventual erosion, and inevitable transience."[45] Jacques Derrida, in his consideration of the photographic trace, likewise points out that
"in photography there are all sorts of initiatives: not only framing but point
of view, calculation of light, adjustment of the exposure, overexposure, un-
derexposure, etc. . . . To the extent that they produce the image and constituted something of an image [*de l'image*], they modify reference itself."[46]

This modification of the referent is precisely what is enacted in the present reading of street art vanished almost a decade ago. The presence of *Halimaw* in the Gerilya's digital archive shifts the meaning of the work from an
ontology of haunted street art to a hauntology of street art—a spectral presence not only of mythological ghosts, but of the transgression of their illegal
installation and their relinquishment to the ravages of natural, cultural, and
sociopolitical seasons.

Gerilya is not unaware of the risks inherent in putting up street art that
is neither commissioned nor sanctioned. In the Philippines, Senate Bill No.
3042, or the Anti-Vandalism Act of 2009, clearly proscribes the following:

    i.  writing, drawing, painting, marking or inscribing on any public
       property or private property any word, slogan, caricature, draw-
       ing, mark, symbol or other thing; or

ii. affixing, posting up or displaying on any public property or private property any poster, placard, advertisement, bill, notice, paper or other document;

iii. or hanging, suspending, hoisting, affixing or displaying on or from any public property or private property any flag, bunting, standard, banner or the like with any word, slogan, caricature, drawing, mark, symbol or other thing.

Street artists may also be liable for malicious mischief according to Article 327 of the Revised Penal Code, which states, "Any person who shall deliberately cause the property of another any damage . . . shall be guilty of malicious mischief." This vulnerability to legal redress and proximity to criminal *mens rea* affirms the "essential subversiveness" of street art,[47] a precondition of the medium that Gerilya is certainly aware of, as indicated in their choice of name, which in the original Spanish means "little war."

Guerilla as a name makes a clear reference to warfare tactics of sabotage, deception, and constantly shifting attack operations; as a mode of creative practice, it similarly takes advantage of spontaneity and improvisation, often for lack of authorization. Yet Gerilya has documented their works religiously from the beginning, since their formation in 2008, signing off on their works with their *baybayin* insignia. One might imagine Gerilya's *Halimaw* slipping conveniently under the radar of the law just for the sheer the number of taggers, graffiti writers, and street artists in Metro Manila. In its myriad hotspots of urban crime, street artists with a cultural agenda that is "inspired by Philippine culture and history, exploring socio-political issues and national identity . . . and drawing influence from Philippine popular and mass culture"[48] apparently occupy an ambivalent space of moderately permissible civil disobedience. During the year that *Halimaw* was installed, it was even featured in the television news magazine show *Kapuso Mo, Jessica Soho* in their Halloween special. For a teaser, in the show's official social media page, they captioned Gerilya's *Manananggal with Tiyanak Horde* in Rizal with "who would have thought that scary concepts. [*sic*] can be cute!"[49] Nevertheless, through the years, Gerilya has taken care to build its reputation as a collective and to work as a crew, not quite committing to secrecy but avoiding whenever possible individual features with the members' full names, even as they began to venture into commissioned street murals and commercial projects in subsequent years.

Amid these conditions of risk, Gerilya's personal project of documenting their street art constitutes a kind of "archival banditry" that redeems these pieces from erasure into perpetuity. In the way that "archive bandits shape their endeavour in a relation of hospitality to the voices which press in from outside the structures and systems they find themselves in, and to the voices from deep inside themselves,"[50] Gerilya's commitment to their cultural and political agenda, their resistance to the hegemonic imperialisms that haunt Manila, drive their impulse to document and preserve the archival trace. It is an effort "at once active and passive,"[51] a simultaneous recording and a remaking of the piece, a new iteration in the impossibility of reproducing the original. Made for the streets, made to obsolesce, the spectralized ghosts of *Halimaw* drive at the "point where the photographic act is not an artistic act, a point where it passively records, and this poignant passivity would be the chance of this relation with death; it captures a reality that is there, that will have been there, in an undecomposable now."[52] The archivy of *Halimaw*'s creatures, with their various significations to cultural erasure, historical violence, and regionalist displacements in contemporary Manila, is an insistence on their existence—and the existence of erasure, violence, displacement—as much as it is a performance of their invisibility. In this way, "the one who has disappeared appears still to be there, and his apparition is not nothing. It does not do nothing. Assuming that the remains can be identified, we know better than ever today that the dead must be able to work. And to cause to work, perhaps more than ever."[53]

The work of recognizing the dead, of acknowledging our ghosts, forces us to realize that:

> the centering idea of a "national history," "national literature," or "nation" is a claim against the reality of many unaggregated, dispersed, and competing versions of community. These versions are generated out of the differences of language, ethnicity, religion, gender, and class. We need to assess the discourse formed by the voices coming from these "localities." We need then to judge what, in the formation of a national discourse, is rendered peripheral, subordinate, or invisible. We need to calculate how the fullness and health of the body is diminished and imperiled by the neglect or suppression of its parts.[54]

The spectralization of *Halimaw* in the digital archive has placed *Halimaw*'s ghosts, and whom/what they represent—those historically "ghosted by power"[55]—in the oddly resilient gap between life/death, existence/nonexistence, expression/erasure, and writing/silencing. Its allegory of our postcolonial yearning for an imagined cultural unity culminates in a terminal loop: erasure reinforcing meaning reinforcing erasure reinforcing meaning. Manila's hauntology is therefore this affliction of soul, "this play of past and future (what we have lost, what we can gain), an ideal always present, always postponed."[56]

But just as these indigenous characters of folk imagination have vexed ideas of identity, they likewise present alternate possibilities for soul recovery. Rarely, if ever, are afflicted souls irrecoverable in the narratives of folk mythology. In fact, what is often imagined in indigenous notions of the soul "is less five or seven souls as a soul fivefold or sevenfold. It is a notion that conveys a native (or, if you will, 'postmodern') passion for what is open and transactional, a wariness of essentialism and exclusion."[57] Mojares's parenthetical reference to the indigenous as postmodern here eloquently placates the postcolonial frustration with perpetually deferred meaning and identity. Through the indigenous imagination of a manifold soul that is able to come to terms with its own disquiets, we might begin to live with our ghosts kindlier. These ghosts of our eternal pursuits—of justice, sovereignty, democracy, emancipation—"[look] at or [watch] us, [these] ghost[s] [concern] us. The specter is not simply someone we see coming back, it is someone by whom we feel ourselves watched, observed, surveyed."[58]

Undone and disembodied, the *Halimaw* of Manila persist now to remain present. They insist, spectrally, on having existed as street art; on continuing to exist as archival markers of Manila's historical shocks, seductions, and sins;[59] and on existing further into an indefinite future in which the aspirations toward a revaluation of Philippine culture continue to be dreamed, processed, and produced. It points to a persistence "to live otherwise, and better. No, not better, but more justly." In this way, for all who are constantly living with and haunted by these ghosts in the eternally vexed spaces of Manila, "being-with specters . . . [is], not only but also, a politics of memory, of inheritance, and of generations."[60] For if what must remain of *Halimaw* is erasure (if erasures can even be said to exist much less remain), it is their haunting that teaches us about the futures that they may yet sojourn to witness. Mojares reminds us:

> Haunting is a form of desire. As the sign of what is amiss, a lack unfulfilled, the shade of something left unfinished, it does not only point to the past but the future. It is what the Tagalog word for memory, *gunita*, signifies: to dream not only of something past but the trace of what one had desired but had not quite accomplished. To be haunted is to be suspended in a dream between past and future.[61]

Certainly, the interwoven power of memory and imagination is located at the heart of every subversive effort in the decolonizing project that remains constant and urgent in postcolonial societies. It is the same messianic impulse that must propel any transgression—or malicious mischief—that the work of cultural rehabilitation may commit. It is the same faith that must drive archival bandits to rescue and redeem the dead and forgotten. Every day, the ghosts of Philippine society multiply; we take responsibility for them and concede we are accountable to our ghosts. The hauntology of

Manila is this vibrant, grisly, haunted, heterogeneous present—what it had been, what else it could be, and what more it can become.

## NOTES

1. Foucault, "What Is an Author?" 301.
2. Del Pilar Blanco and Esther Peeren, "Contextualizing Spectralities."
3. Gerilya, "June 2011 Halimaw Wheatpastes."
4. Escalona, "Duterte's War on Tongues."
5. Macasero, "Does Duterte Have the 'Bisaya Advantage' in Cebu?"
6. Gerilya, "June 2011 Halimaw Wheatpastes."
7. Gerilya, *Gerilya Crew Wheatpaste Sessions: Halimaw 1.*
8. Derrida, *Specters of Marx*, 221.
9. Mary Louise Pratt, quoted in Brody, "Building Empire," 134.
10. Immediately, two iconic resistance movements to come to mind are the Philippine Revolution of 1896, which was initiated by Andres Bonifacio, a worker from Tondo, Manila, and the EDSA Revolution of 1986, which was conducted on the highway the mass movement came to be named after.
11. Camp Aguinaldo is the general headquarters of the Armed Forces of the Philippines, while Camp Crame is that of the Philippine National Police.
12. Mojares, "The Haunting of the Filipino Writer," 308.
13. Not included in this study are Gerilya's *Bakunawa* in Makati City, *Manananggal with Tiyanak Horde* in San Mateo, Rizal, and *Minokawa* in Angono, Rizal, because these are either creatures of a higher strata or creatures installed outside of Metro Manila. The bakunawa is the Cebuano sky dragon that allegedly lies in wait to swallow the moon as it emerges, effectively explaining eclipses and the "scars" on the face of the moon, believed in local legends to be markings from the dragon's teeth. The minokawa is its Bagobo counterpart, known in legends as a great bird with a beak and claws of steel, swallowing the moon so that the world is in darkness until the people sound their *agong* (brass gongs) to draw his attention to the earth, thereby allowing the moon to jump out of its mouth.
14. Ramos, *Creatures of Lower Mythology*, 1.
15. Riggle, "Street Art," 256.
16. All figures included in this essay are photographs taken by Gerilya.
17. Aswang Project, *KAPRE: The Tree Dweller.*
18. Department of Environment and Natural Resources Forest Management Bureau, *Philippine Forestry Statistics 2019.*
19. Clark, "Engkantos and Anitos."
20. Aswang Project, *TIKBALANG.*
21. In the documentary series on Philippine mythological creatures by the Aswang Project, writers like Yvette Tan, Karl de Mesa, and Budjette Tane draw from impressions and memories of their early literary encounters with the tikbalang—often alongside other depictions of half-man, half-horse creatures in Western mythologies—to muse broadly that they may be of Spanish origin. Filmmaker-director Peque Gallaga also imagines an Irish link, associating the tikbalang's legendary speed with the mythological seven-league boots. Canadian researcher Jordan Clark's own historical sojourning has led him to find parallels with Hinduism's Hayagriva through the Malay wave of migration.
22. Aswang Project, *TIKBALANG.*
23. Ubaldo, "Talang Historiko-Kultural Ukol sa Pagpapatiwakal," 115.

24. Clark, "SANTELMO."
25. Evangelista, "The Drug War."
26. Human Rights Watch, "Philippines: 'Drug War' Killings Rise During Pandemic."
27. Weimer, *Seeing Drugs*, 11.
28. Mojares, "The Haunting of the Filipino Writer," 308.
29. Ramos, *Creatures of Lower Mythology*, 3, 7–8, 16.
30. Ogalesco, "Nuno sa Punso."
31. While the tiyanak has been categorized as a dwarf in Maximo Ramos's taxonomy of Philippine mythical creatures in *Filipino Cultural Patterns and Values and Their Mythological Dimensions* (1973), it has been typically described as a vampiric baby in popular imagination, upon which basis I designate it here as aswang.
32. Ramos, *Creatures of Lower Mythology*, 20.
33. Ibid., 2.
34. Ramos, "The Aswang Syncrasy in Philippine Folklore," 243.
35. Gerilya, "June 2011 Halimaw Wheatpastes."
36. Pantoja-Hidalgo, "New Tales for Old," 350.
37. Kumkum Sangari, quoted in Pantoja-Hidalgo, "New Tales for Old," 350.
38. Ibid., 350.
39. Pantoja-Hidalgo, "New Tales for Old," 350.
40. Mojares, "The Haunting of the Filipino Writer," 298.
41. Jonathan Joseph, "Derrida's Spectres of Ideology," 98.
42. Sequeira, "Ephemeral Art in Impermanent Spaces."
43. Ibid.
44. Derrida and Stiegler, "Spectographies."
45. Sequeira, "Ephemeral Art in Impermanent Spaces."
46. Derrida, *Copy, Archive, Signature*, 7.
47. Baldini, "Street Art," 188.
48. "About Gerilya."
49. *Kapuso Mo, Jessica Soho*, "From art to business."
50. Harris, "Hauntology, Archivy and Banditry," 16.
51. Derrida, *Copy, Archive, Signature*, 17.
52. Ibid., 9.
53. Derrida, *Specters of Marx*, 120.
54. Mojares, "The Haunting of the Filipino Writer," 307.
55. Verne Harris, quoted in Lowry, "Archives as a Place for the Soul."
56. Mojares, "The Haunting of the Filipino Writer," 299.
57. Ibid., 307.
58. Derrida and Steigler, "Spectographies."
59. Mojares, "The Haunting of the Filipino Writer," 300.
60. Derrida, *Specters of Marx*, xviii.
61. Mojares, "The Haunting of the Filipino Writer," 309–310.

## BIBLIOGRAPHY

"About Gerilya." Gerilya, accessed May 7, 2021, https://gerilya.tumblr.com/about.
Aswang Project. *KAPRE: The Tree Dweller.* YouTube, December 18, 2015, https://youtu.be/GUrxlu1J0N8.
———. *TIKBALANG: The Horse Demon.* YouTube, October 22, 2015, https://youtu.be/gRUSBSJ39KY.

Baldini, Andrea. "Street Art: A Reply to Riggle." *Journal of Aesthetics and Art Criticism* 74, no. 2 (Spring 2016): 187–191.

Benedict, Laura Watson. "Bagobo Myths." *Journal of American Folklore* 26, no. 99 (1913): 13–63.

Brody, David Eric. "Building Empire: Architecture and American Imperialism in the Philippines." In *The Spectralities Reader: Ghosts and Haunting in Contemporary Cultural Theory*, edited by Blanco Maria del Pilar and Esther Peeren. New York: Bloomsbury Publishing, 2013.

Clark, Jordan. "Engkantos and Anitos: Could Science Be Close to proving They're Real?" *Aswang Project*, January 30, 2016, https://www.aswangproject.com/engkanto-anitos -science/.

——. "Santelmo: Rekindling Philippine Mythology." Aswang Project, December 3, 2016, https://www.aswangproject.com/santelmo/.

Department of Environment and Natural Resources (DENR) Forest Management Bureau. *Philippine Forestry Statistics 2019.* https://forestry.denr.gov.ph/index.php/statis tics/philippines-forestry-statistics.

Derrida, Jacques. *Copy, Archive, Signature: A Conversation on Photography.* Gerard Richter, ed. Redwood City, CA: Stanford University Press, 2010.

——. *Specters of Marx: The State of the Debt, the Work of Mourning and the New International.* Peggy Kamuf, trans. New York: Routledge, 1994.

Derrida, Jacques, and Bernard Stiegler. "Spectographies." In *The Spectralities Reader: Ghosts and Haunting in Contemporary Cultural Theory*, edited by Maria del Pilar Blanco and Esther Peeren. New York: Bloomsbury Publishing.

Escalona, Kim Ashley. "Duterte's War on Tongues." New Mandala, July 19, 2018, https://www.newmandala.org/dutertes-war-tongues/.

Evangelista, Patricia. "The Drug War: Execution at Cessna." Rappler, November 7, 2016, https://r3.rappler.com/nation/146652-war-on-drugs-execution-cessna.

Foucault, Michel. "What Is an Author?" In *Modernity and Its Discontents: Making and Unmaking the Bourgeois from Machiavelli to Bellow*, edited by Steven B. Smith, 299–314. New Haven, CT: Yale University Press, 2016.

Gerilya. *Gerilya Crew Wheatpaste Sessions: Halimaw 1.* YouTube, May 10, 2011, https://youtu.be/EUEcXkK0vVg.

——. *Guerero Lean.* Facebook profile, accessed May 8, 2021, https://www.facebook .com/inihahandognggerilya.

——. "June 2011 Halimaw Wheatpastes (Filipino Lower Mythological Creatures Edition) 1st Batch." Facebook, January 4, 2012, https://www.facebook.com/photo/?fbid =356226137727511.

Harris, Verne. "Hauntology, Archivy and Banditry: An Engagement with Derrida and Zapiro." *Critical Arts* 29: sup. 1 (2015): 13–27.

Human Rights Watch. "Philippines: 'Drug War' Killings Rise During Pandemic, Upsurge in Attacks on Activists, Community Leaders, Rights Defenders." *Human Rights Watch*, January 13, 2021, https://www.hrw.org/news/2021/01/13/philippines-drug-war -killings-rise-during-pandemic.

Joseph, Jonathan. "Derrida's Spectres of Ideology." *Journal of Political Ideologies* 6, no. 1 (2001): 95–115, https://doi.org/10.1080/13569310120040177.

*Kapuso Mo, Jessica Soho.* "From Art to Business, Who Would Have Thought that Scary Concepts Can Be Cute!" Facebook, October 7, 2011, https://www.facebook.com/kap usomojessicasoho/photos/a.10150357737606026/10150357737731026/.

Lowry, James. "Archives as a Place for the Soul: Verne Harris Talks Ghosts of Archive." Society of American Archivists, accessed May 8, 2021, https://bit.ly/3tu6pFw.

Macasero, Ryan. "Does Duterte Have the 'Bisaya Advantage' in Cebu?" Rappler, March 6, 2016, https://www.rappler.com/voices/imho/duterte-bisaya-advantage-cebu.

Mojares, Resil. "The Haunting of the Filipino Writer." In *Waiting for Mariang Makiling: Essays in Philippine Cultural History*, 297–314. Quezon City: Ateneo University Press, 2002.

Ogalesco, John Patrick. "Nuno sa Punso: The Mound Dweller." Aswang Project, November 12, 2016, https://www.aswangproject.com/nuno-sa-punso/.

Pantoja-Hidalgo, Cristina. "New Tales for Old." In *Philippine Studies: Have We Gone Beyond St. Louis?*, edited by Priscelina Patajo-Legasto, 335–362. Quezon City: University of the Philippines Press.

Ramos, Maximo D. "The *Aswang* Syncrasy in Philippine Folklore." *Western Folklore* 28, no. 4 (1969): 238–248, https://doi.org/10.2307/1499218.

———. *Creatures of Lower Mythology*. Quezon City: University of the Philippines Press, 1971.

Riggle, Nicholas Alden. "Street Art: The Transfiguration of the Commonplaces." *Journal of Aesthetics and Art Criticism* 68, no. 3 (Summer 2010): 243–257.

Sequeira, Ágata Dourado. "Ephemeral Art in Impermanent Spaces: The Effects of Street Art in the Social Construction of Public Space." In *Urban Intervention, Street Art and Public Space*, edited by Paula Guerra, Pedro de Neves Costa, and Pedro Soares. Pedro Soares Neves, 2016.

Ubaldo, Lars Raymund. "Talang Historiko-Kultural Ukol sa Pagpapatiwakal." *Malay* 29, no. 1 (2016): 111–124.

Weimar, Daniel. *Seeing Drugs: Modernization, Counterinsurgency, and U.S. Narcotics Control in the Third World, 1969–1976*. Kent, OH: Kent State University Press, 2011.

# *Endo*, Manila Kentex Fire, and Contractualization under Global Capitalism

JEMA PAMINTUAN

F rom manufacturing firms and export processing zones in the 1970s and 1980s, to business centers and shopping malls in the 1990s up to present, Manila served as the Philippines' major gateway through which capital enter and exit the economy. To push for maximization of profits, the least costs of labor are injected into the business structure, allowing the firms' owners to reap the benefits while creating segmentations within the market, such as large differences in incomes and living standards. This is where flexibility in labor figures in the space of the metropolis, as a vital factor in crafting strategies that allow Manila's businesses to thrive using inexpensive labor through contractualization.

Contracting or subcontracting refers to an arrangement whereby a principal agrees to put out or farm out with a contractor or subcontractor the performance or completion of a specific job, work, or services within a definite or predetermined period, regardless of whether such job, work, or service is to be performed or completed within or outside the premises of the principal.[1] It replaces regular workers with temporary workers who receive lower wages with less or zero benefits. International and local firms require labor-intensive manufacturing and processing, thus the need for a flexible work structure with access to cheap labor.

Temporary workers, also called contractuals, trainees, apprentices, helpers, casuals, piece raters, agency-hired, or project employees, do the work of regular workers for a specified and limited period of time, usually less than six months, and they never become regular employees even if they get rehired repeatedly under new contracts.[2] They are also called "555," or "end of contract" ("endo"), which means that the workers can only work for five months at a time. This can be renewable for another two cycles, after which the employee could work as an open contract worker, but it does not guarantee a chance for security of tenure.[3] As early as the Spanish colonial period in the Philippines, there were already records of nonregular employees in the agricultural sector, particularly, the *sakada*—the sugar plantation workers in Negros.[4] These workers are examples of seasonal laborers, and current studies show how underemployment is still being practiced by the rural agricultural economy.[5] Evidence of the continuous increase of workers under the contractual labor scheme is verified by the 2015/2016 press release of the Integrated Survey of Labor and Employment (ISLE). The survey estimated around 1.19 million nonregular workers in the country (pertaining to number of persons engaged in establishments with twenty or more workers per major industry group).[6]

Why contractualization continues to proliferate, why many workers agree to or are pushed to enter into this type of labor arrangement, and how job insecurity becomes a permanent condition for the contractual worker are some of the points that will be highlighted in this essay, using three film texts that portray labor problems in different areas of Metro Manila: *Bangkang Papel sa Dagat ng Apoy* (Paper Boat in a Sea of Fire, Cinesuerte Films, 1984), *Bayan ko, Kapit sa Patalim* (My Country, Gripping the Knife's Edge, Malaya Films, Stephan Films, 1985), and *Endo* (UFO Pictures, 2007). The essay focuses on the films as points of discourse in understanding the structure of contractual labor in select industries in Manila, the workspaces and its players, and the nuances and implications of contractual labor's flexibility/rigidity, stability/fluctuation, to the employer/capitalist and the contractual employee/laborer. It concludes with a discussion of the May 2015 tragedy in a slipper factory in Valenzuela, Manila, and other similar factory fires in South Asian cities where similar labor issues were at play.

## *Bangkang Papel* and *Bayan Ko*: Manila's Factories and Manufacturing Industries in the 1980s

The IBON Foundation, a nonprofit research institution, conducted a case study that explored the predicament of the contractual workers in the manufacturing sector during the 1980s. In a 1981 study on the garments industry, IBON documented the experiences of contractual workers in Triumph International, a Germany-brand undergarment factory located in Taguig, Metro Manila. The workers complained about unreasonably high quota, poor working conditions, lack of job security, lack of safety devices, and a high rate of tuberculosis among rank-and-file employees.[7] Two films in the following section discuss in detail the similar plight of workers during this decade.

*Bangkang Papel sa Dagat ng Apoy* (Paper Boat in a Sea of Fire, Cinesuerte Films, 1984), a film written and directed by Edgardo Reyes, revolves around the lives of the workers in a textile factory in Manila. The factory reflects in its working space a harsh environment unfit for workers. The workers have to toil for long hours without sanitary masks, and the difficulty to breathe comes with the lack of opportunity to vent out grievances pertaining to their harmful work settings. They also have to operate and work with broken machineries while trying to reach the daily quota, which explains how the workspace itself is threatening and detrimental to one's health, productivity, and progress.

In between the cramped spaces and extended labor hours, the workers also deal with unjust working conditions, such as long working hours, but no overtime pay, and violation of rights to tenure and retirement. There are other instances that portray the unfair treatment of workers, including the following: the immediate and sudden regularization of a new employee, as opposed to the stagnant condition of other employees who had been apprentices for a longer period of time; the lack of retirement benefits after twenty-five years of service of an employee; and the absence of cost-of-living allowances and thirteenth-month pay benefits.

Outside the factory and along the streets of Manila, the situation is almost the same: overcrowded streets, cramped shanties, dire circumstances, and the constant need to deal with everyday survival. Similar to the workers' unchanging condition inside the factory, Manila does not offer alternatives nor adequate options for livelihood. The cruel city streets harbor the secret of the mysterious death of a factory worker who was allegedly harassed and blackmailed by the employer. One of the factory employees, Corpuz (Joseph Estrada), decides to oppose and act upon the abuse of workers' rights. He commits to reading the labor code and focuses on the rules pertaining to the regularization of employees. Corpuz, along with some coworkers, eventually organizes a labor union. However, difficult circumstances and lack of freedom to assert their rights plague and burden the union members. In a dark corner of the metropolis, Corpuz, despite all his efforts, meets a tragic end while fighting for the workers' cause.

*Bayan Ko: Kapit sa Patalim* (My Country, Gripping the Knife's Edge, Malaya Films, Stephan Films, 1985) underscores the crises faced by casual employees of a printing shop located in one of Metro Manila's busy streets. Similar to *Bangkang Papel*, the workspace is comprised of workers who have to contend with unreasonable labor conditions, long working hours with little pay, and lack of freedom to speak and advocate for one's labor rights.

The film's main character, Turing (Philip Salvador), is a printing shop employee. His wife, Luz (Gina Alajar), is a casual worker at the printing shop and is undergoing a difficult pregnancy that requires her to stay home and rest. Though the owner of the shop indicates that he would give Luz a full month's pay after Turing relays to him her health condition, he also emphasizes that Luz is not entitled to a sick leave, maternity leave, or any benefits. Even if Turing works overtime, he will not earn enough to buy medicines for his pregnant wife.

Ka Ador (Venchito Galvez), a senior employee at the shop, and some fellow employees, pay Turing and Luz a visit. He explains how their working conditions have pushed some employees to express their complaints and frustrations over drinking sessions. Griping sessions are not enough, according to Ka Ador. He focuses on the need for their situation to change and for their rights to be upheld, justifying the urgency and imperativeness of coming together as a majority and organizing a union. Things will only change if the workers unite and assert their rights. Ka Ador invites Turing to join the union, which the latter politely refuses. Turing explains that he requested in advance for a portion of his salary to pay for Luz's medicines but was forced by the shop owner to sign a waiver, indicating his promise not to join the union. Secret union meetings are held outside the printing shop premises. And yet, similar to the circumstances in the previously discussed film, the right to organization and speech are still under control. The shop owner gains knowledge about the growing union and is threatened by it.

The next scenes of the film portray the silent clamor in the printing shop, where the hushed complaints and whispers of discontent are further stifled by the management when it suddenly comes out with policies such as "no chatting, no socializing, and no talking to each other while working." Ka Ador believes that the owner's actions are forms of intimidation. After an altercation with Hugo (Paquito Diaz), the owner's right-hand man, an employee is unjustly fired from work. It is not clear whether the employee is a regular employee, but his coworkers believe that firing him without any notice goes against his labor rights.

Union members, led by Ka Ador, meet together to plan the strike. They want to consult with a lawyer and make sure that they follow protocol. Once they secure a permit, they show it to the police, who are vigilantly monitoring the protesters' actions. They call on management to rehire their fired coworker. The peaceful protest is disrupted by Hugo and the police. Protesters are told that what they are doing is illegal despite consulting with a lawyer and securing a permit for the strike. Turing is greeted by an angry group of protesters, calling him a "traitor." Being an unwilling ally of Hugo has not improved Turing's overall situation. Violence erupts between the two sides. Ka Ador meets the same tragic end as Corpuz.

The temperament of the two films can be discussed vis-à-vis the social context of the 1970s and 1980s, when the films were released. It was a time of political turmoil in Philippine history essayed by the people's clamor to end the dictatorship, which spurred the revolution in 1986. It was a period that called for communication, purposive dialogues, and campaigns for reform. Professor and critic Alice Guillermo analyzed the use of dialogue in such films, stating that "dialogue is necessary for the exploration of issues, as well as for the portrayal of how the characters reckon with ideas and develop in their social consciousness. These are talky times, because the larger public is largely developing critical awareness, and there is a need for interaction and exchange in the interest of survival."[8] The confrontations between employers/owners and employees/workers were portrayed most effectively through the exchanges and verbal communication between the two sides. The characters of Corpuz and Ka Ador emboldened and sparked consciousness among their peers to uphold their rights and welfare. The workplace did not offer any venue to express and support workers' rights, thus the importance of forming a labor union.

Despite the limitations and restrictions on labor strikes during the martial law period in the Philippines,[9] the persistence of union leaders and members still inspired the formation of unions and the organization of pickets and strikes. The La Tondeña strike in the mid-1970s was known for its workers' outcry to end contractualization and push for regularization. Aside from contracts that lasted for only two months, the workers also grappled with the unjust and arbitrary dismissals of some employees. Despite unsuccessful results of filing petitions to the Department of Labor and Employment (DOLE), the workers went on strike in October 1975 and gained popular attention and support from various sectors of the society. Although not all demands were met, the strike stirred other labor groups to call for fair wages and work security.[10]

Corpuz, Ka Ador, along with their followers, and the La Tondeña protesters showed the importance of recognizing the organization of labor unions, as well as reasonable and necessary protest actions. Unity, dialogue, and clear and just advocacies are essential to the creation of meaningful and safe spaces for workers' voices to be amplified and heard.


## Contractualization in *Endo* and the Services Sector: Flexibility for Whom?

After the revolution in 1986, the country hoped for a better and much improved governance and management of resources, including labor and human capital. One of the objectives of former President Corazon Aquino's

Medium Term Development Plan in 1987 was the "promotion of employment through the utilization of labor-based techniques in all productive sectors."[11] However, these "sectors" mostly pertain to the informal sector, which mainly comprised the services sector, accounting for almost 40 percent of the workforce in 1988,[12] and without government regulation resulted to low productivity and low wages.

With President Fidel Ramos's Philippines 2000 and aim to achieve the newly industrialized country status, liberalization policies and their presumed benefits to the market were introduced and endorsed. Attempts to reform the market included structural adjustment policies in labor; however, the Asian financial crisis in 1997 pushed the economy, especially the businesses, to take steps toward cost cutting, including labor.[13] From 2000 onward, studies on labor flexibility have discussed the negative effects brought about by contractual employment.[14]

Several businesses, including malls, sprouted in the metropolis, creating a bigger need for service labor. In 2020, there were around 232 malls in Metro Manila alone, including shopping centers, community and bargain malls, open-air shopping plazas, duty-free shopping centers, retail podiums, strip malls, and lifestyle malls.[15] This is also proof of the growing number of temporary workers servicing these establishments.

From factories and manufacturing firms in the previously discussed films, *Endo* brings us to spaces that represent the services sector of the metropolis, specifically, fast-food chains and shopping malls. The film's protagonist, Leo (Jason Abalos), is a service crew in a fast-food restaurant. The film opens with a scene showing a customer knocking loudly at the door of I Have Two Eggs, a fast-food diner located in one of Manila's busy streets. The fast-food industry is one of the metropolis's fast-lane businesses that fulfill the need for affordable and fast food, catering to the busy and on-the-go professionals who choose to consume quickly prepared meals.

We see Leo as an obedient and courteous employee; he always arrives at work on time and shows patience despite the crassness of how the customer talks to him and treats him, such as asking Leo to change the order after having just encoded it in the cashier register. Leo's end-of-contract (endo) arrives earlier than expected when he is dismissed from the diner. Personal problems involving a breakup with Candy (C. J. Javarata), his girlfriend/coworker whose contract just ended, affects Leo's performance: he becomes lazy, his work quality worsens, and, unlike his good demeanor in the beginning scenes of the film, he loses patience and yells at the customer who complains about the changes in the menu.

With internet and computer shops on almost every street corner of Metro Manila, ready to service users who do not own a computer and printer and have no personal access to the internet, Leo steps into one of the shops to update and print his résumé. For a contractual worker like Leo, he deems that his viable work option is another contractual job in a different fast-food restaurant or mall store. Evidence of this is a film scene that partially shows Leo's work history, explaining how he spent around five to six months in each mall store or fast-food restaurant he worked for. This explains how the city's economic and labor structure dictates the direction and livelihood of its constituents: to ensure the cheapest cost of operations of the companies and firms, the workers remain temporary instead of acquiring a regular position.

While some institutions[16] trumpet the benefits of contractualization as a stepping-stone for new and first-time workers, eventually leading them (workers) to a secure working position, the film offers counterarguments to this. As seen in Leo's résumé and experience, each time his contract expires, there is no guarantee that he can find another job. Because of the precariousness of his labor condition and the need to support his family, he has no choice but to apply for whatever job is available, even if the type of job has no connection to his previous job and his set of skills. After every five or six months of working, which may not be enough time to assure mastery and efficiency in a set of skills, he has to undergo again a different training to possibly acquire a new set of skills, very much different from his previous training. The caption "work history," which can be read in his résumé, mocks the essence of its meaning—there is no continuity and no trace of progress in his previous set of skills. Leo's work history is in a loop and does not represent any career direction and foresight: salesboy in a toy store[17]; service crew at Wendy's; salesclerk at Bandolino; service crew in a *tapsilogan* (egg, cured beef, and rice diner); salesclerk at a mall; merchandiser in a grocery; service crew in a pizza parlor—all contractual jobs. The city does not offer him exits from these interim workspaces; instead, he is trapped and has not moved forward or upward from these "stepping-stones." With contractualization, there is no "climbing the corporate ladder" and "building one's career" in the metropolis. One's work transitions do not represent progressions, only few and small steps directed toward the next mall boutique, the next fast-food diner, and the next grocery store—all workspaces in need of temporary labor.

Irregularity is experienced on a repeated and consistent basis and becomes a certainty in the lives of contractual laborers like Leo—consulting the newspaper's classified ads after each contract ends, spending time in the computer shop to update and print one's résumé before filing for a job application, falling in line at a service agency to submit the résumé, and once accepted in the job, waiting in anticipation for one's end of contract. And the cycle continues in the next series of job hunting. Temporality is also represented in the following aspects in the film: the unstable concept of savings (Leo's lack of financial savings and lack of skill investment) and the cycle of romantic relationships that coincide with the rhythm of the beginning and end of the worker's job contract, while attempting to consider the company's policies on dating coworkers.

After Leo's failed relationship with Candy, he meets Tanya (Ina Feleo), a saleslady at a mall where Leo happens to work following his termination from the fast-food joint. Tanya eventually becomes Leo's girlfriend. After their contracts are terminated, Leo works as a merchandiser in a grocery store, and Tanya as a chambermaid in a hotel. Tanya has trained for the Safety of Life at Seas (SOLAS) to qualify for a job with a cruise line, but she needs some hotel work experience before she can apply for the job. Tanya urges Leo to train for the SOLAS so they can be together, but Leo insists on finishing his contract at the grocery store. The film shows the contrast between the two characters: though cruise ship employment may also be on a contractual basis,[18] we see Tanya's dreams of getting out of her current work loop and pursuing a different job and, on the other hand, Leo's acceptance of his current state, showing no initiative to abandon his continuously volatile work status. In one scene, Tanya asks Leo his dreams, and Leo answers, "None. It is OK for me just to get by."

Temporality in the film extends to other definitions of short-term, possible "sources of income" and pastimes as exhibited by the preoccupations of the city's unemployed population. Leo's father (portrayed by Ricky Davao) regularly goes to cockfights hoping to win some money from gambling. Tanya's aunt is occupied in playing bingo. The film shows a community of characters from Manila living and moving in an unstable financial environment, resorting to quick fixes (contractual labor, gambling) to aid oneself in surviving the fluctuating economy of the city. And this form of living, a floating and tentative plight, becomes a constant in the characters' lives.

Whenever the company experiences a decline in sales, it is easier to lay off contractual workers because of the shortness of the contract, and it is easier also to hire them if the company needs to, which is why the word *flexible* applies to this arrangement, but only to the employer's advantage. On the other hand, there are no shortcuts on the side of the job applicant's process of entering the company under the contractual employment scheme. The applicant must undergo the usual rigidities that come with job application. Similar to what Leo has experienced in the film, aside from preparing one's résumé and falling in line to submit the application to the service agency, there are other requirements and steps to go through. This includes having a medical exam and getting an NBI (National Bureau of Investigation) clearance, a police clearance, and a barangay clearance.[19] And despite these strictures of entering into contractual employment, some contractual employees do not have medical insurance benefits, SSS coverage, and security of tenure.[20] This contradicts what the *Department Order No. 18-02, Series of 2002* of the Department of Labor and Employment (DOLE) states:

> Section 8. Rights of Contractual Employees. Consistent with Section 7 of these Rules, the contractual employee shall be entitled to all the rights and privileges due a regular employee as provided for in the Labor Code, as amended, to include the following: (a) Safe and healthful working conditions, (b) Labor standards such as service incentive leave, rest days, overtime pay, 13th month pay and separation pay; (c) Social security and welfare benefits; (d) Self-organization, collective bargaining, and peaceful concerted action, and; (e) Security of tenure.[21]

Though not explicitly implied, it is obvious in the film that Leo does not receive any severance pay (he has no extra money to meet daily demands), security of tenure (he needs to look for another job when the contract ends), and any of the other benefits and privileges stated in the department order. In the end, the contractual employee absorbs the volatile conditions of the market.

*Endo* explains the ideology of the current structure of contractual employment, specifically, on the profile and perspective of the workers under this scheme. In contrast to the proactive and vigilant characters of Corpuz and Ka Ador, Leo's silence and passivity shows his point of view, that being in a contractual arrangement is acceptable, decent, and normal. It is a way of livelihood, and it seems that it does not matter to Leo if it is long term. In *Endo*, we do not see protests and mobilizations outside the malls and fast-food chains, nor workers recognizing and upholding their rights and organizing a union, but a culture of complicity numbed by the globally dictated pressures of the market. Leo's submission and resignation to his current condition is a symptom of how, on one hand, society views the contractual worker as unskilled, unworthy of benefits and tenure, and easily dispensable and, on the other hand, how the contractual worker sees himself/herself or responds to his/her situation—unassertive, indifferent, and nonresistant.

## The Illusion of Bridging Socioeconomic Gaps through Contractualization

As more malls, establishments, manufacturing firms, and factories are built in Metro Manila promising job opportunities for people like Leo and Tanya, it may seem that the contractualization scheme adopted by these establishments contributes to the "growth" of the employment sector. According to economics scholar Geoffrey M. Ducanes, "If contractualization leads to greater employment of the unemployed, especially for those with lower skills sets, then we can say it helps in terms of inclusive growth. But this is just one face of the coin, because if the system leads to 'lower labor standards,' it doesn't make a difference."[22] It is not surprising then that the press releases reported by the Department of Labor and Employment about the country's performance in the employment sector would often record an "increase" in the number or percentage of employment,[23] but would not explain the quality of employment experienced by majority of the country's contractual workers.

Ducanes added that the growing percentage of contractual workers has led to a "labor surplus" in the Philippines. As long as more people try to join the labor force every year, the number of contractual workers also increase. In *Endo*, this is characterized by Leo's younger brother, Paul. Paul does not finish his degree despite his brother's persistence to support his studies. Contractualization attracts a bigger population of the unemployed, most of which only has minimal educational attainment, like Paul. It helps the unemployed become employed while making it favorable for businesses to grow. And it is possible that Paul, like his older brother, will yield to the irregularities offered by contractual labor.

## Manila Kentex Fire and the South Asian Factory Tragedies

The previously discussed films showed the cities' workers and workspaces embodying the opposing concepts tied to contractual employment, with workers wrestling with the rigidities of entering, remaining in, and exiting their workplaces, while "flexibility" only applies to the firms' ability to maintain its balance and stability. The ills of contractualization explained in the previous sections are deeply entrenched in the recent Manila Kentex tragedy, where seventy-two people died in a fire that occurred at a slipper factory in Valenzuela, Manila, May 2015. Similar to Corpuz's and Ador's woes, the Kentex workers faced the danger of working in a factory that is equally risky and vulnerable as the economic and material environment of Metro Manila. Investigative articles[24] explained the perilous working space of the factory—overcrowded, no sprinklers, no fire exits, barred windows, iron grills reinforced with fencing wire, lack of training of workers, and lack of knowledge on fire safety standards. The fire, according to the news articles, was caused by the flammable chemicals that were ignited by sparks. It was found that these chemicals had no proper storage.

The instability of the workplace is reflected in its labor arrangement—the hiring of illegally subcontracted workers, job insecurity, and the lack of precautionary measures. The Kentex tragedy challenges the labor agencies, institutions, and individuals who are answerable to the deaths and who should take responsibility for the employees' safety and welfare. After the House Committee Panel on Labor found out that many of the workers of the said factory were subcontracted through an unregistered firm called CJC Manpower Services, the panel's chair, Rep. Karlo Nograles, stated that "the Department of Labor and Employment (DOLE) should not have issued any certification for compliance of labor law and occupational safety and health standards for Kentex because it is engaged in labor-only contracting, which is unlawful."[25] As of October 2020, Kentex Manufacturing Corporation General Manager Terrence King Ong, along with Valenzuela city fire officers charged for reckless imprudence resulting into injuries and multiple homicides, were acquitted.[26]

The reality of contractualization as a labor death trap extends to similar factory tragedies that killed hundreds of workers in some South Asian countries, such as Bangladesh and Pakistan. With the higher labor costs in China, international companies tap the sweatshops and low-cost labor of South and Southeast Asian countries such as India, Pakistan, Bangladesh, Cambodia, and Vietnam, where clothes now make up 75 percent of exports.[27] Most of these factories service global brands and retailers. The Clean Clothes campaign estimated that more than seven hundred people in Bangladesh have died in factory fires over the past ten years.[28] In September 2012, almost three hundred people were killed in two separate factory fires in Karachi (the largest and most populous metropolitan city of Pakistan) and Lahore (the capital city of the Pakistani province Punjab).[29]

The cramped factory spaces were created by the international markets and capitalists' demand for fast-lane production, with stores and global chains competing with one another. The so-called fast-fashion chains such as Zara, the Gap, and H&M aim to quickly produce clothing styles from catwalks to retail stores/outlets,[30] which in turn pushes the factory owners to hire extra workers. This leads to the overcrowding in factories, where contractual workers are pressured to work long hours to meet the chains' demand quotas. The November 2012 Tazreen fire in Bangladesh killed 112 workers, who were reported to be working overtime to reach the requirement for the Christmas rush in the United States:

> The Tazreen fire, which killed 112, was working flat-out to meet the Christmas rush in the West. Survivors claim that managers locked the doors to prevent workers from stealing stock as they fled. Though the article also stated that Wal-Mart had terminated its relationship with the factory due to safety concerns, it was also reported that one of its subcontractors continued to use Tazreen without its consent— Wal-Mart clothes were still being produced there months after the firm had deemed that plant unsafe, remains of the store's "Faded Glory" range were found in the embers.[31]

The dialogues between the three films, the Manila Kentex tragedy, and the South Asian factory tragedies are reminders to revisit and rework the labor policies prescribed by neoliberal schemes and market pressures that only protect the profit-maximizing interests of a few capitalist-driven firms and individuals, and oppose the passivity and complacency in the country's and region's labor culture. What needs to be silenced are not the workers' voices; what ought to be barred are not the fire exits and escapes; what must be trapped and smothered are not the hardworking bodies of workers; but the culture of impunity and the rule of global capitalism that constantly suffocate the workers' rights and welfare.

## NOTES

1. *Department Order No. 18-02, Series of 2002, Rules Implementing Articles 106 to 109 of the Labor Code, as Amended.*

2. Jaymalin, "Contract Workers to Get Full Perks."

3. Lagsa, "Contractualization."

4. Corpuz, *Economic History of the Philippines*, 152.

5. Briones, "Characterization of Agricultural Workers in the Philippines," 2.

6. "Press Release, 2015/2016 Integrated Survey on Labor and Employment Part 1 Reference number 2017-127."

7. *IBON: Primer on the Garment Industry.*

8. Guillermo, "Sister Stella L."

9. Dolan, "Employment and Labor Relations."

10. "On This Day 45 Years Ago."

11. Reyes and Sanchez, "An Assessment of Labor and Employment Policies," 2.

12. Dolan, "Employment and Labor Relations."

13. Tuaño, "The Effects of the Asian Financial Crisis": "Business firms implemented various measures in order to cope with the crisis, such as freeze on hiring, providing smaller salary increases to their workers, suspending work benefits, reducing workdays or work hours, cutting their training budgets, or contracting out company services."

14. Bitonio, "Labor Flexibility and Workers' Representation in the Philippines": "They (non-regular workers) generally get lower pay in comparable jobs, they are very likely to be cut first during periods of market volatility and fluctuation, and the temporary nature of their employment restricts their ability to provide for themselves viable means of social protection."

15. "List of Shopping Malls in Metro Manila."

16. During the mid-1990s, some institutions, including the Center for Research and Communication (CRC), agreed on the benefits of flexible labor, particularly, subcontractual labor. According to Luis Molina, who was then the chief labor sector analyst of CRC, "it provides an opportunity for young, unskilled labor to gain experience, skills and work values, as well as to be paid at least minimum wages and be assured of their rights to self-organization and security of tenure." Reyes, "Labor Subcontracting Needed," 1+.

17. Leo mentions in one part of the film that he used to work in a toy store. His work history can be seen in his printed résumé.

18. Matousek, "Working on a Cruise Ship Can Be Brutal."

19. "Labor Day Blues," 2.

20. Maximiano, "Contractualization," B2.

21. *Department Order No. 18-02, Series of 2002, Rules Implementing Articles 106 to 109 of the Labor Code, as Amended*, 3.

22. Bernabe et al., "Worker Hired-Fired Every Five Months."

23. "Statement of Secretary Rosalinda Dimapilis-Baldoz on the 2015 April Labor Force Survey": "I am pleased to note that the result of the 2015 April Labor Force Survey validates our optimism on the country's overall employment situation. I further note that these results sustain the gains in decent work and Millennium Development Goals (MDG) indicators on employment which we begun to achieve under the administration of President Benigno S. Aquino III. Consequently, the increase in employment resulted to a decrease in unemployment. In the 2015 April, unemployment dropped to 6.4 percent from 7 percent in 2014 April, with the number of unemployed persons recorded at 2.681 million compared to 2.924 million a year ago, a difference of 243,000."

24. See Pante, "Kentex Factory and the Economic Death Trap"; Pietropaoli, "Philippines Factory Fire."

25. Arcangel, "Lawmaker Wants Review."

26. Pabico, "Sandiganbayan Acquits Valenzuela Fire Execs."

27. J.C., "A distinctly South Asian tragedy."

28. Ibid.

29. Ibid.

30. Ibid.

31. Ibid.

## BIBLIOGRAPHY

Arcangel, Xianne. "Lawmaker Wants Review of Labor Code's Contractualization Provisions after Kentex Fire." GMA News Online, May 24, 2015, www.gmanetwork.com/news/story/492250.

Bernabe, Kristin, et al. "Worker Hired-Fired Every Five Months." *Philippine Daily Inquirer*, May 1, 2014, https://newsinfo.inquirer.net/598582/worker-hired-fired-every -5-months#:~:text=In%20its%20many%20forms%2C%20contractualization%20is %20rampant%20in%20the%20country.&text=From%20this%20arrangement%20 stems%20the,not%20make%20them%20permanent%20employees.

Bitonio, Benedicto. "Labor Flexibility and Workers' Representation in the Philippines." Accessed July 31, 2015, http://www.ffw.org.ph/bin/DEPARTMENTS/publications /RESEARCH/Bitonio%20on%20Labor%20Flexibility.pdf.

Briones, Roehlano. "Characterization of Agricultural Workers in the Philippines." *Philippine Institute for Development Studies Discussion Paper Series no. 2017-31.* November 2017.

Brocka, Lino, director. *Bayan ko, Kapit sa Patalim.* Malaya Films, Stephan Films, 1985.

Castro, Jade, director. *Endo.* UFO Pictures, 2007.

Corpuz, Onofre. *Economic History of the Philippines.* Quezon City: University of the Philippines Press, 1997.

*Department Order No. 18-02, Series of 2002, Rules Implementing Articles 106 to 109 of the Labor Code, as Amended*, https://blr.dole.gov.ph/news/department-order-no-18-02 -series-of-2002-rules-implementing-articles-106-109-of-the-labor-code-as-amended/.

Dolan, Ronald, ed. "Employment and Labor Relations." In *Philippines: A Country Study.* Washington: GPO for the Library of Congress, 1991.

Guillermo, Alice. "Sister Stella L, More than Just Entertainment." In *Urian Anthology: 1980–1989*, edited by Nicanor Tiongson, 198–202. Manila: Antonio P. Tuviera, 2001.

*IBON: Primer on the Garment Industry.* Manila: IBON Research, 1981.

Jaymalin, Mayen. "Contract Workers to Get Full Perks." *Philippine Star*, November 30, 2011, https://www.philstar.com/headlines/2011/11/30/753083/contract-workers-get-full-perks.

J.C., "A Distinctly South Asian Tragedy." *Economist*, December 6, 2012, http://www.economist.com/blogs/banyan/2012/12/garment-factory-fires.

"Labor Day Blues: The Blight of Contractualization." *Philippine Human Rights Update*, May-June 1997.

Lagsa, Bobby. "Contractualization: The Workers' Curse." *Sun Star Philippines*, April 27, 2013, https://www.sunstar.com.ph/article/281658/Business/Contractualization-The-workers-curse.

Libcom.org. "A History of Trade Unionism in the Philippines." June 12, 2017, https://libcom.org/history/history-trade-unionism-philippines.

"List of Shopping Malls in Metro Manila." *Wikipedia*, https://en.wikipedia.org/wiki/List_of_shopping_malls_in_Metro_Manila#References.

Matousek, Mark. "Working on a Cruise Ship Can Be Brutal—But 2 Lawyers Who Represent Cruise Workers Explain Why Even Terrible Cruise Ship Jobs Can Be Attractive." *Business Insider*, April 3, 2020, https://www.businessinsider.com/why-cruise-ship-workers-take-brutal-jobs-2018-11.

Maximiano, Jose Mario. "Contractualization: Thorn in Labor's Flesh." *Manila Standard*, September 29, 2003.

"On This Day 45 Years Ago: The La Tondeña Workers' Strike of 1975." *Human Rights Violations Victims' Memorial Commission*, October 23, 2020, https://thefreedommemorial.ph/latest-releases/on-this-day-45-years-ago-the-la-tondena-workers-strike-of-1975/.

Pabico, Gabriel. "Sandiganbayan Acquits Valenzuela Fire Execs, Company Official over Kentex Fire." *Philippine Daily Inquirer*, October 1, 2020, https://newsinfo.inquirer.net/1342676/sandiganbayan-acquits-valenzuela-fire-execs-company-official-over-kentex-fire.

Pante, Biel. "Kentex Factory and the Economic Death Trap." Rappler, May 21, 2015, www.rappler.com/move-ph/ispeak/93879-kentex-death-trap-economy.

Pietropaoli, Irene. "Philippines Factory Fire—72 Workers Need Not Have Died." *Guardian*, June 8, 2015, https://www.theguardian.com/global-development-professionals-network/2015/jun/08/philippines-factory-fire-72-workers-unions-human-rights.

"Press Release, 2015/2016 Integrated Survey on Labor and Employment Part 1 Reference Number 2017-127." *Philippine Statistics Authority*, 2015/2016, https://psa.gov.ph/sites/default/files/attachments/ird/pressrelease/ISLE.pdf.

Reyes, Edgardo, director. *Bangkang Papel sa Dagat ng Apoy*. Cinesuerte Films, 1984.

Reyes, Edna, and Teresa Sanchez. "An Assessment of Labor and Employment Policies in the Philippines, 1986–1988." *Working Paper Series No. 90-09, Philippine Institute for Development Studies*, 1990, http://dirp4.pids.gov.ph/ris/wp/pidswp9009.pdf.

Reyes, Wilfredo G. "Labor Subcontracting Needed if RP Is to Excel—CRC." *BusinessWorld*, July 22, 1995.

"Statement of Secretary Rosalinda Dimapilis-Baldoz on the 2015 April Labor Force Survey." *Department of Labor and Employment*, June 9, 2015, https://www.dole.gov.ph/news/statement-of-secretary-rosalinda-dimapilis-baldoz-on-the-2015-april-labor-force-survey/.

Tuaño, Philip. "The Effects of the Asian Financial Crisis on the Philippine Labour Markets." *EADN Regional Project on the effect of the Asian Financial Crisis*, no. 1, 2002,

http://www.eadn.org/The%20Effects%20of%20the%20Asian%20Financial%20
Crisis%20on%20the%20Philippines.pdf.

Van der Zee, Bibi. "The Inside Story of the Kentex Disaster: 74 Workers Died but No
One Is in Prison." *Guardian*, July 20, 2015, https://www.theguardian.com/global
-development-professionals-network/2015/jul/20/the-inside-story-of-the-kentex
-disaster-74-workers-died-but-no-one-is-in-prison.

# Regime-Made Disaster in Metro Manila

*Beyond an Aesthetics Reading of Photographs*
*of Duterte's "Drug War"*

ROSA CORDILLERA A. CASTILLO AND RAFFY LERMA

## Scene of the Crime

The image unfolds gradually. It is night, and the light is concentrated on a green jeepney, the name "JOANNE" written in bold silver letters on its headboard and on the bloodied face of a man slumped on his back on the hood. A small placard next to the body says "SOCO-MPDCLO-316." On the left side of the vehicle, a scene of the crime operative (SOCO; police forensic investigator) shines a flashlight into the front seat of the jeepney.

The dead man, according to Raffy Lerma, who took the photo, is alleged drug user Gilbert Beguelme, thirty-one years old. He was shot by two unidentified masked men on November 9, 2016.

Beguelme was hanging out on the jeepney with his friends in Sta. Ana, Manila when the latter suddenly ran away after somebody shouted, "Police!" Beguelme's brother, who recounted the events to BBC (Brownstone 2017), said that Gilbert stayed put because "he had no *shabu* (crystal methamphetamine) or marijuana on him. So, he just sat there. That's why he didn't run. When he was all alone, that's when they started shooting him."

When Beguelme was killed, it was just the fifth month in office of newly elected President Rodrigo Duterte, who had declared during his campaign that he would launch a war against drugs. Since he came to power, scenes like this have become common in the capital and elsewhere in the country: dead bodies strewn on sidewalks, inside a shanty house, on the streets, or thrown in a river. Many of the killings, such as that of Beguelme, were conducted brazenly. It has not been easy to ascertain the exact death toll of the

Photo of Gilbert Beguelme. (By Raffy Lerma for the *Philippine Daily Inquirer*, November 9, 2015.)

so-called drug war. Human rights groups estimate that more than twenty-seven thousand have been killed since Duterte was elected president in 2016 and began Oplan Double Barrel, his anti-drug campaign. Meanwhile, police claim that nearly eight thousand deaths are related to the drug war (Servallos 2020), where those killed allegedly resisted arrest or fought back (*nanlaban*) during police anti-drug operations. As for the other deaths, police have labeled them as "homicide cases under investigation" or "deaths under investigation" where vigilante groups and drug gangs could be involved in summary executions. The government is quick to trumpet in their Real Numbers PH website that alongside these figures of deaths, 273,014 people have been arrested, including elected officials and drug group leaders, among others; 57.30 billion pesos worth of drugs and paraphernalia were confiscated (PDEA 2020); and more than 500,000 surrenderees have taken part in the "Recovery and Wellness Program" (Caliwan 2020).

However, government figures on arrests, rehabilitation, and confiscations have been criticized as flawed and inflated (PCIJ 2017), while studies show that the police are likely underreporting the number of fatalities (Coronel et al. 2019; Human Rights Watch 2017). The police claim of *nanlaban* has likewise been disputed by critics who point out that in numerous cases, victims were summarily executed by the police or by auxiliary forces even in cases labeled "vigilante killings" (Amnesty International 2017 in Lamchek 2017; Human Rights Watch 2017; OHCHR 2020). Furthermore, Human Rights Watch (2017) research reveals that police routinely falsified evidence by planting guns, spent ammunition, and drug packets in crime scenes to justify the killings as an act of police self-defense.[1]

These and other incidents led the United Nations High Commissioner on Human Rights (OHCHR 2020, 6) to report that there is "near impunity" in the high numbers of killings, while the International Criminal Court (2020, 47–48) finds that there is "reasonable basis to believe that crimes against humanity" have been committed in the drug war. These killings, according to the Armed Conflict Location and Event Data Project, turned the Philippines into "one of the deadliest places in the world to be a civilian ... despite not facing a conventional war" (Kishi and Pavlik 2019, 6, 40). At the center of this unconventional war is the country's capital.

Lerma succinctly captures this drastic shift in incidences of killings in Metro Manila when he told a rapt audience in Makati during one of his talks in 2018, "I have covered more drug-related deaths, summary executions, and extrajudicial killings in my first month in the drug war in July 2016 than the whole year of 2007 when I was in the nightshift.... Some nights there were no bodies found. But on most nights, there were at least one, two, even five or ten. The most was thirty-two in one night."

This image of Beguelme is one of the photographs that Lerma took of President Duterte's anti-drug policy. He shows these photographs in exhibits and during his talks and tells the stories behind them to various audiences in the Philippines and elsewhere in the world to help disseminate to the public the realities of the drug war, seek accountability for the killings, and humanize its victims. Lerma was staff photographer of the *Philippine Daily Inquirer* for twelve years, covering the daily news beat in Metro Manila. In May 2017, he turned to freelance work to focus on the drug war, becoming part of what came to be known as "the Nightshift," or "the Nightcrawlers." Lerma describes this as an "informal collective of photojournalists, journalists, and filmmakers unofficially 'formed' in the early months of the drug war as freelance and staff photographers began covering the nightly killings in Metro Manila." They play a pivotal role in documenting and making visible the modus operandi of the killings, the plight of the victims, as well as the efforts of victims' families and survivors to resist this violent policy and provide support to each other. Furthermore, they provide evidence of the killings to human rights workers and lawyers. They aim, too, to humanize the victims and thus contest the dehumanization by the state and the broader public. In the process, their photographs give insights into Metro Manila as the site of a "regime-made disaster" (Azoulay 2012) that has been shaped, intensified, and made more visible by Duterte's war on drugs.

## The Drug War as a Regime-Made Disaster

In this chapter, we look at some of the photographs that Lerma has produced and shown to various audiences, and his narratives about these photographs, through what Ariella Azoulay (2008) refers to as the "civil contract of photography." We use her perspectives to illustrate the ways in which these photographs evince Metro Manila as a site of a regime-made disaster. Azoulay asserts that regime-made disasters are produced by, and can produce, democratic regimes (2012, 29). That is, they are "inherent" in these regimes and "organize their entire civil space" (31). The strategies employed in such disasters have become a normal part of the working of the regime, are justified as a necessity, and are oftentimes accompanied by moral claims. Because of these, such disasters are not necessarily recognized or acknowledged by its citizens as a disaster "bearing the imprints of the regime," despite this disaster's visibility (30–31).

A "differential body politic" is crucial to the production of a regime-made disaster. In such a body politic, people are distinguished between citizens on the one hand and "flawed citizens" and "noncitizens" on the other, who are each governed differently by the regime (2008, 30). People are considered "flawed" or "noncitizens" due to their religion, class, gender, and ethnicity, among other categories, and, because of this, their suffering is seen as routine (34). They are therefore not protected. Furthermore, their lives are not publicly mourned and are thus dispensable, as society draws boundaries on whose lives matter and are worthy of being publicly grieved (Butler 2003). A goal of regime-made disasters is to preserve this "existing form and differentiation of the differential body politic" (Azoulay 2012, 30).

We see these strategies in Duterte's drug war. In May 2016, the then-mayor of Davao City won sixteen million votes in the Philippine presidential elections on a campaign centered on a tough stance on law and order. The eradication of drugs in the country was a centerpiece of this campaign. This is a goal that, according to him, must be achieved even if authorities have to resort to violence. Newly elected in 2016, Duterte encouraged vigilantism, saying, "Please feel free to call us, the police, or do it yourself if you have the gun . . . you have my support. Shoot him [the drug dealer] and I'll give you a medal" (Associated Press in Manila 2016). Indeed, he has praised and promoted some policemen accused of human rights violations in their anti-drug operations, reinforcing his rhetoric that strongman tactics are necessary to deal with the drug issue. In glorifying the use of violence to solve the country's drug problem, he compared himself favorably to Hitler (Holmes 2016), for which he had to later apologize amid the ensuing outrage.

Critics of his anti-drug policy and his violent rhetoric accuse him of giving license to the police to use brutal force, specifically extrajudicial killings and summary executions, on suspected drug users and pushers. He has also been criticized for waging a "war on the poor" because a majority of those killed come from poor families (Amnesty International 2017). Furthermore, Simangan (2018) demonstrates that Duterte's drug war rhetoric, policy, and actions, including those of other state agents, are "a textbook case" of genocide that correspond to Gregory Stanton's stages of genocide: classification, symbolization, dehumanization, organization, polarization, preparation, extermination, and denial (87). Duterte has declared that suspected drug offenders are less than human, while his chief of police Ronald dela Rosa justified deaths in police operations as "normal" (Talabong 2017).

## Constructing a National Threat

How big of a threat are illegal drugs in the country? The lack of current credible baseline data on the number of drug users have exposed the figures to arbitrary changes by the president. In effect, he is able to declare numbers that instill alarm and fear in the populace and thus help justify his policy. In 2016, Duterte, citing the Philippine Drug Enforcement Agency (PDEA), pronounced that there were "three million drug addicts" two or three years ago (Rappler 2016). However, this was contradicted by the Dangerous Drugs Board (DDB) chief, who claimed that based on their 2015 to 2016 survey, 1.8 million were involved in drugs, including recreational drug users. The DDB chief was subsequently fired (Sabillo 2017). By May 2017, the figure had jumped to 4.7 million users, according to PDEA. They arrived at this figure based on the assumption that there is one drug addict in every eight households (*Philippine Star* 2017). During the presentation of this number to the public, General Isidro Lapeña of PDEA declared that the drug situation is a "national security threat." A month later, President Duterte said in his 2017 State of the Nation Address that illegal drugs "is the root cause of so much evil and suffering that weakens the social fabric and deters foreign investment from pouring in" (Linao 2017).

Concurrent to his narrative that the Philippines has turned into a narco state and that the police have free rein to deal with it, Duterte sought to delegitimize institutions and groups who are critical of his anti-drug policy, such as church personnel, human rights workers, journalists, as well as international bodies and country leaders, even calling for violence against journalists and human rights workers (Human Rights Watch 2018; OHCHR 2020; Ramos 2016). Meanwhile, in reaction to growing international criticism of his violent policy and rhetoric in his first months in office, Duterte retorted, "When was it a crime to say 'I will kill you' in protecting my country? When did saying 'if you harm my country and my children, I will kill you' become a crime? My God!" (Ramos 2016).

Duterte has styled himself as the father of the country who will stop at nothing to save his children from what his regime has constructed as the number one threat to the very survival of the republic. This is his moral claim. And all of these contribute to normalizing violence—whether perpetrated by police or by other individuals or groups that are connected or not to the police—against certain segments of society.

Sociologist Nicole Curato (2016) points out that the construction of an antagonism between "the people" and "the dangerous other" is part of "penal populism," where "the populist dichotomy is one between virtuous citizens versus hardened criminals—the scum of society who, for Duterte, are beyond redemption" (94). This is particularly pressing given Duterte and his supporters' "false equivalence" of drug users as rapists and murderers (Simangan 2018, 76). Penal populism further entails being "tough on crimes" through harsh punitive mechanisms, the performance of "tabloid-style communication," and the "narrative of crisis" (Curato 2016, 94–95). As discussed above, Duterte's populist rhetoric and performance portray the country as being "on the brink of disaster" due to illegal drugs. And to prevent this disaster from happening requires machismo, which he embodies. Furthermore, Curato argues that Duterte's anti-drug policy resonated with people's latent anxieties for their everyday security that have remained unaddressed by previous governments (100).

Warburg and Jensen's (2018) long-term study on policing strategies in Bagong Silang, Metro Manila, furthermore shows how suspected drug personalities are seen by police and, at times, even by their neighbors and relatives as legitimate targets of violence—that they deserve the fate that befell them. Warburg and Jensen (2018) note, "The dominant state discourse on the securitization of drugs marks a moral boundary about who has the right to protection and who does not" (6). There are thus "hierarchies of misery" where "not all suffering is equal, and compassion must be earned" (Curato 2017). Such moral boundary even within poor communities can also be attributable to neoliberal governmentality and state inefficiency that shape notions of "good citizens" who have self-discipline and who are in antagonism with "evil others" who have bad habits (Kusaka 2020). These attitudes are further informed and exacerbated by, among others, the demonization of suspected drug personalities by media practitioners (Castillo 2021; Lasco and Yu 2021) as well as by religious leaders (Cornelio and Medina 2019); the "exceptionalism" attributed to *shabu* as a violence-inducing drug (Lasco and Yu 2021); and the Catholic Church's decades-long propagation of a moral panic about illegal drugs (Cornelio and Lasco 2020, 328).

Consequently, for the broader Philippine public who continue to support Duterte and his anti-drug campaign with high approval ratings, these killings of "flawed citizens" are not seen as "emergency claims" (Azoulay 2008). Their suffering is nonexceptional, and thus their lives are not publicly mourned (Butler 2003). This is in contrast to the grief of affected families, as we will see below in the photographs by Lerma, as well as the grief of activists, artists, and journalists who have been assisting them—grief that has been channeled toward collective political action and forms of care, healing, and solidarity (Castillo 2021; Nonato 2021). Nonetheless, in the broader Philippine society and in Duterte's policies, these deaths are not given public recognition as human lives lost that deserve to be publicly mourned, nor are the deaths accounted for.

The public ungrievability of victims of the drug war is further compounded by another category to which they belong: the urban poor. For urban poor residents, violent state policies are nothing new: they have had to contend with violent demolitions of their homes and livelihoods and everyday forms of marginalization and other forms of structural violence even before Duterte came to power. The urban poor have been excluded by various regimes' developmental model for Metro Manila that is geared toward attracting foreigners and foreign capital (Tadiar 2004, 83). To contain "the contradictory and antagonistic elements" of capital, Tadiar points out, various regimes from Marcos to the present have employed strategies that "entailed military control, direct domination and bodily repression and territorial confinement" (2004, 84). She cites "slum-clearing operations" as one such strategy to rid the metro of people and structures that Imelda Marcos considered as "eyesores" or at least to hide them from sight. Ortega's (2016, 44, 35) study on the demolition of informal settlements also describe a "violent war against the urban poor" by a "new regime of gentrification . . . grounded upon an on-going neoliberal warfare of accumulation by dispossession." These happen even though the urban poor as informal workers are essential to the workings of Metro Manila. They thus "embody the contradictions integral to the ruling classes' political and economic power. They are at once marginalized and essential" (Tadiar 2004, 83).

Urban poor communities bear the consequences of the drug war even as they must simultaneously contend with long-term multiple layers of vulnerabilities. Yet, their suffering and everyday struggle to survive in Metro Manila are largely invisible. Meanwhile, their visibility among upper and middle classes in the metro are, more often than not, infused with scorn, suspicion, and fear. The urban poor have thus been suffering from a regime-made disaster even before Duterte's drug war. But the drug war heightened their suffering, vulnerability, and status as "flawed citizens" and publicly ungrievable lives.

## The Civil Contract of Photography: Looking beyond the Frame

In order to recognize their suffering as nonroutine and thereby a subject of emergency claims and protection, Azoulay points to the urgency of recognizing this differential body politic. She thus reconceptualizes citizenship "as a framework of partnership and solidarity among those who are governed" that is not dominated by the sovereign (2008, 21). It is in this light that she calls for a "civil contract of photography." The civil contract of photography "assumes that, at least in principle, the users of photography, possess a certain power to suspend the gesture of the sovereign power which seeks to totally dominate the relations between them as governed—governed into citizens and noncitizens, thus making disappear the violation of citizenship" (2009, 1). She asks:

> What conditions prevent photos of horror of certain type of governed from becoming emergency claims? The association of citizenship with disaster and the characterization of certain populations as being more susceptible to disaster than others show that citizenship is not a stable status that one simply struggles to achieve, but an arena of conflict and negotiation. (2009, 3)

For Azoulay, looking at photographs of suffering is a form of citizenship and civil skill because the photograph involves not only the camera, the photographer, and the photographed, but the spectator as well. That is, the photograph is not just determined by the photographer's intentions and style. Rather, it is a product of various encounters. It is relational. She thus argues for a civil view where the spectator bears responsibility to gaze "not only at the photographed person but at all those who took part in the act of photography," including the spectator themselves (2010, 259). In other words, to read the photographs of the war on drugs as evincing a regime-made disaster, and to identify a regime-made disaster as such, it is necessary to develop the "civil skill" to look at these photographs.

Crucial to her political ontology of photography is her opposition to the distinction between the aesthetic and the political in photographs of suffering. She takes to task "the political judgement of taste," where the professional gaze or "expert spectator" judges an image as either "too aesthetic" or "too political" (2010, 245–248). The effect of these judgments, she asserts, is that they shape how audiences view the image, and, consequently, what images are worth looking at. At the same time, these judgments of taste not only deny agency to those who appeared in the photograph but can, in this denial of the agency of the photographed, even inflict violence on them (2015, 51). She argues that such a distinction is untenable because it disregards the co-construction of the photograph between the camera, the photographer, the photographed, and the spectator (2010, 247–250).

Instead of judging a photograph in terms of being "too aesthetic" or "too political," Azoulay directs our attention to viewing these photographs as a document and evidence. This necessitates a "change in the field of vision," in that we view the photograph beyond what is in the frame, to seek "the traces of the citizens or other populations involved in the production of the regime-made disaster" (2012, 30). It includes looking not only at the victims, but also at those who made them victims in order to make visible the role of the regime. One thus needs to consider "the event that took place when the photo was taken and the one taking place now, in front of the photograph with the participation of the spectator" (40). In this way, one enacts citizenship that is marked by a sense of obligation and responsibility to others "to struggle against injuries inflicted on those others" (2008, 14).

It is through this conceptualization of citizenship in relation to photography and regime-made disaster, the political ontology of photography, and the methodology of viewing photographs of suffering that we look at how Lerma's photographs reveal strategies and characteristics of the drug war as a regime-made disaster. While we do not have the space to elaborate on it, it is important to note that alongside providing evidence of this regime-made disaster, members of the Nightcrawlers also utilize various storytelling techniques in collaboration with survivors and other organizations to humanize the victims (Castillo 2021). And even though we focus on Azoulay's methodology, we also recognize that sentiments and feelings provoked by images have political importance (Castillo 2021). Indeed, for Lerma, a strong photo is a compelling and *affective* photo.

What helps one to see beyond the frame and beyond what captions say, as well as what can shape feelings toward images, is one's knowledge of contexts in which the image is embedded. This deeper contextualization is provided by the testimonies and information that Lerma and other members of the Nightcrawlers, as well as survivors and families of victims—who are themselves witnesses to the war on drugs—provide. We take these narratives on board, together with insights from human rights, journalistic, and scholarly investigations as we delineate certain aspects of the "blueprint" (Azoulay 2015, 25) of the drug war as a regime-made disaster. This is not an exhaustive analysis of Lerma's photographic archive of the drug war, let alone the Nightcrawlers' vast body of work, which we will not tackle here. However, our conversations, interviews, and participant observation through the years with some of the group's members inform our discussions of the photographs featured below. Neither is this a comprehensive reading of these photographs, for photographs have multiple meanings and affects across time and space. Nor do we aim to offer a comprehensive discussion about the drug war. Nevertheless, we hope that this is a step at laying bare some of the characteristics of this regime-made disaster in Metro Manila.

## Laying Bare the Drug War as a Regime-Made Disaster

*A Tale of Two Cities*

The quickly rising body count in Metro Manila since Duterte came to power and began implementing his national anti-drug policy led human rights advocates to compare it to his time as the mayor of another major urban city in the south, Davao City. It is in this city in Mindanao where the so-called Davao Death Squad vigilante group, which was allegedly under Duterte's command, is reported to have killed 1,424 people, including 132 children, from 1998 to 2015 (Picardal 2016). These comparisons are not surprising given that Duterte himself said during the presidential campaign, "If I make it to the presidential palace, I will do just what I did as mayor. You drug pushers, hold-up men and do-nothings, you better go out. Because as the mayor, I'd kill you" (Agence France-Presse 2016).

His national war on drugs has thus linked Metro Manila and Davao City in particularly brutal ways. Warburg and Jensen suggest that Davao "has emerged as a central inspiration" for Duterte's anti-drug strategies at the national level (2018, 2). "Counter-insurgency policing strategies," they write, "including spatial bordering strategies, militarization, civil-military partnerships, infiltration and killings" that were developed in Davao and elsewhere in the countryside have been transplanted to urban poor areas in Metro Manila that are targeted in the drug war. These strategies include the transfer of police personnel from Davao City to Metro Manila and other urban cities at the center of Duterte's war on drugs, as well as the implementation of Oplan Tokhang (Warburg and Jensen 2018, 4–5). Tokhang, first launched in Davao City in 2012, derives from the Bisaya phrase *toktok hangyo*, for "knock and persuade." In this policy, cops visit the houses of suspected drug users and pushers and ask them to turn themselves in and seek rehabilitation. These suspected drug personalities are known to police through lists drawn up by local watchmen who are hired to provide information and names of individuals that can be included on the government drugs watch list (Jensen and Hapal 2018, 56). This is in conjunction with the Department of Interior and Local Government's (DILG) anti-drug program called Masa Masid. Translating as "the masses watch," it is the DILG's community-based anti-crime, corruption, and illegal drugs monitoring program. In using community members, including kin, as informers, the drawing up of the drugs watch list consequently increases suspicion within families and communities (Lamchek 2017; Warburg and Jensen 2018, 12). Moreover, devoid of investigation or judicial scrutiny, the drugs watch list serves simultaneously as a form of surveillance, humiliation, and kill list where those on the list have oftentimes ended up dead (Lamchek 2017; Reyes 2016; Simangan 2018; Warburg and Jensen 2018).

Investigative journalist Patricia Evangelista (2018a) further reveals how police have tapped civilians to carry out the killings on their behalf. They are considered as "force multipliers" (2018b), not unlike the paramilitary system in rural areas (see also Amnesty International 2017). Given the similarity of the policing strategies in the war on drugs with counterinsurgency tactics, as well as the existence of violent policing and military tactics in the country even prior to Duterte's presidency, Warburg and Jensen (2018, 6) thus emphasize that the war on drugs is "more than simply a passing phenomenon but as something embedded in Philippine history." Yet, Duterte's violence exceeds those of previous presidents (Reyes 2016).

## Riding-in-Tandem, Criminalizing Tambays

Let us return to the photograph of Beguelme. The perpetrators were reportedly two masked men on a motorbike. This method of killing is nothing new. Activists have been killed by similar motorbike-riding men even before Duterte's drug war. It has become such a common modus operandi that the phrase "riding-in-tandem" has taken on ominous connotations for those who are potential targets or who have received death threats in relation to their political work. The brazenness with which the killers shot Beguelme is also nothing new. That they can kill him in front of other people signifies two things: one, there is impunity for such killings; and two, the perpetrators intended for his death to be visible to others to instill fear or to make an example out of Beguelme. The latter starts to make more sense after Lerma tells his audience in one of his talks that a few weeks before Beguelme was killed, Beguelme witnessed the murder of another person. He was asked by the family of the deceased to testify in the case that they filed against the perpetrators. Alas, Beguelme was killed before he could give his testimony. He was prevented from talking. At the same time, his murder signaled to others who might have been thinking of coming forward as witnesses that the same fate could happen to them. As the 2020 UN report notes, such intimidation and harassment of witnesses and families who wanted to pursue cases are not uncommon (OHCHR 2020, 7).

Another aspect stands out in Beguelme's case. Even without his brother's statement, one gets the impression from the photograph that he seemed to have been hanging out casually, enjoying the company of friends, right before he was killed. The photograph thus shows that a casual hanging out with friends in the neighborhood, that quintessential Filipino pastime of *tambay*, especially in poor areas, has turned deadly. Derived from "stand by," this social practice, translated by the government as "loitering," has also been a subject of governmental control and criminalization. In June 2018, Duterte ordered cops to apprehend loiterers as threats to public order. Within five days of his directive, three thousand were apprehended, including nine hundred minors (Talabong 2018). Cops claim they violated local ordinances. Yet this is another policy that targets the poor, which follows the same social cleansing logic of the drug war. Furthermore, what were once safe, casual spaces in urban poor neighborhoods have become sites of suspicion and death.

## Nanlaban?

In another photo, a hand rests on the ground, grasping a gun. An initial impression might be that this was a man who had fought back against the police and was killed. He seems to fit the bill of the *nanlaban* scenario. But Lerma would urge the audience to look closer at the photograph. "Look at the wrist," he would say. There are cuff marks. This realization often elicits an audible gasp from the audience. How could he have fought back if he was already cuffed? As with other victims, Lerma names him to humanize him and counter the anonymity of statistics. It is the hand of policeman and alleged drug pusher Bobby Orit, forty-one, killed in a supposed "shootout" during a drug buy-bust operation on July 21, 2016. The police, Lerma narrates, claimed that Orit and his companion Danilo Guevarra sensed the undercover operation and fired at the cops. Orit was a policeman who was absent without leave (AWOL) and was on Tondo's drugs watch list.

Following Azoulay's stance to look beyond the image, one can surmise that Orit was already captured and handcuffed, and then released, only to be killed, and that the gun had been planted in his hand to stage a *nanlaban* scenario and justify his death. This is not a unique photograph. There are several similar cases documented by other members of the Nightcrawlers, linking this incident with other allegations of police systematically planting evidence in crime scenes, such as in the case of seventeen-year-old Kian delos Santos, whose death sparked massive protests and a Senate investigation (ABS-CBN News 2017). These allegations were vindicated when, in February 2021, a government official admitted for the first time that crime scenes classified as *nanlaban* were not always processed properly (Navallo 2021). Thus, this photo of Orit is evidence of and speaks to broader police strategies in the drug war and contests the authorities' *nanlaban* narrative.

## *Bordering In, Bordering Out*

Another photo is even more disturbing. A body lies on the ground, hands bound together by packaging tape. His face cannot be seen. It is wrapped in packaging tape, upon which was drawn a smiley face with a black tip pen. Beneath the tightly packed tape is a clear plastic that seems to have been used

Photo of Bobby Orit. (By Raffy Lerma for the *Philippine Daily Inquirer*, July 21, 2016.)

to suffocate the victim. His name, Lerma would say in his talks and write in the caption, was Efren Escrupulo.

All photos of the drug war that depict the victims are evidence of how they have been dehumanized by their killers. Yet, this photograph, and others similar to it, for this is not the only one, stands out for its viciousness. For the killers, Escrupulo is not a human being. And they made sure that others see how they have inscribed this onto his body. The effect that they aim for is fear on the part of criminals, would-be criminals, and the broader public. In the context of drug gangs fighting against each other, the desired effect is to teach a lesson and intimidate their opponents. Reyes further argues that in situations where the dead is wrapped in masking tape and a placard is placed next to the body stating, "I am a drug pusher, do not emulate me," the human body is used as a "spectacle of humiliation and violence" to boost Duterte's popularity on the one hand and demonstrate and consolidate state power on the other (2016, 128). Meanwhile, for cops, who in the first months of the drug war were more than willing to let photojournalists take photos of those killed to show to the public that they are doing their job, images of people they killed "enforced a political promise (of salvaging the nation) by inscribing the notion of order in and on the bodies of those supposedly breaking the law" (Warburg and Jensen 2018, 10).

Instilling fear on the populace is a necessary condition for making the streets more peaceful, according to police that Warburg and Jensen talked to. Their study also discusses how violence in the drug war "is a means by

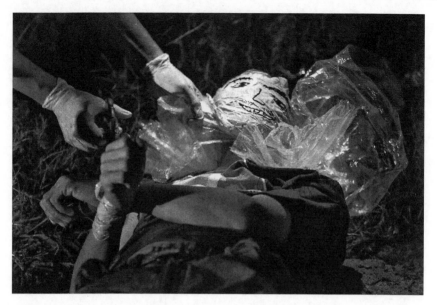

Photo of Efren Escrupolo. (By Raffy Lerma for the *Philippine Daily Inquirer*, November 16, 2016.)

which to border in and border out," delineating zones that have a high likelihood of killings and where counterinsurgency strategies are enacted (Warburg and Jensen 2018, 7). An effect of these police bordering practices and the hypervisibility of the summary killings and police anti-drug operations is the shifting of sociality in these communities where fear and mistrust of each other and of the state have increased. These occur even as urban poor residents sought to adjust their previous strategies of interacting and negotiating with the police to stay alive or not to earn the latter's ire.

### Extortion

One of these police practices that urban poor residents have to negotiate with is extortion (Jensen and Hapal 2018). In a police station in Tondo, Manila, a dozen men and women were discovered hidden in a locked cell behind a bookshelf by a Commission on Human Rights (CHR) team and journalists, including Lerma. In this photo, the door had just been opened during the unannounced jail visit by the CHR and journalists, revealing men and women crammed in a small room. Lerma would tell the audience as he showed the pictures that many of the detainees claimed that they had been held inside the cell without formal charges for almost a week. They further claimed that the police demanded an amount ranging from 25,000 to 300,000 pesos from each of them for their release. They said that some of

(Photo by Raffy Lerma for the *Philippine Daily Inquirer*, April 27, 2017.)

them were released and detained several times, each time having to pay the police for their release.

Urban poor residents have had to deal with extortion even before Duterte's drug war in exchange for relatives who have been incarcerated, wrongfully or rightfully. However, the drug war shifted this exchange relations, making it "more expensive, expansive, and unstable" (Jensen and Hapal 2018, 42). The discovery of this illegal holding cell provides evidence that the police involved in extortion have a new and bigger cash cow in the drug war.

### The Drugs Watch List as a Tool for Revenge

This fear and mistrust are not just due to police operations, the use of surveillance, or the unknown identities of the killers of some of the summary executions. It is also brought about by the use of the drugs watch list to exact revenge on one's enemy, such as what happened to the son of Luzviminda Siapo. In one of Lerma's photos, Luzviminda is embracing the coffin of her dead son Raymart. She had just arrived from Kuwait, where she worked as a domestic helper. Raymart, nineteen, Lerma said, was tagged as a drug suspect by the village hall after a heated argument with a neighbor. A day after the complaint, the teenager was abducted by armed men on motorbikes. He was later found dead with two gunshots on the head. Raymart was

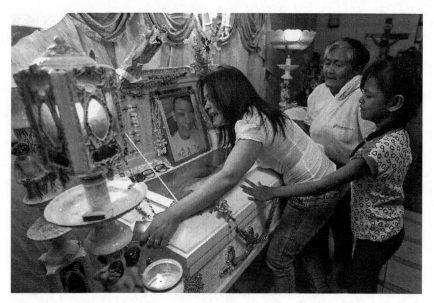

(Photo by Raffy Lerma for the *Philippine Daily Inquirer*, April 9, 2017.)

a person with disability, born with bilateral clubfeet (both feet were deformed). His mother had to beg and kiss the feet of her employer to be allowed to go home and bury her child (See 2017).

In this story, one sees how the drugs watch list can be used in targeting one's enemy, further heightening the fear and mistrust of each other in these communities (see also Lamchek 2017). In Wargburg and Jensen's study, neighbors' relations in Bagong Silang have shifted from one of friendliness to one of "deep mistrust, alertness . . . vigilance" and "guarded suspicion" (2018, 12). They further show that maintaining vigilance and alertness in Bagong Silang is compounded by the congested infrastructure of the city, where "intimacy ensures people's survival," but it is also "unavoidable" (Warburg and Jensen 2018, 12). With privacy virtually impossible, suspicion of each other increases in moments of heightened insecurity and surveillance. One also sees in the Siapo family's story that the war on drugs tentacles beyond the capital and the country and disproportionately affects the most vulnerable: a person with disability and his mother working in unfair working conditions abroad.

### Families Left Behind

Victims of the drug war do not only include those who were killed. Families left behind are victims as well. In one photo, family members of alleged drug peddler Paul Lester Lorenzo cry in anguish after he was killed in a drug

(Photo by Raffy Lerma for the *Philippine Daily Inquirer*, August 19, 2016.)

buy-bust operation in August 2016. Lerma recounts that according to the police, Lorenzo, who was killed along with Danny Laurente, shot at the cops after a drug transaction. The police report further states that recovered from the two victims were ten sachets of *shabu*. In the photo, Lorenzo's body lies on a cart on the *riles*, railway tracks that are bounded on both sides by shanty houses. Lorenzo's brother hugs him, while his daughter, crying, tries to pull her uncle back. A baby is being held by Lorenzo's wife, her eyes closed in pain. A woman also carries a child, and as she cries, she tries to shield the child's face from the scene. At the edge of the frame, Lorenzo's mother seems to be screaming. One does not need to see a video of this scene to imagine the anguished cries of the family. The image itself compels the spectator to share in the family's grief.

Further channeling Azoulay's call for a civil skill, we see in this photo the consequences of the drug war beyond the statistics of those killed. The family's breadwinner gone. Or the hope for a way out of poverty through an educated child, torn, as in the case of Kian delos Santos. The drug war thus not only takes the dead, but also, as Diaz argues, sets "the terms for the living," which "outright rejects Duterte's legitimization of the 'drug war' as a program necessary for improving Filipino life" (2019, 710–711). Thousands of children have particularly suffered physically, emotionally, and economically (Human Rights Watch 2020). Many have been orphaned, both of their parents killed since Duterte came to power. Some of these children witnessed their parents getting killed, and one can only wonder how they will carry this experience with them into adulthood. These children's plight and participation in psychosocial activities aimed at helping them overcome their ordeal have also been the focus of Lerma and his colleagues' photographs.

## Beyond the Symbolism of the Pieta

Lerma is most well-known for his photo that has come to be known as *La Pieta*, which gained national and international attention. It was July 23, 2016, around 1:30 AM, and Lerma had just arrived at the crime scene on EDSA Taft-Pasay Rotunda. He had just come from another crime scene that night outside the Senate. At the end of that night, he would cover four extrajudicial killings in Pasay City. But he would become known for the third killing. There were many people watching the crime scene on Metro Manila's major and busiest thoroughfare. Lerma (2016) writes about that night for the *Philippine Daily Inquirer*:

> In the middle of the police line in which photographers and bystanders are not allowed to cross was the lifeless body of suspected drug pusher Michael Siaron, cradled by [his] partner Jennilyn Olayres. A cardboard sign that read *"Drug pusher ako huwag tularan"* (I am a drug pusher, don't emulate) was left near the body.

An hour had passed after the shooting, according to witnesses. A gunman on a motorcycle driven by an accomplice fired on Siaron and left the cardboard sign beside him. Another person was wounded.

TV floodlights and news cameras popped and flashed as Olayres wept for Siaron while cradling him in her arms like Michelangelo's world-famous sculpture *Pieta*, a depiction of the Virgin Mary mourning over the body of the dead Christ.

In the photo, Olayres is sitting on the road, her face pressed tenderly on the side of her partner's as she holds him up to her chest. Behind her is a huge traffic sign that says, *"Bawal magbaba at magsakay ng pasahero dito"* ("Loading and Unloading are Forbidden"). It is uncanny how this exhortation for urban discipline and subjectivity, what a previous Metro Manila administrator referred to as "Urbanided," serves as a backdrop to another form of discipline through killings and social cleansing in the context of the drug war—articulated ominously in this photo through the placard next to Siaron's body. Behind this sign stands a line of people watching the scene unfolding in front of them.

The experience of taking this photograph marked Lerma. He remembers that night vividly and tells his audiences how Olayres called out to the photographers, journalists, the police, and the numerous onlookers, "That's enough! Help us!"

# PHILIPPINE *Sunday* INQUIRER

BALANCED NEWS · FEARLESS VIEWS

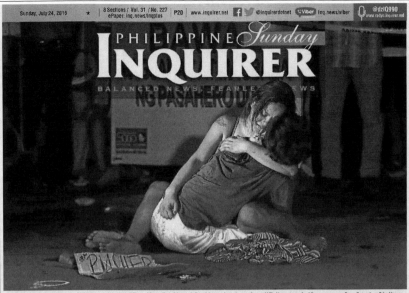

LAMENTATION A weeping Jennelyn Olaires hugs partner Michael Siaron, 30, a pedicab driver and alleged drug pusher, who was shot and killed by motorcycle-riding gunmen near Pasay Rotonda on Edsa. He was one of six killed in drug-related incidents in Pasay and Manila yesterday. (Story on Page A6.) RAFFY LERMA

# Church: Thou shall not kill

## Message to Duterte to coincide with Sona

By Julie M. Aurelio

**SONA 2016**

THOU shall not kill.

The Sixth Commandment is the message for President Duterte that will emanate from a Mass which the Archdiocese of Manila will hold tomorrow afternoon as he delivers his first State of the Nation Address (Sona) to Congress.

The Mass will mark the launching of the "Huwag Kang Papatay" (Thou Shall Not Kill) campaign, which aims to bring together the families of the victims of extrajudicial killings that have come with the

Duterte administration's war on illegal drugs.

Those people—drug users, pushers and dealers—can no longer change their ways because they are already dead, according to an official of the

Archdiocese of Manila.

"We believe, especially in the Year of Mercy, that we have a chance of showing our love of God. But because of this (the extrajudicial killings), there's no more love because there's no more life who will ask for forgiveness and mercy," Fr. Ati-

lano Fajardo said over Radio Veritas yesterday.

Fajardo is the director of the Manila archdiocese's Public Affairs Ministry, which will hold the Mass at St. Vincent de Paul Church on San Marcelino Street in Ermita district.

The Mass, which will start at 5 p.m., includes prayers for the victims of the extrajudicial killings and police operations and their families.

Churchgoers have been asked to wear black and bring candles for a program that will start at 4:30 p.m., by which

**CHURCH/A4**

## Paris pact reversal a big risk, experts say

AS THE UNITED Nations announced plans to fast-track ratification of the Paris Agreement on climate change, President Duterte has announced that he would not honor the country's "crazy" commitment to severely cut greenhouse-gas emission as it would limit industrial growth.

Poor countries such as the

Philippines should be allowed to pursue industrialization to improve the lives of their people, Duterte said in a series of speeches during a visit to Mindanao on Friday.

"If you will not allow us to reach parity, (while industrialized countries) are already there and we are still here, then

**PARIS/A4**

## Young Tawi-Tawi scientist out to save sea of childhood

By Jocelyn R. Uy

THE SEA, with its diverse marine life, and the pristine beaches of his hometown Sibutu Island in Tawi-Tawi were Richard Muallil's playground as a child. Now, as a 35-year-old marine

scientist, Muallil is hoping to transform his old playground into a marine sanctuary, preserving its biodiversity and promoting sustainable fishing.

"Because there are not many programs (either private or gov-

**YOUNG/A15**

## 'Spoiled' Ateneans prove naysayers wrong with village for displaced folk

By Karl Angelica Ocampo

WHEN seven millennials decided to set up a nonprofit organization, a consultant warned that they might be perceived as "snot-nosed, spoiled Ateneans," championing a cause but relying on their affluent parents to fi-

nance their initiatives.

Others doubted their commitment. Could they handle such a huge responsibility? With so many years ahead of them, why spend their youth trying to make the world a better place?

Family and friends wondered why they could not just

focus on their career first and excel in their own fields.

Two years since Taguyod Bayan Foundation Inc. (TBFI) was set up, the group of Ateneon graduates showed that, despite their youth, they had the commitment and the will to pursue their goal.

**SPOILED/A4**

KAYA BA N'YAN MAG-DELIVER NG DAMO?

*Flying donuts make aviation history in US*

WASHINGTON—With a chicken sandwich, hot coffee and donuts, aviation history was made on Friday.

These were among the items in the first drone delivery on US soil approved by aviation officials, made by convenience retailer 7-Eleven and the drone startup Flirtey.

The delivery took place in

**FLYING/A15**

## Polio victim makes limbs for fellow PWDs

By Lyn Rillon

FERNANDO Santos, 56, drives his small automatic vehicle with ease and confidence.

He shows a T-shaped bar he installed in his workshop to control the brake and to change gears.

Another lever he installed below the dashboard is used to manipulate the accelerator using his right hand.

The farthest he has done long-driving on his own, he said, is in Jala-Jala, Rizal province.

Santos was stricken with

polio when he was a year and three months old.

To move around, he uses a wheelchair. He is a person with physical limitations, but certainly not in how he lives.

Santos is the founder and manager of PBF Prosthesis

**POLIO/A13**

---

### WHAT'S INSIDE

| LIFESTYLE | NEWS | ENTERTAINMENT |
|---|---|---|
| **Em-J Pavia:** 'He lived so simply, so passionately, and he cared so deeply for people' / D3 | **Leni on disasters:** It's about being ready, sharing / A9 | **Coco Martin:** Success has its drawbacks / F1 |

Front page of the *Philippine Daily Inquirer* Sunday Edition, July 24, 2016.
(Featuring Raffy Lerma's photo.)

Lerma felt guilty for taking the photos. In talks he gives about his photographs, he would share that he wanted to do something, but he could not because he was not allowed to enter the police line. He would recount, too, that he stopped taking photos and looked for a policeman, asking him, "What are you waiting for?"

To which the policeman replied, "We can't do anything as he is already dead. Let's wait for the SOCO." The ethical dilemmas that Lerma faced at this moment made it clear to him that documenting the killings as evidence and demanding accountability are his ways of helping the victims and their families.

The photo quickly became viral and was featured on the Sunday front page of the *Inquirer*, a day often reserved for feel-good news. It had the headline, "Church: Thou Shall Not Kill." It received massive national and international attention and galvanized a public outcry against the brutal drug war. But it also attracted negative responses, including from Duterte who lambasted the photo as melodramatic during his first State of the Nation Address (Cayabyab 2016). Lerma was accused too on social media of faking the photograph. He was able to disprove these accusations because, first, he was not the only photojournalist covering the crime scene that night. And second, he has other photographs of the crime scene from different angles.

How are we then to read this photograph beyond its aesthetics and the symbolism of *La Pieta*, which is Italian for "pity" and which the Philippine Roman Catholic Church seems to have taken as a cue for their call against the killings as featured on the front page of the *Inquirer*? Azoulay's civil view would insist on looking at the policies and rhetoric we outlined above that led to the death of Siaron and that exposed him and his partner to this event of photography. Even if the perpetrators are vigilantes who may or may not be attached to the police, the fact that the president himself calls for vigilante-style killings is proof that such deaths are linked to the broader climate of impunity enabled by the drug war and his rhetoric. And what about the photographers who were the subject of Olayres's angry plea? Are they "vultures," as Lerma thought? That may or may not be the case. There are various photographic intentions at play, not necessarily directed toward breaking the status quo. Some photographers may not care about the victims and only care about bolstering their careers and in the process do more harm than good. On the one hand, I suggest that in the case of Lerma and other members of the Nightcrawlers, the clarity and consistency of their advocacy for accountability and their collaborations with victims, activists, and lawyers through the years help the spectator read the photograph from a particular critical stance that is infused with a sense of responsibility for the other. Lerma, for instance, has maintained contact with the families of Siaron and Olayres. He also includes in his public talks a photo of Siaron's tiny shanty house built on top of an estuary overflowing with trash to question the po-

(Photo by Raffy Lerma for the *Philippine Daily Inquirer*, August 1, 2016.)

lice's claim that Siaron was a drug dealer. Lerma would ask his audience, "Do drug dealers live like this?" On the other hand, the Nightcrawlers' advocacy has also resulted in Duterte supporters dismissing their photographs as manipulated to destroy the reputation of the president and the country, among other negative reactions (Castillo 2021; Nightcrawlers 2018).

But adapting a civil view necessitates *going beyond* the intentions of the photographer, for the meanings of a photograph does not merely depend on the photographer, as Azoulay has pointed out. We thus suggest that the civil view also directs our attention to the spectators *in* the photograph: those who are in the frame and looking at the crime scene. They were also the subject of Olayres's angry plea. Their gaze could embody that of the spectator who sees the crime scene as a spectacle, in effect distancing oneself from one's responsibility toward the other. Or they could be the spectator who is shocked by the scene and feels helpless to do anything about the situation. Or the spectator who refuses to look. But they can also be the spectator who might look at the crime scene and think that Siaron deserved what happened to him, not unlike some of the neighbors in Bagong Silang that Warburg and Jensen studied, or members of the vigilante group that Evangelista interviewed who believed in the nobility of their work, or a Duterte supporter Castillo talked to who believed such deaths are mere "collateral damage" in a "war." These are among the various ways in which photographs of the drug war have been viewed and have affected viewers as Castillo discusses elsewhere (2021).[2]

Azoulay's civil contract of photography would further insist on shifting our gaze toward ourselves as spectators of the photograph, on how we are coimplicated in this photographic event. That is, how are we, as part of the governed, responsible for this event as well? Here we invoke Butler's (2003) call for a political community that brings "to the fore the relational ties that have implications for theorizing fundamental dependency and ethical responsibility" (12). She calls for thinking about individual fate as inseparable from others so that "the 'we' is traversed by a relationality that we cannot easily argue against." Employing a civil view of photographs of atrocities is a step toward building this political community (Castillo 2021).

## Concluding Remarks

The photographs produced by Lerma that depict intense human pain and suffering as well as the love and palpable grief of families contrast with and contest the dehumanization of poor communities and suspected drug personalities. They are, as Lerma would tell his audiences, brothers, sisters, mothers, fathers. The images are furthermore evidence of a regime-made disaster. In reading these photographs as evidence of a regime-made disaster, we direct our gaze to the differential body politic that underlies and makes possible Duterte's brutal anti-drug policy and the plight of those who are seen as "flawed citizens": excluded, marginalized, subjected to structural and physical violence, disciplining, and cleansing and considered dispensable. This differential body politic is intensified and cemented by the drug war and the high public support for the president and his policy. In taking a civil view, we see the long-running systemic marginalization and violent othering of the urban poor and our role as the spectator of the photograph in maintaining or breaking this differential treatment of those governed. We see as well the forms of violence—emanating from the police, vigilantes who are allegedly on police payroll, and vigilantes from other groups—that are enabled by this differential body politic and by the history of police violence and counterinsurgency measures that inform the current drug war. One can also think of the problematic and overburdened justice and penal system as contributing to this violence, a subject of Lerma's photographs that we do not have the space to discuss in this paper. Beyond the frame of the photograph, it is possible to read the consequences to sociality within targeted communities of the fear and mistrust that are created by the drug war and the hypervisibility and aesthetics of the killings. In turn, the maintenance of this differential body politic helps constitute the current regime. These violent policies do not go unchallenged, however. Lerma and other members of the Nightcrawlers and their collaborators focus on the various ways in which affected individuals, communities, and their allies resist the drug war, stay alive, seek accountability, care for each other, and begin the healing process.

In unpacking the imprint of the regime in the drug war through a civil view of the photographs, we are reminded that this regime-made disaster is not restricted to the current moment. It has been ongoing even before Duterte's ascent to national power. We are also reminded that this regime-made disaster is not just happening in Metro Manila, but elsewhere in the country too. State-sponsored and state-enabled violence against certain segments of society have been experienced in various way and degrees outside of the capital. What sets Metro Manila apart is that a regime-made disaster in the capital gets more local and international coverage than those happening outside the capital, something that the Nightcrawlers are also trying to address despite their limited resources. One wonders, if such brazen killings can happen in the capital, what more for areas of the country that are often omitted from national attention? In a sense, this hierarchy between the capital and the rest of the country is another layer of differentiation among those who are governed. This is another space in which photographs of suffering can make a difference. But to make a difference, spectators of the photographs also have a responsibility to view these images in a manner that reconstitutes citizenship and the relations of those who are governed.

## NOTES

1. Kian Lyod delos Santos in August 2017 was initially portrayed by the police as a drug courier who resisted arrest (ABS-CBN News 2017). But a surveillance video showed plainclothes policemen dragging the defenseless teen away to an alley where he was later found dead. Three cops were eventually convicted of murder.

2. See also Diaz's (2019) analysis of *La Pieta* that focuses on Olayres's grief.

## BIBLIOGRAPHY

ABS-CBN News. "'We Are the Victims': Kian's Dad Rejects Drug Links." ABS-CBN News, August 21, 2017, https://news.abs-cbn.com/news/08/21/17/we-are-the-victims-kians-dad-rejects-drug-links.

Agence France-Presse. "Presidential Favorite Duterte to 'Butcher' Criminals." Inquirer. net, May 8, 2016, https://newsinfo.inquirer.net/783964/philippine-presidential-favorite-duterte-to-butcher-criminals?fbclid=IwAR31ih1YYEaUsuHCxrLcx44K-yRZoui CNWEXnZ085r_LX3ouZ4XAsFYYPkQ.

Amnesty International. "Philippines: The Police's Murderous War on the Poor." *Amnesty International*, January 31, 2017, https://www.amnesty.org/en/latest/news/2017/01/philippines-the-police-murderous-war-on-the-poor/.

Associated Press in Manila. "Kill Drug Dealers and I'll Give You a Medal, Says Philippines President." *Guardian*, June 5, 2016, https://www.theguardian.com/world/2016/jun/05/kill-drug-dealers-medal-philippines-president-rodrigo-duterte.

Azoulay, Ariella. *The Civil Contract of Photography*. New York: Zone Books, 2008.

————. *Civil Imagination: A Political Ontology of Photography*. Translated by Louise Bethlehem. New York: Verso, 2015.

————. "Getting Rid of the Distinction between the Aesthetic and the Political." *Theory, Culture, and Society* 27, 7–8 (2010): 239–262.

————. "On Her Book, *The Civil Contract of Photography*." Rorotoko, January 22, 2009, http://rorotoko.com/interview/20090123_azoulay_ariella_book_civil_contract _photography.

————. "Regime-Made Disaster: On the Possibility of Nongovernmental Viewing." In *Sensible Politics: The Visual Cultures of Nongovernmental Politics*, edited by Yates McKee and Meg McLagan, 29–42. New York: Zone Books, 2012.

Brownstone, Andrew. "Duterte Drug War: Manila's Brutal Nightshift." BBC, August 20, 2017, https://www.bbc.com/news/av/magazine-38181753.

Butler, Judith. "Violence, Mourning, Politics." *Studies in Gender and Sexuality* 4, 1 (2003): 9–37.

Caliwan, Christopher Lloyd. "Over 500k Wellness Programs Held for Drug Surrenderees: PDEA." Philippine News Agency, September 25, 2020, https://www.pna.gov.ph /articles/1116630.

Castillo, Rosa Cordillera A. "A Politics and Ethics of Viewing Photographs of Duterte's 'Drug War:' Towards a Reconceptualization of the Political Community." *Akda: The Asian Journal of Literature, Culture, Performance* 1, no. 2 (2021): 54–70.

Cayabyab, Marc Jayson. "Duterte Hits 'Melodramatic' Inquirer Front Page Photo." Inquirer.Net, July 25, 2016, https://newsinfo.inquirer.net/799260/duterte-on-photo-of -wife-cradling-slain-drug-pusher-nagda-dramahan-tayo.

Cornelio, Jayeel, and Gideon Lasco. "Morality Politics: Drug Use and the Catholic Church in the Philippines." *Open Theology* 6 (2020): 327–341.

Cornelio, Jayeel, and Erron Medina. "Christianity and Duterte's War on Drugs in the Philippines." *Politics, Religion & Ideology* 20 (2019): 151–169.

Coronel, Sheila, Mariel Padilla, David Mora, and the Stabile Center for Investigative Journalism. "The Uncounted Dead of Duterte's Drug War." *Atlantic*, August 9, 2019, https://www.theatlantic.com/international/archive/2019/08/philippines-dead-rodrigo -duterte-drug-war/595978/.

Curato, Nicole. "In the Philippines, all the President's People." *New York Times*, May 31, 2017, https://www.nytimes.com/2017/05/31/opinion/philippines-rodrigo-duterte.html.

————. "Politics of Anxiety, Politics of Hope: Penal Populism and Duterte's Rise to Power." *Journal of Current Southeast Asian Affairs* 35, no. 3 (2016): 91–109.

Diaz, Josen. "Following *La Pieta*: Toward a Transpacific Feminist Historiography of Philippine Authoritarianism." *Signs: Journal of Women in Culture and Society* 4, no. 3 (2019): 693–716.

Evangelista, Patricia. "Get It from the Chief." Rappler, October 6, 2018a, https://r3.rappler .com/newsbreak/investigative/tondo-vigilante-gang-war-on-drugs-series-part-three.

————. "What Did the CSG Do Wrong?" Rappler, October 8, 2018b, https://r3.rappler .com/newsbreak/investigative/tondo-vigilante-gang-war-on-drugs-series-part-four.

Holmes, Oliver. "Rodrigo Duterte Vows to Kill 3 Million Drug Addicts and Likens Himself to Hitler." *Guardian*, October 1, 2016, https://www.theguardian.com/world/2016 /sep/30/rodrigo-duterte-vows-to-kill-3-million-drug-addicts-and-likens-himself-to -hitler.

Human Rights Watch. "'License to Kill': Philippine Police Killings in Duterte's 'War on Drugs.'" *Human Rights Watch*, March 2, 2017, https://www.hrw.org/report/2017/03/02 /license-kill/philippine-police-killings-dutertes-war-drugs.

———. "'Our Happy Family Is Gone': Impact of the 'War on Drugs' on Children in the Philippines." *Human Rights Watch*, May 27, 2020, https://www.hrw.org/node/342197.

———. "Philippines: Duterte's 'Drug War' Claims 12,000+ Lives." *Human Rights Watch*, January 18, 2018, https://www.hrw.org/news/2018/01/18/philippines-dutertes-drug -war-claims-12000-lives.

International Criminal Court, the Office of the Prosecutor. *Report on Preliminary Examination of Activities*. 2020, https://www.icc-cpi.int/Pages/item.aspx?name=2020 -otp-rep-PE.

Jensen, Steffen, and Karl Hapal. "Police Violence and Corruption in the Philippines: Violent Exchange and the War on Drugs." *Journal of Current Southeast Asian Affairs* 37, no. 2 (2018): 39–62.

Kishi, Roudabeh, and Melissa Pavlik. "ACLED 2018: The Year in Review." *Armed Conflict and Location Data Project*, January 11, 2019, https://acleddata.com/2019/01/11/acled -2018-the-year-in-review/.

Kusaka, Wataru. "Disaster, Discipline, Drugs, and Duterte: Emergence of New Moral Subjectivities in Post-Yolanda Leyte." In *Ethnographies of Development and Globalization in the Philippines: Emergent Socialities and the Governing of Precarity*, edited by Koki Seki, 91–97. London and New York: Routledge, 2020.

Lamchek, Jayson. "A Mandate for Mass Killings? Public Support for Duterte's War on Drugs." In *A Duterte Reader: Critical Essays on Rodrigo Duterte's Early Presidency*, edited by Nicole Curato, 201–220. Manila and New York: Ateneo de Manila University Press and Cornell University Press, 2017.

Lasco, Gideon, and Vincen Gregory Yu. "'*Shabu* Is Different': Extrajudicial Killings, Death Penalty, and 'Methamphetamine Exceptionalism' in the Philippines." *International Journal of Drug Policy* 92 (June 2021).

Lerma, Raffy. "The Story behind the Viral Photo." Inquirer.net, July 31, 2016, https:// opinion.inquirer.net/96101/the-story-behind-the-viral-photo#ixzz5dHDiHtU9.

Linao, Girlie. "Duterte Vows Philippines' Drug War Will Not Ease in Face of Criticism." dpa.international, July 24, 2017, https://www.dpa-international.com/topic/duterte-vows -philippines-drug-war-will-ease-face-criticism-170724-99-363168.

Navallo, Mike. "Guevarra: Weapons in 'Nanlaban' Cases Not Examined but Justice System Working." ABS-CBN News, February 24, 2021, https://news.abs-cbn.com/news /02/24/21/guevarra-weapons-in-nanlaban-cases-not-examined-but-justice-system -working.

Nightcrawlers. "Beyond the Death Toll, Humanizing the Victims." *Philippine Center for Investigative Journalism*, May 4, 2018, https://old.pcij.org/blog/2018/05/04/beyond -the-death-toll-humanizing-the-victims.

Nonato, Vince. "Losing Her Son Due to 'Mistaken Identity,' Mother Channels Grief to Helping Other Victims of Drug War." *One News*, January 18, 2021, https://www .onenews.ph/losing-her-son-due-to-mistaken-identity-mother-channels-grief-to -helping-other-victims-of-drug-war.

Ortega, Arnisson Andre. "Manila's Metropolitan Landscape of Gentrification: Global Urban Development, Accumulation by Dispossession, and Neoliberal Warfare Against Informality." *Geoforum*, 70 (2016): 35–50.

Philippine Center for Investigative Journalism (PCIJ). "#RealNumbersPH Unreal, Inexact, Locked in Riddles." *Philippine Center for Investigative Journalism*, June 8, 2017, https://pcij.org/article/832/realnumbersph-unreal-inexact-locked-in-riddles.

Philippine Drug Enforcement Agency (PDEA). "Real Numbers PH." 2020, https://pdea .gov.ph/2-uncategorised/279-realnumbersph.

*Philippine Star.* "PDEA: Philippines Has 4.7 M Drug Users." *Philippine Star,* May 4, 2017, https://www.philstar.com/headlines/2017/05/04/1690823/pdea-philippines-has-47
-m-drug-users.
Picardal, Amado. "The Victims of the Davao Death Squad: Consolidated Report 1998–
2015." *CBCP News,* April 27, 2016, http://www.cbcpnews.com/cbcpnews/?p=76531.
Ramos, Marlon. "Duterte Threatens to Kill Rights Activists if Drug Problem Worsens."
Inquirer.net, November 29, 2016, https://newsinfo.inquirer.net/848933/duterte-threat
ens-to-kill-human-rights-activists-if-drug-problem-worsens.
Rappler. "Full Text: The President's First State of the Nation Address." Rappler, July 25,
2016, https://www.rappler.com/nation/rodrigo-duterte-speech-sona-2016-philippines
-full-text.
Reyes, Danilo Andres. "The Spectacle of Violence in Duterte's 'War on Drugs.'" *Journal
of Current Southeast Asian Affairs* 35, no. 3 (2016): 111–137.
Sabillo, Kristine Angeli. "Duterte Fires Dangerous Drugs Board Chief for 'Contradicting'
Stats." Inquirer.net, May 24, 2017, https://newsinfo.inquirer.net/899267/duterte-fires
-dangerous-drugs-board-chief-for-contradicting-stats.
See, Aie Balagtas. "Drug War Sends OFW Rushing Home for Son Who 'Couldn't Run.'"
Inquirer.net, April 9, 2017, https://newsinfo.inquirer.net/892868/inside-secret-cell
-youre-like-pigs.
Servallos, Neil Jayson. "PNP: Nearly 8,000 Suspects Slain in Anti-Drug War." Philstar
Global, November 5, 2020, https://www.philstar.com/headlines/2020/11/05/2054720
/pnp-nearly-8000-suspects-slain-anti-drug-war.
Simangan, Dahlia. "Is the Philippine 'War on Drugs' an Act of Genocide?" *Journal of
Genocide Studies* 20, no. 1 (2018): 68–89.
Sontag, Susan. *Regarding the Pain of Others.* New York: Picador, 2003.
Tadiar, Neferti. *Fantasy-Production: Sexual Economies and Other Philippine Consequenc-
es for the New World Order.* Quezon City: Ateneo de Manila University Press, 2004.
Talabong, Rambo. "Rise in Deaths in Police Operations 'Normal'—Dela Rosa." Rappler,
August 18, 2017, https://www.rappler.com/nation/deaths-one-time-big-time-opera
tions-normal-dela-rosa-pnp.
———. "What You Should Know: Duterte Administration's Crackdown on 'Tambays.'"
Rappler, June 8, 2018, https://www.rappler.com/newsbreak/iq/things-to-know-anti
-loitering-campaign-duterte-administration.
United Nations Office of the High Commissioner on Human Rights (OHCHR). *Situation
of Human Rights in the Philippines: Report of the United Nations High Commissioner
on Human Rights (Advance Edited Version),* 2020, https://www.ohchr.org/EN/News
Events/Pages/DisplayNews.aspx?NewsID=25924&LangID=E - :~:text=BANGKOK%2
FGENEVA (4 June 2020,Human Rights Office said Thursday.
Warburg, Anna Bræmer, and Steffen Jensen. "Policing the War on Drugs and the Trans-
formation of Urban Space in Manila." *Society and Space* (2018): 1–18.

# Contributors

Paul Michael Leonardo Atienza (@pmlatienza) is Assistant Professor of Asian American Studies in the Department of Critical Race, Gender and Sexuality Studies at Cal Poly Humboldt. Atienza's multidisciplinary scholarship examines beliefs and practices on and about mobile digital media technologies among queer Filipina/o/x in Metro Manila and the U.S. diaspora. His writing has been published in *The Asia Pacific Journal of Anthropology* and in the edited volume, *Q&A: Voices from Queer Asian North America* (Temple University Press, 2021). He is currently coediting a special issue of *Philippine Studies: Historical and Ethnographic Viewpoints* with Dr. Kathleen Cruz Gutierrez focused on a transnational and transgenerational Philippine science and technology studies (STS). Atienza received his Ph.D. in anthropology with a graduate minor in gender and women's studies at the University of Illinois, Urbana-Champaign. He was also a research affiliate with the Seeing Systems INTERSECT group, an interdisciplinary collaboration among Urbana-Champaign scholars interested in the role of vision in technological systems. He is one of the first to receive a master of arts degree in Southeast Asian Studies at the University of California, Riverside's Southeast Asia: Texts, Rituals, Performance (SEAT-RiP) program. He also collaborates with drag performance artist Ma. Arte Susya Purisima Tolentino (@dragmaarte). Contact him at pmla1@humboldt.edu.

Christine Bacareza Balance is Associate Professor of Performing and Media Arts and Asian American Studies and Core Faculty in the Southeast Asia Program (SEAP) at Cornell University. Her first book, *Tropical Renditions: Making Musical Scenes in Filipino America* (Duke University Press, 2016), examines how the performance and reception of post–World War II Filipino/Filipino American popular music compose Filipino identities, publics, and politics. With Lucy San Pablo Burns (UCLA), she coedited the recently published artist-scholar collection *California Dreaming: Movement & Place in the Asian American Imaginary* (University of Hawai'i Press, 2020). Her current book project, *Making Sense of Martial Law*, analyzes the twenty-one-year dictatorial rule of former Philippine President Ferdinand Marcos and how U.S.- and Philippines-based performances and events critique the "Marcosian imaginary." Balance is a proud board member of Cinema Sala, a screening and workshop series that showcases Filipinx work from the film and performing arts industries (cinemasala.org).

**Vanessa Banta** is a postdoctoral fellow at University of Toronto-Scarborough. She holds a Ph.D. in human geography from the University of British Columbia. Born and raised in the Philippines, she also used to teach at the theatre department of the University of the Philippines. Currently, her research lies at the intersections of labor migration, critical development, and urban mobilities.

**Rosa Cordillera A. Castillo** is an anthropologist and engaged scholar based at Humboldt-Universität zu Berlin's Institute for Asian and African Studies. She works on peace and conflict studies, with a particular focus on violence and subjectivity, othering, moral and ethical self-formation, affect and emotions, resistance, and solidarity in national and transnational contexts. She is also interested in and writes on the anthropology of Islam, state and religion, decoloniality, critical research ethics, and engaged scholarship. Castillo received her Ph.D. at the Institute for Social and Cultural Anthropology and the Berlin Graduate School Muslim Cultures and Societies, Freie Universität Berlin. Born and raised in the Philippines, where she was trained in anthropology and taught at the University of the Philippines, Castillo continues her research on the country and its diaspora. She is also the founder of Philippine Studies Series Berlin, project leader of Advancing Philippine Studies at Humboldt-Universität zu Berlin, editorial team member of the Affect and Colonialism Web Lab, and inaugural board member of *Alon: Journal for Filipinx American and Diasporic Studies*.

**Roland Sintos Coloma** is Professor of Teacher Education at Wayne State University (Michigan). A scholar of history, cultural studies, and education, his work addresses critical questions of race, gender, and sexuality from transnational and intersectional perspectives. His publications include *Asian Canadian Studies Reader* (2017), *Filipinos in Canada: Disturbing Invisibility* (2012), and *Postcolonial Challenges in Education* (2009). For his research, he has garnered over $2 million of external funding. Coloma has served in various university leadership roles as assistant dean, department chair, graduate coordinator, and center codirector. He was president of the American Educational Studies Association (2018–2019) and editor of the *Educational Studies* journal (2014–2017). In 2017, he received the Distinguished Scholar Award from the Research on the Education of Asian Pacific Americans special interest group of the American Educational Research Association. In 2020, he was appointed to the governor of Michigan's statewide Asian Pacific American Affairs Commission.

**Gary C. Devilles** is the author of *Sensing Manila*, editor of *Pasakalye: Antolohiya ng Panitikang Filipino*, and coeditor of *Espasyo ng Kulturang Popular* with Roland Tolentino, all published by the Ateneo de Manila University Press. He graduated with a bachelor of arts in philosophy and a master of arts in literature at Ateneo de Manila University and a Ph.D. in media studies at La Trobe University, Melbourne, Australia. Devilles is the current Chair of Manunuri ng Pelikulang Pilipino (Filipino Film Critics) that gives the annual Gawad Urian Awards.

**Robert Diaz** is Associate Professor in the Women and Gender Studies Institute at University of Toronto. His research examines the experiences of sexual minorities, with particular focus on Filipinos in the diaspora. His writing has been published in *Signs*, *GLQ*, *TSQ*, *Journal of Asian American Studies*, *Asian Diasporic Visual Culture and the Americas (ADVA)*, *Women and Performance*, *Topia*, *Filipino Studies: Palimpsests of Nation and Diaspora* (New York University Press, 2016), and *Global Asian American Popular Cultures* (New York University Press, 2016). He is coeditor of *Diasporic Intimacies: Queer Filipinos and Canadian Imaginaries* (Northwestern University Press, 2017), and his book *A Confetti of Ordinary Dreams: Queer Filipinos and Reparative Acts* is forthcoming with Duke University Press.

**Dr. Faith R. Kares** is a mixed methods researcher who specializes in neoliberal political economy, urban development, housing activism, diaspora, and social movements. She has nearly twenty years of experience conducting ethnographic research in Metro Manila and among the Filipino diaspora in the United States. Dr. Kares's work raises broadly questions of power, (in)equity, in/exclusion, and belonging. Through an enduring commitment to participatory action research and other equitable research methods, she is dedicated to engaging wider audiences and making research relevant and accessible to *all* communities. Currently she serves as the Senior Director of Research and Impact of Beloved Community, a Diversity, Equity and Inclusion (DEI) nonprofit organization based in New Orleans. Additionally, she teaches courses at the University of Illinois at Chicago and leads trainings for federal government entities on how to mitigate bias in research. She holds a Ph.D. in cultural anthropology from Northwestern University.

**John B. Labella** is the head of Filipinas Heritage Library, a cultural advocacy unit of Ayala Foundation. The library specializes in books, images, and archival records related to the Philippines' emergence as a nation. His engagement with urbanist thought recently led the library to convene a set of online talks called "Shaping City Sense," now viewable on YouTube. A former Fulbright fellow, Labella continues to work on studies about transnationalism in Philippine literature and literary relations between the United States and Latin American. He has taught at Ateneo de Manila University and the University of Illinois at Urbana-Champaign. He holds a doctorate degree from Princeton University.

**Raffy Lerma** is a freelance photojournalist and documentary photographer based in Manila, Philippines. For twelve years, Lerma worked as a staff photographer for the *Philippine Daily Inquirer*, covering the daily news beat in Metro Manila. He has shifted into working independently to focus on his documentation of the Philippines' war on drugs. He has received numerous awards for his work in the Philippines' war on drugs, including the Society of Publishers in Asia (SOPA) for best news photograph and a recognition of distinction from the Center for Media Freedom and Responsibility, and he was a finalist twice for the W. Eugene Smith Memorial Grant in 2017 and 2018. Lerma has been exhibiting his photographs and giving talks in different parts of the Philippines and the world to help disseminate to a broader audience the realities of the drug war in the country.

**Bliss Cua Lim** is Professor of Cinema Studies at the University of Toronto. She is the author of *Translating Time: Cinema, the Fantastic and Temporal Critique* (Duke University Press, 2009; Ateneo de Manila University Press, 2011). She is a member of the Editorial Collective of the journal *Camera Obscura: Feminism, Culture, and Media Studies*, published by Duke University Press, and serves on the advisory board of *Plaridel: A Philippine Journal of Communication, Media and Society*, published by the University of the Philippines College of Mass Communication. Her next book, *The Archival Afterlives of Philippine Cinema* (forthcoming from Duke University Press), analyzes state, private, and informal archival efforts as well as the tenacious advocacy movement that arose in response to the crisis-ridden history of film archiving in the Philippines.

**Ferdinand M. Lopez** is a retired associate professor in literary and cultural studies at the Faculty of Arts and Letters of the University of Santo Tomas. SHe is currently completing her Ph.D. in women and gender studies at the University of Toronto.

**Martin F. Manalansan IV** is Beverly and Richard Fink Professor in Liberal Arts and Professor of American Studies at the University of Minnesota, Twin Cities. He previously taught at the University of Illinois, Urbana-Champaign, University of the Philippines, New York University, New School University, and City University of New York. Manalansan is the author of *Global Divas: Filipino Gay Men in the Diaspora* (Duke University Press, 2003; Ateneo de Manila University Press, 2006). He is editor/coeditor of five anthologies namely, *Filipino Studies: Palimpsests of Nation and Diaspora* (New York University Press, 2016), *Cultural Compass: Ethnographic Explorations of Asian America* (Temple University Press, 2000), *Queer Globalizations: Citizenship and the Afterlife of Colonialism* (New York University Press, 2002), *Eating Asian America: A Food Studies Reader* (New York University Press, 2013), and *Q & A: Voices from Queer Asian North America* (Temple University Press, 2021). He has edited several journal special issues, which include an *International Migration Review* volume on gender and migration and the *Journal of Asian American Studies* issue entitled "Feeling Filipinos." He has published in numerous journals, including *GLQ, Antipode, Cultural Anthropology, positions: east asia cultures critique*, and *Radical History*, among others. Among his many awards are the Ruth Benedict Prize from the American Anthropological Association in 2003, the Excellence in Mentorship Award in 2013 from Association of Asian American Studies, the Richard Yarborough Mentoring Prize in 2016 from the American Studies Association, and the Crompton-Noll Award for the best LGBTQ essay in 2016 from the Modern Language Association. His current book projects include the ethical and embodied dimensions of the lives and struggles of undocumented queer immigrants, Asian American immigrant culinary cultures, affect and nationalism, urban studies, and the politics of decolonizing social science in the Global South. Before going back to academia, he worked for ten years in AIDS/HIV research, program evaluation, and prevention education at the Gay Men's Health Crisis and the Asian Pacific Islander Coalition on HIV/AIDS, both in New York City.

**Paul Nadal** is Assistant Professor of English and American Studies at Princeton University. His most recent essay, "Cold War Remittance Economy," *American Quarterly* 73.3 (2021): 557–595, received the 1921 Best Essay Prize, which is annually awarded by the American Literature Society for "the best article in any field of American literature." He received his Ph.D. in rhetoric at the University of California, Berkeley.

**Jema Pamintuan** earned her Ph.D. in Philippine studies from the University of the Philippines, Diliman. Some of her critical essays appeared in positions: *east asia cultures critique, Thesis Eleven, Plaridel Journal*, and the *Cultural Center of the Philippines Encyclopedia of Philippine Art* (literature and music volumes). Her film scores for *Ang Sayaw* *ng Dalawang Kaliwang Paa* (coscored with Christine Muyco, 2011) and *Tuos* (2016) won Best Original Music at the Cinemalaya Independent Film Festival (2011 and 2016) and the Gawad Urian Award for Best Music (2011 and 2017).

**Oscar Tantoco Serquiña Jr.** is Faculty in the Department of Speech Communication and Theatre Arts at the University of the Philippines. He obtained his Ph.D. in Theatre Studies from the University of Melbourne. He has received study and research fellowships from the National University of Singapore, Sciences Po in Paris, the National Library of Australia, and the University of Michigan. His essays have appeared in *Public Books*, *Theatre Research International, Humanities Diliman, Kritika Kultura, Philippine Political Science Journal*, and the *Philippine Humanities Review.*

**Louise Jashil R. Sonido** teaches at the University of the Philippines Department of English and Comparative Literature. As a teacher, scholar, multimedia artist, and cultural worker, she has a range of research interests transecting literary criticism, intellectual historiography, media and film scholarship, performance curation, and ethnographies of multimedia production. She is a member of the Congress of Teachers and Educators for Nationalism and Democracy (CONTEND-UP), the Concerned Artists of the Philippines, and the Performance Curators Initiatives. For her master's thesis, she worked on a history of film critical practices in the Philippines during the period of early cinema. She was part of the curatorial team for *Scenes Reclaimed: CCP 50 x Cinemalaya 15* (2019) and the video artist for *Con.Currents: Points of Sublation* (2017) and *Lupang Hinirang: Mga Kwento ng Pagsasalugar ng UP Diliman* (2019).

**Rolando B. Tolentino** is Faculty of University of the Philippines Film Institute, former dean of the UP College of Mass Communication and former director of Likhaan: UP Institute of Creative Writing, where he is also a fellow. He has taught at the Osaka University, National University of Singapore, and University of California, Berkeley. His research interests include Philippine literature, popular culture, cinema and media, and interfacing national and transnational issues. He writes fiction and creative nonfiction. He is Chair of the National Committee on Cinema and Commissioner for the Subcommission on the Arts of the National Committee for Culture and the Arts and is a board member of the Film Development Council of the Philippines. He is a member of the Manunuri ng Pelikulang Pilipino (Filipino Film Critics Group), Congress of Teachers and Educators for Nationalism and Democracy (CONTEND-UP), and Altermidya (People's Alternative Media Network).

# Index